GAIA,
the Thesis,
the Mechanisms
and the Implications

D1321835

GAIA,
The Thesis, the Mechanisms and the Implications

edited by

Peter Bunyard and Edward Goldsmith

First published 1988
Wadebridge Ecological Centre
Worthyvale Manor,
Camelford,
Cornwall.

ISBN 0 950411 18 3

Printed in Great Britain by Quintrell & Company Limited, Wadebridge, Cornwall.

CONTENTS

This book has been printed on recycled paper.

PREFACE

These Proceedings are the first of a series of Symposia organized by the *Wadebridge Ecological Centre* in Cornwall on *Gaia and its implications* for the different fields of study into which knowledge is now divided. This first Symposium, held on 21-24th October 1987, was in the nature of an introduction to the theme. One of the reasons why this series of Symposia is being held in Cornwall is that Jim Lovelock lives on the Cornwall/Devon border and nearby is the city of Plymouth, home of the Marine Biological Association of Great Britain. Michael Whitfield and Andrew Watson both of whom played a key role in developing the Gaia Hypothesis with Jim Lovelock and Lynn Margulis, work at the MBA. Jim Lovelock is currently president of the Association and Michael Whitfield its director. Furthermore, Lynn Margulis is a frequent visitor to this part of Britain, remaining in close touch with the other originators of this critically important thesis.

While Jim has been concerned with the overall concept of Gaia, though especially the atmosphere, and Lynn with biological aspects and the role of the microcosm, Peter Westbroek and his colleague Gerrit-Jan de Bruyn, from the Netherlands, have looked into the geological implications. Both participated in the symposium as did Lynn's young colleague Greg Hinkle from Boston University and her son Dorion Sagan, with whom she has written many books and articles on related subjects.

We were also fortunate in having with us Jacques Grinevald from the University of Geneva who has been working for some time on a History of the idea of the Biosphere which will be published in the form of a report to Ecoropa, the European Ecological Action group that co-sponsored this symposium.

The implications of the Gaia hypothesis are multitudinous. Three of them stand out as particularly important. To begin with nature can no longer be seen as a random assortment of different forms of life. Instead it is a single organization of living things and therefore a natural system as is a cell, an organism, and an ecosystem.

The second important implication of the Gaia thesis is that living organisms, instead of being predominantly egostistical, competitive and aggressive must on the contrary cooperate with each other in order to enable the natural system of which they are part to function properly and achieve stability.

This point brings us to the third main implication which is that Gaia is best seen as a cybernetic system capable of maintaining its stability in the face of environmental challenges as do biological organisms, and other natural systems.

At this meeting we could do no more than provide some idea of what the implications might be for selected fields of study. To do this required asking scholars to reconsider basic assumptions underlying the disciplines in which they worked. That in itself is a very difficult task which very few academics are willing to undertake since it means questioning the validity of much of the work that they have been involved in over the course of many years.

We were fortunate in obtaining the cooperation of a number of scholars who, over the years, have been willing to undertake this thankless task, among them Jerry Ravetz, possibly the leading philosopher of science in this country, Mae-Wan Ho, one of the best known and outspoken critics of neo-Darwinism, Martin von

vii

Hildebrand, who works closely with Gerardo Reichel-Dolmatoff in Colombia on what one might refer to as the cybernetics of Amazonian Indian social groups; Matthias Finger, one of the leading lights of Ecoropa and an outspoken critic of the present mechanistic and reductionist approach to the social sciences and David Abram who has undertaken the philosophical implications of the Gaia thesis.

In addition to the key speakers an extremely interesting group of participants also attended the Conference (see list of participants page 247).

The finance for the conference was provided by the Ecological Foundation to which all thanks are due. We also thank Ecoropa for its sponsorship and participation. We thank the Parsons family of the Camelford Conference Centre and also Hilary Datchens for her help in organising the symposium and in preparing the proceedings, deciphering the almost undecipherable tapes of the discussions and typing out the various drafts and preparing the material for publication. We must thank Katherine Goldsmith for the party she held for all the participants at her home, Whitehay and for the highly polished floor shows provided by our two magicians Dorion Sagan and David Abram, cellist and guitarist Amyra and Peter Bunyard, as well as Sara Kalim for her reciting in the ancient Greek the Homeric poem, *Hymn to the Mother Goddess* (Gaia).

SKETCH FOR A HISTORY
OF
THE IDEA OF THE BIOSPHERE

by Jacques Grinevald

"Until recently the historians and the students of the humanities, and to a certain extent even the biologists, consciously failed to reckon with the natural laws of the biosphere, the only terrestrial envelope where life can exist. Basically man cannot be separated from it; it is only now that this indissolubility begins to appear clearly and in precise terms before us."
Vladimir Vernadsky (1945).

"Therefore the explanation, which is given of the different phenomena of the Earth, must be consistent with the actual constitution of this Earth as a living world, that is, a world maintaining a system of living animals and plants."
James Hutton (1795)

"Yet ignorance dominates the science of the biosphere, the focus of our Project."
Jerome R. Ravetz (1986).

The Discovery of The Biosphere

This meeting on the Gaia hypothesis, with the participation of Lynn Margulis and James Lovelock, is a good opportunity to emphasize the need for a historical perspective of the scientific idea of the Biosphere. My intention is not to trace its history but only to propose a historical overview, just a sketch.

The emerging planetary ecological perspective in terms of which we are, together with all other living beings, from microorganisms to giant redwoods or whales, not apart but a part of the Earth's Biosphere is now, in my mind, the major cultural and scientific revolution of our time and perhaps of the history of mankind in its relationship with Gaia.

The classical paradigm of European scientific development emphasized the *telescopic* and *microscopic* instrumental exploration of the world and neglected the *macroscopic* understanding of the complexity and the unity of the globe as a single living system including humans and their 'exosomatic instruments' (H. Odum, 1971, Lotka; 1925; Georgescu-Roegen, 1976).

In his 1749 thesis at Leiden entitled *De sanguine et circulatione in microcosmo*, James Hutton (1726-1797) the enlightened Scottish physician who turned farmer and natural philosopher emphasized the cyclic organic view of the Earth. Hutton's proposition was eventually superseded by the triumphant lifeless mathematical science of *Rational Mechanics*. Hutton often referred to the whole Earth as 'macrocosm' and an equivalent of an 'organism'. The parallel between the physiological microcosm of our body and the geological macrocosm of our planet Earth was accentuated in his holistic natural philosophy. His 'Theory of the Earth'

1

saw the "mechanism of the globe, by which it is adapted to the purpose of being a habitable world" as a cycling steady-state system, including degenerating and regenerating processes (Hutton, 1788:211).

In his final book entitled the *Theory of the Earth with Proofs and Illustrations,* James Hutton (1795,11:545-6) wrote:

> "We live in a world where order everywhere prevails; and where final causes are as well known, at least, as those which are efficient.... Thus, the circulation of the blood is the efficient cause of life; but, life is the final cause, not only for the circulation of the blood but for the revolution of the globe.... Therefore the explanation, which is given of the different phenomena of the Earth, must be consistent with the actual constitution of this Earth as a living world, that is, a world maintaining a system of living animals and plants."

In 1796, in Paris, the mathematician and astronomer Pierre Simon Laplace (1749-1827) published his popular *Exposition du Système du Monde* in which the stability of the world system was clearly demonstrated and therefore the quiet fate of the habitable planet Earth assured in the cyclic steady-state Solar system.

Hutton's work, popularized by John Playfair's 1802 *Illustrations of the Huttonian Theory,* is now credited for the discovery of the cyclical nature of geological changes and, together with Buffon, of the immensity of the duration of nature. C. A. Basset, the French translator of Playfair in 1815 pointed out in a long note the parallel between Hutton's theory of the Earth and Laplace's stability of the word system. But the first publication of Hutton's theory in 1788 produced no reaction; it was ignored because catastrophism dominated.

Lamarck

Although the term and the modern idea of Biosphere does not appear in Lamarck's work, it is relevant here to mention the French naturalist Jean-Baptiste Lamarck (1744-1829), Buffon's protégé. Compared with Lamarck's fame as a botanist and a zoologist or as the debated originator of biological evolution, Lamarck's contribution to geology, biogeochemistry and environmental sciences is more difficult to evaluate because it has been neglected by the historians of Earth sciences and ecology.

Significantly, it is in his little-known but highly original geological treatise, printed at his own expense, under the title *Hydrogéologie,* that Lamarck introduced the science of *Biology* appropriately within the theory of the Earth:

> "A sound Physics of the Earth should include all the primary considerations of the Earth's atmosphere, of the characteristics and continual changes of the Earth's external crust, and finally of the origin and development of living organisms. These considerations naturally divide the physics of the Earth into three essential parts, the first being a theory of the atmosphere, or *Meteorology*, the second, a theory of the Earth's external crust, or *Hydrogeology*, and the third, a theory of living organisms, or *Biology*. (Lamarck, 1802:7-8; trans. by Carozzi, 1964:18)

Only the second part of his *Physics of the Earth* was published in what Lamarck presented as a "very condensed and rather short" volume. Indeed, he was not a narrow specialized scientist, but, like his mentor Buffon, a philosopher viewing Nature as a whole. Like Sadi Carnot's pathbreaking (1824) memoir which brought about the new science of power or thermodynamics, Lamarck's *Hydrogéologie* was a work of genius, although completely neglected by the scientific establishment of his time. With the notable exception of Vernadsky it was disregarded by the early historians of science until the publication of the 1964 critical edition in English by the historian of geology, Albert V. Carozzi, a former professor at the University of Geneva.

As Jordanova (1984:45) emphasizes in his monograph, the science of life, in Lamarck's scientific philosophy, "only made sense in the context of parallel studies of the Earth and the atmosphere. Living phenomena did not stand alone, but had to be seen as part of a larger whole, nature; indeed, they were only comprehensible when their constant interaction with the non-living world was recognised."

Prior to Humboldt and more latterly Vernadsky, Lamarck's holistic point of view was a precedent to our global ecological worldview. However, with reason, the very term biosphere is not used in Jordanova's *Lamarck*. As a naturalist with an encyclopaedic mind, nurtured by the pre-industrial tradition of the Enlightenment, Lamarck was not only a botanist and a zoologist, but also a mineralogist and meteorologist, yet the basic concept of the biosphere was still foreign to him and the time was not yet ripe for global ecology.

Lamarck fully realized the enormous importance of the action of living organisms on the changing surface of the Earth's crust. A century before Vernadsky and even longer before the formulation of the Gaia hypothesis, he conceived the planetary role of life, the geochemical importance of the intricate interactions between living matter, as Vernadsky understood it, and the terrestrial environment, and then the links betwen geology (including mineralogy, petrology, sedimentology), meteorology and evolutionary biology.

Well known to the geologist Charles Lyell (1797-1875), Lamarck's contribution to the theory of the Earth, recognized the unity and the temporal aspect of nature, emphasizing the great antiquity of the Earth and the continuity of the great processes of nature within the immensity of geological time. Independently of Hutton's *Theory of the Earth*, of which he was unaware, Lamarck discovered the grandeur of the coevolution of Life and its affect upon the face of the Earth.

However the notion of the long duration of geological time had been noted - very much in opposition to the ideas of his time – by Buffon in his *Theory of the Earth* (1749) and in his monumental *Natural History* in which he linked the peculiar constitution of vegetable and animal life with the environmental circumstances of the globe of the Earth variously heated by the Sun (see Buffon, ed. by J. Piveteau, 1954:37).

For a long time, Lamarck's biogeochemical ideas were ignored. The advancement of science, through scientific institutions and the ideology of industrialisation, created compartmentalized and specialized disciplines without paying much attention to the unity of Nature as a whole or biospheric evolution. That Darwin was also a geologist was forgotten: geological sciences and biological sciences advanced separately.

3

Humboldtian Science: a Holistic Epistemology

Opposition to the fragmentation of knowledge is clearly expressed in the works of Buffon, Hutton, Lamarck, Goethe and of the German romantic natural philosophers. Connections, inter-relationships and the unity of nature were very much part of the grand cosmological view of Romanticism.

For the Romantics all the sciences of nature were seen within a unique cosmological framework. The Earth, with its inhabitants was considered as a whole, with holism not being considered in opposition to rationality. Such a scientific approach was admirably illustrated by the influential works of the great German geographer and natural philosopher Alexander von Humboldt (1769-1859).

The 'coevolution' of living organisms, climate, ocean and the Earth's crust is in fact a grand scientific idea deeply rooted in the nineteenth century scientific world-view associated in particular with Humboldt..

> "And at the very core of this Romantic view of nature," Worster (1977:82) remarks, "is what later generations would come to call an ecological perspective: that is, a search for holistic or integrated perception, an emphasis on interdependence and relatedness in nature, and an intense desire to restore man in to a place of intimate intercourse with the vast organism that constitutes the Earth."

Alexander von Humboldt is now considered a true forerunner of our global ecological view of the Earth in the Cosmos. Vernadsky, in common with his master Dokuchaev and the Russian geographers, often quoted Humboldt's *Ansichten der Natur* and other of his works. Written after his famous expedition to the Americas with Aimé Bonpland, Humboldt's *Essai sur la géographie des plantes* (1807) was a classic in early biogeography and ecology. The impact of Humboldt's writings upon Darwin is well documented.

But plant geography was only one of the illustrations of Humboldt's new paradigm or *épistémé*. His holistic scientific research programme, where sensitivity and synthesis complemented rationality and analysis, was Man's new dialogue with Nature.

Beside the rather neglected Hutton's *Theory of the Earth*, it is to Alexander von Humboldt, and among geographers also to his younger contemporary Carl Ritter (1779-1859), that the idea of the whole Earth as a "Tout pénétré d'un souffle de vie" and as a functioning vast organism may best be traced. The links between Humboldt, the German holistic tradition, geography, botany and ecology are particularly well illustrated by the Russian scientific school including Dokuchaev, Woeikof, Berg, Vernadsky and later Sukachev.

Humboldt, author of a multi-volume synthesis appropriately entitled *Kosmos* (4 vols., 1845-58), conceived early "L'idée d'une physique du monde" (letter to Pictet of 1796). Here the term *physique* is not equivalent to our standard concept of physics; it is near to the idea of a World's Natural History or the old Greek word *physis*.

This tradition was later shared by Teilhard de Chardin with Helmut de Terra (1900-1981), his German-American fellow-traveller in Asia who as a geologist and paleontologist, was also author of an important study published in 1955 on Humboldt.

Humboldt, trained as a geologist under Abraham Gottlob Werner (1749-1817) at the famous Freiberg *Bergakademie* where he adopted Wernerian Geognosy, which studies both organic and inorganic bodies in the history of the Earth. *Geognosy*, a term still used in the mid-nineteenth century as in the *Lehrbuch der Geognosie* published by the German mineralogist Karl Freidrich Naumann (1797-1873), has come back into use through the originators of the Gaia theory.

Besides being a great scientific traveller and explorer, a distinguished founding father of modern human geography, a cosmopolitan versatile liberal man, Alexander von Humboldt was also a pioneer in the early organization of international scientific relations as a means of studying the globe, and in particular geomagnetism.

Eduard Suess: Geology and Biosphere

"If we imagine an observer to approach our planet from outer space.."
Eduard Suess
Das Antlitz der Erde (vol.1,1885)

The Austrian geologist Eduard Suess (1831-1914), first coined the term 'Biosphere' in 1875. He was a natural philosopher within the Humboldtian tradition, viewing nature as a whole, the living world, with its geological substrate as an integral part of the Earth's surface. He was looking at life as a planetary phenomenon not just as something occurring inside a laboratory, and from a global macroscopic viewpoint rather than through a microscope.

In his great book *The Face of the Earth*, Suess imagined a space traveller discovering the face of the planet Earth. It was a striking illustration of the whole-Earth approach.

In fact, during Suess's lifetime, several scientists attempted to apply the whole-Earth approach such as Friedrich Ratzel (1844-1904), a German student of the naturalist Haeckel who turned from ecology to geopolitics, and was author of a massive book entitled *Die Erde und das Leben* (Leipzig, 1901-2). The French anarchist and encyclopaedic geographer Elisée Reclus (1830-1905) was the author of many books including *La Terre* (Paris, 2 vols., 1868-69), *Nouvelle Géographie Universelle* (Paris, 19 vol., 1875-93) or *L'Homme et la Terre* (Paris, 6 vols., 1905-8). In this latter book, Reclus declared: "L'Homme est la nature prenant conscience d'elle-même."

Eduard Suess, was born in London of a Jewish merchant family, but after 1845 went to live in Vienna. Partly educated in Prague with French, German and English teachers, he became a great engineer and scholar and also a prominent citizen of Vienna.

As a liberal, he achieved a brilliant political career, beginning just after the success of his 1862 book entitled *Der Boden der Stadt Wien*, a pioneering essay in human geology. Two major civil engineering projects brought Suess great fame including an aquaduct that gave Vienna its drinking water supply from the mountains (1873) and the Danube canal (1875).

He had a long and fruitful academic career at the University of Vienna, first appointed as professor of paleontology (1857-62)), then for nearly forty years as professor of geology. His long involvement with the Imperial Academy of Science began in 1860. In 1893, he was elected vice-president and in 1898 president of the Academy. Like Vernadsky in Russia, he had much influence on science policy and was largely responsible for many reforms of Austrian scientific institutions. He also believed in the universal value of scientific research and devoted a great deal of energy to international scientific relations and organization.

He died in April 1914, just before the Great War.

In 1981, the 150th anniversary of Eduard Suess's birth was commemorated by the *Österreichischen Akademie der Wissenschaften* which in its special publication completely ignored Suess's idea of the biosphere.

Although the entry 'Suess' in the *Dictionary of Scientific Biography* rightly declares that "emphasizing the unity of the living world, in 1875 he created the concept of the biosphere", many statements about the origins of the term biosphere neglect the name of Suess.

For instance, the widely-read unofficial 1972 Stockholm UN Conference publication: *Only One Earth* declared that it was "the Soviet physicist, Vladimir Ivanovich Vernadsky, who invented the word 'biosphere' (Ward and Dubos 1972-76).

In his book *La Biosphère*, Vernadsky (1929:93) wrote:

"The importance of life in the whole structure of the Earth's crust penetrated only slowly the mind of scientists, and it is not yet appreciated today in its full extent. It was only in 1875 that E. Suess, professor at the University of Vienna, one of the most eminent geologists of the last century, introduced into science the notion of biosphere, as the idea of a particular envelope of the terrestrial crust penetrated by life."

That the concept of the Biosphere must be traced to Suess was confirmed by the eminent Yale ecologist George Evelyn Hutchinson, first in the chapter on The Biosphere in his book entitled *The Ecological Theater and the Evolutionary Play* (Hutchinson, 1965) and five years later in his authoritative article introducing the September 1970 issue of *Scientific American* devoted to 'the Biosphere'.

Published in Vienna, and only in a German edition, just three years before the first International Geological Congress in Paris, Suess's 1875 book must be considered as a milestone in the development of geotectonics. But the title, *Die Entstehung der Alpen*, of this booklet which provided the "theoretical basis of much of Suess's later work" and in itself was "influential out of all proportion to its size" (Greene, 1982:148), was rather misleading.

It is clearly not only about the development of the Alps. First in Suess's view, mountains, in this instance using the paradigm of the Alpine chain, were the key to problems of geological thinking; second, only the first two chapters are concerned with the Alps. In fact *Die Entstehung der Alpen* provided a sketch of Suess's global tectonic views later fully developed in his masterpiece *Das Antlitz der Erde*.

In the final chapter of *Die Entstehung der Alpen*, Suess presented his holistic view of the development of the Earth. He explained that the Earth consists of several concentric structures, with a core and a mantle, and that the Earth's crust consists of several spheric 'envelopes' which in fact are in multiple interrelationships. In addition to the *atmosphere*, a term that had already been in use for a long time in the scientific literature, Suess coined the terms: the *hydrosphere* and the *lithosphere*. The idea of the Earth as made up of and surrounded by different spheres was not new, it was part of an intellectual tradition derived from Aristotle's *Meteorologica* and the best Greek science viewing the Earth as a globe in the sky.

However, as Suess emphasized, "one thing seems strange on this spheres-built celestial body, namely organic life." The plant, which deeply roots in the soil to feed and at the same time rises into the air to breathe, wrote Suess, is a good illustration of the situation of life in the zone of interaction between the atmosphere and the lithosphere.

Thus, according to Suess, we can distinguish on the surface of the Earth, at the interface between the hydrosphere, the lithosphere and the atmosphere, another specific planetary sphere or envelope, that of living organisms or biological processes, and we can name it the *Biosphere*. The German word used by Eduard Suess (1875:159) is "eine selbstandige Biosphare", a sustainable Biosphere. Unfortunately Suess never defined his new concept of Biosphere more precisely than that and it was not discussed by others during his lifetime.

In 1875, this birth through geology of the idea of the Biosphere was, to the best of my knowledge, a silent event, the new term remaining apparently unnoticed by natural scientists.

French and Swiss Alpine geologists were deeply impressed by Suess's 1875 book. This impact is emphasized in several memorial books by the French geologist Pierre Termier (1859-1930), a friend of Teilhard and the uncle of Henri Termier who together with his wife eventually published in 1952, a *Histoire géologique de la biosphère*. In his book entitled *A la gloire de la Terre,* which contains many pages on the life and work of Eduard Suess, Pierre Termier (1922) notably described the enthusiasm of his master Marcel Bertrand (1847-1907), a Corps des Mines engineer working with the Geological Survey of France, discovering *Die Entstehung der Alpenan*. After reading it he decided to become an Alpine geologist.

Suess's work owed a great deal to the rise of mountaineering, of which Horace-Benedict de Saussure was a founding father. The early alpinists are not only part of the Romantic movement but also of the scientific development of physics and what was later called geophysics.

Parallel to ocean discoverers like James Cook or George Forster, early mountaineers were scientific explorers interested in geology, mineralogy, botany, zoology, meteorology, calorimetry, physics and the chemistry of gases. Scientific instruments like thermometers and barometers played their part in de Saussure's ascent of Mont Blanc.

It is not completely by chance that the term Biosphere appeared in the final chapter of Suess's 1875 book. The original notion of Biosphere which went practically unnoticed when first introduced in the scientific literature, was also the final word of *Das Antlitz der Erde*, that monumental book published in several tomes towards the end of the nineteenth century.

7

Suess's *The Face of the Earth* was a massive international publishing enterprise and a scientific work of art. His aesthetic approach was a typical result of Viennese culture in old Austria. In the mind of Pierre Termier (1922), it was "a sumptuous temple", an "extraordinary book", a "poem", a "work of genius". In German, the first volume appeared in 1883; the others appeared in 1885, 1888, 1901, and the final volume in 1909.

The English translation, *The Face of the Earth* (5 vols., 1904-24), was made under the direction of William Johnson Sollas (1849-1936), a versatile scientist who combined geological investigations and biological research, his wife Hertha providing the translation. In English-speaking countries Suess's concept of Biosphere was not apparent and it was generally ignored by those following the history of ideas. It is even excluded from the recent Macmillan *Dictionary of the History of Science* (Bynum et al., 1981).

The Face of the Earth reflected the state of science near the end of the nineteenth century. "The title of the book was chosen as an honest statement that geology was not the science of the Earth - merely of its face", Robert Muir Wood (1985:32) remarks in *The Dark Side of the Earth*. In his essay Wood devotes himself to the birth of science of the whole Earth, or rather global geophysics, while still disregarding the Earth's Biosphere.

Suess's great book had the deepest influence on geological thought since the publication in the 1830s of Charles Lyell's *Principles of Geology*. It was not an original revolutionary work as was Alfred Wegener's controversial book *Entstehung der Kontinente und Ozeane* first published in 1915, but the final synthesis of an epoch, comparable with Humboldt's *Kosmos*.

Nevertheless, we have neglected the Biosphere message, and the present environmental/ecological crisis is well captured by the dramatic shift from Suess's *The Face of the Earth* to Jonathan Schell's *The Fate of the Earth*.

In line with Humboldtian science, Suess's monumental work was 'the geological synthesis' of the nineteenth century, according to the Austrian physicist Ludwig Boltzmann (1844-1906), a colleague of Suess's at the Vienna Imperial Academy of Sciences. It was a true geological synthesis, according to the leading historian of science George Sarton (1919).

From our present scientific viewpoint, Suess's work is a classical description of the globe's surface before the rise of the concept of continental drift of Wegener. In fact, as argued in particular by Brouwer (1981) and Sengör (1982), the work of Eduard Suess was not only an intellectual background for the promoters of 'mobilism' (1924:290), but a pivotal and decisive scientific source for the Swiss Emile Argand, the German Alfred Wegener, the American Frank B. Taylor and the South African Alexander Du Toit.

Suess's Biosphere and Teilhard de Chardin

"Tous les êtres organisés, du plus humble au plus élevé, depuis les premières origines de la vie jusqu'au temps où nous sommes, et dans tous les lieux comme dans tous les temps, ne font que rendre sensible aux yeux une impulsion unique, inverse du mouvement de la matière et, en elle-même, indivisible. Tous les vivants se tiennent, et tous cèdent â même formidable poussée."
Henri Bergson, Evolution créeatrice1907)

8

It is ironic that the interdisciplinary idea of Biosphere, closely linking biology and geology, and even astronomy, was a novelty much more difficult to accept than the debated hypothesis of continental drift. However, interdisciplinarity and holism were embodied in Wegener's book, *The origin of continents and oceans* (the third German edition was translated into English and French in 1924): here biogeographical and palaeontological aspects, together with climate change, were explicitly presented in support of the migrating continents theory. Alfred Wegener (1880-1930), who considered himself a revolutionary and geology as an integrative, holistic Earth science, was exasperated by the conservatism of his critics and the resistance of the narrow-minded scientific world.

The term 'biosphere' never clearly defined by Suess, appeared several times through the volumes of *The Face of the Earth* (see Index), but it is the final chapter which emphasized it. Although the last chapter of the French 1918 final volume entitled "La Vie" was described by the historian of science George Sarton (1919) as a "large biogeographical synthesis relating to various geological periods", the term 'biosphere' was completely missed in Sarton's work. Curiously, it is also neglected by historians of geology, including specialists of Suess's work, as well as historians of ecology. However, as the French geologist Pierre Termier remarked in his epilogue to *La Face de la Terre*, the biosphere seems to be the final word of Suess's life-work.

Suess recalled the term *biosphere* (Suess's italicizing) in the beginning of his final chapter entitled "Life" without mentioning his own 1875 precedent. In this volume, which appeared in German in 1909, the word biosphere was not associated with the concentric shells of the Earth's spheric structure, but with the idea of the 'solidarity of all life'.

In Suess's opinion, the idea of the biosphere as the unity of flora and fauna covering the Earth's face emerged out of the revolution in natural history introduced by Lamarck and Darwin: "it is thanks to Lamarck and Darwin that we succeeded in coming to this conclusion", he remarked.

For many students of the 1920s, the Suessian term biosphere appeared to resemble closely the idea expressed in Bergson's great 1907 book *L'Evolution creatrice*. In German-speaking countries, vitalism (often associated with energetics) was in vogue and the idea of the Earth as an organism often expressed.

Indeed, just after the First World War the long awaited publication of the final volume (1918) of *La Face de la Terre* ending with its chapter entitled 'La Vie' ('*Das Leben*', The Life) took place in France. The Suessian notion of Biosphere, although not precisely defined, yet consonant with the idea of the unity of life, and even the old concept of the Great Chain of Being, was accepted within the cultural context of a spiritual revival as synonymous with Life in the sense of Bergson's vitalist metaphysics.

In France, whereas establishment geologists were sceptical of Wegener's ideas, considered by Pierre Termier (1928) as "the dream of a great poet", a "seductive", "unnecessary" and excessively "convenient" hypothesis, they more readily accepted the term 'biosphere' proposed by the respectable Austrian master. Among this scientific circle of Earth scientists, was the Jesuit father Pierre Teilhard de Chardin (1881-1955), then professor of geology at the Institut Catholique of Paris. In the 1920s, the close friend of Teilhard was the mathematician-turned-philosopher, Edouard Le Roy (1870-1954), Bergson's interpreter and successor at the Collège de France. Together, the two unorthodox Catholic thinkers discussed the new scientific idea of the biosphere and, in collaboration with the Russian scientist Vladimir Vernadsky, then in Paris, developed the notion of the noosphere (Teilhard, 1956; Vernadsky, 1945).

Teilhard first used the term Biosphere in a laudatory review of *The Face of the Earth*, in 1921. He then used it in all his philosophical essays, particularly in *Le Phénomène humain,* written in 1938-40 in China, and only published after his death in 1955, becoming a bestseller in the 1960s. As we know, the Biosphere, with a capital 'B' is a very important concept in Teilhard de Chardin's philosophical work.

According to Teilhard, the Biosphere (a term he credited to Suess and never to Vernadsky) is only the organic totality of living beings, forming a continuous thin layer around the face of the Earth, distinct and in addition to the other geospheres. That concept is similar to what Vernadsky called living matter and others biomass or biota. Problems with terminology and conceptual confusion still persist.

In 1969, the following misleading terminological note written by A. Gillard, was published in *Nature:*

> "The term of biosphere was defined by J. B. Lamarck as the rough total of the matter of all living beings. The tenor of the term has greatly altered since. By biosphere, modern biologists mean the part of the Earth's crust (lithosphere and hydrosphere) and of the lower parts of he Earth's atmosphere (trophosphere) where life is present. Accordingly, the biosphere consists of living and non-living components. It is the total complex of soil, water, air and living organisms that forms a complete ecosystem. Many authorities even go a step further. They define the biosphere as "the space of our planet that is taken up by living beings" or as "the part of the Earth's crust, of its hydrosphere and atmosphere, that builds the environment for life" (compare Suess). Here, the biological components fall into the background and the notion biosphere has changed from biological into geobiochemical.
>
> P. Teilhard de Chardin has quite rightly pointed out that by biosphere is not to be understood "the peripherical surface of the globe to which life is confined, but the actual skin of organic substance which we see today enveloping the Earth." His definition then runs parallel to the original definition by Lamarck.
>
> I think it would be useful to propose a new term, viz. 'ecosphere', for that part of our sphere in which there is life together with the living organisms it contains. In the same way as the 'biosphere' is the rough total of all living organisms, the 'ecosphere' is the rough total of all ecosystems (of the hydro-ecosphere, the litho-ecosphere and the atmo-ecosphere)." (Gillard, 1969).

Professor Marcel Florkin (1900-79), an eminent Belgian biochemist, first President of the newly formed International Union of Biochemistry in 1955, correctly introduced the Vernadskian biogeochemical concept of "the biosphere" in his 1943 textbook *Introduction à la biochimie générale*. Another Belgian scientist, the plant ecologist Paul Duvigneaud, a friend of Florkin, emphasized in the first 1962 edition of his masterly textbook in ecology (see Duvigneaud, 1980), the Vernadskian idea of the Biosphere as a fundamental concept of the science of ecology which he called 'synthesis science'.

A. Gillard, in quoting Florkin, was apparently ignorant of Vernadsky, overlooking him for Teilhard, and adding the term 'ecosphere', without credit to LaMont Cole (1958), as well as to the radical ecologist Barry Commoner (1971) who discussed the concept in his bestseller *The Closing Circle*. The emerging popular vogue for the term ecosystem, associated with the fierce politization of ecology in the 1970s, was certainly responsible for this preference for the term ecosphere to that of biosphere. In his first popular book entitled *Science and Survival*, published in 1966, and in a 1969 famous paper in *Science* entitled 'Evaluating the Biosphere', Commoner correctly used the term biosphere. More recently, the terms biosphere and ecosphere were used synonymously in Jonathan Schell's 1982 bestseller *The Fate of the Earth*.

Gillard's 1969 note in Nature is the basis for several reference books, including the *Vocabulaire d'écologie* (Hachette, 2nd ed. 1979) edited in cooperation with ACCT (Agence de cooperation culturelle et technique), CILF (Conseil international de la langue Française) and CNRS (Centre d'études phytosociologiques et écologiques L. Emberger Montpellier), in which Lamarck and Teilhard are quoted but not Vernadsky.

Teilhard's evolutionary cosmic philosophy, long repressed by religious authority, received acclaim only after his death in New York in 1955. Teilhard's work was an inspiration to many people all over the world, including some in Marxist circles. Indeed the Teilhardian idea of the biosphere (and of the noosphere) is still accepted by many, as for instance by the New Age movement. Nevertheless, Teilhard's views are of an extreme anthropocentric nature, influenced as they are with ideas taken from the Western philosophy of progress and development. Such views are now rejected by radical thinkers, including deep ecologists.

While not entering into a discussion over Teilhard's thinking, we must note that there is a profound link between Teilhardism and several recent mystical interpretations of Gaia (see for example Russell, 1984). The point here is that the Teilhardian philosophy or theology of the Earth is not Gaian, because of its strong anthropocentrism, it being contrary to the idea of the Biosphere as a global ecological system in which the coevolution of living organisms (including humans) together with their planetary environment has taken place. Indeed Teilhard's Biosphere is not the result of a biocentric, but of a zoocentric approach. Perhaps because he was obsessed with his discovery of time and the irreversibility of the evolutionary process, Teilhard disregarded the stability of the self-regulating planetary ecosystem.

Although having often talked many times with Vernadsky in Paris, where they had several friends in common at the Museum d'Histoire Naturelle, including the mineralogist Alfred Lacroix, Teilhard apparently never understood Vernadsky's teachings on biogeochemical cycles. This point is ignored by biographers and commentators of Teilhard de Chardin. In fact the peculiar ideas of Teilhard are not consonant with those of Vernadsky, adopted later by ecological scientists and more recently by James Lovelock and Lynn Margulis in their Gaia hypothesis.

The biosphere in Teilhard's sense is not an ecological concept at all; it is not associated with a system view of grand cycles linking the biota, the atmosphere, the hydrosphere and the lithosphere of our moving, dynamic and living planet. Nevertheless, the Teilhardian Biosphere is a living force, with a geological significance and a time's arrow essentially opposed to the processes of entropy in the physical world; it is, however, a pre-ecological view and one which is wholly anthropocentric.

Vladimir I. Vernadsky (1863-1945)

We have celebrated Teilhard de Chardin and ignored Vernadsky, emphasizing the anthropocentric idea of evolution and ignoring the true holistic idea of global ecology, now synonymous with the international concern over the fate of our global living environment, *The Biosphere*. While noting the divergence between Teilhard and Vernadsky regarding the very concept of Biosphere, we have to point out that both these Earth scientists had several points of view in common, the first being a real sense of the wholeness, and of the unity of nature.

Like Teilhard, Vernadsky recognized the great contribution of naturalists such as Buffon and Lamarck. He also paid homage to the profound influence that Goethe and Humboldt exerted over him, often neglected within the dominant mechanistic philosophy of science. Helmut de Terra, a biographer of Humboldt, and a travelling companion of Teilhard, sees Teilhard as belonging to the same holistic tradition as Alexander von Humboldt.

Our ignorance of Vernadsky is a good reminder of our lack of knowledge of the history of ecology in Russia and the part played by Vernadsky's Biosphere concept in the rise of the Soviet tradition of environmental studies and global ecology.

To investigate further the Soviet scientific tradition following Vernadsky's biospheric perspective, I refer you to Kamshilov (1976), Budyko (1980, 1984), Fortescue (1980), and especially Lapo (1987), author of a book first published in 1982 and entitled *Traces of Bygone Biospheres*. These authors link Vernadsky's scientific heritage and the Gaia hypothesis with its emphasis on the transformation of the Earth's environment by living organisms and notably by microorganisms.

In 1963, the Soviet Academy of Sciences, celebrated the centenary of the birth of the Academician V. I. Vernadsky. On that occasion, the Soviet biogeochemist and oceanographer Alexander P. Vinogradov (1895-1975), a former pupil and collaborator of Vernadsky, declared: "Much time will have to pass before the historian of science will be able to review the vast scientific legacy of Vernadsky and fully detail the depth and many-sideness of his influence."

Since that time and stimulated by rising environmental concern, Vernadsky's work gained considerable interest in Russia, but not without some ideological difficulties, as pointed out by Kendall Bailes, an American historian well versed in Soviet studies and a rare expert of Vernadsky's life and work. In a well-documented article,[1] Bailes (1981) commented on the Soviet appraisals of Vernadsky in the framework of the relationship between science, philosophy and politics:

---

1   I am indebted to Frank Egerton for this very useful reference.

"The interpretation of Vernadsky's thought and career in the Soviet Union, I would suggest, has been important for Soviet ideologists, both in order to blunt the more radically anti-Marxist implications of his work and thus his appeal to many Soviet dissenters and at the same time to render his reputation useful to official Soviet goals."

Kendall Bailes is also the author of a long paper entitled *Vernadsky and the Biosphere*, which, as far as I know, is still unpublished[2]. In this work, written presumably in 1978, he remarked: "Yet, due no doubt in part to the barriers of both language and politics, Vernadsky's scientific legacy is given scant and not always complimentary attention by Western ecologists."

Significantly, in a book review (*New Scientist*, 17 July 1986) of the recent first English translation of Vernadsky's *The Biosphere*,[3] James E. Lovelock declared:

"When Lynn Margulis and I introduced the Gaia hypothesis in 1972 neither of us was aware of Vernadsky's work and none of our much learned colleagues drew our attention to the lapse. We retraced his steps and it was not until the 1980s that we discovered him (Vernadsky) to be our most illustrious predecessor."

Born in St. Petersburg on 12 March 1863, to a liberal learned family, Vladimir Ivanovich Vernadsky graduated from the University of his native city, where the famous chemist Dimitri Ivanovich Mendeleev (1834-1907) and the geographer and soil science pioneer Vasili Vasilevich Dokuchaev (1846-1903) got him interested in the sciences of nature and especially in Earth sciences. He became an internationally reputed mineralogist, one of the founders of modern geochemistry and a pioneer in radiogeology. He placed great emphasis on the need to study Precambrian formations with the aim of finding the oldest rocks of the Earth's crust in relation to the idea of life as the most powerful geochemical agent. That self-same idea has since 1977 been pursued within the International Geological Correlation Programme.[4]

But, above all Vernadsky is now considered the creator of biogeochemistry and the founding father of the contemporary conception of the Biosphere.

In fact, Vernadsky was a versatile scientist, an early promoter of the history of science, a true natural philosopher, and a man with a holistic vision. He had high moral standing and was an active organizer of scientific activity in his country, working with the old and new Academy of Sciences and was closely associated with those concerned with the economic development problems of Russia.

For our historical perspective of the idea of the Biosphere, the most interesting period of Vernadsky's life was the 1920s, after the October Revolution and the First World War, especially his fruitful stay in France from July 1922 to December 1925.

He was invited there by the Rector of the University of Paris, the mathematician Paul Appell, to deliver lectures on geochemistry at La Sorbonne.

Founder in 1921 of the Radium Institute in his native country and friend of Pierre Curie, who accidentally died in 1906, Vernadsky frequently visited Marie

---

2 I am indebted to Professor G. E. Hutchinson for sending me a copy.
3 On this very abridged and misleading English translation based on the French edition of 1929, see my critical review (Grinevald, 1986).
4 See IGCP Project 157, "Early Organic Evolution in Relation to Minerals and Energy Resources": Holland and Schidlowski, Eds., 1982; Nagy et al. Eds., 1983; Schopf, Ed., 1983, Schidlowski, 1985).

Curie-Sklodowska in Paris. At the Museum, he worked again with his old friend Alfred Lacroix (1863-1948), whom he had met many years before, in 1888, at the Collège de France laboratory of mineralogist Ferdinand Fouqué (1828-1904). Lacroix, who was the Secrétaire perpétual de l'Académie des Sciences (1914-1948), was instrumental in the editing of Vernadsky's lectures on *La Géochimie* (Vernadsky, 1924).

He was also a friend of Teilhard and as a result Vernadsky met Teilhard and his friend Edouard Le Roy. The Abbé Christophe Gaudefroy (1878-1971), mineralogist at the Institut Catholique, was perhaps also instrumental in the memorable encounter between Teilhard, Le Roy and Vernadsky.[5] Curiously, studies on Teilhard make no mention of this relationship, and references to Vernadsky's works in Edouard Le Roy's two books (Le Roy, 1927, 1928) in which he emphasizes the notions of the biosphere and noosphere, remained unnoticed.

According to my own research, this encounter seems to me very important for Vernadsky as well as for Teilhard and Le Roy. Many ideas on Life on Earth and especially the idea of human development as a powerful geological force became crystallized during discussions between those remarkable holistic thinkers. This historical fact was mentioned in the last papers of Teilhard (1956) and Vernadsky (1945), both posthumously published.

Vernadsky adopted Suess's term *biosphere* after the First World War in his early biogeochemial studies, but it was only during his stay in Paris that he developed a theory of coevolution which he called the 'living matter' and the planetary environment of life, partly created and controlled by life, *The Biosphere*.

In spite of their conceptual differences, both Teilhard and Vernadsky shared a common cosmic and planetary perspective of Life. They were forerunners of '*macroscope*'. (H. Odum, 1971), our new global outlook. They shared the idea of the whole Earth as a peculiar living planet and a single gigantic evolving organism. As geoscientists, or perhaps biogeoscientists, they discovered the immensity of nature's duration. They thought in terms of genesis, global-scope, coevolution and long-term irreversible development.

Vernadsky may well have derived some of his ideas from his uncle Yevgraf Maximovich Korolenko, an amateur philosopher familiar with the works of great naturalists. According to Balandine (1982:24), one of self-taught Korolenko's views was that: "the Earth is a living organism"! A sort of precedent for Lovelock's Gaia hypothesis!

It is important for a historical perspective to remark that Vernadsky's ideas on the very concept of the Biosphere were not immediately clear and his own concept was not fully developed until the writing of his monograph *Biosfera*, published in Leningrad in 1926, just after his return from France, and later published in a French revised and expanded edition in Paris in 1929. Consequently, Teilhard's major essays (dated from 1925) and the two books of Le Roy (1927, 1928), where the doctrine of the Biosphere and the Noosphere was established, were written before the publication of *La Biosphère* by Vernadsky. This latter book was never

---

5   Abbé Christophe Gaudefroy (1878-1971), mineralogist at the Institute Catholique, was perhaps instrumental in the encounter between his colleague Teilhard, Edouard Le Roy and Vernadsky. Recently published letters of Teilhard to Gaudefroy contain no mention of Vernadsky.

later quoted by Teilhard, and all popular subsequent studies on Teilhard ignore it. This fact is of enormous cultural significance: the concept of the Biosphere, in the sense in which Vernadsky uses the term and as adopted by global ecology, has been superseded by Teilhard's idea of the Biosphere.

In France, Vernadsky tentatively introduced his new biogeochemical ideas in a series of articles published after 1923 in the *Revue générale des sciences*. But in no paper did he provide a precise definition of the concept of the Biosphere.

Many interesting ideas belonging to the prehistory of the Gaia hypothesis can be found in the numerous bio-bibliographical notes added by Vernadsky in the publication of his Sorbonne lectures on Geochemistry (biogeochemistry would be a better title). In particular, Vernadsky pointed out the contribution of the founders of organic chemistry, Justus von Liebig (1803-1873) in Germany, Jean-Baptiste Boussingault (1802-1887) and Jean-Baptiste Dumas (1800-1884) in France as to how chemical cycles connected all living organisms, including microorganisms, soils and the atmosphere.

In 1841, Dumas and Boussingault published their views on the grand chemical cycles of nature in a remarkable small book entitled *Essai de statique chimique des êtres organisés*. Based on a lecture concluding Dumas's course at the Ecole de Médecine in Paris, the book was a durable success, with several reeditions and translations, including in the United States in 1844 under the title *The Chemical and Physiological Balance of Organic Nature*. It emphasized the cycling relationships and the chemical equilibrium that unite animals and plants through the biochemistry of the atmosphere. The animal machine (before the thermodynamical paradigm still to be born) was already being compared with a heat engine!

The most important thesis of this early organic chemistry of nature was that animal, vegetable and atmosphere, through the grand carbon, hydrogen, nitrogen and oxygen cycles form a vast system.

The physiological concept of metabolism, appeared in the middle-nineteenth-century Germany under the term *Stoffwechsel* and later in the French literature, being applied not only to individual living organisms, but also to the vast organism of nature, that comprised a Geophysiology of the Biosphere.

In a paper published in 1842, Dumas, Liebig's rival, claimed that his and Boussingault's work was done independently of Liebig's as expressed in his book of 1840.

Today, inspired by a recent paper on "Boussingault and the nitrogen cycle" (Aulie, 1970), James Lovelock and Lynn Margulis have cited Dumas and Boussingault: "The atmosphere, therefore, is the mysterious link that connects the animal with the vegetable, the vegetable with the animal kingdom." (Margulis and Lovelock, 1975a; Margulis, 1981:347).

Vernadsky was the first scientist to be concerned with the boundaries of the Biosphere as "the domain of life" (second part, in Vernadsky, 1929). He devoted a special article in 1937 to "the limits of the biosphere". Many difficulties remained. In his posthumous 1965 book, *The Chemical Structure of Earth's Biosphere and its Surroundings* (only in Russian), "Vernadsky had not defined what he implied by the 'surroundings' of the biosphere" (Lapo, 1987:59). At the time, solving the question concerning the upper boundary of the Biosphere was as complicated as that

15

concerning the lower boundary. Thus he was interested in atmospheric ozone,[6] notably in the work of the physicists Fabry and Buisson, being deeply concerned with the links between geophysical, geochemical and biological processes. He considered the stratospheric ozone shield as the upper limit of the Biosphere, created by the biota for biota, admitting of course that the living beings are confined within narrower limits: "La vie créant l'oxygène libre dans l'écorce terrestre, crée par là même l'ozone et protège la biosphère des rayonnements pernicieux des ondes courtes des astres célestes." (Vernadsky, 1929:147)

In fact the chemist Christian Schönbein (1799-1868), the originator in 1838 of the term Geochemistry, as the study of the chemical make-up of the Earth's components, a friend of the *Naturphilosopher* Schelling, first discovered ozone in his laboratory at the University of Basel, in 1840. But it was not until 1858 that ozone (O_3) was discovered in the atmosphere. Later, through the study of the total ozone content of the vertical distribution of the atmosphere, ozone was found to be responsible for ultraviolet absorption. Ozone was the subject of a first international congress in 1929, in Paris, the principal convener of the conference being the French physicist Charles Fabry (1867-1945). In 1929, ozone was not seen as part of a problem as it has now become, notably after Lovelock's observations, and still more so with the discovery of the Antarctic ozone hole.[7] Yet, we must remember it was Vernadsky who discerned the interactive link between the ozone shield and the Biosphere. But during Vernadaky's life-span, man-made pollution of the Biosphere was still negligible.

Vernadsky considered Life on Earth as a whole, as an extraordinary single cosmos phenomenon. He viewed his conception of The Biosphere as a "scientific discovery" (Vernadsky, 1929, 23), affecting all fields of natural sciences and social sciences, considering it in the light of the history of scientific revolutions, part of the twenty-century intellectual movement or the contemporary "revolution of ideas" (Vernadsky, 1924, 6).

He always pleaded for an integration of the sciences, emphasizing the idea of *Wholeness.*

In the "considérations générales" opening his book *La Géochimie*, directly written in French with the help of his wife Nathalie, Vernadsky wrote:

"On peut dire que jamais dans l'histoire de la pensée humaine l'idée et le sentiment du Tout, de l'union causale de tous les phénomènes scientifiquement observables, n'avait une profondeur et une clarité comparables à celles qu'ils ont attreints au XXe siècle." (Vernadsky, 1924:2)

In France, Vernadsky was deeply impressed by Bergson's philosophy of living. He agreed with Edouard Le Roy that Bergson's work provided "a new philosophy".

---

6   See Ch. Fabry, *L'ozone atmosphérique*, préface de J. Cabannes, Paris, CNRS, 1950. 1. See J. Lecomte et al., "Charles Fabry", *Applied Optics*, 1973, 12(6), pp.1117-1129. A brief historical review is given in G. Brasseur, "The endangered ozone layer", *Environment*, 1987, 29(1), pp.6-11, 39-45.
7   The scientific and 'ecologist' literature is becoming immense. See John Gribbin, ed., *The Breathing Planet*, A New Scientist Guide, London, Blackwell, 1986. J. Gribbin, *The Hole in the Sky, Man's Threat to the Ozone Layer*, London, Corgi, 1988. R. Clarke, *The Ozone Layer*, Nairobi, UNEP/GEMS Environment Library No. 2, 1987

He also agreed with Bergson's message in *L'Evolution créatrice* that:

"All the living hold together, and all yield to the same tremendous push. The animal takes its stand on the plant, man bestrides animality, and the whole of humanity, in space and in time, is one immense army galloping beside and before and behind each of us in an overwhelming charge able to beat down every resistance and clear the most formidable obstacles, perhaps even death."

La Géochimie was apparently not widely read by biologists. Consequently, in the preface of the French editions of *La Biosphère,* Vernadsky emphasized:

"Le but de ce livre est d'attirer l'attention des naturalistes, des géologues, et surtout des biologistes sur l'importance de l'étude quantitative de la vie dans ses rapports indissolubles avec les phénomènes chimiques de la planète." (Vernadsky, 1929, vii).

Vernadsky's energetic and biogeochemical approach to the whole Biospheric system powered by the Sun's energy flux only had, at the time, a decisive influence in his native country. It influenced the rise of environment movement and community ecology, and the Russian trend towards systems thinking (Douglas Weiner, 1988, p.80).

Perhaps the only notable continuing work associated with Vernadsky's ecological heritage was that represented by the school of the great Russian botanist (in fact a plant ecologist) Vladimir Nikolaevich Sukachev (1882-1967). With the late synthesis of 1964 translated into English under the title *Fundamentals of Forest Biogeocoenology* (Sukachev and Dylis, 1968), which represents the long-life school of Sukachev, we can rediscover the profound impact of Vernadsky's holistic biogeochemical concept of the Biosphere on Russian ecology. The concept of *biogeocoenose* developed by Sukachev's school of thinking, which was similar to that of ecosystem coined in 1935 by the English botanist Arthur Tansley, was broader in scope and emphasized the biogeochemical cycling aspects in line with Vernadsky's Biosphere concept.

Unfortunately, by the mid-1930s, the Russian school of ecology and the early movement for the conservation of nature fell into oblivion. The scientific activity as well as the entire country entered into a dark period! The Lysenko syndrome was in germ. As were Bukharin, Boris Hessen and other Soviet delegates to the 1931 Congress of London, which was later considered as a turning point in the history of science, many early Russian ecologists and conservationists were officially denounced as "traitors" and "counter-revolutionaries". Ecology was already considered politically a subversive science!

Vernadsky's Biosphere concept was forgotten until the 1960s. Vernadsky himself died before the Science of the Biosphere or Global Ecology he founded became the focus of international scientific concerns and of several big interdisciplinary research programmes.

Vernadsky, Hutchinson and Ecology

The dark turbulent situation in Russia after the October Revolution caused the emigration of the Vernadsky family; temporary for the Academician Vladimir and his wife, definitively for the son and the daughter. Thanks[8] to the Russian naturalist Alexander Petrunkevich (1875-1964), a former student and friend of Vladimir Vernadsky who was forced to leave his country to escape arrest and had been in America, at Yale University, since 1903, George Vernadsky (1887-1973), the scientist's only son, had been invited as a historian of Russia to Yale in 1927. The next year, George Evelyn Hutchinson, then returning from South Africa, was appointed professor of biology at Yale. The three men became colleagues and close friends.

G. E Hutchinson was born in Cambridge, England, in 1903. His father, Arthur Hutchinson, F.R.S., was a mineralogist and a friend of the Norwegian, Victor M. Goldschmidt, another great name in the rise of modern geochemistry. The career of Hutchinson[9] was that of a great naturalist, limnologist, zoologist, population ecologist and an interdisciplinary scientist. He participated at the famous Macy Foundation conferences on cybernetics after the Second World War, together with Norbert Weiner, John von Neumann, Gregory Bateson and Margaret Mead. As a result, he developed the circular causal systems thinking in ecology with applications to "the large self-regulatory of cycles of the biosphere" (Hutchinson, 1948a).

Hutchinson, as Frank Egerton notes (1983: 262-3) founded "a significant school of ecology at Yale University." The school included such famous ecologists as Howard T. Odum, Robert MacArthur, Lawrence B. Slobodkin, John Vallentyne and Ramon Margalef, a Spanish ecologist who later published his book *La Biosfera entre la termodinamica y el juego* (Margalef, 1980).

Vernadsky's work had a strong influence on many aspects of Hutchinson's ecological thinking. In an autobiographical book, he wrote: "I did my best to help Petrunkevich and George Vernadsky to make his ideas about the biosphere better known in English-speaking countries. Though I came to biogeochemistry through Vernadsky, I soon realized the great importance to biology of the concepts introduced by my father's friend Viktor M. Goldschmidt. Putting these two together in an ecological context I think did something to further the more chemical aspects of ecology."[10]

In a letter (October 1, 1985) Professor Hutchinson wrote: "I can find no mention of *La Biosphere* in my own writing before 1943. The whole concept of the work was however well known to Lindeman and myself mainly through Alexander Petrunkevitch."

---

8   G. E Hutchinson writes: "Petrunkevitch had arranged for George Vernadsky to come to Yale in the late 1920's, I think." (Personal letter from October 1, 1985). In the Archives of the Academy of Sciences in Paris, I have found several letters from Vernadsky to A. Lacroix speaking of his family life and of the emigration of his children.

9   In 1962, Hutchinson received the Eminent Ecologist Award of the Ecological Society of America, and in 1979 the Franklin Medal of the Franklin Institute for the development of the scientific basis of ecology. See *Limnology and Oceanography*, 1971, vol. 16, no. 2, issue dedicated to G. Evelyn Hutchinson, including a Bibliography and notably a paper by Yvette H. Edmondson, "Some components of the Hutchinson legend", pp.157-172; and E. S. Deevey, Ed., *Growth by Intussusception, Ecological Essays in Honor of G. Evelyn Hutchinson*, Hamden, Connecticut, Archon Books, 1972, 441p. See also Saarinen (1982); McIntosh (1985).

10   G. E. Hutchinson, *The Kindly Fruits of the Earth, Recollections of an Embryo Ecologist*, New York, Yale University Press, 1979, p.233.

Already in 1940, reviewing Frederic E. Clements and Victor E. Shelford's famous book *Bio-Ecology* in 1939, Hutchinson wrote:

"The gravest defect of the book, in the reviewer's opinion, lies in its total neglect of certain very important approaches to the subject, in which its technical language is of no assistance. If, as is insisted, the community is an organism, it should be possible to study the metabolism of that organism. The neglect of this aspect of ecology, and of the fact that the living matter of the whole earth may be considered as a unit of higher order than the biome, leads the authors to make the following extraordinary statement, "from the very nature of the medium, the reactions of plants upon the air are usually less definite and controlling than upon the soil." Photosynthesis is discussed briefly on the next page, but no idea of the fact, apparent to Joseph Priestley on the conclusion of his experiments, is given that here we are in the presence of the grest controlling reaction of them all. This neglect of the biogeochemical approach is due in part to the authors' insistence that the community and the environment must be separated and should be considered as forming part of the same ecological unit." (Hutchinson, 1940).

Hutchinson, a man of unusual foresight, was instrumental in the publication in America of two of Vernadsky's works on the Biosphere, George Vernadsky being the translator. The first work, "Problems of Biogeochemistry, ll", dated from 1938, was under the editorship of Hutchinson himself and was published in 1944 in the *Transactions of the Connecticut Academy of Arts and Sciences* (Vernadsky , 1944); the second, more diffuse entitled "The Biosphere and the Noosphere", was published in *American Scientist* in January 1945, a few days after Vernadsky's death on January 6, 1945, in Moscow.

In a foreword the Editor (inspired by Hutchinson, I presume) wrote this laudatory presentation: "The two contributions together present the general intellectual outlook of one of the most remarkable scientific leaders of the present century" (Vernadsky, 1945a). At the time, Vernadsky's ideas made no impression, but later these two references were included in the standard bibliography of Eugene Odum's (1971) *Fundamentals of Ecology*.

In 1943, during the World War II, while the physicists of the Manhattan Engineer District Project worked on the atomic bomb the great Yale ecologist ended the introduction to his series "Marginalia" published in the *American Scientist* with these still relevant words:

"The most practical lasting benefit science can now offer is to teach man how to avoid the destruction of his own environment and how, by understanding himself with true humility and pride, to find ways to avoid injuries that at present he inflicts on himself with such devastating energy."[12]

During World War II, Hutchinson published several important studies of *Biogeochemistry,* including on the atmospheric part of the Biosphere. As we have

---

12   Editor's note in G. E. Hutchinson, "Marginalia: What is science for?", *American Scientist*, 1983, 71, pp.639-644

seen, he was inspired by Vernadsky's teachings. In a paper of 1943, Hutchinson credited "Academician W. I. Vernadsky" for the term biogeochemistry (Vernadsky, 1939); and a photograph of the great Russian scientist, given by George Vernadsky, illustrated this American living homage:

> "The most fruitful approach to the fundamental problems of ecology lies in a synthesis of the results of Vernadsky, Goldschmidt, and certain other investigators entirely outside the traditional field of the biological sciences."[13]

In the second volume of "The Solar System" series edited by the prominent astronomer Gerard Kuiper (1905-1973) and poignantly entitled *The Earth as a Planet*, G. E. Hutchinson wrote an important chapter entitled "The biochemistry of the terrestrial atmosphere" (Hutchinson, 1954). In this text he showed that the Earth's atmosphere is almost entirely of secondary origin as pointed out in 1949 by the late geochemist Harrison Brown[14] and independently by Hans Suess, and as previously anticipated by Vernadsky, Hutchinson emphasized the immense role played by living organisms at the surface of the Earth.

Hutchinson's biogeochemical studies link the work of Vernadsky with that of Lovelock and Margulis. In several papers by Lovelock and Margulis on the Gaia hypothesis, as well as in Lovelock's first book on Gaia (1979), Hutchinson's inspiration is clearly recognized, as in an early paper on Gaia entitled "Homeostatic tendencies of the Earth's atmosphere".

The history of the extraordinary chemical composition of the atmosphere of our planet is one of the main arguments for the Gaia hypothesis, but it is not until the mid-1970s that "the influence of the Biosphere on the Atmosphere" (Dütsch, ed. 1978) became a new scientific consensus, after several decades of discussions on the origin of life on Earth and hence on the early evolution of the Biosphere (not without confusion about the very term), the latter being now considered far older than previously assumed.[15] Already, prophetically, Vernadsky and Teilhard de Chardin, as holistic geologists, imagined the evolution of the Biosphere within the entire history of the Earth. At the same time, by 1970, atmospheric pollution and more generally "Global Chemical Cycles and Their Alterations by Man" (Stumm, ed. 1977; Breuer, 1978) had become a major scientific concern of growing social relevance.

Other contributions to the Gaia concept have been acknowledged by Lovelock and Margulis, notably those of the Swedish geochemist Lars Sillen, the German-born American paleontologist Heinz A. Lowenstam and Alfred Redfield, the latter being a long-life member of Harvard University and Woods Hole Oceanographic Institution. Redfield's 1958 paper entitled "The biological control of chemical factors in the environment" became a classic, partly reedited in *Readings in*

13 G. E. Hutchinson, "The biogeochemistry of aluminium and of certain related elements", *Quarterly Review of Biology*, 1943, 18(1) pp.1-29.
14 H. Brown, "Rare gases and the formation of the Earth's atmosphere", in G. P. Kuiper, Ed., *The Atmospheres of the Earth and the Planets*, Chicago, London, University of Chicago Press, 1949, pp.258-266.
15 The scientific literature on the origin of life and the early evolution of the biosphere (with various definitions!) is a fast growing library since the first international symposium held in Moscow in 1957. See especially Breuer, 1980; Holland and Schidlowski, Eds., 1980; Schopf, ed., 1983; Margulis, 1984; Day, 1984; Schidlowski, 1985; Boureau, 1986; Lapo, 1987; Locquin, ed., 1987; Margulis and Sagan, 1987. One of the pioneers, the noted Russian biochemist Alexander Ivanovich Oparin (1894-1980), who adopted the Marxist-Leninist philosophy, was a critic of Vernadsky!

Ecology by Edward J. Kormondy (1965). However until the 1980s, the historiography of the theme, including Vernadsky's work and terminological issue, was practically ignored.

The general public, political leaders, and even philosophers and historians of science were, in principle, ignorant of the development of biogeochemistry of the Biosphere. Great exceptions included American scientists Barry Commoner, David E. Gates and Eugene Odum, the Belgian Paul Duvignaud and the French François Ramade, as well as several other scientists not normally referred to as ecologists.

The theme of the Biosphere threatened by Man's activities began to emerge during the 1960s. The very term of Biosphere gained currency at the international level with the so-called "Biosphere Conference" convened by UNESCO in Paris in September 1968 (the Proceedings being published in Paris by UNESCO in 1970), with the first International Conference on the Environmental Future, held in Finland during the summer of 1971 (see "The Biosphere Today", by Polunin, 1972), with the widely read unofficial report *Only One Earth* (Ward and Dubos, 1972) to the 1972 Stockholm Conference and many other publications in the fields of ecology and environment. However the general neglect of the Gaia hypothesis and Vernadsky's work illustrated a vast ignorance concerning the fundamental holistic concept of the Biosphere.

In 1965, the first chapter of Hutchinson's book *The Ecological Theatre and the Evolutionary Play* was entitled "The Biosphere or volume in which organisms actually live" (Hutchinson, 1965) and it contained a brief story of the concept of the biosphere.

In his important article introducing the September 1970 issue of *Scientific American* devoted to "the Biosphere", Hutchinson wrote:

> "It is essentially Vernadsky's concept of the biosphere, developed about 50 years after Suess wrote, that we accept today." (Hutchinson, 1970).

In the early 1970s, Hutchinson's writings on Vernadsky's tradition were still largely ignored, even by the scientific community in the United States. Even ecologists such as Paul Ehrlich or Barry Commoner ignored it. But, since the early 1980s, the situation has changed. In *Carbon Dioxide Review: 1982*, edited by William C. Clark (1982:22), we can therefore read:

> "The last several years, however, have brought a growing recognition of the critical role played by the oceans' biological processes in determining the effects of increasing CO_2. This trend is part of a wider resurgence of the biogeochemical perspective of life on Earth, sketched almost half a century ago by Vernadsky and now elegantly remodeled by Lovelock as the "Gaia hypothesis."

William C. Clark, systems ecologist educated at Yale University and coeditor of *Environment* magazine, member of the US National Academy of Science's Board on Atmospheric Sciences and Climate and its Committee on the Applications of Ecological Theory to Environmental Problems, was to be leader of the first phase, during 1983-1987, of the interdisciplinary research project on "Ecologically

21

Sustainable Development of the Biosphere" at the International Institute for Applied Systems Analysis (IIASA), Laxenburg, Austria.

Within the IIASA Biosphere Project, Vernadsky's perspective is considered as "prophetic" (Clark and Munn, eds., 1986:10) and the Gaia hypothesis is taken very seriously by several prominent global geoscientists and ecologists.[16]

The theme of Biosphere has also been taken on board by several other large environmental research projects of the international scientific community, especially the "Global Change", International Geosphere Biosphere Programme 9IGBPO, officially launched in 1986 by the International Council of Scientific Unions (ICSU).

In that respect we must note the Preface signed by Thomas F. Malone in the book on the ICSU Symposium on *Global Change* (Malone and Roederer, eds., 1985), considered by Professor Polunin as "the first multidisciplinary symposium of the world's scientific summit."

In an important report entitled *Atmospheric Carbon Dioxide and the Global Carbon Cycle* edited by John R. Trabalka and published by the U.S. Department of Energy in December 1985, we can read the following "concluding comments":

> "The system comprising the Earth's surface, atmosphere, and the biota might be viewed as if in homeostasis so that the chemical composition of the atmosphere and the climate are both regulated by biota to its preference. No intricate planning, foresight, or cooperation appears to be needed. Regulation can arise as a simple colligative property of life and its environment. One such view, after Vernadsky (1926) and Hutchinson (1954), was recently restated as the Gaia hypothesis (Hitchcock and Lovelock 1967; Lovelock 1979, 1983). It offers a challenging perspective on the natural cycles of the elements."

"The biological Earth is now recognized to exert a major influence on global processes", declares the report entitled *Earth System Science: Overview, A Programme for Global Change*, dated from May 1986, of the Earth System Sciences Committee (ESSC) to the NASA Advisory Council. In the report entitled *Earth System Science: A Closer View*, dated from January 1988, the theme is more deeply developed and a brief history of the term biosphere, with credit to Vernadsky, is given. Perhaps the Institute of Ecotechnics publication of *The Biosphere Catalogue* (Snyder, ed., 1985), including a paper entitled "The Real Deficit: Our Debt to the Biosphere" signed by Lynn Margulis and Dorion Sagan, will be later considered as a landmark.

The problems recommended for inclusion in the "International Geosphere Biosphere Programme" or "Global Change", with *"biospheric interactions* as the focus and discriminator in setting priorities and principal emphases", are considered as "urgent, fundamental and hard" by the National Research Council (U.S. National Academy of Sciences) in its 1986 report entitled *Global Change in the Geosphere: initial Priorities for an IGBP*, which emphasizes the need for a global

---

16 See also Rafal Serafin, *Vernadsky's Biosphere, Teilhard's Noosphere, and Lovelock's Gaia: Perspectives on Human Intervention on Global Biogeochemical Cycles*, Laxenburg, Austria, International Institute for Applied Systems Analysis, 1987; and his paper entitled "Noosphere, Gaia and science of the biosphere", *Environmental Ethics*, 1988, 10(2), in press.

ecology - "a way to perceive and predict biological consequences of global change in the environment."

Global Ecology: The Earth as a Living Planet

"Although the word 'biosphere' has indeed come into general use,
the meaning of the word in all its subversive richness has not yet
penetrated into the consciousness of the world leaders who now
employ it."
Walter Truett Anderson[17]

Since his first paper entitled "Gaia as seen through the atmosphere", Lovelock (1972) considers Gaia as "a living entity". According to Lovelock and Margulis, Gaia is not the Biosphere, if the latter term designates only the part of the Earth's surface where living beings naturally exist (and not "the total ensemble of living organisms", as defined by Lovelock and Margulis in the papers of 1974) nor is it the biota, that is simply the totality of all individual living organisms (often also named the biosphere!). So what is the difference between *Gaia* and the *Biosphere*? And first of all, what is the definition of our concept of the Biosphere bearing in mind that Vernadsky referred to "the living organism of the biosphere" (Vernadsky, 1929:21)?

The notion of Gaia indicates a self-regulatory bio-geo-chemical mechanism with the capacity to keep the planet Earth living by controlling the global environment of the face of the Earth. Gaia is synonymous with the Earth as a planetary living being. But the Geosphere is not the Biosphere.

If the basic idea of the Gaia hypothesis is that the atmosphere is an extension of the Biosphere, this revolutionary idea was already stated by Vernadský and embodied in his biogeochemical conception of *The Biosphere*. Consequently a closer view including a historical perspective is now necessary to understand the filiation between the Gaia concept and Vernadsky's concept of the Biosphere. Cooperation with Russian scholars, experts in Vernadsky's work and subsequent Biospheric studies, is more necessary than ever.

The real meaning of the concept of the Biosphere proposed by Vladimir Vernadsky is not easy to examine, partly because Vernadsky's ideas underwent considerable evolution. In addition, several important texts are still unavailable outside the Russian culture.

According to Vernadsky, the Biosphere is not simply the part of the Earth in which organisms live; life and its accelerated evolutionary dynamics (a point emphasized by the French epistemologist François Meyer) play a major role in the Biospheric environment, transforming together the lithosphere, the hydrosphere and the atmosphere. But of course, the evolution of the Biosphere is *biocentric* not at all *anthropocentric* as Teilhard believed it to be! Indeed only several hundred million years after the formation of the planet Earth (as Vernadsky pointed out from the

---

17   W. T. Anderson, *To Govern Evolution, Further Adventures of the Political Animal*, Cambridge, Mass., Harcourt Brace Jovanovich, 1987, p.255.

beginning!), the Biosphere was already expanding: hence the fate of the Biosphere is truly *The fate of the Earth* (see Schell, 1982; Weiner, 1986).

Were Gaia and geophysiology also conceived by Vernadsky? Here we must leave the question open. We are only beginning to read Vernadsky's works and his last unfinished important book on the Biosphere, written in Russian at the end of his long working life, is still unpublished outside the Soviet Union where it was only published in 1965.

Hutchinson's 1970 article on 'the Biosphere' marked, for our Western scientific culture, the watershed in the recognition of the holistic concept of the Biosphere. But, in the mind of many people, the term Biosphere was often simply considered as synonymous with the global environment. The idea of an 'ecosystem' (Evans, 1956) at the global scale of the planet was better and adopted by several holistic ecologists such as like Eugene Odum.

The year 1970 marked an epoch: the emerging recognition of our global ecological crisis and the adoption of a cosmic perspective on the ecology of the whole Earth. As the celebrated astronomer Carl Sagan wrote in his book *Cosmic Connection*:

"The current resurgence of interest in the ecology of the planet Earth is also connected with this longing for a cosmic perspective. Many of the leaders of the ecological movement in the United States were originally stimulated to action by photographs of Earth taken from space, pictures revealing a tiny, delicate, and fragile world, exquisitely sensitive to the depredations of man - a meadow in the middle of the sky."

Ecology in a broad sense, the recent plate tectonics revolution in the Earth sciences, space exploration and counter culture provided new views of the old planet we live in. During 1970-72, essentially in the United States, many important popular and scientific books were published adopting a global perspective – a symbolic *macroscope*' according to the systems ecologist Howard T. Odum – on 'Man in the Biosphere'.

The age of global ecology, of the coming of a holistic science of the Biosphere, unfortunately is also the nuclear age. The present concern for changing atmosphere is also connected with the Nuclear Winter theory, Alvarez's Mass Extinctions theory, and it is mainly through our threatened global atmospheric environment that Vernadsky's concept of the Biosphere, Global Ecology and the Gaia theory are linked together.

Now, with the rise of Global and Deep Ecology concerns as well as Lovelock's proposal, the time is ripe to the recognition of Gaia and all its implications.

I propose the concept of the Vernadskian revolution as a prerequisite for the discovery of Gaia and the adoption of a bio(spheral)economics.

In this new intellectual, Vernadsky's *La Biosphère* must become a classic, within environmental education as well as scientific learning. A critical edition is needed. Of course, many of Vernadsky's statements are now outmoded but that is the case for all classical ideas in the history of science. We can also discuss several of Vernadsky's ideas on the transition between the Biosphere and the Noosphere. The debate is now open.

We should also agree with the author of *La Géochimie* that: "We are living in a critical epoch of the history of mankind", and what is presently emerging is "the idea and feeling of the wholeness".

We should also credit Vladimir Vernadsky, as a prophetic thinker, with the title of father of the Global Ecology of the Biosphere. Indeed he is the most illustrious precedent for the current Gaia theory. And because we have neglected his biospheric message, and the early warnings of ecologists, we are in the midst of a grave planetary crisis. That situation is well captured by the dramatic historical shift from Eduard Suess's *The Face of the Earth* to Jonathan Schell's *the Fate of the Earth*.

References

Abram, D., The Perceptual Implications of Gaia, *The Ecologist*, Vol,15 No. 3, pp.96-103. 1985.

Bailes, K. E., Vernadsky and the Biosphere, Irvine, University of California, History Department, 1978, 79p. unpublished.

Balandine, R., *Vladimir Vernadsky*, trans. from the Russian, Moscow, Mir, "Outstanding Soviet Scientists", 1982, 107p.

Batisse, M., Man and the Biosphere, *Nature*, 1975, 256, pp.156-158.

Bergson, H., *L'Evolution Créatice*, Paris, Alcan, 1907, p.271. English translation by A. Mitchell, *Creative Evolution*, London, Macmillan, 1911, p.271.

Blum, H. F., Evolution of the Biosphere, *Nature*, 1965, 208, pp.324-326.

Bolin, B., Global Ecology and Man, pp.27-56, in *Proceedings of the World Climate Conference*, Geneva, WMO, No. 537, 1979, xii+79lp.

Bolin, B., *Climatic Changes and their effects on the Biosphere*, Geneva, WHO, 1980, xiv+49p.

Bolin, B., and Cook, R. B., eds., *The Major Biogeochemical Cycles and their Interactions*, SCOPE, Report 21, Chichester, Wiley, 1983, xxi+532p.

Bolin, B., and Boos, B., Eds., *The Greenhouse Effect, Climate Change and Ecosystems*, SCOPE, Report 29, Chichester, Wiley, 500p.

Botkin, D. B., Can there be a theory of Global Ecology?, *Journal of Theoretical Biology*, 1982, 96, pp.95-98.

Budyko, M., *Ecologie globale*, trad. du russe, Moscow, Editions du Progres, 1980, 336p.

Budyko, M., *Evolution of the Biosphere*, trans. from the Russian (1984), Dordrecht, Reidel, 1986, xv+423p.

Caldwell, L. K., Science will not save the biosphere but politics might, *Environmental Conservation*, 1985, 12(3), pp.195-197.

Castri, F., Twenty years of international programmes on ecosystems and the biosphere: an overview of achievements, shortcomings and possible new perspectives, pp.314-331, in Malone, T. F. and Roedere, J. G., Eds., *Global Change*, ICSU Press, Cambridge, Cambridge University Press, 1985, 512p.

Clark, W., and Munn, R. E., Eds., *Sustainable Development of the Biosphere*, Laxenburg, IIASA, Cambridge, Cambridge University Press, 1986, 491p.

Cloud, P., The Biosphere, *Scientific American*, 1983, 249(3), pp.176-189.

Cole, L. C., The Ecosphere, *Scientific American*, 1958, 198(4), pp.83-96.

Commoner, B., *The Closing Circle: Nature, Man and Technology,* New York, Bantam Books, (1971) 1972, 344p.

Cook, R. B., Man and the Biogeochemical Cycles: Interacting with the Elements, *Environment*, 1984, 26(7), pp.11-15, 38-40.

Cowen, R. C., The Biosphere and the Atmosphere: A Global Picture, *Technology Review*, 1986, 89(3), pp.17, 71.

Dasmann, R. F., *Planet in Peril: Man and the Biosphere Today,* New York, Harmondsworth, Unesco-world, Penguin Books, 1972, xii+242p.

Davis, C. B., Imperatives, Strategies, and the World Campaign for the Biosphere, *Environmental Conservation*, 1984, 11(4), pp.291-292.

Day, W., *Genesis on Planet Earth. The Search for Life's Beginning*, foreword by Lynn Margulis, New Haven, Yale University Press, second edition, 1984, xx+299p. ('Gaia', pp.255-264).

Dickinson, R. E., Ed., *The Geophysiology of Amazonia. Vegetation and climate Interactions,* The United Nations University, New York, Chichester, Wiley, 1987, xvii+526p.

Dubos, R., The biosphere: a delicate balance between man and nature *The Unesco Courier*, January 1969, pp.7-16.

Dubos, R., *A God Within,* New York, Charles Scribners' Sons, 1972, ix+325p.

Dubos, R., Gaia and creative evolution, *Nature*, 1979, 282, pp.154-155.

Dumas, J. B., and Boussingault, J. B., *Essai de statique chimique des êtres organisés*, Paris, Fortin et Masson, 1841, 2e éd., 1842, 3e éd., 1844. Recent edition; Bruxelles, Editions Culture et Civilisation, 1972.

Dumas, J. B., Essai de statique chimique des êtres organisés, *Annales de chimie et de physique*, 1842, e3 série, 4, pp.115-126

Duvigneaud, P., *La Synthèse écologique. Populations, communautés, écosystèmes, biosphère, noosphère,* Paris, Doin, 1974; 2e ed. Revue et corrigée, 1980, 380p.

Egerton, F. N., The History of Ecology, *Journal of the History of Biology*, 1983, 16, pp.259-310; 1985, 18, pp.103-143.

Ehrlich, P. R., Sagan, C., Kennedy, D., Roberts, W. O., *The Cold and the Dark. The World after Nuclear War,* New York, Norton, 1984, 229p.

Evans, F. C., Ecosystem as the basic unit in ecology, *Science*, 1956, 123, pp.1127-1128.

Florkin, M., Approches molèculaires de l'intégration écologique. Probléms de terminologie, *Bulletin de l'Académie Royale de Belgique, Classe des Sciences*, 1965, 5e série, 51, pp.239-256.

Forey, P. L., Ed., *The Evolving Biosphere,* British Museum (Natural History), Cambridge, Cambridge University Press, 1981, viii+311p.

Fortescue, J. A. C., *Environmental Geochemistry: A Holistic Approach*, New York, Berlin, Springer-Verlalg, 'Ecological Studies 34', 1980, 347p.

Gates, D. M., The flow of energy in the biosphere, *Scientific American,* September 1971, incorp. in *Energy and Power,* A Scientific American Book, San Francisco, Freeman, 1971, pp.41-52.

Georgescu-Roegen, N., *Energy and Economic Myths,* New York, Pergamon Press, 1976, xxviii+380p.

Gillard, A., On terminology of biosphere and ecosphere, *Nature,* 1969, 223(5205), pp.500-501.

Goody, R., Ed., *Global Change: Impacts on Habitability: A Scientific Basis for Assessment,* A Report by the Executive Committee of a Workshop held at Woods Hole, Massachussets, June 21-26, 1982, Pasadena, Cal., California Institute of Technology, JPL, NASA, 1982, 19p.

Gribbin, J., Ed., *The Breathing Planet.* A New Scientist Guide, Oxford, Basil Blackwell & New Scientist, 1986, 336p.

Grinevald, J., The Forgotten Sources of the Concept of Biosphere. Some historical notes for the study of origins of a holistic concept, contribution presented at the Annual Meeting of World Council for The Biosphere and joint Planning Session with International Society for Environmental Education, Les Avants sur Montreux (Switzerland), 18-22 June 1985, 26p. unpublished.

Grinevald, J., Biosphere et politique internationale: de la guerre froide à l'hiver nucléaire, in B. Jurdant, Ed., *Senses of Science,* European Association for the Study of Science and Technology, IVth meeting, 29 sept./1 Oct. 1986, Strasbourg, Conseil de l'Europe, Université Louis Pasteur, GERSULP, 1986.

Grinevald, J., The Biosphere, by V. I. Vernadsky, *Environmental Conservation,* 1986, 13(3), pp.285-286.

Heintze, C., *The Biosphere: Earth, Air, Fire and Water,* New York, Thomas Nelson, 1977, 128p.

Henderson-Sellers, A., The Earth's environment - a uniquely stable system? *Geophysical Survey,*1981, 4(3), pp.297-329.

Hughes, C. J., Gaia: a natural scientist's ethic for the future, *The Ecologist,* 1985, Vol. 15, No. 3, pp.92-95.

Hughes, J. Donald, Gaia: an ancient view of our planet, *The Ecologist,* 1983, 13(2), pp.54-60.

Humboldt, A. de, *Essai sur la géographie des plantes, accompagné d'un Tableau physique des regions équinoxiales.* Paris, Levrault, Schoell et Cie, 1805, 155p.

Humboldt, A. de, *Cosmos; essai d'une description physique du monde,* Trans. from the German by H. Gaye et Ch. Galusky, Paris, Gide, t.1, 588p.; t.647p.; t.III, 771p. t.IV, 810p. 1847-1859.

Humboldt, A. de, *Tableaux de la Nature,* trans. by M. C. Galusky, Paris, Guérin, 1866, 736p.

Hutchinson, G. E., Bio-Ecology, *Ecology,* 21(2), 1940, pp.267-268.

Hutchinson, G. E., The biochemistry of the terrestrial atmosphere, pp.371-433, in Gerard P. Guiper, Ed.,*Th e Earth as a Planet,* Chicago, University of Chicago Press, 1954, 751p.

Hutchinson, G. E. , The Biosphere or volume in which organisms actually live, pp.1-26, in *The Ecological Theater and the Evolutionary Play,* New Haven, Yale University Press, 1965, xiii+139p.

Hutchinson, G. E., The Biosphere, *Scientific American,* 1970, 223(3), pp.45-53.

Hutchinson, G. E., *the Kindly Fruits of the Earth: Recollections of an Embryo Ecologist,* New Haven, Yale University Press, 1979, 277p.

27

Hutton, J., Theory of Rain, *Transactions of the Royal Society of Edinburgh*, 1, part 2, pp.41-86, (lu le 2 février 1784). 1788a.

Hutton, J., Theory of the Earth; or investigation of the laws observable in the composition, dissolution, and restoration of land upon the globe, *Transactions of the Royal Society of Edinburgh*, 1, part 2, pp.209-304. 1788b.

Hutton, J., *Theory of the Earth with Proofs and Illustrations*, Edinburgh, William Creech, London, Cadell and Davies, 2 vols. 1795 (new edition New York, Stechert-Hafner, 1959).

Hutzinger, O., Ed., (1980-85), *The Natural Environment and the Biogeochemical Cycles*, The Handbook of Environmental Chemistry, Berlin, New York, Springer-Verlag, vol.1, A, 1980, 258p. B, 1982, 317p; C, 1984, 220p; D, 1985, 246p.

Huxley, T. H., *La place de l'homme dans la nature*, trans. from the English (1863), Paris, Baillière, (1868).

Ingersoll, A., L'atmosphère, Pour la Science, 73, pp.122-136. 1983.

International Council of Scientific Unions (ICSU), *The International Geosphere Biosphere Programme: A Study of Global Change*, Final report of the Ad Hock Planning Group, prepared for the 21st General Assembly, Berne, September 14-19, 1986, Paris, ICSU, August 4, 27p.

Imshenetsky, A. A., Lysenko, S. V., and Kazakov, G. A., Upper Boundary of the biosphere, *Applied and Environmental Microbiology*, 35(1), pp.1-5. 1978.

Jaworski, H., *Géon ou la Terre vivante*, Paris, Gallimard, 1928.

Jessop, N. M., *Biosphere: A Study of Life*, Englewood Cliffs, N.J., Prentice Hall, 1970, 954p.

Jones, R. L., *Biogeography: structure, process, pattern and change within the biosphere*, Amsterdam, Hulton Educational Publications, 1980, 192p.

Kamishilov, M. M., *Evolution of the Biosphere*, trans. from the Russian (1974), Moscow, Mir, 1976, 269p.

Khozin, G., *Biosphere and Politics*, trans. from the Russian (1976), Moscow, The Progress Publishers, 1979, 229p.

Kovda, V. A., et al, Contemporary scientific concepts relating to the biosphere, pp.13-29, in *Use and conservation of the biosphere*, Paris, UNESCO, 1970, 272p.

Le Roy, E., *L'Exigence idéaliste et le fait de l'evolution*, Paris, Boivin, 1927, 270p.

Le Roy, E., *Les Origines humaines et l'évolution de l'intelligence*, Paris, Voivin, 1928, 337p.

Lorenz, E. N., *The Nature and Theory of the General Circulation of the Atmosphere*, Geneva, WMO, 1967, xxv+161p.

Lotka, A. J., *Elements of Physical Biology*, Baltimore, Williams and Wilkins Company, 1925, xxx+460p. xxx+465p (new edition ements of Mathematical BiologyNew York, Dover, 1956).

Lovelock, J. E., Gaia as seen through the atmosphere, *Atmospheric Environment*, 1972, 6, pp.579-580.

Lovelock, J. E., *Gaia: A New Look at Life on Earth*, Oxford, Oxford University Press, 1979, 157p. (paperback: 1982)

Lovelock, J. E., Are we destabilising world climate? The lessons of geophysiology, *The Ecologist*, 1985, 15(1-2), pp.52-55.

Lovelock, J. E., Geophysiology: A New Look at Earth Sciences, *Bulletin of the American Meteorological Society*, 1986, 67(4), pp.392-397.

Geophysiology: A New Look at Earth Sciences, in Robert E. Dickinson, Ed., *the Geophysiology of Amazonia: Vegetation and Climate Interactions*, Chichester, Wiley, 1986, pp.11-23.

Lovelock, J. E., The Prehistory of Gaia, *The New Scientist*, 17 July 1986, p.51. (review of The Biosphere, by V. I. Vernadsky).

Lovelock, J. E., and Epton, S. R., The Quest for Gaia, *New Scientist*, 6 February 1975, pp.304-309.

Lovelock, J. E., and Margulis, L. Atmospheric homeostasis by and for the biosphere: the Gaia hypothesis, *Tellus*, 1974, 26, pp.1-10.

Lovelock, J. E., Margulis, L., Homeostatic tendencies of the Earth's atmosphere, *Origins of Life*, 1974, 5, pp.93-103.

Lovelock, J. E., and Margulis, L., Gaia and geognosy: towards a science of the biosphere, in M. B. Rambler, Ed., Global Ecology: Towards a Science of the Biosphere, Boston, Jones and Bartlett Publishing Co., 1986.

Lovelock, J. E., Gaia: the world as living organism, *The New Scientist*, 18 December 1986, pp.25-28.

Lovelock, J. E., and Whitfield, M., Life span of the biosphere, *Nature*, 1982, 296, pp.561-563.

Lowenstam, H. A., Minerals formed by organisms, *Science*, 1981, 211, pp.1126-1131.

Malone, T., Biogeochemical Cycles: A New Research Agenda, *Environment*, 1984, 26(7), pp.4-5, 45.

Malone, T., Mission to Planet Earth: Integrating Studies of Global Change, *Environment*, k1986, 28(8), pp.6-11, 39-42.

Margalef, R., *La Biosfera entra la termodinamica y el juego*, Barcelona, Ediciones Omega, 1980, 236p.

Margulis, L., and Lovelock, J. E., The Biota as Ancient and Modern Modular of the Earth's Atmosphere, in H. U. Dutsch, Ed., *Influence of the Biosphere on the Atmosphere*, Basel, Stuttgart, Birkhauser, 1978, pp.239-243.

Margulis, L., and Lovelock, J. E., Biological modulation of the Earth's atmosphere, *Icarus*, 1974, 21, pp.471-489.

Margulis, L., and Lovelock, J.E., The atmosphere as circulatory system of the biosphere - the Gaia hypothesis, *The CoEvolution Quarterly*, 1975, 6, pp.30-40.

Margulis, L., and Lovelock, J. E., Atmosphere and Evolution, pp.79-100 in John Billingham, Ed., *Life in the Universe*, Cambridge, Mass., MIT Press, 1981, xv+461p.

Meyer, F., Temps, devenir, évolution, *Communications*, 1985, 41, pp.111-122.

Moisseiev, N. N., et al., Biosphere Models, pp.493-510, in R. W. Kates et al., Eds., *Climate impact Assessment: Studies of the Interaction of Climate and Society*, SCOPE Report 27, Chichester, Wiley, 1985, 625p.

Myers, N. Ed., *The Gaia Atlas Planet Management*, Garden City, New York, Anchor Books, London, Pan Books, 1985, 272p.

National Research Council, *Toward an International Geosphere-Biosphere Program*, A Study of Global Change, Report of a National Research Council Workshop, Woods Hole, Massachusetts, July 1983, Washington, D.C., National Academy Press, 1983, 81p.

Odum, E. P., *Fundamentals of Ecology*, Philadelphia, W. B. Saunders Company, 3e éd., 1971, xiv+574p.

Odum, H. T., *Environment, Power and Society*, New York, Wiley-Interscience, 1971, 331p.

Odum, H. T., *Systems Ecology: An Introduction*, New York, Wiley-Interscience, 1983, xvii+644p.

Oparin, A. I., *The Origin of Life on the Earth*, revised and enlarged, trans, from the Russian, New York, Academic Press, Edinburgh, Oliver & Boyd, 1957, 495p.

Polunin, N., The Biosphere Today, pp.33-52, in N. Polunin, Ed., *The Environmental Future*, London, Macmillan, New York, Barne & Noble, 1972, xiv+660p.

Polunin, N., Environmental Education and the Biosphere, *Environmental Conservation*, 1980, 7(2), pp.89-90.

Polunin, N., To Battle for the Biosphere, pp.1-9, in T. N. Veziroglu, Ed., *The Biosphere: Problems and Solutions,*, Amsterdam, Elsevier, 1984, xv+712p.

Ramade, F., *Ecologie des ressources naturélles*, Paris, Masson, 1981, vi+322p.

Redfield, A. C., The biological control of chemical factors in the environment, *American Scientist*, 1958, 46, pp.205-221.

Riedl, R., Die Biosphare und die heutige Erfolgsgessellschaft, *Universitas*, 1973, 28 (6), pp.587-593.

Rosnay, J. E., *Le Macroscope. Vers une vision globale*, Paris, Seuil, 1975, 295p.

Russell, P., *The Awakened Earth. The Global Brain*, L ondon, ARK Paperback, 1984, 228p.

Sagan, C., *Cosmic Connection, An Extraterrestrial Perspective*, New York, Doubleday, 1973, p.60.

Sagan, D., and Margulis, L., The Gaian perspective of ecology, 1983, 13(5), pp.160-167.

Schell, J., *The Fate of the Earth*, New York, Knopf, 1982, 244p.

Schneider, S. H., and Londer, R., *The CoEvolution of Climate and Life*, San Francisco, Sierra Club Books, 1984, xii+563p.

Schopf, J. W., Ed., *Earth's Earliest Biosphere. Its Origin and Evolution*, Princeton, Princeton University Press, 1983, xxv+543p.

Senise, F., *Biosfera in agonia*, Roma, Barone, 1972, 158p.

Siever, R., The Dynamic Earth, *Scientific American*, 1983, 249, pp.46-55.

Sillen, L. G., Regulation of O_2, N_2 and CO_2 in the atmosphere: thoughts of a laboratory chemist, *Tellus*, 1966, 18, pp.198-206.

Snyder, T. P., Ed., *The Biosphere Catalogue*, Orale, Arizona, London, Synergetic Press, 1986, vii+240p.

Suess, E., *Die Entsehung der Alpen*, Wien, W. Braunmuller, 1875, iv+168p.

Suess, E., *The Face of the Earth*, trans. by Hertha B. C. Sollas, under the direction of W. J. Sollas, Oxford, Clarendon Press, 1904-1924, 5 vols.

Sukachev, V., and Dylis, N., *Fundamentals of Forest Biogeocenology*, trans. from the Russian (1964) by Dr .J. M. Maclennan, Edinburgh, London, Oliver and Boyd, 1968, viii+627p.

Taube, M. *Evolution of Matter and Energy on a Cosmic and Planetary Scale*, New York, Berlin, Spriger-Verlag, 1985, xiv+289p.

Teilhard de Chardin, P., *Le Phénomène humain*, Paris, Seuil, 1955, 348p.

Teilhard De Chardin, P., *Le Groupe Zoologique humain. Structures et directions évolutives*, préface de Jean Piveteau, Paris, Albin Michel, 'Les savants et le monde', 1956, xiv+172p.

Teilhard de Chardin, P., L'Hominisation. Introduction à une étude scientifique du phénomène humain (1925), *Ouvres*, Paris, Seuil, t.3, 1957, pp.75-111.

Teilhard du Chardin, P., L'Histoire Naturelle du Monde (1925), in *Ouvres*, Paris, Seuil, t.3, 1959, pp.201-231.

Teilhard de Chardin, P., The Antiquity and World Expansion of Human Culture, in W. L. Thomas, Ed., *Man's Role in Changing the Face of the Earth*, Chicago, University of Chicago Press, A Phoenix Book, t.1, 1956, pp.103-112.

Teilhard de Chardin, P., *Man's Place in Nature*, London, Collins, 1966.

Thomas, L., *The Lives of a Cell. Notes of a Biology Watcher*, New York, Viking Press, 1974, 153p.

Vallentyne, J., Geochemistry of the biosphere, *MacGraw-Hill Encyclopedia of science and Technology*, 1960, 2, pp.239-312.

Vernadksy, V. I., *Le Géochimie*, Paris, Félix Alcan, 'Nouvelle collection scientifique', 1924, iv+404p.

Vernadsky, V. I., L'autotrophie de l'humanité, *Revue générale des sciences*, 1925, 36, pp.495-502.

Vernadsky, V. I., *Biosfera*, Leningrad, Nauchnoe Khimikoteknicheskoe Izdatelstvo, 1926, 150p. (rééd. Moscow, Nauka, 1967, 374p).

Vernadsky, V. I., *Geochemie*, Leipzig, Akademische Verlagsgesellschaft, 1930. xii+370p.

Vernadsky, V. I., L'étude de la vie et la nouvelle physique, *Revue générale des sciences*, 1932, 43, pp.503-514.

Vernadsky, V. I., Le problème du temps dans la science contemporaine, *Revue générale des sciences*, 1934, 45, pp.550-558; 1935, 46, pp.208-213, 308-312.

Vernadsky, V. I., Problems of Biogeochemistry, Trans. by George Vernadsky, edited and condensed by G. E. Hutchinson, *Transactions of the Connecticut Academy of Arts and Science,*, 1944, 35, pp.483-517.

Vernadsky, V. I., The Biosphere and the Noosphere, *American Scientist*, 1945, 33, pp.1-12.

Veziroglu, T. N., Ed., *The Biosphere: Problems and Solutions*, Amsterdam, Eslevier, 1984, xv+712p.

Vinogradov, A. P., The origin of the biosphere, in Marcel Florkin, Ed., *Aspects of the Origin of Life*, Oxford, Pergamon Press, 1960, pp.15-29.

Vinogradov, A., The development of V. I. Vernadsky's ideas, *Soviet Soil Science*, 1963, 8, pp.727-0732.

Vinogracov, A., Centenary of the birth of V. I. Vernadsky, *Geochemistry*, 1963, 3, pp.211-213.

Vinogradov, A., The scientific legacy of V. I. Vernadsky, in A. P. Vinogradov, Ed., *Chemistry of the Earth's Crust: Proceedings of the Geochemical Conference Commemorating the Centenary of Academician V. I. Vernadsky's Birth,* trans. from the Russian by N. Kaner, Jerusalem, Israel Program for Scientific Translations, Vol. 1, 1966, pp.1-8.

Wallen, C. C., *A brief survey of meteorology as related to the biosphere,* Geneva, WMO, 1973, x+54p.

Ward, B., and Dubos, R., *Only One Earth,* Harmondsworth, Penguin Books, 1972, 304p.

Watson, L., *Heaven's Breath. A Natural History of the Wind,* London, Hodder & Stoughton, Coronet Books, 1985, 384p.

Weiner, D.,*Models of nature: ecology, conservation and cultural revolution in Soviet Union,* Indiana, Bloomington, London, Indiana University Press, 1988, p.80.

Westbroek, P., Life as a geologic force: new opportunities for paleontology? *Paleobiology,* 1983, 9, pp.91-96.

Whittaker, R. H., and Likens, G. E., Eds., The Primary Production of the Biosphere, *Human Ecology,* 1973, 1(4), pp.299-369.

Woodwell, G. M., The energy Cycle of the biosphere, *Scientific American,* 1970, 223(3),pp.64-74.

Worthington, B. Barton, World Campaign for the Biosphere, *Environmental Conservation,* 1982, 9(2), pp.93-100.

End Notes
Pierre Teilhard de Chardin (1881-1955) *The Phenomenon of Man.* Glasgow, Collins, 1959.
Book One: Pre-Life
Book Two: Life

"Firstly the initial mass of the cells must from the start have been inwardly subjected to a sort of inter-dependence which went beyond a mere mechanical adjustment, and was already a beginning of 'symbiosis' or life-in-common.

However tenuous it was, the first veil of organised matter spread over the Earth could neither have established nor maintained itself without some network of influences and exchanges which made it a biologically *cohesive whole.* From its origin, the cellular nebula necessarily represented, despite its internal multiplicity, a sort of diffuse super-organism. Not merely a *foam of lives* but, to a certain extent, itself a *living film.* A simple reappearance, after all, in more advanced form and on a higher level of those much older conditions which we have already seen presiding over the birth and equilibrium of the first polymerised substances on the surface of the juvenile Earth. A simple prelude, too, to the much more advanced evolutionary solidarity, so marked in the higher form of life, whose existence obliges us increasingly to admit the strictly organic nature of the links which united them in a single whole at the earth of the *biosphere.*"

Vladimir I. Vernadsky (1863-1945)

"L'homme en tant qu'être vivant es indéfectiblement lié aux phénomènes matériels et énergétiques d'une des enveloppes géologiques de la Terre: la Biosphère. Et il ne peut en être physiquement indépendant un seul instant."

DISCUSSION

Alwyn Jones   What is the message of Vernadsky - what has he said?

Jacques Grinevald   Vernadsky's main idea was that life was a planetary phenomenon, indeed a cosmic phenomenon, because he considered life to exist only on this planet within the solar system, life being powered by the Sun's radiation. From the perspective of the biosphere, he pointed out that the Earth-Solar system was a closed thermodynamical system. In maintaining that a theory of the Earth must be integrated inside a cosmic perspective Vernadsky reintroduced cosmology into the scientific establishment.

Bernard Zamaron   The Catholic Church has failed to come up with any statement on ecology. We must fight to restore the right thinking that man has to live with the Earth and not just conquer it.

Jacques Grinevald   Lynn White's famous paper on the "historical roots of the ecological crisis" emphasized the religious background of the ecological crisis. At the same time we have to appreciate that in antiquity when one spoke of the Earth one meant the land and not the planet as a whole. Today our knowledge of the planet is a consequence primarily of European expansion all around the globe. Our Western civilization now assumes this new knowledge of the planet because it is the first civilization to embark on extra-terrestrial travel. Indeed, our artificial satellites give us a knowledge that no other culture has ever had.

Carl Amery   I think in the light of what Jacques just told us it would be very awkward for the church to rehabilitate Teilhard now, because if I understood Jacques correctly Teilhard believed in some sort of Platonic dualism, a hierarchy of things going from matter to spirit.

Jacques Grinevald   We have celebrated Teilhard and ignored Vernadsky. Now we can celebrate Vernadsky and forget Teilhard a little because the concept of biosphere in Teilhard's work is not the same as Vernadsky's. For Teilhard the biosphere is only biological matter and not the global ecosystem with living things. The difference is very important.

Ulrich Loening   Could you comment on what is happening in the Soviet Union? I have been there twice this year and there is an enormous Vernadsky revival.

Jacques Grinevald   The centenary of Vernadsky's birth in 1863 was celebrated with a great manifestation in the Soviet Union and from that time Vernadsky has been considered a State hero. However, Vernadsky's work was claimed to be part of mainstream communist materialistic ideology and was therefore completely misunderstood within the Soviet Union because Vernadsky was never a Marxist. Indeed, he was never a materialistic dialectician, but rather was for ever in battle against the Soviet authorities. Indeed he was once put on trial and then went into exile; so his situation was very ambiguous. I am acquainted with the recent speeches of the Soviet authorities, but now is the time to look into the French and American archives concerning Vernadsky. In that respect the publication by the Synergistic Press in English of Vernadsky's work on the biosphere is very misleading because it is only an extract of the book and it contains not just a biography of Vernadsky but also of the translator. We need a critical academic edition, published together with scientists and historians of science.

Nicholas Guppy You have given us a very good outline of the growth of the scientific concept of the biosphere but you have only hinted at the growth of the philosophical idea that really came from Bergson. I wonder if you could just broaden that out and show where Bergson himself got his ideas from, for example were they derived to some extent from oriental philosophy? What in fact were his roots? He has played a big part in our present conception of the biosphere.

Jacques Grinevald I think that Bergson's sources were only western and mainly in the scientific tradition of the 19th century, similar to those of the French chemist, Jean Baptiste Dumas, and Jean Baptiste Boussingault. Dumas and Boussingault made valuable contributions to our knowledge on the nitrogen and carbon cycles and therefore to the notion of biogeological cycles, and here I think, Bergson's ideas were the same as Vernadsky's. Thus life was conceived to be a planetary phenomenon and not something restricted and microscopic being separate from the earth's matter. Bergson was aware of the interrelation between matter and life, between the planet and life. Nevertheless, Bergson interpreted the second law of thermodynamics as being opposed to life owing to the definition of thermodynamics in his time. Thus the classical thermodynamics in his time was defined for a closed system not for one which was dissipative, and therefore not for an open system such as is apparent in living organisms. We therefore have to retrace the history of the biosphere in parallel with all the sciences, including the history of thermodynamics. As we all know here, the history of thermodynamics is fraught with difficulty, with many philosophical battles over the word entropy.

We should also be aware that Vernadsky was well acquainted with the work of the great Swedish scientist Arrhenius, and in my opinion Vernadsky was ahead of his time in being aware of cosmic influences on Earth. Thus the discovery of the ozone layer and the work of Fabri and Buisson in France in the 1920s indicating that the newly discovered ozone layer would absorb ultra-violet radiation emphasized to Vernadsky the interrelation between the Earth and the Sun.

THE GAIA HYPOTHESIS
by Jim Lovelock

What I am going to do in my talk is to concentrate much more on the hard science of it, after all I am a scientist and I think it is necessary to kind of stick to one's own, so to speak.

As I see it there are three principal scientific theories about life on a planetary scale and the first of these is the *traditional view* and the one to which I subscribe. It goes right back and sees the Earth as a living organism. I suppose probably the first humans that could talk may have discussed this idea long, long ago but every year, almost every month, I have come across a new statement or I receive a letter in the post, that tells me of an old ancient scientist who had said something about the Earth as a living system on a scientific basis. The earliest one I have been able to get so far was a good European, and Englishman: James Hutton. He took his degree in Leiden somewhere back in the 18th century and the remarkable statement he made, which was in a lecture to the Royal Society of Edinburgh in 1785, was long before anybody else that I can find. He said "I consider the Earth to be a super-organism and its proper study should be by physiology."

He was not just saying that as a kind of off-the-cuff statement, he based his thoughts on quite a lot of work of his own on the cycling of the elements in the hydrological cycle whereby water comes from the oceans to the land and flows back down again. He was much moved by the science of physiology which was almost the whole of biology then, since science had hardly separated at all. Indeed I think it was Harvey's work on the circulation of the blood that influenced him considerably. There was then the circulation society that thought in those ways. This tradition of physiology I think actually runs through into the tradition described by Jacques Grinevald because Vernadsky's mentor was a man called Correlenco who was a philosopher and in the best biography I have ever found of Vernadsky one by Bolandin, it is claimed that the young Vernadsky often went for walks with Correlenco in the forests near Kiev and the old man would talk about the Earth being alive; quite clearly he was aware of the older scientific tradition. Of course, science in Victorian times in Britain and right the way across Europe had fragmented into numerous separate expertises and disciplines and Correlenco was a kind of link back to the past. It was probably very important in establishing Vernadsky's view of the Earth.

This notion 'alive' bothers a lot of my scientific colleagues and if any of them are here present and are worried by it for the moment just think of it as no more than the capacity of the Earth to regulate itself and to keep cool when things are changing adversely. It is a characteristic which physiologists always refer to by their 'buzz word' homeostasis. This then is the first tradition, that sees the Earth as a living organism. It is the view to which I subscribe, and I believe it to have a firm scientific basis.

Secondly there is the liberal view which is often called '*the co-evolutionary theory*'. In this the organisms are only seen as loosely coupled with their physical and chemical environment. Co-evolutionists accept that organisms may change the composition of the material world but they do not accept the possibility that life has a constructive influence so that organisms alter the material world in a way that affects their own selection. I have been able to trace this theory back as far as Lamarck, the same as Jacques Grinevald did, and of course he was the first biologist. There may have been earlier scientists who thought this way and I would not be in the least surprised to discover it. I think, in fact, one can over do the business of attaching ideas to names, they are pretty common currency and go round and all of us mix up and share in the whole of the thinking. I have never been very clear in my own mind whether Vernadsky was of this liberal co-evolutional middle view of the Earth or whether he subscribed to the first traditional view. I suspect that he probably would have liked to have subscribed to the first traditional view but the pressures of scientific rectitude in his days and in particular the political pressures on him in Russia probably kept him down towards more the middle of the road 'liberal'.

Then lastly we have the scientific theory which we can describe as *the conventional wisdom*. Now this is something that is neither conventional nor wise. Indeed it has much more in common with trades union politics than with science. In this very Victorian theory of the Earth the Earth and life sciences exist in separate buildings of the university and meet only to discuss administrative and territorial matters. The life scientists in this kind of theory see the evolution of organisms proceeding according to their personal interpretation of Darwin's great vision. And Darwin, like all other great scientists, suffers the disciple phenomenon. Hence the Earth scientists see the evolution of the material world proceeding strictly according to the rules of physics and chemistry with organisms on the planet merely passengers.

Those then are the three main theories of the Earth in science. In science we are now usually bothered too much about absolute truth; we are much more concerned about having a theory that is useful in predicting experiments and in helping us to pick winners. After all, most working scientists depend on getting grants to fund themselves and it is no use subscribing to theories that pick losers. Let me therefore try to tell you why I think that *Gaia theory*, that's the first, the traditional theory, is the best predictor for the Earth's future.

Let us go back some twenty years ago to when we first saw those pictures of the Earth from space. We had that vicarious vision of stunning beauty, that dappled white and blue sphere and it stirred all of us, no matter that by now it has just become a visual cliche. I have always thought that our sense of reality comes from matching our personal mental image or model of the world with that we are receiving through our senses and that I think is why that vision - an astronaut's eye view - of the Earth was so disturbing. It showed us for the first time just how much from reality we had strayed.

The Earth was also being viewed from space by the more discerning eye of scientific instruments and it was this view that confirmed James Hutton's vision in the 18th century of the Earth as a super-organism. When you see the Earth in infra red light rather than visible light it is seen immediately as a strange and wonderful anomaly amongst the planets of our solar system. Our atmosphere, the air we breathe, is revealed this way to be outrageously out of equilibrium in a chemical sense. It is more like the mixture of gases that enters the intake manifold of your car, with hydrocarbons mixed with oxygen and if it were more concentrated it would be combustible or explosive. In total contrast the atmospheres of our dead partner planets, Mars and Venus, have atmospheres like those gases exhausted by combustion.

This unorthodox composition of the Earth's atmosphere radiates such a strong signal in the infra red that if there were a space craft right outside the solar system the information received would give *prima facie* evidence that the only planet in the solar system that bore life was the Earth. But much more than this, if the observer stayed there for some time he would see that this very unstable, almost combustible, atmosphere persisted at a steady state and if he were a scientist he would know that this 'stability' required some powerful regulation process operating at the surface that was controlling it and keeping it constant for very long periods of time. It was this kind of evidence from space research that led me to postulate the Gaia hypothesis and led me to a long and fruitful collaboration with Lynn Margulis who was at that time the only scientist I could talk to about it.

To sum up the evidence of 15 years ago: the presence of life on Earth was revealed by its intensely unusual atmosphere and it was the persistence of this instability for geological periods of time that suggested the presence of the controller Gaia. It is important to recognise that the atmosphere is the smallest compartment of the Earth and yet through it flows most of the elements that go to make up living systems. Thus the carbon, nitrogen, oxygen and hydrogen of living organisms are all flowing through the atmosphere and that is why Gaia was first seen in the atmosphere. The oceans are similarly affected but, as my friend and colleague Mike Whitfield will be telling you later, to find and see Gaia in the oceans is a much more difficult task because the effects of life are so diluted by the vast volumes of water and salt that are there.

Let us go back and look critically at those three theories of the Earth that I mentioned in the light of the evidence that has come along in the last 15-20 years since the hypothesis was first proposed.

The third theory that life evolved separately and independently of the Earth although still widely held and the conventional wisdom expressed in many text books is an accident of the 19th century development of science; and is quite wrong. If the physics and chemistry of the Earth were evolving independently of life and if organisms were simply adapting to the changes that took place then there would be no reason whatever to find any marked chemical disequilibria in the Earth's atmosphere. The Earth might have a different composition from the other planets but there is simply no way that lifeless chemistry could lead to an atmosphere that was rich in reactive gases. According to the third theory we could have, for example an atmosphere with 21 per cent oxygen, but we could not have methane and hydrogen present at the same time. We could have 90 per cent of hydrogen and methane in the atmosphere, as do the larger outer planets, but we could not have oxygen as well. This type of argument, that can be extended at considerable length, always renders the conventional wisdom as presented in the textbooks untenable. It is sometimes said that the eminence of scientists is measured by the length of time that they hold up progress in their field; the Victorians included a great many of these golden 'oldies' and it was inevitable that in the last century, with so many exciting discoveries about the world to be made, such scientists had little time or inclination to think about the total picture, the larger view of the Earth. They were really in the position of the assemblers of a vast jigsaw puzzle and as you know the first task is to collect the pieces into categories: in fact you collect the edges and the blue bits that make the sky, you do not think about the assembled picture until you have got a good chunk of it together. It is easy to be critical of them but with hindsight it is understandable why they were narrow in their view.

The second theory that I mentioned, the co-evolutionist theory which perhaps originated with Lamarck is the basis of the modern science of biogeochemistry which Vernadsky founded. It states that life and the environment interact - that gases like oxygen and methane are biological products - but it does not recognise the existence of any tight coupling between the organisms and their environment, nor the active regulation of the chemical composition and climate of the Earth. Most importantly it does not see the Earth as alive. The co-evolutionists recognise the folly of separating the Earth and life sciences but dare not or will not take the full leap to Gaia. They stay with the liberal middle of the road science of biogeochemistry or co-evolution. The second theory also is I think untenable, although it is considerably more difficult to dispose of than was the third theory.

Before I go on to Gaia theory and to show why I think co-evolution is inadequate to explain the facts of the Earth, I think first we need to look at the viewpoint of the biologists.

Biologists amongst you may wonder why I have not mentioned the biological viewpoints so far in these three theories. I have not done so because, apart from the entertaining criticisms of Gaia by Richard Dawkins and Ford Doolittle, biologists in general have tended to ignore both Vernadsky and Gaia.

Instead they have tended to assume that the physical and chemical world evolves according to the rules laid down in the geology or biogeochemistry department of their university and the details of this material evolution need not be their concern. If the environment changes then organisms adapt to the change. They had very good reasons to think this way. There were and still are so many fascinating developments in evolutionary theory and molecular biology that why should biologists bother with controversial matters outside those interests. But the notion of adaptation is all too easily misused to justify ignorance. Somehow both geologists and biologists have failed to note that their separate researches have clearly demonstrated that the world is massively affected by the presence of life. The air we breathe, the ocean and the rocks are all either direct products of living organisms, think of the chalk cliffs of Dover, just one gigantic pile of shells, or else they have been greatly modified by their presence, and this even includes the igneous rocks coming from volcanos. Indeed organisms are not just adapting to a dead world determined by physics and chemistry textbooks alone, they live with a world that is the breath and the bones and the blood of their ancestors and that they themselves are now sustaining.

The abundant evidence that exists of an essentially recursive interaction between life and its environment is fatal to the old conventional wisdom of a completely separate evolution of the Earth and life. It is also *destructive to the co-evolutionary argument.*

If organisms are adapting to a world whose material state is determined by the activities of their neighbours then changing the environment becomes part of the game. It would be absurd to suppose that organisms would avoid the act of changing their environment if by so doing they left more progeny.

To believe in the loose uncoupled interaction of co-evolution or biogeochemistry as a description of the Earth is to my mind as difficult a position to maintain as believing that a pair of naked teenagers who climbed into bed together would remain separate and engage in polite conversation rather than exploring the joys of close coupling.

There are I think three main reasons why Gaia theory has not been taken seriously. First of all it is old fashioned and goes right back to the Greeks and earlier and must therefore be out of date. Secondly I chose to present it somewhat poetically and unfortunately most scientists, probably as a result of a faulty education have an instinctive distrust of anything of science that is presented without recourse to scientific jargon. And lastly detail was lacking as to how it worked and very few of us are happy with a theory if we cannot envisage a mechanism. The preliminary nature of the theory led to those entertaining criticisms from Richard Dawkins and Ford Doolittle. Richard Dawkins in *The Extended Phenotype*, expounds at great length and with considerable fluency that Gaia is impossible since planets do not reproduce and therefore there would be no natural selection of the most fit planet. Ford Doolittle, in Canada, rejected Gaia on somewhat more solid grounds. He said that planetary self regulation needs foresight and planning by the biota and that there is just no way for global altruism to evolve through natural selection. He was happy with symbiosis and even with Lynn's endosymbiosis but, he claimed these associations were always between closely connected entities and Gaia would require the existence of a committee of the species to meet annually somewhere to bargain for next year's climate and chemical composition. This global-scale cooperation was out of the question: as equally was the idea of a gigantic Panglossian nanny who had looked after the Earth ever since life began.

These criticisms derive from dogma and are absurd. Even so they are hard to answer. For a while I wondered if Gaia was just another one of those untestable notions like the antropic principle or Rupert Sheldrake's 'morphogenetic fields', something to be talked about over coffee or a few beers rather than be investigated.

In fact, the feedback loops that link life with its environment are so numerous and so intricate that I could see little hope of ever quantifying or understanding them. Then it occurred to me over Christmas 1981 that you could do in science as both artists and composers do, which is to make an abstraction; an invention that nonetheless captured the essence

Daisy World

Think of a portrait artist who with a few swift strokes drawn on a canvas, can capture the likeness of his subject and then spend months filling in the details. As scientists we can do the same kind of thing and what I want to try and show you is how we did it. We make our sketch by reducing the environment to a single variable, temperature, and we reduce the biota to a single species, daisies. Now I want you to imagine a planet which is very like the Earth, although in fact it is actually a computer model of a planet that is spinning like the Earth. As you can see it has no clouds, and it has an uncomplicated atmosphere without any greenhouse gases or pollutants to complicate its climate. It is also travelling in orbit around a star, the same mass and composition of our own sun and like our own sun it warms up as it grows old. As physicists have discovered it is a property of stars to do this; it is the reverse of a bonfire, the older it becomes the hotter it gets. From straightforward physics it is relatively easy to calculate what would be the mean surface temperature of this imaginary world. Indeed, once we know the colour and hence the albedo of the planet we know its temperature. In the conventional wisdom diagram, we see what happens to that world as its star warms up from the time of the beginning of life to its present luminosity. What we see is a steady warm up of the planet with the temperature rising as the star heats up. Meanwhile the conventional biological wisdom indicates that daisies like any other mainstream plant do not grow if the temperature is below 5°C, it is too cold: nor do they grow if the temperature is above 40°C, it is too hot. In fact they grow best in the middle, round about room temperature. Now I think this view is replete with nonsense. Instead this is what would happen on our imaginary planet if we seeded it with dark and light coloured daisy seeds. When the temperature reached 5°C the daisy seeds would germinate, but as you can see immediately, once they started to grow the darker ones would be at an advantage since it is very cold; indeed it is only five degrees, thus they can hardly grow at all. However, the dark ones absorb sunlight which makes them warmer so that they grow better; whereas the light coloured ones actually reflect sunlight and are cooler so they do not grow well at all. At the end of the first season many more dark daisy seeds are left compared with light ones, giving dark daisies a head start at the beginning of the next season. By spreading out over an increasing area the dark daisies would soon be warming not just themselves but the region as well. The result is an explosive positive feedback growth in the dark daisy population, and a sharp rise in the temperature of the planet. However it would not go on rising indefinitely because in time it would become too hot for the dark daisies; moreover once the planet became warm the light coloured daisies would start growing well and begin competing with the dark form. Thus simple competition and natural selection of the two daisy species as the star warms up can be seen to keep the planet's temperature very close to the optimum for daisy growth. That little model, therefore, is a definitive answer to the criticisms of Ford Doolittle and Richard Dawkins. It is a system that has no purpose in it. It does not require committees or anything like that; rather it follows from the process of natural selection tightly coupled into the physical evolution of the planet.

Many of my biological friends are hard nosed and they said "Oh yes that's a very pretty model but what would happen if there were grey coloured daisies in it? Surely they are not going to waste energy making pigment and they would take over, so that the system would never work."

It is not very difficult to put another equation in the model for grey daisies and when you do you find that the planet regulates just as well or slightly better than before. The reason is obvious; when it is very cold only dark daisies are fit to grow, the grey ones do not stand a chance and when it is very hot only the light coloured daisies are fit to grow. The only place that grey coloured daisies can grow is in the middle where their growth is not needed, where they are just passengers in a system. So much for that.

When I made the three daisy species model I was quite unaware that I was breaking all of the rules of population biology, since it had been known for 60 years in population biology that you cannot model the competition of more than two species simultaneously. If you try to do so the mathematics blows up and the whole system gets drawn away into outer space by a modern type of a demon called a strange attractor. But because I had been brought up in the tradition where you never read the literature before you do an experiment, since, if you read it before you get discouraged and never do the experiment, I had a few qualms at making a ten daisy species model. With competition between the ten daisy species (as their star that was warming their planet evolved) there are no signs of instability, the system works very well. The climate is regulated even better than it was with two daisies; much more smoothly. But the most exciting result is found with the ecologist's parameter 'diversity'. For the first time we have a theoretical justification for diversity within ecosystems and quite the opposite of what theoretical ecologists have been telling us for sixty years, namely that the more complex an ecosystem gets the more unstable and fragile it becomes. For this little ecosystem, anyway, the more species the more stability.

Alfred Lotka

At this pooint I went back and read the literature, coming across a scientist who is even more unknown than Vernadsky and yet I think as important. Alfred Lotka, who was a contemporary of Vernadsky, was a professor at John Hopkins University and in 1925 he wrote a book called *Physical Biology*. On page 16 he says "this fact deserves emphasis. It is customary to discuss the evolution of a species of organisms. As we proceed we shall see many reasons why we should constantly take in view the evolution as a whole of the system, organisms plus environment. It may at first sight seem as if this should prove a more complicated problem than the consideration of the evolution of a part only of the system but it will become apparent as we proceed that the physical laws governing evolution in all probability take on a simpler form when referred to the system as a whole than to any portion thereof. It is not so much the organism or the species that evolves but the entire system, species and environment, the two are inseparable."

Now in Alfred Lotka's time there were no computers and I have calculated to do that model by hand using ordinary analytical mathematics and working an eight hour day and a five day week, but otherwise never stopping it would take one and a half years. Obviously Lotka was in no position to test his notion but his intuitive insight was immense and it is very sad that 60 years of population biology should have followed their founder, Alfred Lotka, and have got it all wrong and never gone back to read his book.

Daisy world as I have described it is just an invention and Andrew Watson in his talk will tell you how much more it is than just that and that when the details are fleshed out how it can become a generality and a theoretical basis for Gaia.

Naturally I do not mean to suggest that the Earth regulates its temperature by growing daisies. The purpose of daisy world is to provide insight into the mechanisms of the real world and of Gaia.

That then is how I think it works, at the present stage of its development, as I said earlier, it matters little whether the theory is right or wrong for already it is providing a new and more productive view of the Earth and the other planets. In

41

fact it is not difficult for it to do so, for the conventional theories of ecology and biogeochemistry are crippled by the apartheid that separates the sciences.

There are two principal things that Gaia theory provokes us to consider. The first is the same conclusion as Vernadsky came to, namely that life is a planetary scale phenomenon. But I think I go farther than Vernadsky in saying that you cannot have sparser life on a planet any more than you can have half of an animal. Living organisms have to regulate their planet otherwise the irresistible forces of physical and chemical evolution will soon render it uninhabitable. And this is very true of our own planet now.

The second thing is that the Gaia theory adds to Darwin's great vision. It does not contradict it, but it is no longer sufficient to consider the evolution of the species separate from the evolution of their environment. The two processes are tightly coupled, as Alfred Lotka said, in a single indivisible process. It is not enough to say that the organism that leaves the most progeny succeeds. Success comes only to the organism that also maintains a benign relationship with its material environment.

A helpful thought I find in connection with the difficult idea of the Earth as alive was put to me by the physicist Jerome Rothstein. What he suggested was compare the Earth with a tree and he took as an example a giant redwood tree. Imagine you have gone through a grove of those gorgeous trees on the west coast of America and have come across a stump of one that has been cut down. Let us hope it was cut down because it was diseased and not just for lumbering. As you walk on to the platform of the stump, standing on 3,000 years of history, the interesting thing to remember is that nearly all of the tree was dead when the tree was alive. In fact the middle of a living tree is dead wood with just a think skin of living tissue around the circumference and beyond another dead layer, the bark, which protects the tree from the rigours of the environment, although not from the chainsaws of the loggers. Now the Earth is very much like that; you have the middle, molten, dead, incandescent but around the circumstance that same thin skin of living tissue and beyond it the atmosphere which is just like a bark of a tree, therefore not formally alive like living tissue but it is still a protective layer against the rigours of the environment, which for the Earth is space.

For some time after the Earth was first formed, 4½ billion years ago, it must have been sterile and evolving quite rapidly in a geological sense by the laws of physics and chemistry alone and at some time during that evolution of the Earth as a physical planet a time window opened when the material conditions of our planet were right for life. It was neither too hot nor too cold and the right chemicals were lying around in the environment.

I am not concerned with whether life originated spontaneously, floated in on a bit of cometary flotsam or was put here by visitors from somewhere else. The origin of life to me is, as my theological friends say, ineffable. When life started or arrived there must have been a period of co-evolution, with life evolving in its way and the Earth evolving inexorably away from the environmental state that just happened to be favourable for life.

Thus Earth did go through a co-evolutionary phase just after life started, but there must have come a moment when the evolution of the organisms and the evolution of their host planet fused into a single evolutionary process, rather like the moment of conception when the sperm and the egg fuse, if you want a poetic

42

analogy. I think that that moment marked the beginning of the system we are calling Gaia.

I said earlier that theories are judged useful in science if they make predictions that are useful or can be tested by experiment. At first sight it would seem that doing planet scale experiments is likely to be both very expensive and reprehensible. But they are happening whether we like it or not as a result of our own activities. Perhaps the largest and most reprehensible of all these experiments is the removal of the forests of the humid tropics, next probably comes the burning of fossil fuels. Gaia theory predicts different consequences for these activities than do those of either conventional science or of biogeochemistry.

In particular Gaia theory sees the Earth as a responsive living organism that will at first tend to resist adverse environmental change and maintain homeostasis. But if stressed beyond the limits of whatever happens to be the current regulatory apparatus, it will jump to a new stable environment where many of the current range of species will be eliminated.

In spite of such excitements as the hurricane force winds over much of Britain in early October 1987 or the ozone hole over Antarctica, and other things, nothing much is yet apparently happening to the environment that suggests an imminent jump to a different state. But even so such surprises should be looked on perhaps as harbingers of larger non-linearities to come if we persist in our experiments with the planet.

One recent discovery that illustrates the value of Gaia as a predictor is last year's finding of a connection between cloud cover over the open oceans and algae that live on the surface layers of the sea.

It all began because Gaia theory required the production of large quantities of special compounds able to transfer the elements sulphur and iodine from the sea where they are abundant to the land surfaces where they are depleted, by the wash off of rainfall and transport by rivers. Curious about this I set sail aboard the research vessel Shackleton in 1971 on its journey from Wales to Antarctica and back and wherever the ship sailed in the oceans the sulphur compound, dimethyl sulphide and the iodine compound methyl iodide were found. Their abundances in the sea were sufficient to allow a flux to the atmosphere enough to make up the needs of the land surfaces. Had it not been for the predictive value of Gaia theory both of these compounds I think would have remained as curiosities of algal biochemistry rather than be looked upon as major carriers of the sulphur and iodine cycles of nature.

But the story did not end there; for within the last two years with my colleagues Andi Andreae, Robert Charlson and Steven Warren we have argued that the output of this sulphur gas, dimethyl sulphide, from the marine algae over the open oceans is the largest if not the only source of the nuclei on which cloud droplets form over the oceans.

Cloud density, if it can be linked with algal growth on the ocean surfaces, can be shown to have as large an effect on global climate as the burning of fossil fuels and that of the CO_2 greenhouse. From the viewpoint of Gaia it is an extremely economic way to manage the climate.

Andi Andreae has found that the output of this compound from the oceans does not much depend upon productivity but on speciation. Indeed it is highest over the desert regions where the ocean is clear, hot and deficient in nutrients. It is likely to be quite a complicated story before it is finally unravelled but the link between clouds and algal growth as a meteorological one is already becoming established by meteorologists themselves.

The dimethyl sulphide producing algae, by nucleating the water above them and producing clouds, are of course acting just like the white daisies in those models I first showed you. My last slide is from a photograph taken while on an expedition I was on with Lynn in Hawaii. The postcard shows the onshore breeze coming on to one of the islands and you can see the mist coming up off the sea. In fact that is not water vapour mist, but dilute sulphuric acid. Indeed there is acid rain even way out in the middle of the Pacific which is natural acid rain that is not coming from the burning of fossil fuels. The cloud layer, you can just faintly see the clouds, is up at several thousand feet so the relative humidity close to the surface is much too low for water to condense out as clouds; yet it will do so around the microdroplets of sulphuric acid. This brought me to an incredibly interesting quote which I picked up on the big island off Hawaii from a Polynesian. He told me he had read Captain Cook's journals because he was rather a noted figure on those islands and in Captain Cook's journals, it said "it is a dispensation of providence that wherever the ship sails in tropic waters there is a golden haze that protects the skins of the men and the rigging of the ship from the fierce rays of the sun". Now that was long before any pollution and we must assume it was just such an acid haze that he was talking about.

When thinking of the oceans we must bear in mind perhaps the most important point of all: that while water may have been needed for the start of life the persistence of water on this planet is another of the consequences of the Gaia system. Venus and Mars once had abundant water but having no life could not keep it. We have water because we have life.

So what is the message from Gaia for human ecology?

First and foremost Gaia forces upon us a concern for the planet and its state of health and offers an alternative to our near obsessive concern with the state of humanity.

It is in our own interest anyway to live well with the Earth. If we do not Gaia will live on but with a new biosphere that may not include humans. It is this thought that makes me part company with many environmentalists especially those who claim to be friends of the earth but in fact are friends of humanity. I recognise that we share the same objectives at heart but where we differ is in the priorities. To a friend of Gaia, ozone depletion and Chernobyl are minor problems affecting mostly white people. The demolition of the forests of the humid tropics and the ever increasing burden of greenhouse gases are real threats to Gaia and humanity alike.

We are in many ways in the same state with regard to the health of the Earth as were the early physicians towards the health of their patients. We have an impressive array of scientific equipment and expertise but so did the nineteenth century physicians. There was microbiology and microscopes and the bacterial theory of disease. There was biochemistry and an understanding of many metabolic disorders. But there was almost nothing a physician could do other than comfort and relieve pain or do simple surgery. It was not until after World War 2 that hi-tech medicine came of age.

So it is with the Earth. We have theories and equipment but there is little that science has to offer for the cure of the ills of Gaia. One thing though we can learn from the physician that is invaluable in our professional practice as planetary physicians is the hippocratic oath - do nothing that would harm the patient.

In our enthusiasm or belief in some new nostrum we should take care that the cure is not worse than the disease.

The other and more optimistic message is that the evolution of Gaia seems to depend upon the activities of individual organisms. If these are favourable for the environment they succeed. If not they are doomed but life goes on.

To me this means that it is more important to try to live in harmony with the Earth at a personal level than to allow any of the numerous human collectives and parties to take that responsibility away from us.

DISCUSSION

Peter Bunyard Could life have gone a very different way from the way it has and yet still given us a planet which is at the right temperature and so on for it still to be comfortable for life today?

James Lovelock I don't think I can answer that one; all I can say is that the changes in the physical environment that have occurred during the evolution of the Earth have been profound and that without the presence of a regulating capacity of the biota and of their environment operating together as a system, we wouldn't be talking about it now.

Ted Pawloff There have been a number of abrupt changes during the Earth's history, some of which appear to have resulted in mass extinctions. Here we seem to have a synthesis broken at great cost: can those changes be easily incorporated into the mathematics behind the models of Gaia?

James Lovelock On the historical side catastrophists, including some of the people talked about by Jacques Grinevald, have been around for a long time. You are quite right in that the type of modelling we are doing suggests that sudden jumps are the norm and to be expected, but also long periods of stasis in between. So you can have gradualism and jumps and there is no inconsistency between the two; it's not a case of either or.

Pierre Lehmann In describing Gaia you have shown us your 'Daisy World' models. As we know there are more complicated things for Gaia to regulate: for instance it is necessary that the cat should eat the mouse. Do you think we might have a way one day to introduce into the explanation of Gaia the reasons that would promote the cat to eat the mouse?

James Lovelock Strangely enough the mathematics of this kind of model operates very smoothly, as I have shown when seeing what happens after putting in several species of daisies that are eaten by rabbits and the rabbits are eaten by foxes. The generality you obtain from such models is that the more species and the more interactions you put into the system the more stable it becomes. Whether that as a model answers your question I wouldn't know, but at least it goes in the right direction.

Nicholas Guppy You mentioned that both Mars and Venus had abundant water at one time. Can you give us more information about that phase in those planets?

James Lovelock It is much easier to do so with respect to Mars because there is very little evidence at the moment about the earlier state of Venus. Nevertheless there are good grounds for believing that a quantity of water was outgassed from Venus in about the same proportions as the oceans on Earth, and of course there is none there now. On Mars you can actually see water channels, or at least it would be difficult to explain those channels on any other basis. One would therefore have expected considerable amounts of water to have been outgassed from Mars. It has recently been suggested that Mars once did have life on it, kept warm by a methane greenhouse, and it will be very interesting to find out with future expeditions to the planet if there are microfossils of an archean type.

Vanya Walker-Leigh One of the basic tenets of ancient mystical ideas is that the entire cosmos is a living self-regulating organism. Can you relate Gaia theory to that?

James Lovelock I conceive of Gaia as a metaphor of science, and speaking as a scientist I would rather handle what I call manageable topics. Concepts that are ineffable, such as whether the Universe is alive, one just cannot get at.

Nedira Bunyard Your theory sounds very optimistic but it does not appear to me to be very anthropocentric, so is your optimism in a sense detached from human concerns?

James Lovelock Thank you for asking that question. I often find myself in a difficult position in environmental groups. My heart is with them but Gaia really parts company from most of environmental thinking because it is speaking for the planet and not for the people on it, and I often feel that, although I am a member of Friends of the Earth, they really are friends of humanity and not *friends of the earth*. I don't feel any need to apologise for taking an anti-environmental ideal because there are millions who speak for people but hardly anyone speaking for the planet; yet it is in our interests to do so.

Ted Pawloff In the sense that the concept of noösphere was brought up earlier on, it might well be that the noösphere is part of the global necessity for the evolution of what at this time we may call Gaia. At the same time it appears that we are in a situation in which the noösphere, of which the technosphere is part, is not fully integrated with the evolution of the biosphere and unless we manage this integration we shall ourselves disappear.

James Lovelock That is a fascinating way of putting it. I have always found the concept of the noösphere very difficult because it is unmanageable in my terms. I think one should always remember that Gaia has been in operation for at least 3½ billion years without us hardly involved in it and so it is right really to put the noösphere into the context of a possible future rather than something that is here now.

Andrew Watson If there does turn out to have been evidence for past life on Mars that would seem to be at variance with the theory of planetary-scale life that you put forward, because if life gets control of the environment, what would cause it suddenly to cease?

James Lovelock Let's imagine there was life on Mars (my mentioning that life may have been once present on Mars was just an entertaining thought); if so it would have been over 2½ billion years ago. The Earth in those times was probably having trouble keeping warm because the sun was a lot cooler; on Mars it would have been a desperate problem, I would have thought, and if by some fortunate 'window' Mars had picked up life early on it would have been much more vulnerable to freeze out and some catastrophic event which was either internally driven or else was the result of a planetesimal impact. People tend to forget how exceedingly violent such events are; we have had some 30 on earth and they have been some 1000 times more powerful than all-out nuclear war involving all weapon-stocks. Undoubtedly such events would be hazardous for a planet that perhaps was struggling on the edge of sustaining its life. Ironically, the Earth will be in that state at some future date when the sun has warmed up a bit more: it will then be quite difficult to sustain the system.

Simon Bradley   In your book you played down the scare of aerosols, is that still part of your thinking?

James Lovelock   I haven't changed my views on that very much. I look on the current ozone hole issue, which certainly is attributable to the presence of CFCs in the atmosphere, as a kind of indicator, like a litmus paper. It's not an effect that has any appreciable effect on the amount of UV-B getting through to the Earth, which has been persistently diminishing as time has gone by. I personally think we have now reached the time when the emission of chlorofluorocarbons to the atmosphere should be curtailed. We need to have monetary inducements to encourage a more sensible use of these compounds, for instance by recycling them from old refrigerators instead of just dumping them. On the other hand I don't regard the ozone issue as a serious environmental one. The people who really are suffering from environmental depredation are those living in the Third World in the humid tropics, and to them the ozone scare is almost a non-issue.

Gregory Hinkle   Could you comment on how long you think the window might have been open for the origin of life and if the window is open does life necessarily have to evolve?

James Lovelock   You could put outer limits to it. The Earth formed 4.55 billion years ago and was then probably a pretty hot, sticky place. I don't know how rapidly it cooled to a point where life could have originated, but the time keeps being put back - 3.8 billion years was the last date I heard as a possibility. The window may have been short in geological terms - a million years or so.

Alwyn Jones   As was said earlier your theory was somewhat optimistic, but is there a pessimistic side? Is there a single threatening force which could undermine Gaia - for instance deforestation?

James Lovelock   The reason I am optimistic is not on a human personal basis but because the insults that the system has withstood in the past, like the planetesimal impacts, have been so huge compared with what we are doing at the moment, that it gives one a kind of comfort that no matter what we do life will go on on the planet, but of course it might be a totally different place to the one we know.

Alwyn Jones But it seems from hearing what you said this morning that you seem inclined to think that deforestation may be a crucial factor, which if it goes too far could be irreversible?

James Lovelock Yes, it could be a crucial factor in the current global ecosystem which includes us.

Marcus Colchester I can't understand why if Gaia is so self-sustaining you feel it necessary to speak out for it rather than concerning yourself to the more immediate problems that face us?

James Lovelock That's well said; I don't know, I have got myself landed with it!

JIM LOVELOCK'S GAIA
by Lynn Margulis

I am very grateful to have been invited here to this corner of England, to Cornwall, the native habitat of Jim Lovelock.

My plan is to state 'Gaia'as a scientific hypothesis. Having recognised the Gaian phenomenon I would like to explain where I think Gaia comes from and ask for how long this Gaia phenomenon has persisted on the surface of the Earth. And then I would like to raise some of the objections to the Gaia hypothesis. To my knowledge the Gaia hypothesis has never been discussed in polite scientific society by sympathetic scientists; this is an all time first.

We have now come 25 years. Here I show you a list of all the scientific papers Jim and I know about that are explicitly in the Gaian context (Table 1). For the first ten years or so it was known as "Life as seen through the atmosphere" – and other phrases. It was not called the Gaia hypothesis until, as you all know, Jim (with the help of William Golding) found a good four letter word to focus the attention of his colleagues on his ideas.

The Gaia hypothesis is the offspring of Jim Lovelock's fertile imagination and the US space programme. The hypothesis is concerned primarily with the lower atmosphere that is, the trophosphere. With respect to the chemical composition of the reactive gases of the lower atmosphere, the oxidation/reduction state and the pH (i.e., acidity and alkalinity), the Gaia hypothesis states that these attributes of the atmosphere are actively maintained by the activities of the biota. "The biota" refers to the sum of all living organisms: flora, fauna and especially microbiota. At current estimates we are talking about 30 million or so species.

I reject Jim's statement "The Earth is alive"; this metaphor, stated this way alienates precisely those scientists who should be working in a Gaian context. I do not agree with the formulation that says "Gaia is an organism". First of all in this context no-one has defined "organism". Furthermore I do not think that Gaia is a singularity. Rather Gaia is an extremely complex system with identifiable regulatory properties which are very specific to the lower atmosphere.

Equally I think there are no fundamental inconsistencies between the Gaia hypothesis and the basic tenets of Darwinian evolution, despite some Neo-Darwinian latter-day saints. This gang, led by Richard Dawkins, solipsistically wallow in their own zoological, capitalistic, competitive, cost-benefit interpretation of Darwin - having miss-taken him. Gaia is a hypothesis that can be tested just as Darwinian evolution is a testable scientific hypothesis. Gaia definitely falls within the realm of science even though scientists themselves may be ignorant or small-minded in denying that the hypothesis is testable. Like evolution as a hypothesis, it is testable but complex and requires many observations.

Why do so many people disagree, why do they tend to reject the Gaia hypothesis? My reading of the reasons are as follows: they ask how possibly can the mere biota regulate the planet Earth? How on this gigantic scale, can the temperature and the reactive gases of the planet be maintained? How does some little organism that is just trying to 'maximise its fitness' or increase its rate of reproduction in a thoroughly selfish way, possibly contribute to global regulation in a Panglossian

50

way? Since no mechanism for regulation appears to exist these investigators deny the existence of the gaian phenomenon.

Lack of evidence of control mechanisms is the usual kind of complaint. Scientists do not believe that planktonic algae in the sea produce sulphur gases just to 'benefit' the trees on the land. To summarise: Jim and I identify at least two objections. Our critics argue first that Gaia has not been stated properly as a scientific hypothesis and second that we lack a tangible mechanism of environmental control. But both of these objections can be countered.

As scientists, we cannot deny the existence of phenomena simply because we have failed to see mechanisms. The response the Gaia hypothesis is encountering is very much like the reception, in the 1920's of the ideas of Swiss meteorologist Alfred Wegener. He saw a phenomenon, "continental drift" as he called it, but it was not until the early sixties, that many scientists - those dragging magnetometers behind ships, those studying deep earthquakes, those recovering deep sea drilling cores – discovered a mechanism that brought about the acceptance of Wegener's

GAIA HYPOTHESIS COMES OF AGE. TWENTY-THREE YEARS OF
SCIENTIFIC PUBLICATIONS ON THE GAIA HYPOTHESIS (1965-1988)

Date	Authors	Title	Journal & Reference
1965	Lovelock, J.E.	A physical basis for life detection experiments	Nature 207:568–569
1967	Hitchcock, D.R. and Lovelock, J.E.	Life detection by atmospheric analysis	Icarus 7:149–159
1969	Lovelock, J.E. and Giffin, C.E.	Planetary atmospheres: Compositional and other changes associated with the presence of life	In: Advanced Space Experiments. Vol. 25. D.L. Tiffany and E. Caltzeff, eds. American Astronomical Society, Washington, DC
1972	Lovelock, J.E. and Lodge, J.P.	Oxygen—the contemporary atmosphere	Atmospheric Environment 6:575–578
1972	Lovelock, J.E.	Gaia as seen through the atmosphere	Atmospheric Environment 6:579–580
1974	Lovelock, J.E. and Margulis, L.	Atmospheric homeostasis, by and for the biosphere: The Gaia hypothesis	Tellus 26:1–10
1974	Margulis, L. and Lovelock, J.E.	Biological modulation of the Earth's atmosphere	Icarus 21:471–489
1975	Margulis, L. and Lovelock, J.E.	The atmosphere as circulatory system of the biosphere—The Gaia Hypothesis	CoEvolution Quarterly 6:30–41
1975	Lovelock, J.E.	Thermodynamics and the recognition of alien biospheres	Proc. R. Soc. Lond. B 189:167–181
1977	Margulis, L. and Lovelock, J.E.	The view from Mars and Venus	The Sciences Mar./Apr. pp. 10–13
1978	Watson, A., Lovelock, J.E., and Margulis, L.	Methanogenesis, fires, and the regulation of atmospheric oxygen	BioSystems 10:293–298
1980	Margulis, L.	After Viking: Life on Earth	The Sciences Nov., pp. 24–26
1980	Margulis, L. and Lovelock, J.E.	L'atmosphère est-elle le système circulatoire de la biosphère? L'hypothèse Gaia	CoEvolution 1:20–31
1981	Dastoor, M., Nealson, K.H. and Margulis, L., eds.	Interaction of the biota with the atmosphere and sediments	NASA Workshop Report, meeting Oct. 18–19, 1979, Washington, DC
1981	Doolittle, W.F.	Is nature really motherly?	CoEvolution Quarterly 29:58–63
1981	Margulis, L., Nealson, K.H. and Taylor, L., eds.	Planetary Biology and Microbial Ecology: Biochemistry of carbon and early life	NASA Technical Memorandum 86043 (Summer program research report, 1982)

GAIA HYPOTHESIS COMES OF AGE (continued)

Date	Authors	Title	Journal & Reference
1982	Lovelock, J.E.	Gaia: A New Look at Life on Earth	Oxford University Press, Oxford and New York
1982	Lovelock, J.E. and Watson, A.J.	The regulation of carbon dioxide and climate: Gaia and geochemistry	Journal of Planetary Science 30:795–802
1982	Margulis, L.	The biological point of view: The effect of life on the planet	In: Formation of Planetary Systems. A. Brahic, ed. Centre d'Etudes Spatiales. Capadues Editions, Toulouse, pp. 891–893
1983	Lovelock, J.E.	Gaia as seen through the atmosphere	In: Biomineralization and Biological Metal Accumulation. P. Westbroek and E. de Jong, eds., Reidel Publishing Co., Dordrecht, Holland, pp. 15–25
1983	Margulis, L. and Lovelock, J.E.	Le petit monde des pâquerettes: Un modèle quantitatif de Gaia	CoEvolution 11:48–52
1983	Margulis, L. and Stolz, J.	Microbial systematics and a Gaian view of the sediments	In: Biomineralization and Biological Metal Accumulation. P. Westbroek and E. de Jong, eds., Reidel Publishing Co., Dordrecht, Holland, pp. 27–53
1983	Sagan, D. and Margulis, L.	The Gaian perspective of ecology	The Ecologist 13:160–167
1983	Watson, A. and Lovelock, J.E.	Biological homeostasis of the global environment: The parable of Daisyworld	Tellus 35B:284–289
1984	Sagan, D. and Margulis, L.	Gaia and philosophy	In: On Nature. Leroy Rouner, ed., 6:100–125. Boston University Studies in Philosophy and Religion. University of Notre Dame Press, Notre Dame, Indiana
1985	Sagan, D., ed.	Planetary biology and microbial ecology: The global sulfur cycle	NASA Technical Memorandum (Summer program research report, NASA Ames, Jun.–Aug. 1984)
1986	Margulis, L., Lopez Baluja, L., Awramik, S.M., and Sagan, D.	Community living long before man	In: Man's Effect on the Global Environment, D. Botkin and A. Orio, eds. Vol. 2, Elsevier Science Publishers, Amsterdam; The Science of the Total Environment 56:379–397
1987	Lovelock, J.E.	Gaia: A New Look at Life on Earth, 2nd ed. Oxford University Press, Oxford and New York
1988	Lovelock, J.E.	The Ages of Gaia	W.W. Norton Co., New York

Table 1 Nearly 30 years of Gaia publications (from *Global Ecology: Towards a Science of the Biosphere* edited by Mitchell Rambler, Rene Fester, Lynn Margulis. Academic Press, San Diego 1989.

phenomenon. Together, through the impetus of great minds such as Donald Mackenzie and Fred Vines the concept emerged of plate tectonics as the mechanism of continental drift. Today the phenomenon of 'drift' is generally believed because the mechanism 'plate tectonics' has been revealed.

The other serious objection to the Gaia hypothesis has to do with time scale, argue the Neo-Darwinists of this world. The question is posed more or less like this: since living organisms are only interested in their immediate survival and the leaving of more offspring, how can the Earth have been regulated for more than 3,000 million years? How indeed can fast-acting organisms contribute to some million years of regulation and stability?

I now want to show you how the hypothesis came to be and what is the status of its testing. Then I think we can counter totally within the realms of ordinary science these objections.

One of the major tools of the Gaia hypothesis is the intrinsic global level of observation it employs. Let us compare planetary phenomena of the Earth with those of the 'sister' or flanking planets, Mars and Venus. Let us start with Venus. The Russians are now up to their 16th or so soft-landing mission on Venus. A view of the surface of Venus from Venera space flight 9 (which was launched on October 27th 1975 and landed on the planet in January 1976) is shown in Fig.1. The camera had just 45 seconds to operate, because conditions on Venus were so highly acidic and hot. The major features of the atmospheres of Venus as detected by the Soviet Venera space shots merely confirm what astonomers had detected using telescopes. We see here the Venus regolith, a surface littered with rubble. The surface is composed primarily of ejecta material from meteorite impact or volanic debris. Conspicuously missing are the sedimentary rocks, the open bodies of water like those found on Earth. Furthermore the atmosphere of Venus is far richer than Earth in carbon dioxide.

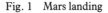

Fig. 1   Mars landing

Photograph: NASA

52

The Russians are now taking direct meso-scale measurements using orbitors and they have confirmed that Venus is an extremely dry planet. The clouds are extraordinarily acidic because they are composed of sulphate particles. To sum up Venus has a carbon dioxide-rich atmosphere with fewer than 3 per cent nitrogen and with high temperatures of about 400°C.

The other 'sister', the planet out just beyond Earth is Mars, with its polar ice caps; we know there is some water on its surface. In the late 1960s the US planned the Viking spacecraft, with two orbitors and landers. Launched in 1975, Viking reached its target in 1976 and made two landings, one at Chryse and one at Utopia. The dedicated reason for the mission was to find out if the planet Mars had life. Jim Lovelock had already predicted there was no life on Mars, But NASA hardly wanted to hear about his theories when they were spending a 1,000 million dollars on the "biology package" to detect life on the red planet. Jim was correct, employing the Gaia hypothesis, he predicted no life would be found on Mars at a time when none of us, myself included, understood what the Gaia hypothesis was.

What was the logic behind his assertions? As we approach Mars we see what Jim referred to yesterday; features from the orbiter that look as if they should be interpreted as riverine, and as having once contained flowing water (Fig.2). These features have since been cratered through impacts which means that the features are very ancient. The water was probably out-gassed from Mars over 2,000 million years. Most of it was lost although some remains frozen. Today there is no liquid water, although most agree that the evidence suggests there once may even have been Martian oceans. Like Venus, the atmosphere of Mars is primarily composed of carbon dixoide: 95 per cent of it is that gas. Like Venus Mars is very dry. On Mars too sulphur, conferring acidity, is thought to be present although the surface

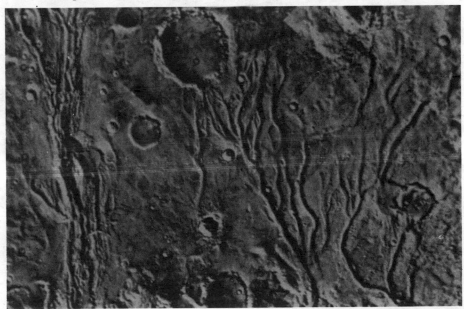

Fig. 2   Mars rivers

Photograph: NASA

temperature of Mars is very cold whereas that of Venus is very hot. Toby Owen Professor at the State University of New York at Stony Brook calls it the 'Goldilocks syndrome': one planet, Venus, is too hot, the other Mars, is too cold. The Earth is just right.

In contrast to the complex naive 'chicken-soup'and photosynthesis experiments that NASA scientists set up to test for life on Mars is Lovelock's concept. He stated his request very clearly: just give me the gas exchanges, just tell me how much of each gas is produced over what period of time; just measure the endogenous Martian surface gas fluxes. If NASA had provided Lovelock that information for the surface of Mars he could have tested the Gaia hypothesis directly. The rates of removal and production of various gases on Mars and Venus can be explained completely on the basis of physics and chemistry alone. Any such analysis was then grossly inadequate for the Earth's atmosphere. But NASA nor the Russian space programme never have undertaken a serious chemical analysis of the Martian or Venus surface nor of their unperturbed gas fluxes. Perhaps, for the intellectual climate at the time, it was premature to ask for those sorts of measurements.

If we interpolate what to expect of an Earth placed right between Mars and Venus in a 'gedanken' experiment we should see a carbon dioxide rich atmosphere, fewer than 3 per cent nitrogen, and a surface temperature somewhere betweeen that of Mars and Venus. We should expect a very acidic planet. The Apollo mission has provided us many pictures of the Earth taken from the Moon. If we had an orbiter that landed in the middle of the Colorado desert, as you can see from Fig. 3 we would not even find evidence of life on Earth. Even in Colorado we cannot expect giraffes or elephants to signal the existence of life by walking in front of the camera.

Fig. 3   Earth regolith: Hawaii   Photograph: Carmen Aguilar-Diaz

So what is here on Earth to tell us about the ubiquitous surface distribution of life? To detect life on Earth too we need gas exchange measurements telling us which gases are to be found and in what amounts.

Figure 4 compares the atmosphere of Venus with those of the other planets. Note it is composed of 96.6 per cent carbon dixoide. Mars' atmosphere has roughly the same composition as Venus at 95 per cent, each planet has between two and three per cent nitrogen. Regarding gases such as argon that are inert, and 'noble' they behave more or less as expected for unreactive substances. We find the concentrations to be similar in all three instances. Thus, the planetary reactive gas behaviour is best understood by the Gaia hypothesis. On Venus and Mars we have barely detectable amounts of water and oxygen. Then if we look at the Earth as if we were equilibrium chemists, we are totally flabbergasted. What we find makes little sense. The atmospheric composition of gases on Earth is like a mixture that goes into an automobile, not like the 'spent' gas mixture that comes out. Indeed the Earth's atmosphere is composed of a reactive mixture of gases. For instance nitrogen plus oxygen reacts to form nitrogen oxides which in the presence of water become nitrite and nitrate ions. Yet the Earth is composed of nearly 80 per cent gaseous nitrogen (N_2) and 20 per cent oxygen (O_2). What is worse is that a whole suite of gases - hydrogen, methane, ammonia, all of which react directly with oxygen - can always be detected in air samples. Finding hydrogen and oxygen together that have not reacted to produce water reflects some active and dynamic phenomenon that is generating those reactive gases. The same can be said for nitrogen in the presence of oxygen.

The Earth has far too much oxygen. Oxygen appears to have been around at approximately 20 per cent for at least 600 million years. The other striking difference between the Earth and her neighbours is that the carbon dioxide on

Fig. 4   Comparison of planetary atmospheres

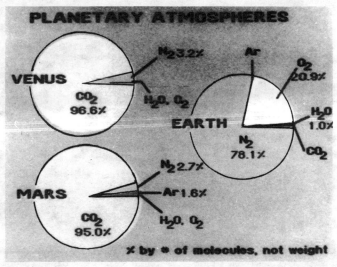

Photograph: Jeremy Sagan

55

Earth has virtually disappeared. Only 0.03 per cent is left. To the chemist and physicist the Earth is a planetary anomaly. Meanwhile the Gaia hypothesis states that this anomalous situation is generated and maintained by life, that the reactive aspects of the atmosphere are products of the evolution of life.

The next question is for how long has the Earth been a planetary anomaly? I want now to show you why I think the Gaia phenomenon has been going probably for 3,500 million years. *Homo sapiens sapiens,* our species, is maybe 40,000 years old. All this time the Gaia phenomenon of the atmosphere of the planet has been going on in the absence of *Homo sapiens*. Gaia hardly requires man, indeed we are just another one of these mammalian "weeds"; species that come and go every million years or so.

A prime question is "where did the carbon dioxide go?" Many people think that the carbon dioxide is in the biota, within the bodies of animals, trees and plants, but in fact fewer than one part per million is found in the bodies of such organisms. An astounding observation, made also by Toby Owen is that if we converted all the limestone deposits of the sediments into carbon dioxide gas of the air then our planet would become just like Mars and Venus.

The particular rock beside the tall Canadian shown in Fig. 5 is in North West territories. The rock represents what Dorion and I have called in *Microcosmos* bacterial skyscraper. The rock was made by bacteria. The particular rock in this photograph has been dated around 2300 million years old. To keep a time perspective any kind of animal, including those like trilobites or brachiopods that make chitinous or limestone shells, are only 570 million years old. Indeed the

Fig. 5   PrePhanerozoic stromatolites from the Kilohogok Basin, Victoria Island, N.W. Territories, Canada. These domed ancient stromatolites are about two billion years old and over two meters high.

tropical forests and African elephants that are so dear to our hearts are just latter-day epiphenomena of the effects of life on the planet. They are the Bachs and Beethovens of an orchestrated system that has been playing for 3500 million years. Fundamentally the crucial Gaian mechanism is a bacterial system. The bacteria-made rocks are an analogue to coral reefs of the much later Phanerozoic aeon. They follow a similar pattern of growth, precipitation, and subsidence so that a gigantic reef is formed that reaches the sea surface. Such rock-making phenomena of life take place over thousands and even tens of thousands of years. An area that today is the Canadian Arctic was tropical when the rocks in Fig. 5 were first formed. These bacterial rocks, ancient reef-like systems are called stromatolites. The oldest stromatolites known (much smaller than those in Fig. 5) are 3400 million years old. Such communities of organisms that formed these rocks were at the high point of their development just before 700 million years ago. From then on they were eaten back by animals, faced competition from algae and were subjected to other factors that altogether led to their demise. The important point to realise is that these stromalitic structures tell us that bacteria have been removing carbon dioxide from the atmosphere from some 3500 million years ago to the present. Such really huge stromatolite deposits are no longer being made; they have become extinct. How do we know that stromatolites were made by bacteria? Because we are lucky. In western Australia in places such as Shark Bay, 800 miles north of Perth the salt content is very high. In Hamelin Pond of Shark Bay we can find scenes today that we imagine are quite similar to ancient ones. Bacterial calcium carbonate structures being made today are remarkably similar in detail to those made 2000 million years ago.

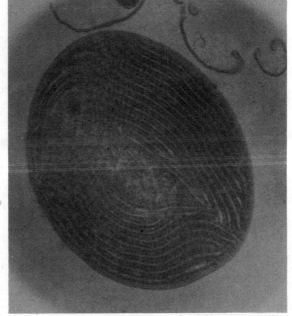

Fig. 6   Thylakoids in Aphanetheca

Photograph: John F. Stolz

57

What are they? Primarily composed of limestone, calcium carbonate, the blue-green sheen on top is due to carbonate-precipitating oxygen-producing bacteria. We need to remember that the action of the whole Gaian phenomenon may be on the micron and sub-micron level (10^{-6}m). Yet there is so much action in so many dynamic populations that the phenomena are actually detectable on a planetary scale. We are extending ourselves from microns to kilometres in scale. Today the largest living stromatolites we know of are about a metre across. Nevertheless the action, the place where the carbon dioxide is actually removed from the atmosphere, is a membrane which is thinner than one tenth of a micron. This here (Fig.6) is the membrane through which salt is pumped. The concept here is that microscale actitivies result in macroscale phenomena - which Jim Lovelock calls the colligative (collective) properties of life.

We have two major reservoirs of carbon at the surface of the planet; one is the much larger reservoir found in rocks and the other is the carbon in the cell material as well as that in fossil fuels. As the deposits are laid we simultaneously obtain free oxygen. The same process: oxygenic photosynthesis, gives us both deposited carbon and atmospheric oxygen. Probably many different types of cyanobacteria are involved, these bacteria being the heroes of a saga in which they have been truly responsible for global change.

We see here in Fig. 7 an organism called *Microcoleus*: it looks like a bunch of insulated telephone wires, made of long thin fibres encased in a sheath. The organisms move rapidly towards the light; if impeded by sediment, they trap particles together. They will 'trap' carbon dioxide precipitated by other

Fig. 7 *Microcoleus*

Photograph: John F. Stolz

cyanobacteria as sediment clasts. Layer upon layer of rocky sediment is produced. *Microcoleus* never lives by itself alone; it is always found in a community.

In addition to the lack of carbon dioxide in Earth's atmosphere and over-abundance of oxygen we have too much free hydrogen, too much methane and too much ammonia. All of these are extremely hydrogen-rich gases that react with oxygen. The reason for their presence is simple. Methane comes exclusively from anaerobic methanogenic bacteria which produce some million tonnes per year. The only way we can explain the presence of 1 to 2 parts per million of methane in today's atmosphere is by realizing it is bacterial excrement. Some of these methanogenic bacteria are found in huge numbers in the guts of ruminants such as cows, which Sir David Smith, FRS., calls "40-gallon methane generators on four legs."

Hydrogen is a well-known product from photosynthetic fermenting bacteria, microorganisms that always grow under anaerobic conditions. Every one of such reactive gases (e.g. hydrogen, methane, ammonia, hydrogen sulphide) is a product of life. Almost all are the products of microbial life. Even when these gases are produced by animals or plants the fundamental metabolism is either due to associated microorganisms or is represented in the bacteria. Hence animals and plants do no more than add to that which bacteria do and have been doing for aeons. Thus although trees can photosynthesise to much greater heights compared to bacteria, they are essentially photosynthesising using the same biochemical mechanisms. Furthermore, major cycling like the production of methane or hydrogen sulphide, or the fixation of inert atmospheric nitrogen, cannot be carried out at all by animals and plants. These gas emissions require bacteria either alone or in symbiotic concert. The vast complex and diverse metabolism that run the Earth system are all found in bacteria. Occasionally some of them were amplified by the later evolution of animals and plants. Already in the Archean Aeon (3500-2500 million years ago) we have direct evidence of bacteria's oxygenic ability, methanogenic ability, sulphate reduction and oxidation ability, nitrogen fixation ability. This diversity of pathways is found in seaside communities of microorganisms, like that which *Microcoleus* dominates.

Because the ancient limestone has been infiltrated with chert silica in the formation of rock some microbial communities became silicified. We see excellent preservation including some of cyanobacteria – produced oxygen and – removed CO_2. Under favourable conditions the rocks can be sliced and examined under the light microscope. Just the kind of organisms that today reside in the intertidal zones and are laying down the calcium carbonate can be found in some ancient cherts. On the basis of microfossils we say that these organisms flourished at least 2,000 million years ago and probably as much as 3500 million years.

If we had found laminated '*Microcoleus*-like' sediment on Mars or Venus we might have an incentive to ask if Gaia had ever occurred on these planets. Indeed these bacterial communities - only a few of which preserve as stromatolites - are surface structures: the skin tissue of the Earth. Evaporate is on top and sometimes carbonate is found underneath. The quantity of carbonate depends on the extent weathering of rocks has taken place. Salt (sodium chloride, magnesium chloride) and gypsum (calcium sulphate) are also found. Right beneath the evaporate layer is the community of microorganisms, the "telephone-wire community" that carries

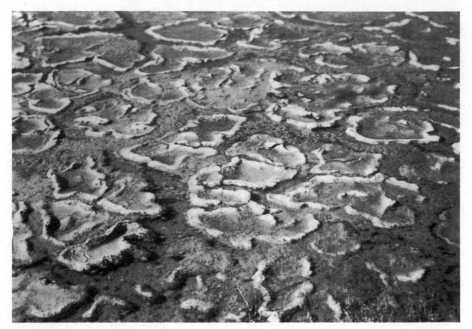

Fig. 8   Modern *microcoleus* mats

Photograph: Stanley Awramik

out much of the oxygenic photosynthetic activity. The modern mats we see in Fig.8 may be 100 or more years old. They are totally organised, packed with diversity, and it is through them that the essential gas exchanges take place, contributing to the Gaian phenomenon by their growth and metabolism. Yet we walk over them as if they were dirty sand. We must recognize this continuous covering of the Earth as living; the Earth's living surface coat has been responsible for the global-level regulation and exchanges of reactive gases. Particular organisms, for instance, take in hydrogen sulphide and carbon dioxide and produce sulphur globules which are later metabolised and become sulphate particles. These organisms are to be found in mat layers shown here. The mat layers go on and on, extraordinarily complicated, with bacterial cells arranged in organised communities.

During the winter of 1979 a disastrous storm destroyed the *Microcoleus* mats you have been seeing. Jim Lovelock, Claude Monty and I went to visit these mats that spring but all we found was a big puddle of water. Desperately, I said "the mats must be here, they have got to be here". Claude Monty quipped that if I expected such communities to have been around for 3500 million years a little spring flood was hardly going to bother them! Nevertheless that spring flood had destroyed one particular community because this one, the *Microcoleus* community requires intertidal exposure. For two years *Microcoleus failed to get such intertidal exposure yet the remnants of the community survived incognito* under the water. We had lost *Microcoleus* and instead certain red organisms had colonised the community, some of which eat cellulose, while others precipitate metallic iron and manganese. We witnessed a total change of details in the community. The flood experience was

60

informative; it was like an extinction at a large level, followed by colonisation with all kinds of new organisms that had not been there before. Most of them were anaerobic bacteria. The mud laid by the storm - to a bacterium inside - was equivalent to dumping 20 metres or more of mud and debris on New York City. However, from 1981 to the present, conditions returned to what they were before - the normal intertidal conditions.

The first thing we noticed was that a mud layer with the capacity to preserve the microbes had been laid down and probably this kind of process accounts for why we have preservation of any mat communities in the fossil record. Today that particular microbial community of Baja California Norte, Mexico, is back in the recovery stage. Here we see at the local microscale the kind of discontinuities that we find exemplified in Jim Lovelock's 'Daisy world model'. We have a carbon dioxide removal-oxygen release system, followed after the catastrophe by sulphur-colonising bacteria and then back again to what I call the normal condition: oxygenic photosynthetic mat-building communities.

The Gaia hypothesis was invented for the atmosphere - the trophosphere's chemical and temperature regulation. We, (John Stolz, Peter Westbroek, Greg Hinkle, Ricardo Guerrero and I) are beginning to believe that Gaian regulation must be considered a property of the Earth's surface sediments too.

I conclude with just one more example of sedimentary Gaia: enormous guano nitrate and phosphate deposits on the islands off the coast of Peru. These rock piles were laid down, as you well know, by generation after generation of sea birds. Such a sedimentary feature is wholly impossible on lifeless Mars or Venus. Surely guano islands are Gaian features that are completely out of equilibrium from the 'chemistry and physics of planets' point-of-view. The rock islands are basically produced because of an upwelling in that part of the world. Phosphate and other minerals lead to phytoplanktonic blooms. The fish then eat the phytoplankton, predatory fish eat smaller fish. Birds eat the larger fish and year after year these guano birds nest in the same place. The guano mountains represent thousands of years of accumulation of bird droppings. This particulate matter here on the surface of the planet, extremely phosphorus rich - on the Gaian view - is something entirely unknown on Mars and Venus. Other atmospheric particulates too would be impossible without Gaia. Some people call them sea birds, some people call them guano birds. Whatever they are called they are clearly metre-wide phosphorus-nitrogen-sulphur-rich locomotory volatiles in the atmosphere. Until the geologists, geophysicists and atmospheric chemists realise that these volatiles cannot be modelled by equilibrium chemistry or Newtonian physics but require an understanding of the exponential growth potential features of all the components in the surface layer called life, they will not succeed in intellectual comprehension. Indeed until they become Gaian in outlook these physical scientists will not have a proper model for climate or temperature or atmospheric composition. Until the Neo-Darwinists replace their abstruse and inappropriate mathematical masturbation with solid knowledge of metabolic and atmospheric chemistry these biological scientists will not have a proper model for the evolutionary history of life.

In 1664 Sachs Von Lewenheib wrote a book entitled *Oceanus Macromicrocosmicus*. He was a champion, as I understand it, of Harvey's physiological view of the cycling of the blood. He said that when the blood cycles it does not mean that it makes a "perfect circle" rather it is part of a closed system phenomenon. He rejected the idea of open systems in which the blood just seeped out of the heart, as previously thought. Von Lewenheib used 'meteoric' (rain, fog, snow) water taken from a weather example to defend blood physiology. He pointed out that when the water runs off it does not just vanish but it forms a circle, not in a geometric sense but in a figurative sense. Thus it evaporates and then precipitates over the mountains collecting into rivers and then into lakes and lakes into more rivers and ponds and so on until it collects in the ocean.

Now Lovelock has the Harvey-Von Lewenheib problem in reverse. Today we all accept that our blood circulates in our bodies. Everybody realises that we are not "being teleological" when we say that bicarbonate has a function in the blood, that mechanisms exist which keep our blood temperature constant, that mechanisms maintain sodium, chloride, and potassium ion concentrations within physiologically appropriate bounds. These are not teleological matters but they are scientific ones. What are the mechanisms that maintain the properties of circulation, of physiology of the blood? Here Jim and I are in the reverse of the situation in which Harvey and Von Lewenheib found themselves. We ask what mechanisms are there for maintaining the methane in the atmosphere, or dimethyl sulphide; indeed what physiological mechanisms maintain these and so many other phenomena of Gaia planetary control? Like those enlightened scientists of three hundred years ago we find we are being criticised by the geophysical scientists for our inability to produce precise mechanisms. We are accused of teleology. But like the modern physiologists and plate-tectonic geologists we shall overcome. That the air is regulated by life will soon seem obvious to biologists and climatologists. Scientists will feel compelled to read his new book (Lovelock 1988). Jim Lovelock will be recognized as the latter day William Harvey, and the *science* of planetary biology will begin.

References

Lovelock, J.E. *Ages of Gaia*, W. W. Norton, Co. New York, NY, 1988.

Margulis, L. and Sagan, D., *Microcosmos: Four billion years of evolution from our microbial ancestors.* Allen and Unwin, London, 1986.

Acknowledgements

We acknowledgement the financial support of the NASA life sciences office (NGR-004-052 to LM) and the Richard A. Lounsbery Foundation, N.Y. We are grateful to Rene Fester, Gregory Hinkle and Lorraine Olendzenski for aid with manuscript preparation.

DISCUSSION

Marcus Colchester   When we saw those two pictures of Mars and Venus and compared their atmospheres with that of the Earth, in particular you pointed out the difference in the oxygen and carbon dioxide content, but you didn't signal the extraordinary one of nitrogen. I am just wondering why you left it out of the story?

Lynn Margulis   I'm glad you brought up the question of nitrogen. Professor Tobias Owen (State University of New York Stony Brook) with others have carried out a 'gedanken' experiment in which they let all the carbon dioxide and other sources of carbon in the lithosphere go back into the atmosphere. They then look at the ratios of carbon dioxide in the atmosphere to nitrogen and to the other gases and they find 96 per cent CO_2 compared with 2 to 3 per cent nitrogen. The nitrogen on the Earth is therefore not in excess but it has no place to go in the rocks as it is now basically in its volatile phase. Relative to carbon dioxide, if the CO_2 were in the atmosphere and not in the rocks the nitrogen proportion in the Earth's atmosphere would be typical of that of any inner planet.

Ulrich Loening   It's left over in other words?

Lynn Margulis   Yes. Nitrogen gas is left over because nitrates are uncommon on our wet hungry planet and free nitrogen gas is not reactive in the making of any other common rock.

Ted Pawloff   Why does the scientific community have a problem with this way of looking?

Lynn Margulis   Physical scientists attempting to model the atmosphere on the basis of gaian concepts have a serious problem: they have to teach microbiology to their students. For the neo-Darwinian types their problem is that they only see one kind of metabolism, namely carbon dioxide releasing — oxygen in-taking animal metabolism, everything else they see as sort of 'selfish' or 'competitive'.

Elizabeth Sahtouris   One of the big problems the scientific community has is that in general it thinks of all the gaian organisms as separate entities that have somehow to get together in order to regulate. My point is that we never talk about our bodies as being regulated by the sum of the cells. What is required is for scientists to recognize the gaian system as having diversified from a unity that was never split apart.

Ulrich Loening   A parallel reason why it is not accepted is that it is so obvious and self-evident if one thinks about it.

Bernard Zamaron   Where did the bacteria come from?

Lynn Margulis   There is always an evolutionary sequence from previous bacteria. The question then becomes where did the first bacteria come from? That is the 'origin of life problem' – where fools walk in and angels fear to tread. All I will say is that we know that life originated by the Archeon Aeon, the time with which we are concerned. Indeed, there were definite communities of bacteria by the time solid rocks appeared and were preserved, on the Earth, maybe 3.8 billion years ago. Now where did those communities of bacteria come from? My personal opinion is that they evolved from complex chemical systems acted upon by solar radiation on the surface of the early Earth, but I don't defend that opinion other than through being acquainted with a whole series of reasonable hypothesis in the scientific literature. Everything I have described in my talk definitely occurred after the origin of life. Thus we take as given the origin of life. Nevertheless, I think the origin occurred on Earth and believe there are good arguments that it did.

Mae-Wan Ho   How long did it take for the carbon dioxide composition to go down to the present level and also what sort of mechanisms are actually operating these communities so that they lay down calcium carbonate?

Lynn Margulis   Geochemists tell me that before the Phanerozoic Aeon, (from 570 million years ago until the present) the carbon dioxide content could have been up from 0.03 to maybe 8 per cent, but even that is quite high. At the most in the recent geological past it might have been 10 per cent. As far as the precipitation mechanism is concerned, it's not exactly straightforward. There are three kinds of bacteria all of which are superficially the same. In one you will find perfect tiny crystals of aragonite and in the other calcite whilst in the third there won't be any precipitation at all; yet all are living in the same water under parallel conditions. These sort of observations tell you that it is genetic differences in the organisms given the same environmental conditions that allow some to precipitate and some not, some to make skeletons and some not. For instance Steve Weiner at the Weizmann Institute in Israel has some beautiful data on peptides, partial proteins, which act like a template for calcium carbonate precipitation. Change one of the amino acids and precipitation fails to occur. The feeling is that relatively small genetic changes can lead to great changes in precipitation.

Mae-Wan Ho   Are they actually symbiotic communities in any sense at all?

Lynn Margulis   If you define symbiosis as organisms, individual members of different species in protracted physical association throughout most of the life cycle of at least one of them, if you have that kind of definition, you could say yes, they are. In any case these microbes are tightly and regularly associated with each other.

Jerry Ravetz   I have got a gedanken experiment and that would be to take some of the criticisms of Dawkin and Doolittle and wherever they say Gaia to put in natural selection.

Lynn Margulis   That is one of David Abram's major points. He asks 'who is doing the selection'? In fact 'natural selection' is a very bad metaphor since it implies a conscious 'selection' – it is a shame we let Darwin get away with it to begin with! All you need to do is to replace 'natural selection' with 'Gaia'. In other words 'Gaia' defined as "the regulatory system comprised of the sum of the rest of the organisms and their environment". The mechanisms of gaian regulation is known and familiar: differentiated growth and survival of active organisms. 'Gaia' selects and, as you say becomes the selective agent.

Edward Goldsmith The Frenchman, Pierre Paul Grassé, who recently died, stated quite explicitly that all Neo-Darwinism has done is to substitute the word natural selection for the word 'God'.

THE GAIA HYPOTHESIS-
MECHANISMS AND TESTS
by Andrew J. Watson

It is argued that Gaian homeostasis may be a natural consequence of an intimate 'close-coupling' between the biota and the global environment. This possibility is illustrated by a discussion of 'Daisyworld', an imaginary planet where the environment has been simplified to a single variable, planetary temperature, and the biota consists of only one or two species of daisies.

From the Gaia hypothesis one may make predictions about the evolution of the global environment and its present stability, and these may be used to test the hypothesis according to the scientific method. In particular, an environment which evolves by long periods of stasis punctuated by short periods of change would be consistent with Gaia, whereas a history of rapid and continuous fluctuation would not. Major changes in the environment should occur simultaneously with sudden changes recorded in the fossil record.

The Gaia hypothesis as originally stated by Lovelock and Margulis (1974) was this: the environment at the surface of the earth is actively homeostated by the biota for their own benefit. At the time that it was first proposed, most Earth scientists thought of life (when they thought of it at all) simply as an opportunist adapting to the global environment. Life rarely had any actual influence on the environment, let alone controlled it in any sense. During the past 15 years this perception has changed greatly, and most scientists today would probably agree that it was the emergence of life on Earth, more than any other single factor, which caused our planet's evolution to diverge from that of Mars, Venus or the Moon.

However while acknowledging that life has influenced the environment, mainstream science still stops well short of accepting the Gaian notion of homeostasis by and for the biota. This idea, it has been argued, is teleological, implying that life has some underlying purpose which was designed into it at the beginning -- a notion which belongs to philosophy and religion, not science. My purpose here is to show that some form of regulatory behaviour may actually follow as a natural consequence of the close relationship between the biota and the global environment which scientists already accept, and that the hypothesis is in fact open to test using the classical scientific method.

More than anything else, it is the composition of the atmosphere which shows us that life is a global geological force. Table 1 lists the major sources of the most abundant atmospheric gases, rare gases excepted. With the exception of water vapour they all derive either directly or indirectly from the organised activity of life. (In this context, the products of industry may legitimately be regarded as 'life processes'). This conclusion is not altered if the table is extended to include trace gases at lower and lower concentrations; on the contrary, it is reinforced.

There is nothing controversial about this table; it reflects the established scientific wisdom regarding the sources of atmospheric gases, and it clearly shows that on Earth organisms have a profound influence on the environment. Now, the

TABLE 1: SOURCES OF ABUNDANT ATMOSPHERIC GASES

Gas	Major Source	Biological/Industrial
Nitrogen	Denitrification	Yes
Oxygen	Photosynthesis	Yes
Water vapour	Evaporation	No
Carbon dioxide	Respiration	Yes
Methane	Methanogenesis	Yes
Hydrogen	Natural hydrocarbon Oxidation/anthropogenic	Yes
Carbon monoxide	Methane oxidation/ anthropogenic	Yes
Nitrous Oxide	Nitrification/ Denitrification	Yes

converse is also true and has been recognised since the time of Darwin. That is, organisms are influenced by the environment. To take atmospheric composition as an example again, plants and animals are obviously dependent on the oxygen, carbon dioxide and nitrogen in the air. In other words, life and the global environment are two parts of a close-coupled system, where the two components are arranged in a feedback loop (Figure 1). Perturbations of one will affect the other and this will in

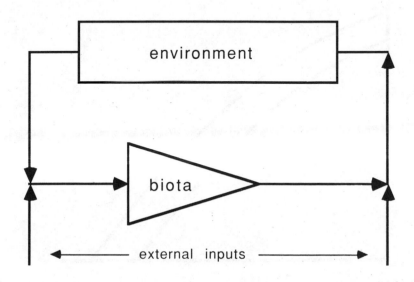

Fig. 1   Schematic to illustrate the biota and the environment as a closed loop.

turn feed back on the original change. The feedback may be positive or negative, but it will not in general be non-existent. Figure 1 includes provision for external variables to be taken into account, because the system is not completely closed. Examples of external perturbations might be changes in the solar output, meteorite impacts, orbital wobbles etc.

We would like to know what properties this close-coupling between life and the environment might confer on the system. Might it, for example, confer increased stability? The difficulty here is that the diagram is too simplistic: in reality both the biota and the environment are vastly complex entities, multiply interconnected, and there is hardly a single aspect of their interaction which can as yet be confidently described by a mathematical equation. To make progress, and as an exercise to illustrate the possibilities, we must make some drastic simplifications. We shall reduce the environment to a single variable--say temperature, and the biota to a single species, namely daisies.

Daisyworld

Daisyworld is a cloudless planet with a negligible atmospheric greenhouse on which the only kind of life is daisies, which for the moment we will assume to be white. Because the daisies are lighter than the ground they cover, they tend to increase the albedo of the planet and thus to cool it. The mean temperature of the planet as a function of the area covered by daisies will have a form like figure 2a. The

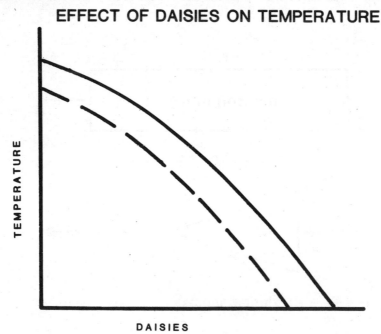

EFFECT OF DAISIES ON TEMPERATURE

Fig 2a   Dependence of mean planetary temperature on the number of white daisies. Decreasing the solar luminosity shifts the curve to the dotted line.

dotted line shows how the curve might shift following a change in some external variable which influences the temperature. As an example of such a variable we will take the luminosity of Daisyworld's sun.

Now, let us assume that the daisies grow best over a restricted range of planetary temperatures. The temperature-versus-growth curve peaks at 20° celsius say, and falls to zero much below 5° or much above about 40°. As a function of temperature, the steady-state population of daisies will look like figure 2b. Figures 2a and 2b both relate the temperature to the daisy population at steady state, so that the steady state condition of the system as a whole must be specified by the intercepts of the two curves. In figure 2c they are superimposed, and it can be seen that there are two possible steady state solutions for the particular case drawn here. It turns out that the solution where the derivatives of the two curves have opposite signs is unconditionally stable, whereas the other solution tends to instability so that the system will normally come to rest at the stable solution.

Consider now what happens to the stable solution when some change in the external environment alters the planetary temperature. Suppose for example that Daisyworld's sun warms up, as ours is supposed to be doing. If the daisy population is held constant, we get a much larger change in the planetary temperature than if we allow the daisies to change to their new steady state. In the stable configuration, the daisy population alters so as to oppose the original change.

Notice that here we have made very few assumptions: we have assumed that the daisies can affect the temperature, but the mechanism works equally well whatever

EFFECT OF TEMPERATURE ON DAISIES

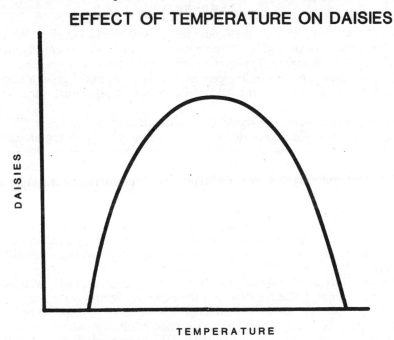

Fig. 2b   Dependence of daisy population on temperature.

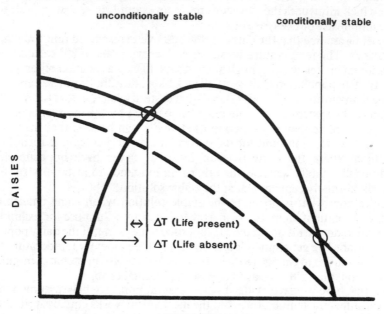

Fig. 2c Simultaneous solution of these functions.

direction they affect it. That is, they could just as well be black daisies. We have assumed that they can only grow within a restricted range of our environmental variable, but all mainstream life requires temperatures above freezing and below about 50 centigrade, and indeed the general picture of a peaked growth curve is common to a number of environmental variables besides temperature, for example pH.

Lovelock and I discussed this model in some depth in a paper in *Tellus*. (Watson and Lovelock, 1983). We emphasised there that the exercise was being conducted, not because we believe that daisies, or any other plants, regulate the Earth's temperature by this mechanism, but because it provides an easily understood model of close-coupling between the biota and the environment. The daisy populations were modelled by differential equations borrowed directly from population ecology, and we considered also the case of competitive growth of white and black daisies. Figures 3a, b and c show the results of a few computer calculations for the mean temperature of the planet, for varying assumptions. In each case, the mean planetary temperature at steady state has been plotted as a function of the luminosity of Daisyworld's sun.

For the case illustrated in figure 3a only one species of daisy (black in this case) was allowed to grow. Some regulation of the planetary temperature is apparent, though in this case over a rather limited range of luminosity. When both black and white daisies are included (figure 3b) we get good regulation over a much wider range of input luminosities. The regulation has the peculiar characteristic that the mean temperature actually tends to decrease as the luminosity increases. This type

70

Fig. 3 Steady state solutions of daisy population and planetary temperature as a function of solar luminosity

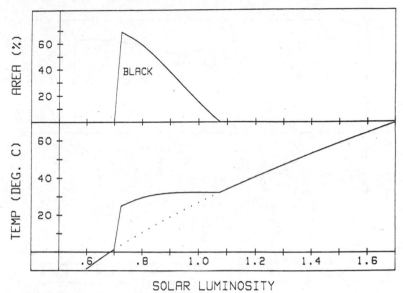

Fig. 3a Black daisies only.

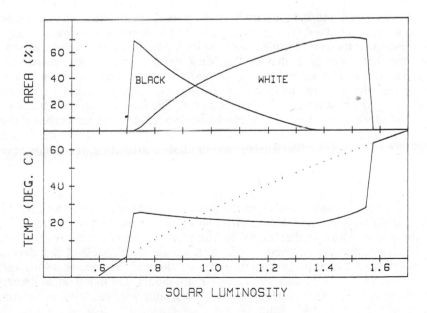

Fig. 3b Black and white daisies in competition.

71

Fig. 3c Same as 3b but black daisies are covered by white cloud.

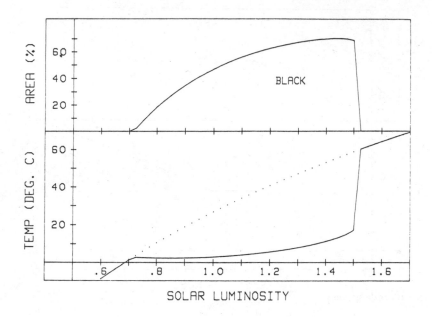

of behaviour is not unusual for a multiple loop, non-linear system such as we are dealing with here, but it is quite impossible in simple single loop feedback systems.

In these simulations we assumed that the local temperature of the white daisies was somewhat lower than that of the black daisies because they absorb less radiation. As a result, white daisies grow best when the planetary temperature is warmer than the optimum temperature of the growth curve. Black daisies on the other hand grow best when the planet is cooler. The feedback on each species of daisy is in this case self-limiting: white daisies 'prefer' a warm planet, but if they grow to cover too much ground they tend to cool the whole planet and thereby inhibit their own growth. Black daisies are similarly self-limiting. It is not however necessary to set up the system in this civilised configuration for it to exhibit homeostasis. We can if we like contrive to make the feedback on one or both types self-reinforcing. In the calculations for figure 3c we retained the assumption that black daisies prefer colder conditions but pretended that a white cloud formed over each black daisy. Thus more black daisies mean more white clouds which tends to cool the planet, which further stimulates the black daisies and inhibits the white. The result is again excellent homeostasis over a wide range, but the black daisies, which now push the temperature in the direction that they themselves favour, out-compete the whites which always go extinct in this model. The moral is that if we try to set the system up in a way which is unstable, it simply adjusts itself by deleting unfit species until it is stable again.

What relevance does this contrived, idealized world have to the Earth? That

72

depends on how general are our assumptions and how strong are the postulated feedbacks between organisms and their environment. To illustrate, we can sketch out the elements of a feedback loop, analogous to that on daisyworld, which might conceivably have helped to stabilise the Earth's temperature over geological time.

First, it is necessary to assume that the biota have a net effect on the temperature of the Earth. For the purposes of this argument the direction of this effect is immaterial, but we have argued that the net effect of life on Earth may be to depress the planetary temperature by 'pumping down' atmospheric carbon dioxide considerably, thus reducing the efficiency of the atmospheric 'greenhouse' (Lovelock and Watson, 1982). The reasoning goes as follows. Over geological time, the main removal process for carbon from the biosphere is by the chemical weathering of silicate rocks in the soil (Walker *et al.*, 1981). In soils the partial pressure of carbon dioxide is much higher than in the atmosphere because of the decay of organic matter by soil microbes (Holland, 1978). In the absence of life, presumably atmospheric carbon dioxide would have to be much higher to produce the same weathering rate.

Secondly we have to assume that there is a net effect of temperature on the biota. A good case can be made that the biosphere is low-temperature limited. That is to say, a general cooling of the planet would lead to less biological activity over the Earth as a whole, perhaps an extension of the barren polar regions and a contraction of the fertile tropics. In particular it would lead to less soil respiration, hence slower removal of carbon dioxide, which would then build up in the atmosphere and tend to oppose the original change. Although in detail this mechanism is quite unlike that on Daisyworld, the principle is really the same. One needs only to assume that the biota affect the temperature and that the temperature in turn affects the biota in a consistent manner, to be led to the conclusion that the net effect of these interactions will be regulatory. Positive, destabilising feedback loops can of course also exist. However, if the biota-environment is a strong interaction these states will be highly unstable and will therefore be transitory; most of the time the system will reside in the stable configurations where negative feedback dominates. The Gaia hypothesis of global regulation by the biota may follow as a natural consequence of the intense and vital interaction between the Earth and the organisms which inhabit it.

Tests for Gaia

According to Karl Popper (1963), science proceeds by logically unjustified and unjustifiable conjectures, theories or hypotheses. These generate predictions which are open to refutation, or testing. One problem with the Gaia hypothesis is that, in common with other conjectures in the field of Earth history, its subject matter is remarkably difficult to test by direct experiment. However it is certainly possible to make some predictions about what the course of Earth history should have been like to be consistent with Gaia, and I think it is worth outlining some of them. We are all the time adding to our knowledge of the environment in the geological past, so these predictions do have a fighting chance of being tested.

1. STASIS THE NORM

If there is any truth in the idea of Gaian homeostasis, it follows that stasis must be the norm of affairs on Earth. This applies equally to the biota and to the environment in which it resides, for a substantial change in one will provoke a response by the other. However, there is no doubt that major changes have occurred in the past and that the system is not immovably frozen in one state. There are for example, several major extinctions in the fossil record (i.e. Raup and Sepkoski, 1982) and there is one generally agreed major change in atmospheric composition; that is, the appearance of free oxygen. Following Gaia we would expect that these changes would be relatively rapid episodes where the system 'flips' from one stable state to a new one, accompanied by a temporary failure of the regulatory mechanisms. Similar behaviour can be seen on Daisyworld at the extreme limits of regulation, where a slight increase in solar luminosity causes the sudden extinction of the daisies. We therefore predict that the atmosphere should have evolved by a kind of punctuated equilibrium, long periods of stasis being interrupted by short periods of rapid change. Furthermore, the shifts should occur at the same time as major changes in the fossil record. For example, there is not much evidence to constrain speculation about the history of atmospheric oxygen after its appearance about two billion years ago. There are indications that it had reached a level comparable to that of today by the time of the Carboniferous, (Watson, 1978) but there appears to be no geological reason why oxygen should not have varied widely and quite rapidly over the intervening 1700 million years.

But that is not the Gaian prediction. Gaia would regulate the oxygen level most of the time, with major changes occurring only at crisis points in the history of the Earth. If, as we piece together the history of the atmosphere, it becomes clear that atmospheric components typically vary widely and continuously over geological time, this will be evidence against Gaia. But if the major changes occur in synchrony with a punctuated fossil record, then we should take this as evidence consistent with the hypothesis. Sometimes it may be possible to pinpoint an event which caused the initial change, but it is probably irrelevant to ask whether these punctuations are caused by changes initially in the environment, or in the biota, since these two components are so intimately linked together.

2. MARS

There is increasingly good evidence that Mars was once a much warmer planet with running water on its surface. This has led some scientists to speculate that, though Mars is now definitely a dead planet, it may have supported a thriving biosphere in the distant past. If a future Mars mission finds evidence for fossil life on Mars, we should regard this as evidence against the Gaia hypothesis, unless we can also find evidence for a really cataclysmic planetismal impact which might have sterilised the planet. A biosphere that was 'in control' of the planet's geochemistry would not have succumbed quietly to a slow cooling of the planet.

3. GAIA AND POLLUTION

We can also describe the response of Gaia to the relentless exploitation and pollution of the biosphere by our own species. At first the system will tend to respond so as to minimise the changes we are inflicting. In a global sense, little harm will therefore be done providing we do not stress the present state too far. But suppose that we apply so much stress that we push the system beyond the limits of regulation; it may then begin to change *of its own accord* to a new state. If that occurs we will find ourselves powerless to reverse the changes. Eventually the system will come to rest in a new stable state, but that state may not include most of the animals and plants that enrich our present Earth; it may not even include *Homo sapiens*. Given our present ignorance of how much stress the present configuration of the biosphere can take, the Gaia hypothesis should warn us to be very wary of inducing global scale changes in the environment. The danger is not so much that we may kill Gaia; rather it is that we may make her roll over, and that in doing so she may destroy us and everything we care for.

References

Holland, H.D., 1978, *The chemistry of the atmosphere and the oceans*, Interscience, New York.

Lovelock, J.E. and Margulis, L., 1974, Atmospheric homeostasis by and for the biosphere: The Gaia Hypothesis, *Tellus* 6 2.2.

Lovelock, J. E., and Watson, A. J., 1982, The regulation of carbon dioxide and climate: Gaia or geochemistry, *Planet. Space Sci.* 30, 8.

Popper, K.R., 1963 *Conjectures and Refutations*, Routledge and Kegan Paul, London.

Raup, D.M., and Sepkosky, J. J. 1982, Mass extinctions in the marine fossil record, *Science*, 215, 1501.

Walker, J. C. G., Hays, P. B. and Kasting, J. F., 1981, A negative feedback mechanism for the long term stabilization of Earth's surface temperature. *J. Geophys.Res.*86, 9776-9782.

Watson, A. J., 1978 "Consequences for the biosphere of forest and grassland fires", PhD thesis, Reading University, Reading, U.K.

Watson, A. J., and Lovelock, J. E., 1983, Biological homeostasis of the global environment: the parable of Daisyworld, *Tellus* 35B, 284.

DISCUSSION

Peter Westbroek   What happens if you put species together with different growth optima?

Andrew Watson   You mean different temperatures at which they like to grow? We haven't actually tried that as far as I know.

Peter Westbroek   Yes, and which one has got to be controller?

Andrew Watson   My guess would be that whichever one happened to be closest to the optimum would be the one that controls.

Mae-Wan Ho   I was just wondering why you haven't included albedo in the second model? Isn't that supposed to be very important?

Andrew Watson   Not as far as this model is concerned. In reality it is not at all clear that the vegetation of the Earth has a great effect on the albedo of the planet. Something which certainly does have a great effect on the albedo of the planet is the extent of ice cover, for example, and another factor that has a great effect is the amount of cloud cover. Jim talked briefly about a biological feedback in the tropics and sub-tropics whereby cloud or the whiteness of the clouds is increased by there being more life in the oceans underneath, but that's a different model. That suggestion by Jim Lovelock and Bob Charlson is really the first time as far as I know that anyone has proposed that the biota of the planet may control the temperature of the planet by an albedo feedback.

Nicholas Guppy   You have got an increased population of white daisies. Can you break down the effect on temperature?

Andrew Watson   You are asking how much of it heats the atmosphere, how much heats the clouds? On the real Earth or on our Daisy World? The answer on Daisy World is simple: all the heat is re-irradiated into space and through the simple physical law - the Stefan-Boltzmann law - we can determine the temperature of the planet if we know what colour it is. That's easy for the model, that's why we chose it.

Nicholas Guppy   If you heated up the clouds they would tend to dissipate. Has any work been done to show how that works in the real world?

Andrew Watson   In the real world plenty of work has been done, particularly by the Russians. A recent book by M. I. Budyko, *The Evolution of the Biosphere*, a sort of extension of Vernadsky's ideas, gives a good account of where the heat that is re-irradiated from the Earth goes to; it varies very much depending on where you are on the planet.

Peter Bunyard   The change-over from warm periods to ice-age seem to go rather fast. Will such changes be explicable in terms of Gaia theory?

76

Andrew Watson I hope that we are going to get to the situation shortly where we will be able to model the onset and the ending of the ice ages. Apparently over the last few million years the ice ages have been driven by the Milankovic Oscillations, at least that appears to be the case over the last five or so cycles when the correlation between the 100,000 year oscillation cycle and the ice-age cycle has fitted together remarkably well. The oscillations cause slight changes in the amount of sunlight that falls on the Northern Hemisphere as distinct from the Southern Hemisphere. Even so, it has been a puzzle why those changes should cause major glaciations and the answer certainly has to do with biology: it is a biological problem as much as it is a geological one.

We know, for instance, that the carbon dioxide level goes up and down in sympathy with the Milankovic wobble and we know that the marine biota controls the amount of carbon dioxide in the atmosphere in the short term, so clearly the marine biota are changing in accordance with this very tiny wobble, but just how remains to be seen.

Edward Goldsmith Your Daisy World is a self-regulatory system capable of achieving its homeostasis, but it is a very crude self-regulatory system. As an ecosystem evolves from the pioneer to the climax state so self-regulation becomes more sophisticated, while discontinuities or fluctuations are progressively ironed out, and the system thus becomes increasingly stable and hence more homeostatic. This change corresponds to the gradual replacement of external controls, that is to say the system's behaviour is ever less determined by external factors - the ones that monopolise the attention of ecologists and evolutionary theorists today - and are increasingly the product of the system's own initiative. For instance, in a pioneer society population may be controlled by food availability, epidemics, wars and other trauma. In a climax society - a tribal one - they will be determined, on the other hand, by a whole constellation of culturally determined strategies such as taboos against sexual activities during lactation or during the first years of widowhood. My point is that a self-regulatory system at the pioneer stage such as your Daisy World does not appear to be teleological, but once self-regulation becomes internalized its fundamentally teleological character becomes much more evident.

Andrew Watson The point of the exercise was to try and abstract the thing we were interested in, but I do agree with you that as you increase the complexity the very stark relationship between the biota and the environment that our model demonstrates probably breaks down, so that for most organisms their immediate surroundings and other organisms they interact with become more important as it were than their interaction with the wider environment. Nevertheless, I still think there are some very important and rather simple ecosystems where this kind of game may be played. In particular, if you look at what organisms are important globally it seems to me that rather a small number of classes may be involved. For example, the phytoplankton in the sea which appear to have a special geochemical significance, yet at the same time, they do not have such an intimate relationship with other organisms as they have with their environment.

Jerry Ravetz   Why don't the icecaps just progressively cover the Earth through the albedo effect? Ice reflects more sunlight which reduces the temperature still further and so on.

Andrew Watson   It is not simply that. There are a number of complex factors, one of them being the position of the continents on the planet. When the continents are close to the poles then ice can grow more rapidly. The general theory predicts that the ice-albedo system is somewhat unstable and there will come a point where once you get too much ice on the planet the system will runaway so that the entire planet ices over. Meanwhile the temperature zooms down to something like 250° Kelvin, which is about −20 to −30°C, and life at that point would cease. It has to be pointed out that if you model that, then factors such as the marine biological effect start to come into play. Indeed, if you stopped all growth in the oceans the carbon dioxide levels in the atmosphere would rapidly go up and start to counteract that effect. On the other hand it has been suggested that at the peak of the last ice-age the Earth came very close to running away and being permanently iced over.

Peter Bunyard   Could you elaborate as to why that particular ice age?

Andrew Watson   It was a very severe ice age. Even during the summer the North Atlantic remained frozen over from the middle of Spain over to New York, so there was a vast increase in the amount of ice cover. That was some 15,000 years ago; that's all.

Peter Bunyard   So basically the death of large chunks of marine biota brought us back to safety?

Andrew Watson   That is the current theory.

Peter Bunyard   With solar luminosity increasing and carbon dioxide being used to counteract that effect, from the biota's point of view, what happens when there is no more CO_2 to pull out from the atmosphere. Will that mark the end of a steady state system?

Andrew Watson   That is very difficult to predict. One extreme possibility is that the mean temperature would rise by some 20° C. I don't think that that would be the most likely scenario, for example Jim Lovelock's cloud albedo feedback hypothesis might save us.

MECHANISMS OR MACHINATIONS –
IS THE OCEAN SELF REGULATING?
by Michael Whitfield

The oceans provided the cradle for the development of life. For the first three thousand million years of the earth's history, life was confined to the oceans and so it is there that we must turn to identify Gaian control mechanisms and to understand their origins and evolution. The oceans today appear vast, covering more than two thirds of the earth's surface with waters up to ten kilometres deep. Yet if the earth were reduced in scale to a ball of rock a metre in diameter, the surface would just be moist to the touch. It is this thin film of moisture and the tenuous atmosphere that it helps to maintain that make the planet habitable.

All the known elements can be found dissolved in sea water and there has been an intimate relationship between the composition of sea water and the evolution of life. The continued existence of life in the oceans is still critically dependent on the availability of nutrients for plant growth in the surface, sun-lit layers and on the effective control of the concentrations of potentially toxic elements.

The surface of the earth is subject to vigorous geological activity driven by energy from the sun and from nuclear reactions taking place deep within the planet's core. These geological processes are capable of changing the composition of sea water and hence of affecting the ocean's ability to support life. In addition, the earth's climate is influenced by gradual and episodic variations in the sun's luminosity and by periodic wobbles in the earth's orbit. If we add to this the suggestion that the earth has been bombarded on occasion by large meteorites (planetismals) that have caused mass extinctions, we can see that any biological control systems that have evolved must be extremely resilient.

To appreciate how rapidly the geological processes work, we need to view the earth's history on a timescale that we can comprehend. Let us compress the whole of the earth's history into a single day. On this timescale, one second is equivalent to eighteen million years! Simple bacterial cells first appear in the fossil record at about eight o'clock in the morning on the Earth-day timescale and it is not until eight o'clock at night that the first evidence of nucleated cells, the precursors of all higher life forms, is observed. The colonisation of the land by higher organisms does not begin until ten o'clock at night. Against this leisurely progression the geological processes within the ocean appear quite frenetic.

The oceans are stirred at a rate of three thousand revolutions per minute, and the water in the oceans is renewed through the hydrological cycle once every second. enough sediment is discharged into the oceans by the world's rivers to completely fill in the ocean basins in a little over an hour. Over the same period, the rivers introduce enough dissolved material to double its salt content. Volcanic processes occurring along the mid oceanic ridges as a result of continental drift have a comparable impact on the chemistry of the oceans. The current episode of continental drift, driven by convective processes deep within the earth's mantle, is only one and a half hours old.

The individual elements dissolved in sea water are rapidly turned over by these geological processes. In general the more concentrated an element is in sea water, the longer is its residence time. Biological processes at the cellular level have apparently evolved to take advantage of the most concentrated elements in sea water that are capable of performing a particular function thereby minimising the effects of variations in sea water composition. As a corollary to this, the elements that are most toxic to organisms tend to have short residence times and be present at low concentrations. In the Earth-day essential nutrient elements such as nitrogen and phosphorus have a residence time in the oceans of a few minutes and the residence time of essential trace metals such as iron and manganese are measured in milliseconds on this timescale. Even the most concentrated elements such as sodium and chlorine have residence times of only an hour or so. Consequently in a completely unregulated system the oceans could have fluctuated rapidly and erratically from rich pastures to sterile deserts throughout the earth's history. Some kind of control mechanisms must have been at work in the oceans to enable life to evolve continuously over such a long period.

CONTROL MECHANISMS IN THE OCEAN

The vigour of the geological process and the general relationship between residence time and concentration appear to suggest that the oceans may simply be controlled by geological processes. Two kinds of processes can be invoked and these can be illustrated by considering the problem of maintaining a constant level in a tank of water which has both an inlet and an outlet.

In the normal lavatory cistern, any removal of water is counterbalanced by an inflow of water triggered off by the opening of the ball valve. This active process is very effective in maintaining the level so long as there is sufficient time for the inflow to refill the tank. The geochemical equivalent of this system is an equilibrium reaction in which the dissolved component reacts with a solid mineral phase. If the component is too concentrated in the solution, more mineral is deposited to remove the excess. If too little is present, the mineral dissolves to increase the solution concentration. The actual level in solution is fixed by thermodynamic laws. For such a process to be effective, there must be at least one pure mineral phase responsible for maintaining the concentration of each element in sea water and there must be sufficient time for the equilibrium to be established. In practice this would require the presence of more than ninety different mineral phases all at equilibrium. When we look at the ocean sediments we find an abundance of mineral phases but these are rarely pure and hardly ever at equilibrium either with the solution or between ourselves.

The alternative geochemical mechanisms of regulation is the passive or *steady state* system. In the case of our tank of water this is equivalent to having both the inflow and outflow switched on at the same time. Given favourable conditions the water level will rise until the rate of addition equals the rate of removal. Clearly such a system is open to considerable fluctuations since the water level will change whenever there is a change in the flows into or out of the tank. There will also be occasions when the tank will dry out or overflow because there is no active control of the water level. It is possible that such a mechanism is at work in the ocean with the

80

input of elements from the rivers and the atmosphere being balanced by removal in the sediments. This implies that the levels of all the essential and toxic elements have been fortuitously balanced at about the correct levels for the last three or four thousand million years despite the vigour of the geochemical cycle and the relatively short residence times of the elements in the oceans.

What sort of an ocean can be achieved by applying a steady state model? In the simplest model we can consider the ocean chemistry as being controlled by the exchange of elements between sea water and the large quantities of rock fragments fed into the oceans each year by the world's rivers. At steady state, with input rates from the rivers matching removal rates in the sediments a simple relationship would be expected between the concentrations of the elements in sea water and the concentrations of the elements in the deep sea clays being deposited on the ocean bed. Using information on the binding of chemical elements to particles such correlations can be shown to exist for more than sixty elements over twelve orders of magnitude (a million millionfold change) in concentration in sea water. There is therefore a basic geochemical rationale behind the composition of sea water and geochemical processes set a framework within which biological systems must work. However, when we look more closely at these simple geochemical rules we find that there is considerable flexibility in the composition of sea water that they predict. In general, concentrations one hundred times greater or one hundred times less than those observed for most elements today would be equally compatible with our present rather crude understanding. Yet the requirements of living organisms are not as tolerant as those of geochemical exchange reaction and a much tighter control of sea water composition is implied by the continuous development of life.

While it is possible that a combination of equilibrium and steady state might exert this degree of control, we must also explore the potential of a third mechanism – control by *feedback*. Again turning to the analogy of the water tank, a sensor could be placed at the bottom of the tank which would respond to the water depth (or pressure). This could be linked to the tap controlling the inflowing water with a valve designed to slow down the flow as the depth increased (negative feedback). A system of this kind actively responds to changes in the system and is consequently much more effective at maintaining a level in a system subject to considerable variability. The Gaia hypothesis suggests that organisms have become so intimately involved in the cycling of the elements in the atmosphere and in the oceans that, through a complex series of feedback mechanisms, they actually control the fluid environment. This control must be robust enough to counter so far as possible the effects of external variations through negative feedback. When the system is stressed beyond the limits of control it should also be able to move rapidly, by positive feedback, to another state which is capable of controlling the critical environmental parameters under the new circumstances. This is an extension of the concept of evolution as a progressive testing of organisms for their fitness and ability to adapt to a changing environment. According to the Gaia concept an ability to modify the environment to suit the requirements of living things is just as valuable an attribute as the ability of an organism to adapt it own characteristics to take advantage of the changing environment.

To test the Gaia hypothesis in the oceans we must answer three questions. The first question we must consider is "Do the biota influence the composition of the

81

oceans on a global scale?". It seems unlikely at first sight that a dilute soup of predominantly microscopic marine creatures, largely confined to the sunlit surface of the ocean, could significantly affect the composition of such large volumes of water. The second question is "Can the changes brought about by the biota be seen as components of a feedback system?". If there is no evidence of the potential for feedback then the influence of life on the composition of the oceans could be considered simply as an adjunct to the geochemical cycles. The final question we must consider is "Are the biologically controlled feedback systems significantly powerful to control the environment?". If feedback loops are overwhelmed by the geological forces at work on the earth's surface then, again, the biological processes should be considered as incidental to the geochemically-driven cycles.

DO THE BIOTA INFLUENCE THE OCEANS

Through photosynthesis by microscopic plants in the surface layers of the ocean, carbon dioxide is drawn down from the atmosphere and oxygen is released. The exchange of oxygen and carbon dioxide (and a range of other volatile compounds produced by the phytoplankton) has a profound effect on the suitability of the atmosphere for higher life forms. In addition, carbon dioxide and other trace gases influence the earth's climate by affecting the efficiency with which heat is trapped by the atmosphere. The global impact of this exchange of gases at the sea surface will depend on the processes which control the fertility of the oceans. To understand the role that living organisms play in such processes we need to look at the impact on the oceans of the organic material produced by photosynthesis.

Some of the carbon fixed by the photosynthesis sinks from the surface layer either because the plants themselves die or because they are eaten by grazing animals which defæcate and their pellets fall down into the deep ocean. It is a sobering thought that the main Gaia mechanism at work in the oceans may be driven by a steady rain of animal droppings.

The flow of material is impressive with approximately 400 million tons of carbon per year cascading into the deep ocean. The total mass of material is much greater than this since only 25 per cent by weight is organic material. The rest is made up of shell fragments (calcium carbonate or silica) produced in the surface layers (70 per cent by weight) or mineral debris introduced by the rivers or by wind-blown dust (5 per cent by weight).

Along with the carbon, essential elements such as nitrogen, phosphorus, iron and manganese are removed from the surface layers in the particulate material. Consequently, in productive areas the essential nutrients tend to be stripped out of the surface layers by the rain of particles. If all of this material was buried in the deep sea sediments the oceans would rapidly turn into a sterile desert fed only by the slow trickle of nutrients from the land. For life to continue to thrive in the oceans it is essential that the nutrients trapped in the particulate debris are recycled to the ·surface from the deeper layers of the ocean. The bulk of the material leaving the surface layers is indeed redissolved in the deep ocean – the organic matter through rapid decay via the action of bacteria and the shell material by the corrosive effects of the immense pressures exerted at depth (up to one thousand times greater than atmospheric pressure at the greatest ocean depths). This process continues within the sediment to such good effect that only 0.1 per cent of the organic carbon which leaves the surface layers is permanently removed. The nutrients released in this way are recirculated to the surface by ocean currents. The result of this very effective recycling is that the composition of the deep water, so far as the nutrient elements are concerned, closely follows the composition of the organic matter raining down from the sea surface and the concentration of carbon, nitrogen, phosphorus and various trace elements are closely correlated with one another in the deep ocean.

The cycle of surface removal, deep ocean regeneration and circulation back to the surface dominates the distribution of a wide range of elements in the ocean including biologically essential elements (such as carbon, phosphorus, zinc, copper, selenium, iodine), elements taken up by shell formation (calcium, strontium, silicon) and elements taken up by the growing phytoplankton because their chemistry is similar to that of essential elements (arsenic, cadmium, germanium). In addition the particles falling down from the ocean surface can remove trace metals from the ocean by geochemical scavenging reactions at the particle surface. Toxic elements such as beryllium and lead are removed in this way as are essential nutrient elements such as iron and manganese. All together, the biologically driven particle cycle dominates the distribution of more than three quarters of the elements dissolved in sea water. This impact is felt worldwide. The global ocean circulation transports material from one region to another as if on a conveyor belt. Cold water with a high salt content is formed in the North Atlantic and drops to the bottom of the ocean from where it follows a slow journey passing via the Indian Ocean to the Pacific, picking up additional deep water supplies from the Southern Ocean. As the water ages *en route* it picks up higher and higher concentrations of the elements released by the breakdown of particles so that the concentrations of the nutrients and related elements are greater in the deep Pacific than they are in the deep Atlantic. In contrast the elements that are scavenged from the water column by particles have lower concentrations in the deep Pacific than in the Atlantic because they have been stripped by a continuous flux of particles during their one thousand year journey.

In summary we find that the major impact of living organisms on the ocean is to control the distribution of most of the elements dissolved in sea water. Through this parsimonious recycling the removal of essential nutrients from the ocean is delayed – phosphorus for example is recycled ten times through this active particle pump before being finally removed in the sediment. The answer to our first question is therefore a resounding 'yes' – the biota *do* influence the composition of the asmosphere and the oceans on a global scale. This brings us to the second question.

ARE THE CHANGES BROUGHT ABOUT BY THE BIOTA COMPONENTS OF A FEEDBACK SYSTEM?

Beginning again at the ocean surface we can begin to identify some potential feedback mechanisms. We have seen that the productivity of the oceans depends in large measure on the efficiency with which nutrient-rich deep waters can be stirred back to the surface layers by ocean currents. These currents are driven by the earth's rotation and, more significantly, by the temperature differences between the poles and the equator. Thus we can see the beginnings of a feedback loop since photosynthesis in the oceans influences the climate by the exchange of gas, particularly carbon dioxide, across the sea surface. The climate in turn influences the productivity of the oceans by providing the driving force behind ocean circulation which recycles essential nutrient elements from the deep ocean to the sea surface. Furthermore the seasonal warming of the ocean surface at mid to high latitudes ensures good conditions for the growth of phytoplankton in the spring and summer. There is therefore a very close link between the growth of plants in the ocean, the earth's climate and the circulation of the oceans.

A further subtle link exists since phytoplankton growing in the open ocean also release a gas called dimethyl sulphide which is transformed into strong acids (sulphuric and methyl sulphuric acid) in the atmosphere. These acids provide cloud condensation nuclei and, in regions remote from land, can control size of the cloud droplets and hence influence the clouds' ability to reflect the sun's radiation. This in turn influences the cooling effect of clouds on the earth's atmosphere and provides another biologically driven mechanism that affects the earth's climate.

There are also possibilities for feedback within the oceans since the cycles of so many elements are interlinked by their involvement in the biologically driven particulate cycle. Consider phosphorus which is, in geological terms, the nutrient whose availability will control plant growth. When particles containing phosphorus fall into the deep ocean they are attacked by bacteria which use oxygen to break down the organic matter and thereby release the phosphorus. If the input of phosphorus from the land to the ocean surface was rapidly increased (e.g. by man's intervention) the productivity in the surface layers would rise and more particles would fall into the deep ocean. The oxygen levels in the deep water would be depleted by the increased demand as more particles are broken down by bacterial action. However, as the oxygen levels fall the breakdown of particles becomes less efficient so that more phosphorus will be sequestered into the sediments. Consequently the recirculation of phosphorus to the surface layers will become progressively less efficient. The feedback provided by the linking of the elemental cycles provides an active control mechanism.

Numerous other examples can be described but two more will suffice to make the point that we can discern possibilities for feedback within the oceans. The first example concerns the availability of tracemetals for phytoplankton growth. We know that a scarcity of phosphorus and nitrogen can, on occasion, limit the growth of plants in the surface layers of the ocean. There are also a number of trace metals which might be close to their limiting concentrations either because they are too dilute to support phytoplankton growth (e.g. iron, manganese, zinc) or because they may be approaching the toxic limit and may therefore restrict growth (e.g. copper, lead). Careful research over the past decade has shown that the availability of such trace metals to phytoplankton can be strongly influenced by the presence of organic compounds in the water which react with the metals in solution. These organic complexes are in turn produced by biological processes. We therefore have a system which can be fine-tuned to regulate productivity by feedback since phytoplankton growth may be controlled by trace metal availability which may, in turn, be controlled by phytoplankton growth! For iron the picture is made more subtle by the release of readily available reduced iron by photochemical processes dependent on the presence of biologically produced photosensitive compounds. The presence of such compounds brings us to the final example of feedback.

Continued photosynthesis in the oceans depends on the transparency of sea water. Much of the organic matter produced in the oceans is designed to trap light and many of the condensation products produced after the death of the plankton give a yellowish tinge to the water. If such material were to accumulate in the oceans, the progressive deepening of the water colour would gradually reduce the useful depth for photosynthesis and hence restrict the productivity of the oceans. In fact a very complex but very effective pattern of light induced chemistry has evolved to remove such material and, incidentally, to release nutrient metals such as iron and manganese which are normally in short supply. Here we can see the possibility of a Gaian type of evolution in which control of environment and fitness to survive are closely linked. Organisms which produced non-degradable coloured compounds would shade themselves out whereas organisms which produced degradable products which did not disturb the transparency of the water would remain productive.

Given these few examples it is clear that the dominant influence of life on much of the chemistry of the oceans can provide ample opportunity for the development of feedback mechanisms. This brings us to the third and final question in this brief assessment of the importance of the Gaia hypothesis in the oceans.

ARE THE BIOLOGICALLY-CONTROLLED FEEDBACK SYSTEMS SUFFICIENTLY POWERFUL TO CONTROL THE ENVIRONMENT?
This question can be answered very simply – we do not know! Here we could end our discussion if the real answer to the question were not so important to our own survival on this planet. Our mechanised, detached approach is now interfering with the natural regulatory system of the planet on a global scale. Through the destruction of the rain forests, the burning of fossil fuels, the changing agricultural patterns (massively increased rice crops and beef production) and through the release of a myriad of industrial gases we are increasing the insulation efficiency of the atmosphere and thereby triggering a planetary warming. We are interfering with the productivity of our coastal waters by the discharge of sewage and other domestic and industrial wastes and the influence of our activities is felt even out in the open ocean through the transport of massive quantities of sulphur, nitrogen, iron, lead and a host of trace elements via aerosols and atmospheric dust. We know that climate changes, and the injection of key elements into the surface layers are capable of influencing the productivity of the oceans which in turn will influence the climate.

In the past there have been major changes in the earth's climate associated with shifts in atmospheric carbon dioxide levels in the absence of man's interference. The rapid changes in atmospheric composition involved argue strongly for the presence of effective positive and negative feedback mechanisms in the natural control systems.

THE GAIAN PERSPECTIVE

A serious consideration of the Gaia hypothesis demands four important changes to the way we view the world. In the first place Gaia puts life at the centre of our concerns. It suggests that life has had a formative influence on our environment and that biological processes still play an active, central role in ensuring that the planet remains habitable. By inferring that life has such an active role the Gaia hypothesis also makes us focus on the possibility that feedback effects are essential in the control of our environment. This brings us to the second change in perspective demanded by the Gaia hypothesis – that we must consider life on earth to be intimately interlinked. It is not sufficient to consider ecosystems such as the tropical rain forests, the rich salt-marsh zones or the open ocean as separate entities. If the Gaia hypothesis is valid the interconnections between these key ecosystems are as important as the ecosystems themselves. The third major shift in our thinking is that we must consider our planet as a whole and not as a mosaic of independent entities defined by human political systems. If we are to identify and understand the key feedback mechanisms that control our planetary environment we must work internationally and we must consider large areas of the globe. For example, if we are to understand the role of the oceans in climate regulation we must study the behaviour of the system over whole ocean basins and begin to unravel its complexities throughout the seasons. Considering only the exchange of carbon dioxide across the sea surface we know that the major site for transfer into the oceans is at the poles, separated by thousands of miles from the major area of release in the tropics. Furthermore the biological and physical effects controlling carbon dioxide exchange vary strongly with season and are closely interlinked. This brings us to the fourth major effect of the Gaia hypothesis on the scientific approach to the environment – it forces us to consider the inadequacies of the reductionist approach. Scientists are used to dividing our knowledge of the world into neat disciplinary blocks (physics, chemistry, biology etc.) and to progressively subdividing these blocks into more and more specialised and isolated subdisciplines.

There are signs that these shifts in perception are being taken on board by the scientific community – although not always with an explicit recognition of the Gaia hypothesis. An international Joint Global Ocean Flux Study (JGOFS) is now getting underway to study the processes driving the carbon cycle in the oceans and its links to the physics of ocean mixing and to the cycling of the elements. The UK is making a major contribution to this programme through its own Biogeochemical Ocean Flux Study (BOFS) which is based in Plymouth. These programmes have taken heed of the four shifts in perspective required by the Gaia hypothesis and they are beginning to tackle the environmental problems on the right scale and are asking appropriate, holistic, questions about the control processes. A much larger programme, the International Geosphere Biosphere Programme (IGBP), is also being formulated which will seek to relate studies of terrestrial, oceanic and atmospheric systems on a global scale.

This broad perspective has been made possible not only by improvements in our technology (satellite observations, improved measurement systems, computer modelling) but also by an increasing concern over the future of our planet. If the scientific community, working together in international collaboration can demonstrate the importance of biological systems and of feedback on a global scale then that is a message that will surely be heeded by those with the political power.

Acknowledgement
I am grateful to Peter Bunyard for his help in preparing this paper.

DISCUSSION

Marcus Colchester   Can you suggest the points where this system is vulnerable to human interference? Are there any sorts of flashing warning lights?

Michael Whitfield   I think it is becoming much clearer now that the distribution of production on the planet and in the planet's oceans is dependent on the physics and that the physics is dependent on the climate. In that respect there are major shifts in the climate which cause shifts in the stirring of the oceans or certainly shifts in the timing or the period of warming of the surface of the oceans and those could cause significant changes in the distribution of production and maybe in total production.

Another effect is the extreme sensitivity of the phytoplankton in the oceans to changes in trace metal concentrations. For instance, we have been looking at the production of the oceans by standard methods for a long time. If you take a bottle of water, add some carbon-14 incubate it and then count how much carbon-14 is taken up by the cells over a period of time, in other words following standard procedures, you get some very interesting results when you contaminate it with above natural levels of trace metals. For example, if you take the purest possible salt you can buy from the most respected chemical firm and make up a solution of the same to create a concentration of sodium chloride equivalent to the concentration of the oceans you will find concentrations of most of the trace metals that are tens if not hundreds of times higher than in the natural oceans. So simply by putting that salt water in the bottle we can contaminate enough to depress production by a factor of two in some instances. It is therefore clear that the system is sensitive to that kind of contamination.

Pierre Lehmann   In terms of mineralization it would appear that biological processes can play an important role. What about the phenonemon of *El Niño*, which is the result of changes in the balance of pressure in the southern Pacific; El Niño occurs in ways that nobody can forecast. Since it seems to be impossible from physical laws to forecast this climatic phenomenon perhaps some biological phenomena are involved?

Michael Whitfield   I find it difficult just standing here to think of such a mechanism. I would rather see it as the other way round, that a small change in the physics might be accentuated by the impact on the biological process involving the exchange of CO_2 between the surface of the oceans and the atmosphere. I cannot see a way in which biological processes can influence the pressure balances in the oceans unless it is through cloud formation or changes in the heat balance, perhaps through nucleation processes. That is a possibility, but we are still ignorant.

Lynn Margulis   You mention density discontinuities that stabilize the ocean surface, I just wonder what that is and could it be Gaian in some way?

Michael Whitfield   No, it isn't. Basically what happens is that throughout the winter the winds are strong and the atmosphere is cold so that the water is stirred, the extent depending on latitude. For instance at our latitudes the stirring may go down to some 200 metres or so, maybe even more. The water is thus stirred to considerable depths with the result that plankton may be carried down to the depths and up again. Although there are nutrients about and the light is not really limiting it is still not possible for the plankton to grow in profusion.

Lynn Margulis   It is the winds that are actually dictating that process?

Michael Whitfield   It is largely the insulation, the amount of energy coming in, and a point is reached when the amount of heat coming in is sufficient to warm up the surface water while it is at the surface and make it less dense so that it is harder for it to sink. Gradually therefore you reach a point where there is a layer of warm surface water which is still mixed by the wind but because it is warm it doesn't sink effectively. Then you get discontinuity in the density between that warm surface water and the cold ocean water below that remains unaffected.

Roswitha Hentschel   Coming back to the feedback loop which links your research with the Gaia Hypothesis, this feedback by the biota would be cut off by pollution. What are the consequences of that likely to be?

Michael Whitfield   The problem when trying to relate problems with Gaia with pollution problems is that we have to step back from the perspective of what is bad for man is bad for Gaia. That is a real complication because once the oceans are polluted new ecosystems will take over. For instance in the Baltic anoxic bacteria are doing very well and as far as production is concerned the overall changes may not be so great. But if you are worried about the availability of fish or if you are worried about our requirements from the sea, then the effects have been catastrophic. The bulk of production in the ocean is actually in the open ocean even though the coastal shallows are much more productive per acre than the open ocean, there being a lot more ocean than continental shelf.

Wolfgang Sachs   You were saying that in order to prove the Gaia hypothesis we will have to show that biological forces are somehow more important than chemical forces. Could you please comment a bit more on that?

Michael Whitfield   The problem there is getting the information. If you look at the oceans from space then they do not appear uniformly green during the spring in the northern hemisphere. In fact the distribution of the plankton is very complicated; it is complicated by the physics resulting in a pattern of streaks. Hence, going to one place and taking a sample will not show something precise about the interactions of the ocean as a whole. To decide whether gaian mechanisms are as strong as we believe they might be requires that we have some quantitative feel of the relationship between the growth of the surface layers and the draw-down of carbon, as well as of the biological remineralization and physical processes that stir the oceans and dictate the distribution on the surface layer. We therefore need quantitative information about what is actually controlling production in the oceans. When growth stops what is it limited by - is it for instance limited by the lack of nitrogen or the lack of iron or the lack of manganese - and if so what are the biological processes that can make the material available to continue the production through to the end of the cycle?

Paul Blau   I have heard that oil pollution from tanker holds, especially in East and West Africa, hinders evaporation of water from the surface of the oceans and therefore leads to a change in climate, less evaporation resulting in less clouds.

Secondly, there was a discussion decades back whether depth waters exchanged with surface waters and over what time span. Originally it was supposed that, seaquakes aside, there would be no exchange in the short term. Then some Russian research was done and the scientists came up with a theory - it was at the Ocean research Centre in Monaco - that exchange took place with a time span of four decades. Is there any new development in this field of research?

Michael Whitfield   I don't know the answer to the first question. Certainly there are many biologically produced surface active components. Indeed a number of surface active components have been found that are produced biologically which could affect the rate of exchange of water and of other volatiles. The point is that I cannot answer your question on the relative of man-made surface active components to biologically produced ones. I would guess that probably the biologically produced ones are still more effective over larger areas of the oceans compared with man-made ones.

Concerning the exchange of deep waters with surface waters clearly there are major circulations and clearly that is the way that deep waters get up to the ocean surface. If you look at the carbon-14 in deep waters you will find that the oldest deep waters in the North Atlantic are 1500 years old; thus there is an exchange and one of the critical parameters in trying to understand the uptake of carbon dioxide by the oceans is the actual exchange rate across this thermally generated density discontinuity. In the deeper oceans you have several thousand metres of very deep cold water. Some of the work on tracers in the oceans resulting from the atmospheric nuclear tests of the 50s and 60s can give some idea of the rate of transport into the depths. Some work done recently in the Mediterranean indicates that you can get transfer of material down to great depths over short periods of time. Looking at some exotic species like hydrogen peroxide in sea water, which is produced by photochemistry at the surface layers, one finds that they are mixed down to a thousand metres or so within a week as a result of storm events. By using tracer techniques we are getting to know more about that.

Vanya Walker-Leigh   A great deal of radioactive waste has been dumped, supposedly in very secure containers into the ocean. Should such containers split open, what would be the effect on the ocean?

Michael Whitfield   I should be able to get a grant for five years at a million £s per year if I could answer that one!

Ulrich Loening   Only if you could come up with an answer that it doesn't matter.

Peter Bunyard   I would like to ask about a mechanism which has been studied at Harwell. There researchers found that very high concentrations of plutonium and americium could be found in sea spray. Could that be Gaia getting back to us? Is there an easy explanation for such high concentrations in sea spray relative to concentrations in sea water?

Michael Whitfield   If the material is going into the oceans in dissolved form there are two ways it can be concentrated in sea spray: one is by going onto particulate matter and then flotation of that particulate matter by the tides with concentration on the surface and then bubbling, blowing off the surface. The other possibility is through the production of the radioactive substances in aerosol form so that it concentrates naturally on the surface and when it is blown back it will return in about the same concentrations as it went in.

Peter Bunyard   The assumption is that it is going in, being dumped and getting into the sediments and then coming back from the sediments into the water. Could there be any microorganisms involved at all in this release of actinides?

Michael Whitfield   Some of the actinides are very surface active and they will stick to particles. Certainly organisms may be involved in that they might transform the elements to an oxidized state and so increase their mobility through the environment.

MARINE SALINITY; A GAIAN PHENOMENON
by Gregory J. Hinkle

Salt composition and total salinity in the oceans have been constant over geological periods of time (at least the 570 million years since the beginning of the Phanerozoic Aeon). Analysis of sedimentary rocks has provided geological evidence that the concentrations of the major ions have not changed appreciably for hundreds of millions of years (Garrels, *et al.* 1971). Mass extinctions owing to changes in salt concentrations have not occurred despite the very limited salinity fluctuation tolerance of virtually all marine organisms. Attempts to determine the physico-chemical reactions responsible for salt concentration stability in marine systems are underway (e.g. Whitfield, 1981). Although many models have been proposed, none have sufficiently detailed the dynamic mechanisms by which the concentration of all the marine ionic species has been maintained. Attempts to model steady state salinity solely on the basis of chemistry and physics have universally failed.

The Gaia hypothesis, as proposed by James Lovelock, considers the long-term geological effect of everyday biological activity, and provides an alternative perspective from which to view phenomena of salt dynamics. Using laboratory-contained microbial ecosystems and abiological controls, we are testing the hypothesis that evaporite-associated microbial communities (i.e., cyanobacterial mats) actively regulate their environment and in the process contribute to the Gaian phenomenon of ocean salinity regulation.

Gaia and Salt

Is ocean salinity under active, dynamic biological control? Have the biota regulated the salt composition of the oceans for at least 2000 million years? Before the advent of the Gaia hypothesis these unasked questions would have been greeted with cries of derision by leading oceanographic and geological authorities. Against the backdrop of our ever-increasing understanding of the forces that shape and build planets, the Gaia hypothesis has provided a paradigm within which these questions take on scientific meaning (Lovelock, 1987).

One of man's oldest questions was, and still is, "Why are the oceans so salty?" The simple and essentially incorrect answer was that salts, released through the weathering of rocks and transported by rivers, have accumulated in the oceans. The concentration of salt in the ocean was said to increase as a function of time and the process had been going on for so long that the oceans are now very salty. If one calculates how long it would take to accumulate an 'oceans-worth' of salt, one finds that in relation to the age of the Earth (over four thousand million years), accumulation to present salinities would occur within a very short time (fewer than 60 million years, Whitfield, 1982). From a Gaian point of view this old question must then be rephrased as "Why aren't the oceans even saltier?" The two ions comprising 90 per cent of the salts in sea water, sodium (Na^+) and chlorine (Cl^-), are both below saturation by a factor of 10! (Holland, 1978). In other words the present concentrations of sodium and chlorine ions in the world's oceans would have to be 10 times higher for NaCl to precipitate in the open ocean. If salt is added at a rate of approximately one 'oceans-worth' per 60 million years, and if the two ions accounting for 90 per cent of total salinity are a factor of 10 below saturation, then the concentration of salts in the oceans should increase with time. Yet this conclusion is completely at odds with both geological and biological evidence pointing to a constancy of composition and of total salinity in the oceans for well over 500 million years (Whitfield, 1981: Garrels *et al*, 1971).

Once again we return to the question "Why aren't the oceans saltier?" If the oceans have remained very nearly constant in both composition and total salinity for so long given the rapid input of riverine salt, then the many ions making up sea water must also be removed at an equally rapid rate. Many attempts have been made to model the evolution of marine chemistry and much has been learned (Holland, 1978, 1984). However these models have failed to provide a rational explanation (on the basis of the laws of chemistry and physics) for either the composition of the oceans or the constancy of that composition over geological periods of time. All the models to date lack an understanding and appreciation of the effect of biological activities on geological processes. While acknowledging the effects of the environment on the evolution of organisms, the models have ignored the equally important and reciprocal effect of life on the evolution of the environment. The effects of biological activity, the accumulation of wastes and biomass and the use of metabolites within the environment, cannot be predicted solely from the laws of chemistry and physics. In fact most geochemists take great pains to remove any and all traces of life in their experiments for the very reason that 'contamination' (i.e. metabolic activity and its by-products) yields unpredictable and inconsistent results. Until these models see living processes as something greater than an inscrutable, undescribable 'black box' they are likely to remain ineffective tools.

Much recent work has pointed to the crucial role of the biota, in particular microorganisms, in understanding the unexpectedly low concentrations of many biologically important elements in sea water (Whitfield, 1981, 1982: Whitfield and Watson, 1983). Elements required by or toxic to the biota tend to be anomalously low in concentration. The possibility of active biological regulation of salinity has been considered only a few times and then rejected for lack of a plausible mechanism relating rapid biological processes to long-term geological salt removal (Whitfield, 1981). Within a gaian framework this distinction between geology and biology becomes increasingly blurred.

The control of ions across an ion-selective permeable membrane is a central principle of any contemporary definition of life (e.g. Wilson and Maloney, 1976). Intricate and energetically demanding ion pumps (i.e. salt pumps) in the membranes of all cells maintain a consistent osmotic milieu within which proteins and nucleic acids interact. In a gaian framework the control of salinity is then the sum ionic control of the individuals in a community or ecosystem. The small size of bacteria often belies their ecological significance. For instance, although bacteria typically make up just 10-40 per cent of the biomass in a typical open ocean sample, because of their high surface to volume ratio they represent 70-90 per cent of the biologically active surface area (Azam, 1987). The realization that just one ml. of sediment can contain up to 100 million salt-pumping bacteria illustrates the enormous influence the biota necessarily have on global salt fluxes. The abundance, metabolic diversity and rapid turnover rates of bacteria point to their central role in maintenance of all gaian phenomena, as does the fact that these phenomena must have been occurring long before the evolution of eukaryotes. That organisms control the salinity of their internal environment is indisputable. That organisms or groups of organisms can control the salinity of their external environment is the thesis of this work.

The limited ability of all marine organisms to survive changes in the salinity of their environment puts biological constraints on how severe fluctuations in total salinity might have been in the past. The contemporary oceans contain approximately 3.4 per cent salt (100 grams of ocean water completely dried will yield 3.4 grams of salts). If the concentration of salts in the ocean were to increase above 5 to 6 per cent only halophilic bacteria characteristic of evaporitic basins would survive. A barrier exists in the range of 4-7 per cent salt above which osmotic stress becomes overwhelming and basic cellular functions such as ion-pumping and the maintenance of membrane potential fail (Khlebovich, 1969). And since the rate at which salts are transported to the ocean is so rapid, the time required for such a change in salinity is geologically very short. The lack of evidence for mass extinctions through changes in global salinity, despite the potential for dramatic changes in total salinity owing to episodes of glaciation, planetismal impacts, changes in weathering rates and other planet-scale perturbations, demonstrates the stability of the oceans for at least the last 570 million years.

Composition of rocks deposited in paleo-oceans permits geologists to determine with considerable accuracy the composition of the principal ions and total salinity at the time of deposition. The evidence suggests that neither composition nor total salinity has changed appreciably for hundreds of million years and puts a geological constraint on the degree of salinity fluctuations in the ancient past (Garrels, 1971).

Experimental Approach

Inherent in the Gaia hypothesis is the idea that reciprocal relations between the biota (the sum of all living things on the planet) and the environment maintain homeorrhetic conditions on Earth. Salt (i.e. NaCl) is ultimately removed from the oceans via the formation of evaporite basins in the sun-drenched tropical regions of the world (Holland, 1978). An evaporite flat looks like a lifeless geological setting. The conspicuous absence of plants and animals only furthers our perception of an inanimate environment. But intimately associated with all known evaporite basins are communities of bacteria (prokaryotic organisms lacking a nucleus) thriving in waters too saline for most eukaryotic organisms (i.e. the nucleated organisms - plants, animals, fungi and protists).

Through the production of organic sheath material, cyanobacteria trap and bind clastic sediments and form a tough, cohesive scaffold within which the community lives. Contained in the sediments are evaporite salts whose dissolution chemistry may be altered through the formation of organic films (Zutic and Legovic, 1987). A wealth of micropaleontological evidence shows that these mats and their analogues have been growing and subsequently buried on Earth for at least 3,500 million years (Awramik, 1984). The presence of microbial mats through the aeons is consistent with the equally long- term maintenance of ocean salinity. By studying the effect of salt on those communities of organisms intimately associated with the formation of evaporites and, in turn, the effect these microbial communities have on the salt dynamics within the evaporite community, we hope to elucidate a small portion of the global salt cycle.

We are now growing these same bacterial communities (*Microcoleus* dominated cyanobacterial mats) in the laboratory in small-scale evaporite basins. Since all the nutrients cycle within the boundaries of the basin, each set-up is in effect a miniature salina ecosystem. With these miniature ecosystems we can make direct measurements under controlled conditions of the salt dynamics within a salina. By comparing the salt dynamics in the ecosystem containing the microbial communities with the salt dynamics in an identical experimental set-up from which all life has been removed (by gamma irradiation) we hope to assess the extent of biological modulation of what are necessarily chemical phenomena. We expect the presence of these microbial communities to retard the re-dissolution of salts and possibly to act as nuclei in the formation of salt crystals. The deposition of salts within the microbial mats and their subsequent burial provides a plausible mechanism for a biological role in the removal of marine salt.

Experiments incorporating abiological controls are an admittedly crude method for determining the gross effects of life on the sediments, but should provide useful, if putative, tests of the Gaia hypothesis. And since our laboratory-bound microbial mats are wholly functional ecosystems we believe they are ideal models for studying gaian phenomena. Long before the evolution of eukaryotes, microbial mats were the dominant form of life on Earth (Margulis, 1982: Margulis *et al.*, 1986). As analogues of those pre-Cambrian communities, modern microbial mats have the potential to reveal pre-Cambrian gaian processes. Unlike the mathematical model systems generally employed to study the fluxes of elements and energy, a model

 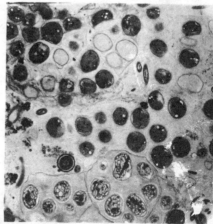

Fig. 1   Salt-encrusted microbial mats at Laguna Figueroa, Baja California, Mexico. Photo courtesy of Robert Horodyski.

Fig. 2   Electron micrograph of the microbial community making up the microbial mats at Laguna Figueroa. Photo courtesy of John Stolz.

system based on a living, gas-exchanging microbial community will contain the one component distinguishing Earth from its barren neighbours Venus and Mars - the biota.

Although the mechanisms controlling the composition and total salinity in the oceans are not known, the Gaia hypothesis provides an alternative to the strictly chemical and physical models which have been proposed to date. In denying the mechanistic view while acknowledging the reciprocal effects between the environment and the biota, the Gaia hypothesis recognizes the potential for life to act as a geological force on the face of the Earth.

References

Awramik, S. M. Ancient Stromatolites and Microbial Mats. In: *Microbial Mats: Stromatolites*. Y. Cohen, R. W. Castenholz, H. O. Halvorson, Eds. 1984. Alan R. Liss, Co. New York.

Azam, Farooq (Personal Communication).

Brown, S. Margulis, L. Ibarra, S. and Siqueiros. D. Desiccation Resistance and contamination as mechanisms of Gaia. *BioSystems* 17:337-360, 1985.

Garrels, R. T. Mackenzie, F. T. *Evolution of Sedimentary Rocks*. W. W. Norton, New York. p.400, 1971.

Holland, H. D. *The Chemistry of the Atmosphere and Oceans*. J. Wiley & Sons, New York, NY. p.351, 1978.

Holland, H. D. *Chemical Evolution of the Atmosphere and Oceans*. Princeton University Press, Princeton, NJ. p.582, 1984.

Khlebovich, V. V. *Marine Biology* 2: 338-345, 1969.

Lovelock, J. E. *Gaia: A New Look at Life on Earth*. Oxford University Press, 1979.

Margulis, L. *Early Life*. Science Books International, Boston, Massachusetts. p.160, 1982.

Margulis, L. Lopez Baluja, L. Awramik, S. M. Sagan, D. Community living long before man. In: *The Science of the Total Environment* 56: 379-397, 1986.

Whitfield, M. The world ocean: mechanism or machination? *Interdisciplinary Science Reviews* vol 6(1) pp.12-35, 1981.

Whitfield, M. The salt sea - accident or design? *New Scientist* 94: 1299 pp.14-17, 1982.

Whitfield, M. Watson, A. J. The influence of biomineralisation on the composition of seawater. In: *Biomineralization and Biological Metal Accumulation*.P. Westbroek, E. W. De Jong, Eds. D. Reidel Publishing Company, Dordrecht, The Netherlands, p.523, 1983.

Wilson, T. H. Maloney, P. C. Speculations on the evolution of ion transport mechanisms. *Federation Proceeding* 35 (10):2174-2179, 1976.

Zutic, V. Legovic, T. Organic matter at the fresh-water/sea-water interface of an estuary. *Nature* 328:612-614, 1987.

Acknowledgements
The author would like to thank Jenny Stricker, Lorraine Olendzenski and Lynn Margulis for their help in the preparation and review of this manuscript. The continued support of the Boston University Graduate School, the Lounsbery Foundation and the National Aeronautic and Space Administration is gratefully acknowledged.

DISCUSSION

Mae-Wan Ho Has anyone tried to analyze the composition of those stromatolites? Are they particularly high in sodium and why do you think they could be useful?

Gregory Hinkle The way evaporites are formed is that the salt water enters, the stromatolites or reefs form a carbonate barrier and the water evaporates behind it.

Mae-Wan Ho Oh I see, you are not proposing that the sodium actually forms some complexes with organic material.

Gregory Hinkle One of the big problems in biology is to understand why the oceans aren't more salty since sodium chloride is so soluble and should therefore have accumulated to an even greater extent in the oceans than it has.

Peter Westbroek In order to make the system gaian you must have a mechanism that really keeps the concentration of salt in check in the main ocean. What do you propose could be such a mechanism? A laguna, for instance, is an evaporite basin so there is bound to be a higher concentration of salt anyway. But how is your organism going to know what the concentration of salt in the ocean is? If you want to make it gaian you have got to have feedback.

Gregory Hinkle I think you have to look at the system as a whole and study the way it might have evolved. It could be that those organisms which help to create conditions of high salinity by forming evaporite basins are doing so in order to keep other organisms out.

Peter Westbroek I don't see the link between the laguna and the ocean. What I would like to see is the link to Gaia.

Ulrich Loening Perhaps there isn't a link because inland seas have a higher salt concentration; the Mediterranean, for instance has higher salinity than the Atlantic, the Black Sea higher still and the Caspian even more so. The process therefore only works on a global scale.

Peter Westbroek I can see that your organisms may affect the concentration of the seas by providing a place, by essentially modulating the removal rate of salt from the ocean. What I don't see is where the feedback is except that if you remove the salt fast enough then the ocean is simply no longer saline. Where in fact is the negative feedback which prevents your organisms from going out of control?

James Lovelock In defence: two years ago we couldn't see any feedback at all between the plant cover of the Earth and the ocean. The point that Greg has raised is that the great bulk of mainstream organisms are exceedingly sensitive to salinity, tolerating just a little above ocean salinity. This raises a big question. How on earth have they survived for all that long time? We can't yet see the link, but at least it stimulates one to go out and look for it.

Ulrich Loening   There is a very attractive idea we mostly learnt at school which I know is now wrong; the question is how and why it is wrong. The sea now is about twice as concentrated as isotonic saline, which I think is 1.7 per cent. The old idea is that organisms like ourselves have an internal salt concentration, very well maintained by our kidneys, at the concentration at which the sea was when we were still sea organisms. How is it that modern animals have come to have their present salt concentrations? What were the origins of this and can one get a clue of what might have happened earlier?

James Lovelock   This is a topic on which I worked extensively many years ago. One of the weak points in the structure of living organisms is that the membranes are not held together by covalent bonds, but instead are held together by the same weak forces that hold a soap bubble together. One of the things such cells cannot tolerate is high salt concentrations since the whole membrane system disperses and dissolves, and you can't run a cell decently if all your bits and pieces are floating miles away. As far as the salt concentration in mammalian blood is concerned, I suppose that is the most comfortable concentration to run at.

Ulrich Loening   So it is a fundamental quality and not a gaian concept at all?

Peter Bunyard   You said, Greg, that there would be no mass extinctions, and that reminds me of something that Jim has written in his book concerning one way we got out of the ice age. He suggested, if I remember correctly, that the sea became much saltier through all the ice forming and the sea level dropping. The sea then became too salty for the algae and their dying off led to a build up in CO_2.

Gregory Hinkle   Actually Andy Watson and I had a talk about this. It's certainly a plausible mechanism for the termination of the glaciation period.

Andrew Watson   The problem with this mechanism is that there was only a 7 per cent change in the concentration of salt in the ocean at the end of the last glaciation, so it's not clear that the changes would be sufficient to kill off the algae. But I was very interested in something that Greg said in his talk that if you want a marine organism to grow faster you just dilute the salts somewhat. It would be interesting to see just how much.

Peter Bunyard   So it would be a slowing down rather than an extinction?

Ulrich Loening   Can we get the facts right. Now you are talking about a 7 per cent change in salt concentration?

Lynn Margulis   No, 7 per cent of the 3.4 per cent.

Ulrich Loening   But you said it was constant and your constancy is within a variance of what actually happened?

97

Andrew Watson   Well it certainly changed by 7 per cent of 3.5 per cent at the end of the last ice age.

Ulrich Loening   So that's within the category of saying it has been stable over the past 500 million years?

Michael Whitfield   I think there is a distribution problem here because if you make the water more salt it sinks to the bottom of the oceans and it is quite a long time before that effect is felt in the surface layers. You have got a delay of maybe a thousand years or so before the effective increase in salinity is felt. But if you decrease the salinity then you melt ice and the fresh water runs out like a fresh water lake across the surface of the ocean. So you are not getting a gradual shift of just 7 per cent and you could be killing off organisms. I think there are problems of timescale here which need to be considered before you can get a nice CO_2 regulator.

James Lovelock   You might be right because it is much more complicated than anybody might think. During the last glaciation the sea level fell I think by 150 metres. That means that all the entrances to the evaporite basins were now high out of the oceans up the mountainside. When it rains water full of salt is going to wash out of those basins down to the sea. Once you start taking the whole picture into consideration it can prove extremely complicated.

THE GEOLOGICAL IMPACT OF LIFE
by Peter Westbroek and Gerrit-Jan de Bruyn

The ozone layer is vanishing, atmospheric carbon dioxide is shooting up, the tropical rainforest is disappearing, deserts expand......this is how the natural environment is being subjected to the rampant growth of our society. Many scientists are concerned and point to the exponential increase in the world's population density, in per capita energy consumption, and in the utilization of raw materials. Their threatening graphs suggest that a catastrophe of global extent is on its way. How far can we go before our planet will be unfit for human life; are the predictions realistic; what can we do to prevent a catastrophe?

Nobody knows. Our knowledge of the Earth is insufficient; it is impossible to predict how the system will react to the enormous changes. We need a grand interdisciplinary research effort on the interaction of the physical, chemical, biological and cultural factors affecting the dynamism of our planet. Under the name of 'Global Change' such a programme is now being launched. It will be a project of unprecedented scope, combining the research of scientists all over the globe. Material fluxes on land, in the sea and in the air will be measured; with remote sensing techniques the information will be mapped out, and computer models will simulate the dynamical behaviour of the planet. Financial support is provided by many governments. Not only the present environment is being studied, but it is realized that a deep insight into the history of our planet is needed to understand the situation today. The coordinator of the project, Thomas Rosswall, of the Swedish Academy of Sciences, speaks of a unique challenge for generations of scientists, allowing them to break through the established divides between their disciplines, so that an integrated science of the system Earth will emerge.

Theory

However important an inventory of global change may be, far more urgent is the need for a comprehensive theory encompassing the dynamics of our planet. A theory is needed to distinguish between relevant and irrelevant information; it provides a source of reference and a guide for observations.

In recent decades a unitary view of global dynamics has emerged. The theory of plate tectonics provides a frame of reference at a physical level. Geochemical models describe the history of the Earth in terms of material fluxes between chemical reservoirs. The art of rock dating is now refined to the point that global events can be distinguished from local perturbations. However, a major stumbling block for the development of a comprehensive theory of Earth dynamics is the traditional concept of life in the geological sciences. Physical and chemical forces are thought to be primarily responsible for the development of our planet; the biosphere (i.e. the thin shell around the earth where life occurs) is thought of as a decoration, an interesting phenomenon, but of trivial importance from a geodynamical point of view. Life would have *adapted* to the ever changing physico-chemical conditions, and never would it have exerted a major influence on the course of Earth history.

In contrast to this traditional view, there always has been a strong undercurrent in Earth science underscoring the geological forces exerted by the 'biota' (a term denoting all living systems together). Hutton, Darwin, Spencer, Vernadsky and Hutchinson are among the leading scientists who advocated this alternative view in the past. In recent years, the idea is becoming widely accepted that the biota have influenced the history of our planet in many important ways. It is realized that without an insight in the nature of this active role of life a proper understanding in the dynamics of our planet is impossible. Bringing together Earth and life sciences is an urgent task, an arrow-head of the 'Global Change' programme, requiring extensive funding, and, more importantly, a change of mind and heart of all the scientists involved.

The Gaia hypothesis of Jim Lovelock and Lynn Margulis is to be considered as an important fruit of this integration between the sciences of life and Earth. In addition to the concept of 'life as a geological force' it conveys the notion of global homeostasis and the maintenance of optimum conditions by and for the biota. Is Gaia to become the leading theory of Earth dynamics, the ultimate frame of reference for global change research? Many scientists gratefully welcome the new look of life on Earth that this hypothesis provides, but others have the uneasy feeling that something is wrong. Here, I shall attempt to bring this contradiction more into the open.

Little mass and major powers

In the gaian perspective the geological forces of life must be enormous. Life is thought to be in charge on this planet, providing salutary homeostasis with regard to climate as well as the chemical and physical constitution of the atmosphere, the oceans and the outer crust. A curious contradiction springs to the mind: the masses of the atmosphere, the hydrosphere, and the Earth's crust are, respectively, 2,500, one million and ten million times the total mass of all living organisms on Earth together. The biosphere is a flimsy film with many holes, vanishingly small in comparison with its environment. How can this insignificant structure influence the huge mills of Earth dynamics? After all isn't the habitability of our planet determined by a lucky combination of physical and chemical constraints?

It is easy to see how, nevertheless, the biota can deploy gigantic forces, despite their trivial mass. In the first place, life is a typical surface phenomenon. The biosphere occupies a strategic position at the interface of rocks, water and air, and is ideally located to influence the chemical traffic between these three phases. In addition, solar radiation has no problem reaching the biosphere, so that the biota can be kept in a strongly energized condition. Another important factor is that living systems can act as catalysts in many reactions - they can hasten the course of geological processes, often by a factor of more than a million. Other processes can be brought to a standstill.

The long time span of life is yet another reason why the biota can have influenced the history of our planet in important ways: life has been around for over 3.5 billion years. Even a minor influence can have a gigantic cumulative effect if sustained for such a period of time. The question is: how dynamic is the Earth, and how do the biota influence this dynamism?

The Earth as a dynamic planet – the rock cycle

If we were in a position to overview the entire Earth from space, and if in addition our perspective of time would be strongly contracted, we would see that our planet is a very dynamic one. Continents would move about in all directions over its surface; sometimes they would cluster together and then they would shatter apart again. We would see how new ocean crust was generated along mid-ocean ridges, how it would shift away on either side, and how, in less than 200 million years, it would be pushed down again into the underlying mantle.

Along these zones of ocean crust consumption (or of 'subduction'), and also where continents collide, mountain chains are formed. The rock masses are pushed up, and as soon as they rise above the surface they are attacked by weather and wind, fragmented and reduced to clay, sand and dissolved materials (weathering). The debris is washed away (erosion), is transported downslope and deposited as sediment. Locally, it may hang on for some time, but eventually it will be pushed back to the surface, crushed or dissolved and deposited further down. Steadily, the mass travels from the continents into the shelf seas, and finally it will be dumped on the deep-sea floor. Now it will be carried along with the shifting ocean crust to a deep sea trough to be plastered onto the continent, or subducted into the deep Earth. It will be compressed, heated, maybe even melted and allowed to re-solidify, and in a subsequent phase of mountain formation it will be pushed up again towards the surface. The whole process will now begin all over again.

The materials at the outside of the Earth are involved in a continuous cyclic motion which may last for hundreds of millions of years, the *rock cycle*. The principle is shown in figure 1. The question is: what is the role of life in this dynamic scene?

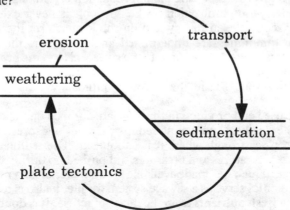

Fig. 1 The rock cycle from a physico-chemical point of view

101

Biosphere and rock cycle

Through their strategic position at the interface of rocks, water and air, and in the light of the sun, living systems can play an active role in particular in those processes of the rock cycle taking place on the outside of the planet: weathering, erosion, transport and sedimentation. The nature of this biological intervention is best revealed by considering the contrast between the slow motion of plate tectonics and mountain formation in comparison with the frantic activity of life. Essential nutrients, such as phosphate, iron, copper or molybdenum are supplied in minute concentrations to the biota from the depths of the Earth. Hence, the biological activity can only be maintained because natural selection has created a huge variety of mechanisms whereby the organisms can exploit the very thrifty nutrient supplies to their own advantage.

Nutrient supplies are increased in the first place by a dramatic speeding up of weathering by the activity of biological systems. Fungi, bacteria, and plant roots penetrate into small cracks in the rocks and create microenvironments where the minerals can readily disintegrate. From a biological point of view, weathering may be compared with mining: raw materials are extracted from the rocks and supplied to living systems.

The nutrients are then kept in circulation by extensive biological recycling. The weathered surface layers or soils play an important role in this repeated utilization. They form an indispensable substrate for vegetation: here, the debris of dead plants are broken down by organisms and the liberated nutrients are made available to the plants again. Excess nutrients are washed out or withdrawn from the biologically catalyzed circulation by storage in the tissues, by precipitation or evaporation, whereas limiting nutrients are usually recycled very efficiently. The nutrient fluxes tend to be diverted by the living communities in such a way that their concentration is adapted to local needs.

Although living systems promote the breakdown of rocks in the weathering process, there are multiple mechanisms whereby the resulting debris are kept in place as soils. Overgrowth, roots and slime production are among the stabilizing factors. Nevertheless, the reutilization of the nutrients is never exhaustive. The biologically catalyzed cycles are leaky and on the longer term the nutrients are diluted. Living communities are undermined and disappear; the soil cover is washed away and fresh rocks are brought to the surface. Now, the process can start all over. Meanwhile, the washed-out nutrients may stimulate biological activity downstream. In this way, life in the oceans is ultimately maintained by these nutrient fluxes.

Ultimately, the used end products of the biota are dumped on the deep-sea floor and enclosed in the slowly accumulating sediments. Sea-floor spreading will bring the refuse to a deep-sea trough where it is subducted. The sedimentary mass is subjected to high temperatures and pressures and pushed up during the formation of a mountain ridge. Thus, it is made available as raw material for a new cycle. Not only does plate tectonics serve as a sewage system for life, it also is responsible for the regeneration of fresh nutrients from the fluxes of refuse. It is doubtful whether life would persist for long in the absence of plate tectonics.

While Fig. 1 shows the classical, physical view of the rock cycle, Fig. 2 shows the same process, but now from a biological point of view.

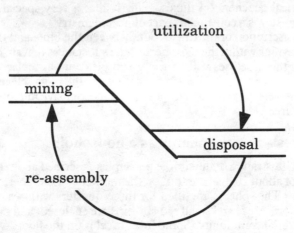

Fig. 2   The rock cycle from a biological point of view

Toxic materials

The behaviour of living systems with respect to toxic materials is totally different. Like the nutrients, these substances may be liberated through the weathering of rocks. In addition, toxic compounds occur in air and in water, and they may even be generated as by-products of biologically catalyzed reactions. A huge variety of mechanisms has been described whereby poisonous materials are actively *removed* from biological systems. For instance, heavy metals may accumulate in the cell walls of many bacteria, so that they are kept away from the cellular machinery.

Dead or living organisms, loaded with heavy metals, are often taken up in sediments, so that the overlying waters are cleansed. In the ocean, poisonous materials are withdrawn from the upper water layers where planktonic organisms may bloom. Toxic nitrogen and sulphur compounds as well as, for instance, mercury, may be volatilized and released into the atmosphere. Thus, in contrast to the nutrients, toxic materials tend to be *withdrawn* from the biological circulation, or are even removed altogether from the biosphere. Some can be converted into useful or harmless materials and then be further channelled through the nutrient cycles. Ultimately, most toxic materials will end up in the deep sea sediment, together with the final remains of the biota. After a very long time they may be brought back into circulation by the internal dynamics of the Earth.

One aspect needs further clarification. The interaction of the biota with the rock cycle is an energy consuming process. Without solar radiation the process would soon come to an end. The light is captured by the biota and transformed into chemical energy. This energy is conducted through a fine network through the biosphere and sets the entire machinery in operation. Ultimately, it escapes in a low-grade form into space.

The biosphere is a flimsy, but exceedingly complex and highly energized shell around the Earth. The geochemical fluxes wind together here into elaborate self-organizing and self-perpetuating networks. In the remote past they have emerged from non-biological geochemical fluxes. This is life: a very special geochemical process. Biochemistry is a constituent part of geochemistry.

This general description of the interaction between the biota and the rock cycle sums up the behaviour within the biosphere of the substances that are important for life. In practice, the processes will be more complex, in particular because non-biological processes continually disturb the activity of the biota. Nevertheless, it is striking that these general rules are supported by an extensive microbiological and ecological literature.

Crystal spheres – the biospheres as a household

The most telling illustration of the simple principles described above are the sealed spheres of glass of about 20 diameter put on the market by EcoSphere Associates in Tucson, Arizona. The spheres are filled for three-quarters with sea water and for one quarter with air. Algae and small red shrimps are enclosed, and no doubt there is also a rich bacterial community. Some fine gravel is on the floor. Only light and heat can be exchanged with the surroundings. The producer claims that the shrimps can survive for 10 years, until they die of old age. Twenty chemical nutrient elements must be recycled most efficiently throughout that period in order to keep this exceedingly complex and fragile system going. Many toxic compounds are continuously kept away from the biochemical circulation. Such sealed-off biological communities may be considered as separate biospheres. Similar systems at a much larger scale are now used in biospheric experiments and for supporting the crews of prolonged journeys in space.

Biospheres, large and small, may be compared with a household. We conduct the fluxes of food and energy through our homes, remove the filth and take care that everything is in place, so that we can live as conveniently as possible. Also in the biosphere the fluxes of nutrients and energy are efficiently utilized, and harmful materials are kept out of the way. Could we not conclude that the chemical constitution of the biosphere is optimised by and for the biota?

The similarity between biospheres and a houschold is no more than an analogy, however, and the comparison should not be pushed too far. It is evident, for instance, that the biospheric order is not the result of intentional judgement of an intelligent being. The only steering factor is natural selection and the organization that we perceive has emerged by itself. Spontaneously the food chains interweave so that a discrimination is made between nutrients and toxic materials. The nutrients are sucked into the biosphere and their availability is enhanced by recycling; toxic materials are chased away. This picture of a self-reproducing biosphere, actively maintaining optimal conditions for its own survival is maybe the most telling and best documented illustration of the Gaia principle.

Gaia undermined

However attractive the Gaia concept may be, it does not fully reflect the real development of our planet. All one may say is that there is a *tendency* in the biosphere

104

towards biologically regulated optimization and stability. But also are countless examples known where a biologically stabilized condition is undermined, not necessarily by external influences, but also resulting from the operation of the stabilizing system itself.

Oxygen

One example is the accumulation of oxygen in the atmosphere, a dramatic event that took place some two billion years ago. It is generally assumed that before this time, the atmosphere contained no, or only very little oxygen. As a result of its strongly oxidizing properties this gas is extremely toxic: as chlorine in the toilet, it readily converts organic matter into carbon dioxide and water. Organisms, like ourselves, that now live in close contact with oxygen can only survive because they have a rich repertoire of detoxifying mechanisms at their disposal.

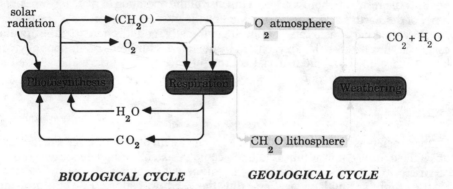

Fig. 3 Coupling of the biological and geological cycles of organic carbon and oxygen; the origin of atmospheric oxygen

Figure 3 represents the mechanism responsible for the accumulation of oxygen. The gas is a by-product of photosynthesis, the process whereby certain microorganisms, algae and plants convert solar radiation into the chemical energy on which all further life depends. The relatively inert carbon dioxide and water are converted into a reactive mixture – organic matter (CH_2O) and oxygen. Respiratory processes reverse the reaction, so that carbon dioxide and water are regenerated. This biologically catalyzed cycle of carbon must have had its beginnings shortly after the origin of life.

The cycle is leaky, however: a small portion of the organic carbon is enclosed in the accumulating sediments and may remain there for a very long time. Thus, a gigantic reservoir of organic matter could be formed in the Earth's crust. For each molecule of organic carbon withdrawn in this way from the biological circulation, one molecule of oxygen was liberated. Originally, however, the gas could not accumulate in the atmosphere. It reacted immediately with reduced iron and sulphur and as a result huge reservoirs of oxidized iron and sulphur (rust and gypsum) were stored in the crust together with the organic carbon. Thus, a steady geochemical trend, whereby ever larger amounts of iron and sulphur were transferred from the reduced to the oxidized state, is characteristic for the early development of the Earth. Finally, the amounts of iron and sulphur appearing at the surface were reduced to a point that oxygen could freely accumulate in the atmosphere.

The original biosphere, adapted as it was to an oxygen-free atmosphere was suddenly exposed to a ubiquitous, poisonous gas. The offspring of this early life still occurs in peatbogs, in marine sediments and in our intestine. Only a fraction of the biota could adapt to the new and hostile environment, and even learned to utilize it. This was the beginning of an impressive new deployment of the biosphere. We ourselves are totally dependent on oxygen for our own survival. The transition of an oxygen-free to an oxygen-rich atmosphere shows how a global environmental crisis may be brought about by biological evolution, and how a stabilizing biological regulatory system was destroyed and replaced by a new one.

It is worth noticing at this point that the presence of oxygen in our atmosphere is not only the result of photosynthesis, but also of the operation of plate tectonics: the relief of the Earth's surface is maintained by the internal movements of the planet. Fresh sedimentary basins are produced continually, and it is here that the organic carbon accumulates so that oxygen can be liberated. Hundreds of millions of years later the occluded organic material is brought back to the surface and allowed to undergo a delayed reaction with oxygen. The cycle is round.

Culture

Human society is a second example of a living system of which the emergence has upset the natural equilibrium. Evolution could be extended outside the constraints of strictly biological organization by a unique combination of tool production, abstract thinking and language, and thus the Earth was subjected to the growing demands of human culture. New geochemical fluxes, comparable in size to the natural ones were set into operation. The heart of the problem is shown in Fig. 4.

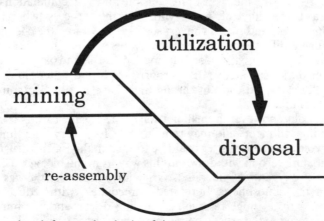

Fig. 4   The rock cycle from a cultural point of view

The extraction of raw materials from the environment, their utilization and also the removal of the refuse are strongly intensified compared with the pristine situation (Fig. 2). New and non-natural chemicals are brought into circulation at a huge scale, and the societal needs for raw materials are qualitatively different from the natural ones. Culture has not yet developed a counterpart of the subtle recycling and detoxification network in operation in nature. Culture overgrows the Earth with an explosive force, and changes in character all the time as a result of the rapid development of technology.

Presently, there is a general awareness that this rampant growth exerts a deep influence upon the global ecosystem. However, in contrast to common wisdom, this influence is also very old. Very early in its existence, far more than a million years ago, humanity has deforested vast terrains by burning. Erosion rates must have increased dramatically, the nutrient fluxes from the continents to the oceans were amplified and algal blooms were stimulated. Carbon dioxide was removed from the atmosphere and deposited as dead organic material on the ocean floor. Carbon dioxide is a major greenhouse gas, and its removal may have hastened a cooling trend of the Earth's climate, already underway since early Tertiary times. It is not unlikely, therefore, that the ice age is the first global environmental catastrophe, literally ignited by our ancestors.

The development of the cultural forces is gaining momentum, and we are tragically uncertain about the outcome. Some draw courage from the Gaia hypothesis, believing that the natural tendency towards salutary homeostasis will protect us from a catastrophe. But are we not destroying the gaian household from which we have emerged? Geological history demonstrates that the Earth is subjected to continual change. Periods of stasis alternate with episodes of rapid change. The Gaia hypothesis relates to only one aspect of this shifting scene: the tendency of the biosphere towards stabilization and optimization of the conditions for life. On the one hand, environmental fluctuations are counteracted, but on the other the system is kept out of equilibrium by the very operation of biological regulation, so that sudden and dramatic changes may ensue.

It is possible that many of the global regulatory mechanisms maintaining suitable conditions for life in the past are presently eradicated by the development of culture. A catastrophe could well mark the beginning of a new and flourishing era in the history of life. But it is questionable whether our progeny would be included. Research programmes such as 'Global Change' may help us to understand the extent of the problem. But it will not be enough. Ultimately, a drastic societal reorganization will be required. If somehow the change can be kept under control, new and unprecedented opportunities may emerge for humanity and nature alike!

DISCUSSION

Peter Bunyard   How important was radioactivity as a driving mechanism for tectonic plate movement and could this now be running down because of the decay of radioactive isotopes such as uranium?

Peter Westbroek   Plate tectonic activity is driven by radioactive decay, mainly of potassium, thorium, and uranium. The heat generated brings about convection currents which then drive the plates around. It's the same as if you take a glass of water and start heating up one side. The water starts flowing round and round. It is generally believed that the amount of heat released by radioactive decay in the deep Earth has diminished over geological time. The Earth is 4.6 billion years old, and the oldest rocks known are 3.8 billion years. The reason why we have no geological record over that earliest period is thought to be twofold: the Earth's surface may have been in a molten state, and a huge meteorite bombardment may have destroyed all crust that was formed. In the time that followed, the geotectonic regime seems to have been a very turbulent one; then, between 3 and 2.5 billion years ago, large-scale production of continental crust took place. Plate tectonics is thought to represent the dominant mode of Earth dynamics from at least 2.5 billion years ago to the present day. This would mean that throughout that time continental crust was predominantly recycled, and that little of it was added to the existing stock. There is reason to believe that the decrease in radioactive decay has resulted in a slowing down of plate tectonics.

Peter Bunyard   I wondered if this might not be a reason why one needs a gaian mechanism, a kind of Gaian action actually to boost something which is physically dying away. It may well be that if the physical processes underlying the recycling of crustal material should diminish then life should take over that function, just as photosynthesis took over from chemosynthesis once the abundant source of energy-rich chemicals had been consumed by the early living inhabitants of Earth.

Peter Westbroek   Of course, life has indeed developed powerful ways for recycling its nutrients. Another possibility is that life actually catalyses the rock cycle and plate tectonics, and that through biological activity conditions are created whereby global geochemical cycling is induced. Personally, I wouldn't dare to make a distinct statement on that. We really don't know how much plate movement depends on life. Yet, it has been *speculated* that in the absence of life there would be no plate tectonics. It is thought that oceans are required for plate tectonics, and that this planet could only have retained its water because its outside remained sufficiently cool. The secret is that the greenhouse gas CO_2 was kept away from the atmosphere and stored in the crust in the form of a huge reservoir of limestone. CO_2 is removed from the atmosphere as bicarbonate (HCO_3-) through the weathering of calcium silicates on the land; calcium and bicarbonate are washed into the ocean and removed from there by the precipitation of limestone ($CaCO_3$). On the present Earth, both weathering and limestone formation are facilitated by the biota. So, one can make a case for a certain degree of participation of the biota in the maintenance of suitable conditions for plate tectonics. However, we don't know how important the biological factor is. Both weathering and limestone production can take place in the absence of the biota. But I agree that the point you raise is an important one that should be given more attention.

Peter Bunyard   How does that relate to the observation that there appears to have been no tectonic plate movement either on Venus and Mars. Jim Lovelock, for instance, sees this difference between Earth and its planetary neighbours as indications that life might really play a role in plate tectonics. Venus and Mars, one suspects, have similar radioactive contents in their internal structure.

Peter Westbroek   Venus and Mars have also lost their water. As I said, it has been suggested that the presence of life is essential for the retention of water, but we cannot be sure.

James Lovelock   One geophysicist seems to be very convinced; that is Don Anderson. He published a major article in *Science* a couple of years ago and he stated quite categorically that without life on Earth there would be no tectonics. He then went on to explain something which I always meant to follow up but never got round to it. It was something to do with the base transitions between the salts.

Nicholas Hildyard   I am wondering whether there is a difference between the geological event we are facing today – the sort of man-made episode – and the ones that have gone previously.

Peter Westbroek   I think that in humans evolutionary change has largely freed itself from its biological constraints. What changes with us are the artificial tools on which we depend, and the ideas that we need to find our way through out artificial environment. Tools are not part of the body; they can be easily exchanged with better ones, and be perfected in the mean time. One may regard humans as animals with exchangeable organs, and our evolution as largely taking place outside our bodies. It is therefore that we can adapt to almost any conceivable environment, and are able to spread out over the entire Earth and beyond. Tool use can only evolve together with abstract thought and speech. This combination represents a tremendous geological force. The human system, as internally divided as it is, is a gigantic productive system consisting not only of us individuals but also of tools, weapons, institutions, ideologies, etc. We are component parts of that system, and seem to have only little control over its rampant growth. It represents a new level of organization on Earth, and indeed I believe that this revolution is unparalleled in Earth history. It seems to me that Gaia is already passé; it is rapidly changing into something else.

Mae-Wan Ho   I feel that people here have become obsessed with homeostatis and stability. But what about development and novelty? They are part of evolution. Have we decided that we have really come to the end of the maturity of this organism and we want to keep it forever as it is? Organisms undergo birth, infancy and maturity, and in the midst of all that we still know that organisms can get ill. As you say Gaia is sick now, and what's important to me, it seems, is what criteria we can identify for Gaia's health.

Jerry Ravetz   Could you imagine Gaia being sick?

James Lovelock   I would go further than that. Our role in the future as ecologists might well be as planetary physicians. The problem is that we are a bit like 17th or 18th century physicians who would do little for their patient except give him some opium to relieve the pain, and we are roughly at that position with regard to the Earth. But one thing those physicians did have apart from physiology was the hippocratic oath to do nothing that would harm the patient, and I would put this forward as a very important tenet to be held by all environmental groups, because in one's desire to do something good one sometimes does something bad.

Nicholas Hildyard   What criteria should we choose to evaluate sickness and health? Isn't it relative anyway because we judge health against the general standard prevailing of health?

Ulrich Loening   As a biologist I would think there is a criterion of health for the planet which is several million, maybe some 100 million years experience of continuous evolution including diversity of species, radiative adaptation and extinction, which has gone on with bumps of various sorts. The notion that one should be trying to preserve it in a static form we can discard. The Earth is evolving and its health is continuous mixed evolution with no dramatic changes owing to one species because that has never happened before.

Peter Bunyard   We heard this morning from Jim that the more diverse a system is the more stable and in a sense strong. Could one propose for instance that the more diversity was maintained, the more in general the richness, the variety, the more it would be a sign of health?

Edward Goldsmith   Both René Dubos and Professor Audy defined a healthy organism as one capable of maintaining its homeostasis in the face of external and internal challenges. If we accept this definition then it is not sufficient to see a disease as being caused by an external challenge - a parasite for instance - it would be more accurate to see the disease as caused by a reduction in the organism's ability to resist the parasite. The organism's resistance can, of course, itself be affected by external challenges. Stress and worry clearly are factors, as is exposure to low levels of radiation and to certain biologically active chemicals which may adversely affect the immune system, making the organism very much more vulnerable to a disease it normally would have taken in its stride. I think this notion of health can be generalized. Both an ecosystem and a climax society for instance can be regarded as healthy to the extent that they can maintain their stability or homeostasis in the face of change.

Nicholas Guppy   I was just thinking that Gaia has evolved a number of mechanisms for maintaining homeostasis. From what I know they are the ocean and its life, the tidal regions and their muds with micro-biological fauna and flora, the rainforests, all the carbon sinks. I think we should see if they themselves are in a

110

state of adequate self-preparedness. In other words is the rainforest regenerating itself adequately, are the wetlands, is pollution in the ocean damaging the ocean mechanism? It's a question of looking at the limbs of Gaia.

Daniel Mayer   It seems to me that the only reason why one would make a medical analogy would be obviously to try and do something. It seems to me that the idea of thinking globally and acting locally is actually a very sensible thing. The Gaia hypothesis would therefore be a way of modelling what the whole picture looks like but when we actually do something we do it on a smaller scale, even though we are keeping tabs on what such actions mean on a large scale. If we think of ourselves as a collective of individuals and our diseases as being part of a collective and then use that back in considering Gaia as a collective of environments, even though on another level we think of it as one organism, then I think the medical analogy becomes much more helpful.

Edward Goldsmith   Today diseases are interpreted in such a way as to make them appear amenable to the sort of management we wish to provide. But if we looked at those diseases in ecological terms we would see that such management was unjustified because, to use an analogy, you don't want to wage chemical warfare against microbes, you want to create conditions in which people can resist these microbes.

Pierre Lehmann   When I look at the Lake of Geneva I would be hard put to say that the influence of man has not been negative because the lake has become very polluted from something that was very clean only 50 years ago. Anyone can see that. Now we are treating the water in special plants, so how can we define new criteria for health when we don't know any more how the lake was before?

PANEL DISCUSSION

Michael Whitfield   Lynn, the non-human protagonist in your drama this morning was an intertidal organism which clearly was very resistant to change in salinity because you showed the Australian version which actually had sodium chloride precipitating on them, but out there in your picture was the vast ocean. I just wondered whether you thought the stromatolites were actually the dominant CO_2 precipitating organisms or whether there is good evidence for non-stromatolitic limestone deposition? What for instance was the role of the open ocean throughout the vast period of time before eukaryotic organisms evolved?

Lynn Margulis   Last year they found the biggest stromatolites alive today; they are not Australian but they are sub-tidal. These stromatolites are thirty feet tall and are found in the Caribbean off the Grand Bahamas Banks. How much stromatolites were built up in the open ocean is debatable, however we don't have such a phenomenon today so I doubt if we had it then. Yet way out on to the whole continental shelf area you have vast limestone deposits. "Stromatolite" is just the word for layered limestone produced by the trapping, binding and precipitation by microorganisms; so basically if you find such layered limestones you have direct evidence of mat communities, hence organisms that form such structures.

Michael Whitfield   So there is no analogue to the White Cliffs of Dover?

Lynn Margulis   I think there are analogues but not in the Archean; in fact the analogues occurred where there were plankton protists.

Michael Whitfield   With regard to limestones that have been deposited by planktonic organisms in the open ocean I am wondering how relevant the contemporary is to the pre-history of Gaia.

Lynn Margulis   As far as I understand, as determined by the acritarch fossil record, the planktonic habit is about 800 million years old, it is really quite recent.

Andrew Watson   Neither is there any evidence that I know of for colonization of the real land surface, the centre of the continents.

Lynn Margulis   I am so glad you raised that. *Microcoleus chthonoplastes* has a relative called *Microcoleus vaginatus* known to many people as "thallophyte" or 'desert crust'. Superficially it looks very much like lichens. There is direct evidence that organisms such as *M. vaginatus* colonized the land at least 2,000 million years ago. The idea that land colonization occurred for the first time only in the Devonian is off by at least a 1,000 million years. Such organisms cannot survive submergence they are completely land adapted deriving water from dew or seasonal rains. Indeed once a year when it rains their filaments shoot out of their sheaths and recolonize the soil. In the Great Lake area we can find terragenous rocks that look very much like terragenous sediment laid down today, the difference is that these soil profiles were created two billion years ago when there were no plants. I agree plants are Devonian

112

but bacteria and protists including algae, which are not plants, existed much earlier. Ecologically such microorganisms do the same sort of things that plants do even better.

James Lovelock Not only that, but you wouldn't have had the weathering of the rocks proceeding at any reasonable pace if the land had not been colonized.

Walter Schwarz I would like Lynn and Jim to comment on to what extent Gaia is an organism and what that means. And also if it is such an organism whether it reacts with other organisms outside it, in other words with the universe. You did say yesterday that you were not interested in this regulation of the universe but nevertheless the Earth obviously reacts with the universe in some ways.

James Lovelock I say "the Earth is alive", "the Earth is an organism", I admit a little provocatively because I think my colleagues need a bit of provoking; they have been sitting on their chairs, a bit too long. You could carry the metaphor a little too far, but on the other hand in many respects the Earth behaves as an organism in the sort of way that James Hutton meant it, as a large biological construct that has the capacity to homeostat itself, which is after all one of the important characteristics of living organisms. In that respect it resembles them and justifies the name organism.
 The other justification is that you cannot have life on the planet except on a planetary scale; anything much smaller than a planet cannot hold life for a virtually infinite space of time as it has been held on the planet, a sparse life on a planet just dies out because the planet evolves and that is the end of it, the life dies. It is on that sort of scale that I am using the word organism but also metaphorically as a provocative statement.

Nicholas Guppy You are changing the definition of the word organism which already has a lot of established usages and pre-conceived images in peoples' minds. Don't you think you could call it something like a super-organism just to draw the thunder away from it.

James Lovelock Well I felt the word super was associated with super-market and hyper is even worse. If I lived in James Hutton's time I certainly would have said it, yes you are right it is a super-organism.

Walter Schwarz What about the interactions between this organism and its environment?

James Lovelock Its environment is of course space and it interacts with it very vigorously because it receives all of the crucial energy that makes it work as sunlight, high quantum energy, and it excretes low grade infra-red to space and this is its interaction with the universe.

Andrew Watson But the same could be said of Mars or Venus.

James Lovelock Surely, and it is the difference in its interaction which makes the Earth recognizable.

Vanya Walker-Leigh   What is the gaian function of *Homo sapiens sapiens*?

James Lovelock   That is a biological question.

Lynn Margulis   To me *Homo sapiens sapiens* is just a very recent weed in the sense that as a species it is actively growing and changing its environment. This kind of bloom behaviour has been known before, it's been known for dinosaurs, and for other organisms for which conditions become conducive to growth. Great population growth follows and just before the demise things look wonderful. This is a very common biological strategy, we see it on Petri plates on a daily basis. Only our unbelievable self-centredness which we can't help prevents us from seeing how ordinary is our example. Part of the explanation of our successful blooming is that which makes us see ourselves as the pinnacle, the centre. These kinds of opportunistic fast-growing organisms usually carry with them the seeds of their own destruction by lack of control of their populations.
   What are drugs, homosexuality and the AIDS virus epidemic but gaian mechanisms of holding us back from reaching our biotic potential? What is biotic potential? Characteristic for any species, it is the potential number of offspring per unit generation per parent organism or per pair. In humans it is something like 20 organisms per couple for 30 years. I don't know anybody with 20 children so let's estimate human biotic potential as 10 children per generation. Well many factors keep human biotic potential from being reached: starvation, hormonal changes, war. This failure to reach biotic potential is called "natural selection" and it restrains the tendency of all life to grow wildly.

Marcus Colchester   You have criticized the physical and chemical sciences for not taking on biology in explaining Gaia. Aren't you making the same error of not appreciating the social cultural dimensions of what is going on now by interpreting it in a purely biological way and isn't that leading us away from a proper sort of gaian perspective?

Gregory Hinkle   If you removed all the humans from the Earth as far as Gaia is concerned virtually nothing would happen, but if you took away the microbes the whole system would crash.

Mae-Wan Ho   That's precisely why natural selection cannot be involved in this. What can be the selection pressure for human beings if they do not serve any function?

James Lovelock   They serve a function as any other animal, consumers eating plants and recycling. We are doing a great deal of use just breathing out CO_2, plants would be in a bad way if we didn't.

Peter Westbroek   I think we should try and see humans as special and not completely biological. I believe that natural selection in humans proceeds outside the body: we use all kinds of tools and apparatus which are exchanged and thrown away when they don't work. They are exchanged for better ones and that really is

114

where natural selection is taking place, not in our bodies because biologically we are not changing very rapidly and certainly not in accordance with the enormous changes that are taking place in society at the moment. We have had enormous development over a time scale of a few hundred years which is not yet reflected in our biology.

Ulrich Loening I think the novel principle is a state of natural evolution of an organism that, by natural selection, developed an incredible brain and made use of it. Nature has always been opportunistic and therefore mankind has now created the facility of using his brain to do incredibly more and be unbelievably successful. That fits exactly in with what Lynn said.

James Lovelock You are leaving out of account the importance of the human being as a social animal; quite clearly the whales and dolphins have brains at least equal to ours, possibly superior, but it has brought them very little advantage. What is so remarkable about humans is their social activity and one only has to consider a termite nest, a most marvellously constructed air-conditioned edifice of huge size that is made by organisms with brains not much more than a micro-computer.

Nicholas Guppy What are the net effects of human societies upon the gaian chemical system and temperature?

James Lovelock It is huge, the increase in carbon dioxide is gigantic. By the middle of the next century, unless something changes very drastically, there will be a much larger increase in carbon dioxide than occurred between the last glaciation and now and the difference between the last glaciation and now is very different climatically. The air would have been frozen totally here now in the last glaciation and we must expect a warm-up by a considerable amount or more.

Jeremy Faull Jim suggested yesterday that the Gaia hypothesis had value as a predictive theory and that it was likely to be a better predictive theory than anything else going. I would like to ask what is the point of trying to establish the validity of the Gaia hypothesis beyond it being a pleasant intellectual enterprise?

Michael Whitfield Clearly it is important if there are positive as well as negative feedbacks. For example, if we are releasing carbon dioxide into the atmosphere and that is going to change the climate which might lower the temperature differential between the poles and the equator then that will be significant since the temperature differential drives the circulation of the oceans. The circulation of the oceans brings the nutrients to the surface which creates biological productivity and that productivity pulls down carbon dioxide so you can imagine a positive feedback effect taking place should the circulation of the oceans be slowed down. Now if that is the case then the horrendous predictions we are making about CO_2 in the atmosphere might be gross underestimates. It is imperative that we find out quickly because if it is the case we will have to think very differently about the way we treat the problem. From an anthropocentric point of view our survival is at stake. I don't

115

think we are worried about Gaia's survival; I am sure Gaia will survive, but there seems to be two levels in the whole of the discussion we have had, one is about Gaia as a concept, Gaia as a long-lived organism or as a long-lived ecosystem and feature of our universe. The other level concerns our own attitude towards our environment because it not only involves curiosity and interest but our own survival.

Alwyn Jones Gaia has been faithful to life on Earth as we know it. In that sense we must be concerned with Gaia's survival preserving what we have now so that we can get back into harmony with the balance of nature. Any other form of Gaia would be inadequate for the protection of our kind of life.

Michael Whitfield The thought of being in harmony is essential if we are going to survive.

Andrew Watson We can't help but be anthropocentric because that is the way we are. But it may help our survival if intellectually at least we grasp what a tiny little wart on the surface of Gaia we are. If we can grasp that this organism is really quite non essential and so to speak with a flick of her tail she can make us extinct and a lot of other things that we value then perhaps we might come to be a little wary of Gaia. She may not just be our mother, she may roll over on us.

Peter Westbroek We need to resolve why the Gaia idea is not falling on fertile ground in the scientific community. I think one of the reasons is that in order to implement this theory within scientific research a gigantic reorganization will be necessary requiring enormous investment. For instance, in geology departments there is no knowledge whatsoever of biology and the whole curricula for students and the entire structure of the various departments will have to be changed completely. What we need therefore is to bring about an integration between the Earth and Life sciences.

Michael Whitfield I believe that there is a movement within the scientific community to try to look at environmental problems in an interdisciplinary way rather than in a multidisciplinary way. The way such problems have been looked at before is with the different scientists looking at the same phenomena but not thinking together. The result has been a kind of reductionism with a failure to answer properly the questions. However today I believe there is a movement in the right direction as for instance with the International Geosphere/Biosphere Programme (IGBP now called "Global Charge") and the joint Global Ocean Study. Attempts are being made to view the Earth as a whole in an interdisciplinary way and I think it is important that people with gaian concepts get into these programmes to make sure that the right kind of questions are asked.

James Lovelock We tend to be impatient with human progress, the time-constant of response for humans to the recognition of environmental programmes seems to be between 20 and 40 years and this is a long time for most of us. Do we in fact have that time?

Lynn Margulis In relation to the interdisciplinary nature of studies we tend to forget that the space programmes were always holistic. Don Anderson for instance, professor of geological sciences at the California Institute of Technology in Pasadena, is a hard core geophysicist yet he is well aware that biology must play some role in his theories of Earth movements. In fact he actually suggested to NASA that they proceed with the "mission to Earth" using the same kind of remote sensing, computer integrative techniques that have been used in the studies of Mars, Venus and the Moon.

Diana Schumacher We have spoken about man as a social animal but not as a consumer and it seems to me that one of the distinctive features about man is his total inability to limit his consumption levels and his impact on the environment. I believe that New York throws away about 24,000 tons of domestic refuse a day and we in this country throw away 30 million tons a year. And it is not recycled so when we talk about nature recycling we have to notice this difference in man as a consumer.

Lynn Margulis It's a time scale difference, throwing away all that garbage puts selection pressure on those organisms, including other people, that recycle the wastes. We are at the beginning of feeling selection pressures because of our continuing human bloom.

Andrew Watson Each individual organism is limited by the resources that it requires within the community. If we don't limit ourselves in an intellectual way Gaia will limit it for us and we may not like it so much.

Sigmund Kvalöy We haven't even begun to study how to carry out really effective interdisciplinary work that I would call generalism as distinct from specialism. When I listen to those of you who are engaged in Gaia research I hear what I would call reductionism coming through. In a Gaia oriented research team it would be vital that people should talk the same language, to break down the old academic values. The other point I would like to raise concerns biotechnology which is now on the increase and has increased tremendously. Could this technology change the regulatory mechanisms of Gaia?

Peter Westbroek We are now trying to use eco-biotechnolgy for changing or cleaning the environment, as for instance using bacteria that can concentrate heavy metals so as to extract heavy metals out of water. If that's what you mean, then that in the long run may have an effect on the management of ecology.

Gregory Hinkle Whatever genetic manipulation we do is essentially fine-tuning a system that has evolved over 3000 million years.

Helena Norberg-Hodge Even though we are taking a very broad view of life on Earth one crucial period seems to have gone amiss and that is what man has been doing since industrialization. Indeed when we talk about man today we tend to confuse industrialized man with human beings and yet there is a tremendous

117

difference even now on this planet between the Ladakhis with whom I have been working for more than a dozen years and modern industrial man and more precisely concerning his impact on nature. We still have millions of people in the Third World who do not have this impact on Gaia and I think it very important in our thinking and in our discussions that we bear this in mind.

Furthermore we often confuse science and technological innovation and the very clever thinking which has gone into the tinkering process over the past 200 years is not an evolutionary process. Maybe some of you would disagree with me but I can assure you that we are not more highly evolved than these Ladakhis, I would say on the contrary the children I have lived and worked with if are anything more highly evolved and certainly more adapted to Gaia. But something very interesting happens with the process of industrialization since it can almost overnight turn human beings who have been having a very low impact on Gaia, an insignificant impact, into people who may have the power with nuclear bombs and other technologies certainly to alter Gaia forever.

Nicholas Guppy We have a reached a point, I think, at which we can actually think in terms of practical recommendations, for instance to protect our carbon sinks, to plant slow-growing carbon-fixing trees, to protect wetlands. We have seen that there can be action over the ozone layer that takes place quickly once people are clear about the issues.

Lynn Margulis Action over Lake Erie is a case in point that's really remarkable; that involved recognition of the problem and the right people at the right time, including the scientific community. Lake Erie water was undrinkable and unswimmable – it was toxic and now it's drinkable, an incredible difference. There are probably certain things on which we would probably disagree: 10 per cent of things we would all completely agree upon and could easily endorse.

Peter Westbroek I believe we should take great care not to break away from the scientific community since if we can convert people within that community to change then things will change very rapidly.

James Lovelock We in the scientific community are aware of the deficiencies we have. I would ask for comparable awareness in the community at large that scientists are not quite stuck in the 19th century reductionistic, tinkering tradition. We are beginning to change too and we would ask you to give us support because it is not an easy process.

THE MECHANICAL AND THE ORGANIC: EPISTEMOLOGICAL CONSEQUENCES OF THE GAIA HYPOTHESIS

by David Abram

Biologist Steven J. Gould, speaking on evolution last spring to a packed auditorium at the State University of New York at Stony Brook, fielded a question from the back of the room. "Could you please", asked the small voice, "could you please comment on the Gaia Hypothesis?" "I'm glad you asked that," said Gould, and he went on: "After each of the last five lectures that I have given at universities, at least one person has asked a question about the Gaia Hypothesis. Yet nothing that I said in those lectures had anything to do with the Gaia Hypothesis! This is very interesting," he said, "people are obviously very curious about the Gaia Hypothesis. Yet I myself can't see anything in it that I didn't learn in grade school. Obviously the atmosphere interacts with life; its oxygen content, for instance, is clearly dependent on living organisms. But we've known this a long time. The Gaia Hypothesis says nothing new, it offers no new mechanisms. It just changes the metaphor. But metaphor is not mechanism!" And that was his final word on the matter.

What Gould failed to say is that 'mechanism', itself, is nothing more than a metaphor. It is an important one, to be sure. Indeed the whole process of modern science seems to get underway with this metaphor. In 1644 the brilliant philosopher Rene Descartes wrote "I have described the earth, and all the visible world, as if it were a machine." In his various writings, Descartes, developing a notion already suggested by other philosophers, effectively inaugurated that tradition of thought we call 'mechanism', or, as it was known at that time, the 'mechanical philosophy.' And his metaphor is still with us today.

But let us see how this metaphor operates upon us. What are the assumptions, explicit and implicit, that we wittingly or unwittingly buy into when we accept the premise that the visible world and, most specifically, the Earth, is best understood as a very intricate and complex machine?

First, the 'Mechanical philosophy' suggests that matter, itself, is ultimately inert, without any life or creativity of its own. The great worth of the machine metaphor is that it implies that the material world is, at least in principle, entirely predictable. According to this metaphor, the material world operates like any machine according to fixed and unvarying rules; laws that have been built into the machine from the start. It has no creativity, no spontaneity of its own. As a watch or a clock ticks away with complete uniformity until it runs down, so the material world cannot itself alter or vary the laws that are built into it. (We don't commonly think that the gears of our clocks can mischievously mutate and thereby alter the time.) The laws of a mechanical world are fixed and unchanging; if we can discover those laws, we will be able to predict with utter certainty the events of the world. Or so the mechanical philosophers thought in the seventeenth century.

Mind you, a thing does not have to be a machine for it to be predictable. Most people that I know are fairly predictable. Other animals and plants are 'roughly' predictable. About as predictable as, say, the weather. But Descartes and his followers chose to view the weather as, in principle, *entirely* predictable. For the material world was not an organism -- it was a machine. It had no life of its own. It had no sensitivity, no intrinsic power, no motive force of its own.

Which brings us to the second assumption implicit in the mechanical metaphor, an assumption rather more hidden than the first. A machine always implies someone who invented the machine, a builder, a maker. A machine cannot assemble itself. Clocks, carriages, or steam-engines do not assemble themselves from scratch -- if they did, they would be very wild and magical entities indeed, and we could not ascribe to them the fixity, uniformity and predictability that we associate with any strictly mechanical object. If we view nature as a machine, then we tacitly view it as something that has been built, something that has been made from outside. This is still evident in much of the language that we use in our science today: we speak of behaviour that has been 'programmed' into an animal's genes, of information that is 'hardwired' into the brain. But who wrote the programme? Who wired the brain? As mechanists we borrow these metaphors from our own experience of built things, things that have been invented and constructed by humans, and then we pretend that the inventor or the builder (or the programmer) does not come along with the metaphor. But, of course, he does. It is a necessary part of the metaphor. You don't get a machine without someone who built the machine.

I am asking you to begin to recognize the way that metaphors work upon us implicitly, even unconsciously. Yet what is largely unconscious today was quite obvious in the seventeenth century. If the material world is like a machine, then this world must have been constructed from outside. *A mechanical world implies a maker.* And *that* is precisely why the mechanical philosophy and mechanism triumphed in the seventeenth and eighteenth centuries to become part of the very fabric of conventional science. Mechanism gained ascendancy not because it was a necessary adjunct of scientific practice, but because it disarmed the objections of the Church, the dominant social and political institution of the time. The mechanical philosophy became a central facet of the scientific world-view precisely because it implied the existence of a maker (a divine inventor, if you will), and thus made possible an alliance between science and the Church.

We moderns tend to assume that the adoption of the mechanical metaphor was a necessary precondition for the growth and flourishing of experimental science. Yet an attentive study of the various conflicts and debates that gave rise to the scientific revolution quickly calls such assumptions into question. Until the latter half of the seventeenth century, the tradition of experimentation was *not* associated with the mechanical philosophy. On the contrary, the method of careful experimentation was associated with those who practised it, those who developed and refined it to the level of an art, individuals who had a very different perspective from that of the mechanists. For these were those who called themselves 'natural magicians', and often, 'alchemists'. They viewed the material world and, indeed, matter itself, as a locus of subtle powers and immanent forces, a dynamic network of invisible sympathies and antipathies. For the Renaissance natural magician, Marcilio Ficino -- the great translator of Plato's works into Latin -- for the Hermetic natural magicians Giordano Bruno and Tommasso Campanella, for the brilliant physician and alchemist Paracelsus (the real father of homeopathic medicine) and, indeed, for the entire alchemical tradition, material nature was perceived as alive, as a complex, living organism with which the investigator - the natural magician, or scientist -- was in relation. The experimental method was developed and honed as the medium of this relation, as a practice of dialogue between oneself and animate nature. Experimentation was here a form of participation, a technique of communication or communion which, when successful, effected a transformation not just in the structure of the material experimented upon, but in the structure of the experimenter himself (Easlea,1980, Yates, 1969).

Many of the great discoveries that we associate with the scientific revolution and, indeed, many of the scientists themselves, took their inspiration from this participatory tradition of natural magic -- one need only mention Nicholas Copernicus, who wrote of the sun as the visible God, quoting the legendary Egyptian magician Hermes Trismegistis, Johannes Kepler (whose mother was imprisoned and nearly executed for practising witchcraft -- on the evidence of Kepler's own writings), William Gilbert (the great student of magnetism, which he termed 'coition' as if it were a type of sexual intercourse that matter has with itself, and who, in his book *Magnete* wrote of the whole earth as a living body with its own impulse for self-preservation), (Easlea 1980, chapters 2-3). And, of course, we must mention Francis Bacon, the 'father' of experimental science, who saw his scientific method as a refinement of the tradition of natural magic and wrote that through his work the term "magic," which "has long been used in a bad sense, will again be restored to its ancient and honourable meaning" (Easlea 1980: 128).

How is it that we have forgotten this intimate link between experimental science and natural magic? How or why was this link with magic so obscured by the subsequent tradition of natural science? Why did Isaac Newton, arguably one of the greatest of all natural magicians, find it necessary to hide and even publicly deny the vast alchemical researches that occupied him throughout his life?

Clearly, the Church in the sixteenth and seventeenth centuries felt itself threatened by this powerful tradition which held that the material world was *a source of itself*, this tradition which spoke of the enveloping Earth as a living being, a living matrix of spiritual powers and receptivities. Such a way of speaking threatened the theological doctrine that matter itself is passive and barren, and that the corporeal realm of nature was a fallen, sinful realm, necessarily separated from its divine source. (I am not referring here, of course, to Christian doctrine in general, but only to the institutionalized Church of the sixteenth and seventeenth centuries - a period, let us remember, that saw hundreds of thousands, if not millions of persons, most of them women, tortured and executed as witches by the ecclesiastical and lay authorities.)

The *true* source, according to the Church, was radically external to nature, outside of the earthly domain in which we are bodily immersed. The teachings of natural magic, however, with their constant reference to immanent powers, implied that the divine miracles reported in the Old and the New Testaments might be explained by subtle principles entirely *internal* to material nature. This was heresy - heresy of the first order - since it enabled one to doubt the very agency and existence of the God outside nature.

Clearly then, if natural experimentation was to become a respectable or even a permissible practice it would have to find a new rhetoric for itself. It would have to shed its origins in the magical and participatory world-view and take on a new way of speaking more in line with Church doctrine.

It was 'mechanism', or the 'mechanical philosophy', that provided this new and much safer way of speaking. For again, a metaphorical machine entails a metaphorical builder, a creator. Like the Church, the mechanical philosophy necessitated an implicit belief in a creative source entirely outside of the material or sensible world. And, like the Church, the mechanical philosophy involved a denigration of corporeal matter, not exactly as fallen, sinful and demonic, but as barren, inert and ultimately, dead.

Here, then, was a perfect cosmology for the experimental scientists to adopt -- one that would allow them to continue to investigate nature without fear of being persecuted, or executed, for heresy. The mechanical metaphor made possible an alliance between seventeenth century science and the Church. And thus mechanism became a central tenet of the scientific world view. (See Endnote).

We are now in a position to discern the third and most powerful assumption implicit in the mechanical metaphor. The only true machines of which we have direct experience are those that have been invented by humans. Hence, if the world really functions as a complex machine, then the one who built that machine must be very much like us. There is, in other words, an implied isomorphism between humans and the one who built or programmed the complicated, vast machine of the world. We are, after all, made in his image. Hence, we alone have a heavenly mandate to manipulate the rest of this world for our own benefit. If the material Earth is a created machine, it falls to us – since we are not just created, but creators in our own right - to figure out how the machine works.

The mechanical metaphor, then, not only makes it rather simple for us to operationalize the world, by presenting nature as an assemblage of working parts that have no internal relation to each other - a set of parts, that is, that can be readily taken apart or put back together without undue damage; it also provides us with a metaphysical justification for any and all such manipulations. Since machines are invented by humans, the human mind necessarily retains a godlike position outside of the mechanical world that it analyzes. This is still evident today. It is neatly illustrated by two recent headlines in the *New York Times*, from a single week in 1987. The first, from April 14, 1987, reads "Physicist Aims to Create A Universe, Literally." The article relates the progress of Alan Guth and his colleagues at the Massachusetts Institute of Technology in their ongoing attempt to create a universe "from scratch" in the laboratory. The second headline, three days later on April 17, reads "New Animal Forms Will Be Patented." This article goes on to describe some of the newly 'invented' animals awaiting patenting, such as the pigs whose genome now contains a human growth hormone gene to make them grow faster. "The animals are leaner than naturally bred pigs, but they suffer from several debilitating ailments, including crossed eyes, severe arthritis in the joints and susceptibility to disease." Hmmm. At any rate it is instructive to string these two headlines from a single week together, in order to see how they read. "Physicist Aims to Create A Universe In The Laboratory: The New Animal Forms Will be Patented." It is like reading the daily newspaper on Mount Olympus!

Within the mechanical metaphor, there is always this implicit parallel between the creative human mind and that which created the universe, between humans and God. The human researcher thus has a divine mandate to experiment on, to operate upon, to manipulate earthly nature in any fashion he or she sees fit. The inertness of matter, the clear lack of sentience in all that is not human, absolves the researcher of any guilt regarding the apparent pain he may happen to inflict upon animals or ecosystems (such pain, as Descartes told us, is entirely an illusion, for automatons cannot really *feel* anything).

The mechanical world-view implicates us in a relation to the world which is that of an inventor, an operator, or an engineer to his machine (many biologists, for instance, now think of themselves as 'genetic engineers'). It is this privileged position, the licence it gives us for the possession, mastery and control of nature, that makes us so reluctant to drop the mechanical metaphor today. If mechanism rose to prominence in the seventeenth century owing to its compatibility with the belief in a divine creator, it remains in prominence today largely due to the deification of human powers that it promotes.

But this deification, this human privilege, comes at the expense of our perceptual experience. Let me explain. If we suspend our theoretical awareness in order to attend to our sensory experience of the world around us (to our experience not as disembodied intellects but as intelligent, sensing animals), we find that we are not outside of the world, but entirely *in* it. We are thoroughly encompassed by the world, immersed in its depths. Hence our sensory relation to the world is hardly that of a spectator to an object. As sensing animals, we are *never* disinterested onlookers but participants in a dynamic, shifting and ambiguous field.

Maurice Merleau-Ponty, the philosopher who has perhaps most carefully analyzed the experience of perception, underscored the participatory nature of this experience by calling attention to the obvious but easily overlooked fact that our hand, with which we touch the world, is itself a touchable thing, and thus is itself entirely a part of the tactile field that it explores. Likewise the eyes, with which we see the world, are themselves visible. They are themselves entirely included within the visible world that they see - they are one of the visible things, like the bark of a tree, or a stone, or the sky. For Merleau-Ponty, to *see* is also, at one and the same time, to feel oneself *seen* and to touch the world is also to be touched *by* the world! Clearly a wholly immaterial mind could neither see nor touch things, could not experience anything at all. *We* can experience things, can touch, hear, and taste things, only because, as bodies, we are ourselves a part of the sensible field, and have *our own* textures, sounds, and tastes. We can perceive things at all only because we are entirely a part of the sensible world that we perceive. We might just as well say that we are organs of that world, and that the world is perceiving itself through us (Merleau-Ponty, 1968, 1962).

But here the main point to get from Merleau-Ponty is that, from the perspective of our lived, embodied awareness, perception is always experienced as an interactive, reciprocal participation. The event of perception is never instantaneous - it has always a duration, and in that duration there is always a movement, a questioning and responding, a subtle attuning of the eyes to that which they see, or of the ears to what is heard, and thus we enter into a relationship with the things we perceive.

When, for instance, my hand moves over the surface of a stone newly found on the beach, my fingers must adjust themselves to the particular texture of the stone's surface, they must find the right rhythm, the right way to touch it if they are to discover its subtle furrows and patterns, as my eyes must find the right way to look at and focus that stone's surface if they wish to disclose the secrets of its mineral composition. It is in this way that the stone teaches my senses and informs my body. And the more I dwell with that stone, the more I will learn. *There is a mutual engagement of my body by the stone, and of the stone by my body.* And so it is with everything that we perceive, constantly, continually - the paved streets we walk upon, the trees that surround our home, the clouds that catch our gaze. Perception is always an active engagement with what one perceives, a reciprocal participation with things. As such, our direct perception always discloses things and the world as ambiguous, animate presences with which we find ourselves in *relation*. That this is our native, human experience of things is attested by the discourse of virtually all indigenous, oral, tribal peoples, whose languages refuse any designation of things, or of the sensible world, as ultimately inanimate. If a thing has the power to 'call my attention' or to 'capture my gaze', it can hardly be thought of as inert. "If this stone was not in some sense alive, you could no longer see it", I was told by an old shaman in the desert near Santa Fe. By which he meant to say, I think, that simply to see something is already to be in an active relationship with that thing, and how could one be in a dynamic relationship with something if it were entirely inanimate, without any potency or spontaneity of its own? How indeed? By implying that matter is utterly passive and inert, mechanism denies our perceptual experience. It denies our sensory involvement in the world.

The scientist who holds to a fundamentally mechanistic view of the natural world must suspend his or her sensory participation with things. He strives to picture the world from the viewpoint of an external spectator. He conceives of the Earth as a system of objective relations laid out before his gaze, but he does not include the gaze, his own seeing, within the system. Denying his sensory involvement in that which he seeks to understand, he is left with a purely mental relation to what is only an abstract image.

Likewise with any particular object or organism that the mechanist studies. There as well, she must assume the position of a disinterested onlooker. She must suppress all personal involvement in the object; any trace of subjectivity must be purged from her account. But this is an impossible ideal, for there is always some interest or circumstance that leads us to study one phenomenon rather than another, and this necessarily conditions what we look for, and what we discover. We are always in, and of, the world that we seek to describe from outside. We can deny, but we cannot escape being involved in whatever we perceive. Hence, *we may claim that the sensible world is ultimately inert or inanimate, but we can never wholly experience it as such.* The most that we can do is to try to *render* the sensible world inanimate, either by killing that which we perceive, or by deadening our sensory experience. Our *denial* or participation thus manifests as a particular *form* of participation, one that does violence to our bodies and to the Earth.

Mechanism, then, is a way of speaking that denies the inherently reciprocal and participatory nature of perceptual experience. It thus constricts and stifles the senses; they are no longer free to openly engage things like trees, bird-song, and the movement of waves. We grow more and more oblivious to the animate Earth as our body becomes closed in upon itself; our direct intercourse with the sensible world is inhibited. Mechanism sublimates our carnal relationship with the Earth into a purely mental relation, not to the world, but to the abstract image of a finished blueprint, the abstract ideal of a finished truth.

This mentalistic epistemology, with its fear of direct relationship and its intolerance of ambiguity, is the mark, I suggest, of an immature or adolescent science, a science that has not yet come into its own. Although it sporadically fosters grandiose feelings of power and godlike mastery over nature, science as mechanism is inherently unstable, since it is founded upon a denial of the very conditions that make science possible at all. Such a science cannot last - it must either obliterate the world in a final apotheosis of denial, or else give way to another mode of science: one that can affirm, rather than deny, our living bond with the world that surrounds us.

The Gaia hypothesis may well signal the emergence of just such a mature science - a science that seeks not to *control* the world but to *participate with* the world, not to operate upon nature, but to co-operate with nature. If the chemical composition of the air that we are breathing is being sensitively monitored and maintained by the sum of all of the Earth's biota acting in concert, as a single, coherent, autopoietic or living system, then the material world that surrounds us is not, in any sense, inert or inanimate. Nor are these insects, these trees or even these boulders entirely passive and inert. For material nature can no longer be perceived as a collection of detachable working parts - it is not a created machine but rather a vast, self-generative, living physiology, open and responsive to changing circumstances. In short, it is an entity.

Of course, we may still attempt to speak of Gaia in purely mechanical terms, or try to conceive of Gaia as a strictly objective set of processes, straining thus to hold our science within the old mechanical paradigm to which we have become accustomed. We may be reluctant to give up the dream of a finished objectivity, and of the fixed reality to which it would correspond. Nevertheless, Gaia will never fit very neatly within the discourse of mechanism. A mechanism is entirely determined. It acts, as we have seen, according to a set of predictable and fixed rules and structures that it itself did not generate. Yet it is precisely such a formulation that Gaia, as a *self*-generating system, resists. Of course, we may say that Gaia is a machine, or a set of mechanisms, that is building itself. Fine! But then we have given up, perhaps without realizing it, that part of the metaphor that makes mechanism so compelling. That is, a machine that creates itself is never entirely predictable. For it is generating itself as it goes, creatively. (We have no guarantee, for instance, that the so called 'mechanisms' that Gaia employs to regulate the salinity of the oceans, or to limit the influx of ultra-violet radiation into the atmosphere, are precisely the same that she will be employing a hundred years from now.) Gaia, as an autonomous self-generating entity, is no more and no less predictable than a living body, and we might as well simply speak of it as such and stop pretending that it is anything like a machine that we could build. The Gaia hypothesis indicates that the world we inhabit is rather more like a living organism than a watch, or a spaceship, or even a computer.

And we are entirely inside of, circumscribed by this organic entity. For the Gaia hypothesis indicates that the atmosphere in which we live and think is itself a dynamic extension of the planetary surface, a functioning organ of the animate Earth. As I have stated in an earlier article:

> It may be that the new emphasis it places on the atmosphere of this world is the most radical aspect of the Gaia hypothesis. For it carries the implication that before we as individuals can begin to recognize the Earth as a self-sustaining organic presence, we must remember and reacquaint ourselves with the very medium within which we move. The air can no longer be confused with mere negative presence or the absence of solid things - henceforth the air is itself a density - mysterious indeed for its invisibility -- but a thick and tactile presence nonetheless. We are immersed in its depths as surely as fish are immersed in the sea. It is the medium, the silent interlocutor of all our musings and moods. We simply cannot exist without its support and nourishment, without its active participation in whatever we are up to at any moment.
>
> In concert with the other animals, with the plants, and with the microbes themselves, we are an active part of the Earth's atmosphere, constantly circulating the breath of this planet through our bodies and brains, exchanging certain vital gases for others, and thus monitoring and maintaining the delicate makeup of the medium (Abram, 1985).

So simply by breathing we are participating in the life of the biosphere. But not just by breathing! If the biosphere is really a coherent, self-sustaining entity, then everything we see, everything we hear, every experience of smelling and tasting and touching is informing our bodies regarding the internal state of this other, vaster physiology - the biosphere itself. Sensory perception, then, is really a form of communication between an organism and the living biosphere. (And this can be the case even when we are observing ourselves, noticing a headache that we feel or the commotion in our stomach caused by some contaminated water. For we ourselves are a part of Gaia. If the biosphere is a living entity, then introspection, listening to our own bodies, can become a way of listening and attuning to the Earth.) Perception is a communication or even a communion - a sensuous participation between ourselves and the living world that encompasses us. Yet we have seen that this is precisely the way that we commonly experience perception - as an interaction, a participation or intertwining between ourselves and that which we perceive. Perception is never strictly objective, since to perceive anything at all is to involve oneself in that thing and to feel oneself influenced by the encounter. We have seen that mechanism denies this dialectic by assuming that the world is a created object, fixed and unchanging, incapable of creative response. The Gaia hypothesis, on the other hand, ultimately affirms the participatory nature of our perceptual experience since it defines the physical environment as something animate and alive, which is precisely the way that our bodies experience it. Thus the Gaia hypothesis enables, quite literally, *a return to our senses*. We become aware, once again, of our sensing bodies, and of the bodily world that surrounds us.

If this world we inhabit is really a machine - a fixed and finished object - then it cannot respond to our attention; there is nothing to participate or to communicate with except ourselves, our own 'creative human minds'. If, however, the Earth is not a finished object, but is continually creating itself, then everything is open to participation. We are drawn out of that ideal, platonic domain of thoughts and theories back into this realm we inhabit with our bodies, this land that we share with the other animals and the plants and the microbial entities who vibrate and spin within our cells and within the cells of the spider. Our senses loosen themselves from the mechanical constraints imposed by an outmoded language - they begin to participate in the ongoing life of the land around us.

We are now in a position to contrast succinctly the epistemology of mechanism with the epistemological implications of Gaia. The mechanical model of the world entails a mentalistic epistemology, the assumption that the most precise knowledge of things is a detached, intellectual apprehension purged of all subjective, personal or perspectival (that is, bodily) involvement. It is an abstract, disembodied knowledge. Meanwhile, the gaian understanding of the world, that which speaks of the biosphere not as a machine but as an autopoietic, living physiology, entails an embodied, participatory epistemology. As the Earth is no longer a machine, so the human body is no more a fixed machine but a thinking, feeling, sensing physiology, a microcosm of the autopoietic Earth. It is hence not as a detached mind, but as a living body that I can come to know the world, participating in its processes, feeling my life resonate with its life, becoming more a part of the world. Knowledge, here, is always carnal knowledge, a wisdom born of the body's own attunement to that which it studies, and to the Earth.

This view is entirely akin to that of Ludwig Fleck, the great epistemologist and sociologist of science, who wrote in 1929 that:

> Cognition is neither passive contemplation nor acquisition of the only possible insight into something given. It is an active, live interrelationship, a shaping and being reshaped, in short, an act of creation (or, we might add, co-creation). (Fleck, 1929).

We may wonder what science will come to look like if such an epistemology were to take hold and spread throughout the human community. It is likely that scientists would soon lose interest in the pursuit of a finished blueprint of the Earth, in favour of discovering ways to better the relationship between humankind and the rest of the biosphere, and ways to rectify current problems caused by the neglect of that relationship. I have spoken of a science that seeks not to control nature but to communicate with nature. Experimentation would come to be recognized once again as a discipline or art of communication between the scientist and that which he or she studies (an interpretation which is not unlike the original understanding of experimental practice, as we have seen). Indeed, I am sure that many scientists are already familiar with the experience of a deep communication or communion with that which they study, although current scientific discourse makes it rather difficult to acknowledge or to articulate such experience. (Unless, of course, one is a physicist). The physicists are freer to articulate such experiences only because their objects remain transcendent to the world of our immediate experience. To participate mystically with subatomic quanta or even with the ultimate origin of the universe does not really force science to alter its assumptions regarding the inert or mechanical nature of the *everyday* sensible world, and so does not really threaten

127

our right to dominate and manipulate the immediate world around us. But biologists, who study this very world - the world that we can directly perceive, often with our unaided senses - are in a much more precarious position politically.) However, in a genuinely gaian science, or in a gaian community of scientists, it will become manifestly evident that one is already involved in that which one studies, and so it will no longer be necessary to try to avoid or to repress this involvement. On the contrary, scientists may begin to openly develop and cultivate their personal rapport with that which they study as a means of deepening their scientific insight.

Biologist Barbara McClintok, who was awarded the Nobel Prize in 1984 for her discovery of genetic transposition, exemplifies the participatory epistemology implied by a gaian science. She insists that a genuine scientist must have "a feeling for the organism" – and not only for "living" organisms but "for any object that fully claims our attention" (Keller, 1985: 166). McClintok describes a rather magical shift in her orientation that enabled her to identify chromosomes that she had previously been unable to distinguish. It is the shift to a participatory epistemology:

"I found that the more I worked with them, the bigger and bigger the chromosomes got, and when I was really working with them, I wasn't outside, I was down there. I was part of the system. I was right down there with them and everything got big. I even was able to see the internal parts of the chromosomes - actually everything was there. It surprised me because I actually felt as if I was right down there and these were my friends. As you look at these things, they become a part of you. And you forget yourself (Keller, 1985: 165)."

As Barbara McClintock came to perceive herself inside of the living system she was studying, so the Gaia hypothesis situates all of us inside of this world that we share with the plants and the animals and the stones. The things around us are no longer inert. They are our co-participants in the evolution of a knowledge and a science that belongs to humankind no more, and no less, than it belongs to the Earth.

ENDNOTE
On this reading mechanistic science went hand in hand with a Christian metaphysics. The schism that we have come to assume today between the scientists and the theologians, or between science and religion, only really gets underway with the publication and dissemination of the *Origin of Species*. For Darwin was beginning to speak of a sort of creative power inherent in nature itself; he spoke of a natural selection – a selective power not outside of nature but internal to nature. Of course, by using the metaphor of selection he was still propagating a metaphysics somewhat similar to that of the Church (in which he had been steeped as a young man). "Selecting" is the kind of thing that an anthropomorphic divinity does; and we can see from newspaper articles of that time that many readers interpreted Darwin's use of the term "selection" as a sort of indirect argument for the existence of God. His correspondence indicates that Darwin, himself, remained somewhat attached to the idea of transcendental divinity: the use of the term "selection", with all its associations of humanlike *will* or *choice*, (see Robert M. Young), *Darwin's Metaphor, 1985*, Cambridge University Press, pp.79-125.) Nevertheless, Darwin's work was the first to imply a creativity inherent in nature itself, and this was a blow to the church. We now are beginning to discern

that if the environment "selects" the organisms that inhabit, so these organisms also "selectively" influence that environment, and so maybe "selection" is not such a great term. This interaction is a much more reciprocal phenomenon than that suggested by the metaphor of selection – it is more a sort of dialogue wherein the environment puts questions to the organism and the organism, in answering those questions, puts new questions to the environment which the environment, in turn, answers with further questions. It is precisely this sort of open dialectic, this mutual participation between the body and the Earth, that the Gaia hypothesis is beginning to thematize and articulate.

References

Abram, David. "The Perceptual Implications of Gaia." in *The Ecologist*, Volume 15, No. 3, 1985.

Descartes, Rene. *Principles of Philosophy*, Part 1V, principle CLXXXVIII, in *The Philosophical Work of Descartes*, translated by Haldane and Ross, 1931, Cambridge University Press.

Easlea, Brian. *Witch Hunting, Magic, and the New Philosophy:* an introduction to the debates of the scientific revolution 1450-1750.980, Humanities Press, New Jersey.

Fleck, Ludwick. "On the Crisis of 'Reality'" (1929), in *Cognition and Fact: materials on Ludwik Fleck*, edited by Robert Cohen and Thomas Schnelle, 1986, D. Reidel Publishing Co. Boston, pp.47-57.

Keller, Evelyn Fox. *Reflections on Gender and Science*. 1985, Yale University Press, p.166.

Merleau-Ponty, Maurice. *The Visible and the Invisible*. Edited by Claude Lefort, translated by Alphonso Lingis, 1986, Northwestern University Press. See also Merleau-Ponty's seminal text *The Phenomenology of Perception*. Translated by Colin Smith, 1962, Routledge and Kegan Paul.

Yates, Frances. *Giordano Bruno and the Hermetic Tradition*, 1969, Vintage Press.

DISCUSSION

Willem Hoogendiyk   Life, including man changes the environment, so is not the Gaia hypothesis an excuse for us to go on building dams, to do our bit of biotechnology, generate nuclear electricity and all our other industrial activities?

Marcus Colchester   My question follows exactly from that: your exposition about the relationship between religion and the development of holistic science was very fascinating, but, of course, these things do not evolve in a social and political vacuum: nor do you imply that. Would you like therefore to single out what are the main forces you believe are determining or influencing the evolution of that form of thought? And whether a sort of gaian perspective, such as you advocate, is a solution to our way of interacting with the planet? Indeed, what sort of political economic changes are necessary on the planet to allow that actually to develop?

David Abram   In my paper I try to articulate what I took to be one or two of the main factors in the development of the most recent form of the kind of distanced mentalistic epistemology which is *mechanism*. In terms of what is needed for the future I did not really want to speak so much about the future since I can't predict. I don't think Gaia is that predictable but I would point, perhaps, toward the new notion of bioregionalism as a partial answer.

Ken Dickinson   Aren't we trying to fit Gaia into an inappropriate discourse given the sort of institutions we have? Aren't you in fact diluting the importance of a very radical conceptual scheme by making it work in this inappropriate way?

David Abram   There is another way to understand that: it's not necessarily a dilution. Gaia, it must be recognized, was first revealed in the midst of normal science, Jim Lovelock and others having glimpsed its first contours. But certainly it will take time for all the implications, for a discourse, for a language, for how to find a way to articulate this vision so that it can all begin to fall into place. Obviously the scientists who are working with Gaia are walking a very fine line; they must necessarily stay in communication with the scientific community.

All I am arguing for is that those scientists, and in some ways I feel myself to be one of them, are aware of this fine line. So just to be aware of the tenuous position that we are in is a very delicate thing. If we hold Gaia and continually keep speaking of it in strictly cybernetic mechanical fashion then what Willem feared would happen will of course happen. If we don't try to borrow as much as we can from physiology, from organisms, then it is likely that the Gaia hypothesis will become just another justification for our manipulation and control of the Earth and we will get more and more books with titles such as: *An Atlas of Planet Management*. I don't think that Gaia genuinely understood allows for such a notion of management.

Pierre Lehmann   Concerning the point you made that if you have a machine then you need an inventor, I would like to refer you to the book by Fred Hoyle in which he introduces the idea of the intelligent Universe. He felt that some relationship between Gaia and the Universe beyond was somehow necessary. In that respect it's not very reasonable to think of Gaia alone; you have to look beyond. In your talk you introduced the idea that we must try to manage perception with scientific insight. I think it vital that we follow that path, since today there is a refusal to acknowledge anything that is not considered truly scientific as a means of making progress in nature. Going the way you suggest might be a way of avoiding that pitfall.

David Abram Certainly one of the keys is to recognize that the relationship we are sustaining with the world as a scientific culture is clearly not very healthy; it looks very immature, very adolescent, and we should realize that perhaps our science has not yet come into its own; it has not yet become a mature form of science, a science worthy of the name: that is what I am trying to suggest.

In response to the first part of your question about Hoyle. I haven't read that particular book, although I am, of course, familiar with his work. What I want to say is that our culture has become very skilled, particularly since the scientific revolution, at looking beyond this world; we are very good at that because it is a way of not perceiving what is in front of our nose. As I mentioned before, physicists are able quite easily to articulate this sort of participation; they say "O.K. We are in a sort of participatory, even a mystical communion with the structure of matter at the sub-atomic level". And now many physicists, especially those who hold to the so-called anthropic principle, are saying that perhaps our viewing of the origins of the Universe is participating in the actual origin itself. In other words the physicists are articulating just this kind of perceptual participation, but notice that this participation remains circumscribed within the sub-atomic or within the super-macroscopic domains. In that way it is kept from infiltrating our immediate experience and really threatening our assumptions regarding the inert and mechanical nature of the direct sensible world around us. That's why it is so simple for physicists to speak in this kind of mystical way and much more difficult for biologists who study the world that surrounds us, this Earth.

Andrea Finger You spoke of the Nobel Prize winner, Barbara McClintok who identified with chromosomes. This can also happen with machines. One nuclear engineer used to feel like the computer and when he saw the temperature curve rising he would close his eyes because it was all getting too hot. Equally the director of Super-Phénix, the fast reactor at Creys-Malville is said to be in love with fast neutrons. It is not rational.

David Abram For sure, I think that once one starts participating with anything besides the strictly human, once one starts participating with anything outside of the human skull, it becomes easier to begin to participate with other things as well. It is important not to keep viewing the organic world as mechanical, but to invert this approach so as to view the mechanical as an extension of the organic, since our artifacts and instruments are extensions of our bodies. For instance in Germany, people are beginning to think of houses as membranes, as a third skin, (with our clothes forming the second skin). That is a very useful way for architects to go. The same with machines: nothing is purely mechanical, not even the machine.

Ted Pawloff We must pay tribute to Jim Lovelock for having had the vision and courage to express his insight in a poetic way and I think he has set an example. It paves the way to some extent for others to follow, since in one sense Gaia is metaphor, in another it is inspiration. Secondly, although I agree to a large extent with what you said, I think it is necessary to consider the importance of evolution. There definitely is an evolution of something I refer to as 'materialization', referred to by other people in the context of 'becoming aware'. The reality of ideas is actually part of the reality of nature but we must try to leave the thing as open-ended as we possibly can, never to close it off. I completely agree with you that we have to get back in touch with our perceptions, but the fact that our ideas are fools of perceptions of the realities themselves can lead us astray. Not to enclose them within our skull as we have been doing but actually see them as part of nature, I believe we have no monopoly on that side of reality as on any of the others.

David Abram That's the point I would want to argue, that whatever the mental, the ideal is, ideas are not strictly human and our species has no special monopoly on them.

Sigmund Kvalöy We require a new sort of science now that mechanistic science has failed. We need to have new conceptions.

David Abram It's not just science for which we need new conceptions but economic structure as well.

GAIA AND THE PHILOSOPHY OF SCIENCE
by Jerry Ravetz

Introduction

As you will see on the sheet that I wrote up this morning and had distributed, what I will be talking about is not the same as what I sent in my preliminary paper. In thinking of what I could accomplish most usefully here, I decided that instead of giving you my opinions on various issues, I would try to clarify the issues on which other people could debate. I will therefore try to raise, in a rather condensed form, the different sorts of philosophical issues that have been in play in all the discussions of this conference. The only positive opinions that I shall offer will be not about Gaia but about philosophy. I do this not in order to convince you of my point of view, but only to help you see why I am doing things in the way I do.

Philosophy and Gaia

I believe that philosophy is directly relevant to real science and to real life. What happens is that when someone (perhaps yourself) is engaged on something that is big and new, either scientific research or even a personal project, there arise difficulties, problems, contradictions of all sorts that cannot be solved within that practice. These threaten you with failure, the loss of your security and of your direction. There are many personal approaches to the resolution of such a crisis. You may try music, dance, loving, or pictures; or you may try some conceptual study of what it is that you are trying to do: that is philosophy. Practical philosophy, as I see it, is a way of thinking in a particular context, when the ordinary approaches fail. It is not the only way to respond, and perhaps not even always the best way, but it is one way, and one that I understand best.

What I have just described is not what professional philosophers, mostly employed in educational establishments do most of the time. One of the complications in practical philosophy is that the conceptual tools we use are generally fashioned by people who are professional philosophers, during a 'pure' research mixed with teaching; and their products may not be exactly what we want. So as practical philosophers we are in a sense amateurs; we can never get complete satisfaction about our philosophizing. Yet somehow out of our reflections we can achieve greater clarity about our enterprises and ourselves.

The relevance of this rather general account of philosophy is that we in this conference have been doing practical philosophy more or less continuously since the moment we arrived here. A number of different positions have been put forward on some quite basic issues concerning humanity and our position in the world. Although we are all in one family, in a sense, people are seeing and feeling things differently. My job here is to make these different standpoints clear and explicit, so that when we reflect at leisure on this conference we will have a better idea of what happened and where we can go from here.

One important thing about philosophy is that it is always studying the same problems. Some people consider it inferior to science on that ground, for it never seems to get anywhere. But as humans we face the same sorts of issues and dilemmas down through the centuries; and an analysis given by a Plato or a Descartes can still be illuminating today. Of course, this is a matter of degree; if you are in a traditional Eskimo culture, or even a traditional Chinese culture, the formulation of the problems will be different to a significant degree. In our European culture, since the times of classical Greece, there has been a remarkable continuity of the great themes around which we do philosophy. It is quite reasonable to speak of the Good, the True, the Real, the Just, the Beautiful, and also the Human, while knowing that for each generation these root ideas must be seen somewhat differently and brought to life again.

It is against this background that I find the Gaia hypothesis exciting. It seems to me that Gaia may become a very important event in our modern intellectual history. I am generally rather sceptical of new titles or new labels about scientific ideas, because most of them come and go very quickly, more like fashions than like truths. There are some grand organizing ideas that sound very exciting, but then they cannot be made into hypotheses for research science, and so they remain external to science, at the level of popularization or propaganda. By contrast, it now seems possible that the Gaia hypothesis will begin to give real coherence to what has hitherto been a rather complex and confused set of ideas about the natural environment. It will thereby become a very powerful organizing principle analogous to continental drift in geology. With that strength, it will affect our perceptions of nature and therefore of ourselves, in a solid and determinate way. Thereby it will change the face of practical philosophy for us here, and perhaps eventually of professional philosophy as well.

In the discussions we have had so far, I have already sensed a variety of contrasting positions, and the potential for conflicts among us. In themselves, these are no bad thing, for they reflect the healthy diversity among our backgrounds and outlooks. But our debates will be more effective and constructive, if we are clear about the issues that may divide us, and also that in our debates we are doing philosophy and not science.

The Nature of Humanity

This is the first big issue to be raised by Gaia. In its old form, it involved the placing of mankind between the apes and angels. Now it concerns our relation to non-human nature. Clearly, in some ways we are part of nature, and in some ways not; just as in some ways we depend on nature and in others we change it from outside. The debates can be on the ways in which these relations work out; or there can be a question of whether there is a decisive, essential answer on one side or the other, and if so which. For we are interested in ourselves, wanting to know whether there is something very special about us as a species, different in some very important way from amoebas and dragonflies and cats. We *feel* as if we are different, and more important in some scheme of things that is bigger than ourselves; and yet that is a philosophical position that can never be conclusively proved.

Gaia introduces a new element into this picture of ourselves in nature. Within the great dynamic homeostat of the planetary system, we are a very little thing in physical terms, comparable to a culture in a Petri-dish. We may not be very long lived as a species, and so in another billion years there may be hardly any trace of our temporary presence. But while we are here, we can have quite significant effects on Gaia in her present phase. We may quite possibly be driving Gaia rapidly towards an unstable boundary, to where she must flip to a new phase, with very destructive consequences for ourselves and much else besides. It is even conceivable that the new phase of Gaia will be one that is at such an extreme of temperature that life as it has built up over the billennia will be extinguished or severely reduced.

Hence, we are now forced to look at humankind as not merely interdependent with nature, or symbiotic with the rest of Gaia. Rather, in these terms we may be a pathogenic parasite on the whole planetary organism. It had done quite well without us for a long time, going through its cycles smoothly or roughly. Then *Homo 'sapiens'* arrives, and within a twinkling, on the scale of planetary time, he (should I use the masculine here?) does such things as to foul the whole system and destroy his nest and much else. To emphasize the point, let me try another analogy: ourselves (and particularly European man) as a weed. When a previously stable system is disturbed, the weeds invade and choke out everything else. Of course, after a while they create a new stability and are themselves squeezed out by a new flora. Is this the best that can be hoped for ourselves? If so, our pride in our accomplishments would become rather muted, and we seriously wonder whether we are some sort of mistake.

Now, this pessimistic way of looking at humanity did not start with Gaia; ever since the Bomb and pollution, people, helped by science-fiction writers and some scientists, have been aware of such possibilities. What is new with Gaia is that the issue now has a basis in science. The possibility that we are, on balance, a bad thing for our planet can now be stated in a precise, even partly testable form. This can cause a change in our image of ourselves comparable to those wrought by, say, Copernicus, Darwin and Freud. The first of these initiated a change in our picture of heaven and earth so that there is no longer a location for the angels up above, and for the damned souls down below. The second showed that no special creation was required to explain the origin of the many non-human species of living things, and so by analogy none was required for mankind. Finally with Freud we discovered the unconscious, so that our reason, what really distinguishes us from the animals, turns out to be not so supreme and independent, but is as much governed by causes as the reactions of a goldfish to stimuli. Each of these scientific discoveries was opposed on the grounds that its philosophical interpretation would deny the dignity and uniqueness of mankind; yet humanity has survived them all, and (we think) with greater understanding and perhaps wisdom each time

The contribution that Gaia makes to this sequence of discoveries is to take the process a step further. We are not merely an integral part of nature, depending on myriads of yet undiscovered natural processes for our very existence. But we are perhaps an unnatural part of nature, uniquely (to our present knowledge) among all species, in that we threaten to destroy the homeostatic balance on which our existence depends. Hence the meaning of our existence on this planet is called into

135

question. We can no longer assume that in some way we as a species are 'good' in the sense that each of us strives to be good to those around us. Perhaps we collectively are 'bad'; and if so, what is it all about, if anything? If by our own criteria of richness, diversity and complexity of organization and life, we as a species now threaten to destroy and degrade all of it on this planet, then our own value to - may I call it - the creation, is seriously put into doubt.

Suppose that Gaia was doing just fine until we came along and introduced our increasingly unstable perturbations into the system, now possibly culminating in something quite planetismic within our lifetimes. What then of ourselves? Of course I am not predicting this; but since the possibility of such a man-made planetary catastrophe cannot be denied, then the philosophical, or existential question is a real one. Thus Gaia raises further disturbing questions about our place in a bigger scheme of things, if there is one; and given the scientific strength of Gaia, the philosophical question, a new form of an old issue, becomes all the more real and urgent.

The Problem of Evil

This more general problem follows on naturally from those discussed just above. It is something that has been with us as a philosophical issue, since Biblical times; we have the book of Job and also the myth of Adam and Eve. Certainly in this century we have seen enough evil, either malevolent as with the Holocaust, or benevolent as with the Bomb. No philosopher or theologian has yet had a permanent success in showing that the apparent evil that pervades, even dominates so much of human activity and human history, is really good in a clever disguise. We have even had people who blame it all on civilization, who imagine what used to be called 'noble savages' as in the eighteenth century, or perhaps 'natural people' now, from Rousseau to Laurens van der Post, contrasting their purity and genuine realization of the values we profess, to our corrupted and sinful state. Others try to find some civilization which seems now, from its records, to have been in an harmonious and stable relation with its environment before some unfortunate accident terminated its life.

Such reflections are the negative reaction to the general optimism that has characterized European civilization for some centuries. We have applied science for the transformation of the means of production, and thereby achieved the solution of the curse of poverty at the material level. It only remains to reorganize our social arrangements, and then there will be enough food and fibre for all, together with an abundance of manufactured goods. And wherever there has been such progress in the material realm, there has been a corresponding improvement in the cultural and spiritual lives of people, with the driving out of the superstition and obscurantism on which a reactionary clergy thrive.

Here then, are the two contradictory views on the human meaning of industrial society. What contribution can Gaia make to this philosophical issue concerning the good society? In a general way, Gaia tells us that what has been going on over the last few hundred years cannot be extended to all mankind, or even sustained for very long. Regardless of its debateable merits for human advancement, it is only a temporary phenomenon. I like to make the point vividly with a question. Can the biosphere support a billion cars and also a billion air conditioners? This would be the load, if a Western standard of living, with instant transport and domestic climate control, were to be shared equally throughout the world. With the help of Gaia one could calculate the impact of the wastes in materials and energy that would be created by such a multiplication, fivefold or twentyfold, of these processes. But if such a burden on the downstream cycles of Gaia are not sustainable, then the vision of a just society being achieved through our present technology is a delusion. We can keep our comforts for some time, and let the world's poor continue to rot; but that would be evil, and would sooner or later become destructive in physical as well as moral terms to us all.

Thus Gaia, as a sharpening of an ecological perspective, provides us with two philosophical issues arising out of the destructiveness of the ordinary operations of our modern industrial technology. In the long run (which may not be very long by planetary standards or even by human ones) the disruptive effects of our material culture will be producing vast and destructive changes; so that our own status as beings endowed with some superior qualities, is called into question. Then, even in the short run, the impossibility of extending the current material benefits of our industrial system to all of humanity means that we are the Rich and they are the Poor; and the evil of injustice on a planetary scale is enforced not merely by consciously selfish politics, but by the exigencies of our productive machine.

Knowledge and Ignorance

The last problem involved waste, and that leads me naturally into my next topic. This is the theory of knowledge, frequently entitled by its Greek name, epistemology. For me the problem needs a new look; for we can no longer maintain the traditional view of science as rolling back the boundary with ignorance, perhaps even approaching truth asymptotically. The lesson of our industrial technology as sharpened by awareness of Gaia, is that ignorance will always be with us (so long as things persist in their present form); and that indeed man-made ignorance constitutes a great and ever-increasing threat to our survival. This is, I believe, a new move in epistemology.

I can illustrate this philosophical point by continuing my discussion of waste; paradoxical, or even perhaps not in the best of taste, but I believe to be relevant to the sort of philosophy that we need. For waste is an increasingly urgent problem in industrialized societies; and yet we know very little about it. A few years ago I gave a lecture-course on waste, and in my preliminary reading I scoured the catalogues of the University of California libraries, to find materials on the problem of waste. There was plenty on particular sorts of waste, but on Waste - nothing. This is probably because the industrial system does not yet recognize that there is a problem of Waste, only of particular wastes. The fact that it is being increasingly threatened with widespread poisoning by toxic wastes, and (in America at least) is becoming choked with nuclear wastes, is not yet seen as a systematic problem.

It can be argued that any culture needs to maintain ignorance, of some sort, about the things that threaten its integrity; we speak of taboos, in both the strict

137

anthropological sense and also in the popular, social sense. Perhaps now, waste, being so nasty, threatening and in the last resort unmanageable by our present approaches, is a taboo of late industrial society. Were we to consider seriously, systematically and publicly what is known of the environmental consequences of its activities, with waste primary among them but including other assaults as well, then so much that we now take for granted as benefits would be revealed as incurring incalculable costs as well. So the system maintains its plausibility by enforcing a sort of 'ignorance of ignorance'. All the concentration is upon our knowledge, of what we understand about nature, and how we can control her. The areas of ignorance, most easily seen in wastes and pollution, are left to the 'garbage sciences' starved of resources, prestige and influence.

One result of this is that we find an increasing number of urgent and intractable problems being thrust upon those with a competence to handle them, ranging from acid rain to CFCs, ozone and greenhouse effect. In every instance our knowledge, at least at the beginning of a study of specific problems, is weak and paltry compared to our ignorance. And the policy implications of their uncertain conclusions are even more open-ended. When should we start making the investments for a planned removal of the world's major coastal cities, in anticipation of the rise in mean sea level consequent on greenhouse heating? Such questions betray our ignorance, which now increasingly swamps our knowledge when we must make long-term decisions.

Of course, science has always had to cope with ignorance; and its progress over recent centuries has seemed so triumphant and inevitable because of the way in which the border with ignorance was rolled back in one field after another. But now we have a new phenomenon, that I call man-made ignorance. This is of systems and cycles that exist out there in the natural world, but which exist only because of human intervention. Most of our wastes are of this character; indeed we may say that the category 'waste' is itself a sign of a bad technology. (Lest I seem to have things too neatly sewn up, I may raise the question, whether there is indeed waste in Gaia, such as the vast quantity of nitrogen in the atmosphere).

Our man-made ignorance can extend quite dramatically to insoluble yet urgent engineering problems, as the design of a repository for nuclear waste that will be safe for some tens of thousands of years. This is a very good example for illustrating the problem; I use it whenever I lecture on such issues. For this impossibly long time-horizon in design is coupled with an urgently brief time-horizon in decision. The American authorities are increasingly anxious to 'solve' the problem of the nuclear wastes, at least in principle, lest there be some nasty accident at a temporary storage place when there is no remedy in sight. But, as Barry Commoner said long ago, everything has to go somewhere, and statistically negligible people can have political bite. So in the disposal of nuclear wastes (perhaps appropriately, given the general nature of the technology), we have this exquisite interaction of knowledge, ignorance, Gaia and dirty politics: the classic case. Please excuse my aesthetic appreciation of what is a very nasty problem; I cannot help it.

When we consider the complexity and interrelatedness of the cycles by which Gaia maintains her balances, the massiveness of the disruptions which we now impose on her, the primitive quality of the scientific materials by which we attempt to decipher her clues; then truly we can speak of a man-made ignorance, criminal or pitiful depending on your point of view, in our relations with Gaia. Let me make it clear, that I do not think that this ignorance is absolute or static; there is much that is being done by science, both inside and outside the establishment, on all these problems. One of the enjoyable and exciting things about being at this conference is seeing science of such relevance, originality and excellence being reported and even being in the making. And certainly, more will be done, as the urgency of these problems becomes plain to us all, except perhaps for the most myopic or tyrannical of politicians. But the questions remain, will enough be done to sort out the existing damage to Gaia; and also will the scientists have the appropriate conception of their task?

Methodology

When we reflect on the interaction of knowledge with ignorance in the scientific problems of Gaia, it becomes clear that a very new conception of what scientific work is about, will become relevant and indeed necessary. This does *not* mean abandoning rigorous research using any appropriate method, be it quantitative, field-research, simulation or what have you. But the relations of the scientists to the materials they explore, and to each other, will have to change. In his classic work on the philosophy of science, Thomas Kuhn described "normal science" as "the strenuous and devoted effort to force nature into the conceptual boxes provided by one's professional education". With such a normality, it is not surprising that attempts to achieve genuine interdisciplinary research always founder. Nor is there any philosophical basis for resisting the inevitable trends for research to become atomised and fragmented, conceptually and socially. How can there possibly be an integration of the various sorts of expertise relevant to any real Gaia problem, except when the research is done by those courageous individuals out on the margin, they and their work surviving precariously on the goodwill of supporters in funding agencies.

I believe that the recognition of ignorance can provide some basis for escaping from the atomism of the scientific life as we have experienced it hitherto. I might here paraphrase Winston Churchill's famous remark about greatness, and say that some research problems are invented (as in basic science), some are presented (as in mission-oriented science), and some are *thrust upon us* (as in problems of an assaulted environment). In this last case, scientists do not have the luxury of satisfying professional standards of rigour. Such problems may be described as having uncertain facts, disputed values, high decision stakes and urgent decisions. When we evaluate solutions to such problems, we broaden our perspective from 'correctness' (relative to the state of the art in experiment and theory), to 'function', in a context that is partly technical and partly societal.

This is not the place to enter into a long discussion of the methodology of 'policy-related research'. Let it suffice for now that I can see this as becoming a crucially important area of science, and one in which the assumptions about who is competent to do science and why, become drastically altered. In this, 'housewives' epidemiology' and TV investigative journalism will have their legitimate place, alongside the more conventional research. I could also argue that without the critical presence of such complementary sciences, it will be all the more difficult for the aware minority within the community of established scientists to make any impression on their colleagues and leaders. There is no need for me to labour this point here, since so much of what *The Ecologist* has published and fostered, is in just this category of science.

As such science matures, there will be problems aplenty, practical and theoretical. One of the thorniest will be quality-control. I wrote on this a long time ago, in my old book; and some of my gloomiest predictions seem to be coming true. We might ask, if the scientists themselves now have difficulty in maintaining good quality in their research, how can there be any chance of this when all problems are confused and conflicted? Well, I think there is an answer to that, not perfect by any means, but at least providing a mechanism. This is, public debate in all forums including those before a mass TV audience. Our system of trial by jury rests on the ability of ordinary people to see through the skills of advocacy, frequently employed on quite abstract and technical arguments. Without proposing any institutional forms at this point. I can imagine how an enrichment of the mechanisms for criticism (which, as Sir Karl Popper saw, is the lifeblood of science) could provide a means of ensuring quality-control in this new sort of science, appropriate to the problems of Gaia.

When it is appreciated all around that a Gaia-problem, either on a large or a small scale, is simply of a different type from that of atomised traditional science, then appropriate techniques will develop naturally. With them will come appropriate conceptions of the objects of enquiry of the sciences. Thus concepts such as integration and complex functionality will emerge from the backroom where biologists have entertained them somewhat shamefacedly, and be recognised as appropriate for Gaia just as much as consciousness is for humans. We may have a very exciting time ahead, in our thinking about what science is for, and is.

Ontology

I cannot resist raising this last philosophical issue, even though it might make some people quite uncomfortable. For 'ontology' is the Greek term for the study of Reality; and with this I might seem to be introducing metaphysics or even religion into a scientific gathering. I should say at the outset that no particular conception of reality is entailed by adherence to the Gaia concept. Clearly, an old-fashioned atomist might have a lot of translating to do, back and forth between his concepts and those of Gaia; but for the human mind few such feats are impossible. At the other end, support of Gaia need not take a person further than acceptance of 'systems' and suchlike as real for the purposes of doing the science. And we all know that when Jim Lovelock chose the name 'Gaia' he was most definitely not implying that the earth is a goddess, or alive, or anything of the sort.

And yet... When we look at the earlier history, perhaps the prehistory, of the scientific conception of the Earth as a great homeostat governed by life-processes, we see what must be called metaphysics. There were some quite amazing people around in Paris in the 1920's, and in their dialogues there could not have been any tight, defensive boundaries around their accepted realities. Vernadsky may have seen the whole thing as a vast harmonious hierarchy of systems; but then Bergson had this *Elan Vital*; and Teilhard de Chardin told explicitly of his experiences of something bigger and more meaningful than any merely perceptual events.

That was all long ago, and now we are all scientists rather than speculators. But, perhaps partly because of the playful name, partly because of the very deep human problems it raises, and also partly because of the approach to science that it fosters, Gaia is likely to make its contribution to the enrichment of realities that we are already experiencing. This is happening mainly on the medical side. When we know that ageing is a disease, and car-accidents are an epidemic, heroic bacteriology is no longer the most effective paradigm for health problems. Also, when so many people are helped by acupuncture and allied techniques, it is hard to continue to say that 'chi' energy is an Oriental superstition. What is to be done with the mind-body interaction, revealed in many manifestations from placebo effect through psychogenic disease and the practical success of healing therapies, is an exciting topic.

When I think of these enriched, perhaps nesting realities from the crudest mechanism out to the visionary, I cannot help recalling that marvellous scientific satire of Victorian England, *Flatland*. There the realities were of dimensions; and the protagonist, a Square, was taken on a journey to see the busy Linelander and also the self-satisfied Pointlander. His education was in a third dimension, which (to his cost) he found impossible to communicate to his countryman; and I must not tell you of the denouement where awareness was shown to have its limits however high you go. We, with Gaia, can look down upon the old-fashioned mechanist; but who is looking down on us?

I cannot make any prediction as to how Gaia will affect our perceived, accepted and in a sense socially constructed realities. But science works in many ways; we know how it was the moon-race, that essentially pointless extravaganza, that gave humanity its first effective vision of Gaia, blue, delicate and alone, What sorts of perceptions and experiences will come now, is beyond my powers or interest to foresee. But once we have Gaia, it is difficult to keep the lines tightly drawn. I have in mind a metaphor that even Jim Lovelock used, namely that Gaia can be 'sick'. Now I am sure that such an anthropomorphism can be translated back down into terms of stabilities, responses to shocks, and suchlike. But the term 'sick' is now in play, along with 'Gaia' herself. If we, so long accustomed to thinking of ourselves as the crown of creation, the only reality that really counts, come to see ourselves as guests of Gaia, and moreover bad guests who have been making our hostess sick, well then our reality will be that bit different, and the challenge of Gaia will have moved on another step.

DISCUSSION

Karl Wagner   My problem is that I find it hard to equate our 1½ days of discussion on Gaia with the real ecological crises facing the world. The system we are confronting is not controlled by insight into the workings of the planet, such as we are obtaining here, it is rather controlled by insight into financial markets.

Jerry Ravetz   Here we have another manifestation of the problem of evil. There's all our intelligence, not only of us in this room, but also for example those working in the World Bank. Yet the World Bank and others are continuing to destroy our habitat and enforcing policies that drive Gaia towards a flip. A particular problem is that we really do not know which of the environmental problems facing us are the most serious from a gaian point of view, for instance Jim Lovelock told us the other day that the ozone hole was probably not so salient in this respect. However there is this enormous gap in our understanding; hence we are partly ignorant about what might be done and very ignorant about how to make it done. It is as if we have no time at all and yet we need more time: these are crushing contradictions that afflict every one of us.

Carl Amery   I think there is still a lot to be learned about decision-making. In this respect the old adage, 'the road to hell is paved with good intentions' is particularly apt insofar as it suggests that we are thinking of trying to improve ourselves, but that we don't have the moral strength to do so. In fact, 90 per cent of the misery of mankind is caused by good intentions and with that in mind we must revise the process of decision-making. Think of the immense effort that has gone into trying to curb the nuclear deterrent business and what do we have now, just 3 per cent of the destructive power of the weapons is to be abolished. It's not that we make the wrong decisions but that we make them at the wrong time.

Ulrich Loening   You have discussed the inadequacy of our science, yet look at the present way in which we actually know perfectly well the answer to the acid rain problems and yet our scientific community is demanding absolute proof. They want proof of guilt but I would say if you put a reactive gas into the atmosphere ten times the concentration put in by Gaia we have to take the simpler scientific approach which assumes guilt unless proved innocent. We actually know the answers but we don't act and that is another dimension to the question.

James Lovelock   May I make a comment on that because it is wrong scientifically. It is more than probable that at least half the acid rain falling on Norway and Sweden is coming from the North Sea by gaian processes which are being over-stimulated by agricultural procedures in Europe and is nothing to do with power stations in Britain. For some peculiar political reason this country is always singled out as the sole source of acid rain in Europe but anybody who has been to Eastern Europe will know that the density of smog and acid that is waffling around there makes this place look clean by comparison. Therefore when the scientists say they don't know they really don't know.

142

Ulrich Loening   If you do something with chemically reactive substances, and let it include agriculture, on a scale which is planetary the first assumption you have to make is that it will affect Gaia. How it will affect Gaia is quite another matter, on this I think we would agree.

Jerry Ravetz   Here we have an example of the way in which a robust and fruitful hypothesis can become very important in debate and discussion. I am thinking for example of when there was a big debate over lead in petrol with big arguments over the methodology of the experiments as well as of the surveys which indicated that children suffered from even low levels of lead. I had a friend at Leeds who was very cautious about the whole thing, until one day he said "well it seems to me that they all agree that we are on the three times less than what seems to be a danger level. I think a factor of three isn't enough". A factor of three isn't enough because next year it may come down. Here we have asserted a principle that if a reactive substance is pumped into Gaia over a fairly large area, perhaps globally, at a much higher concentration than Gaia has, one can assume without being a gaian mystic but simply through knowing about cycles, that things will happen downstream. In that way if Gaia is accepted as a hypothesis we can avoid an artificially high criterion of proof because then you have a general principle.

Wolfgang Sachs   It is important that we do not get too complacent about the Gaia hypothesis. For instance David Abram was praising Gaia as an alternative to mechanical philosophy. Now I am not so sure about that. I see for instance, that Gaia very much deepens a basic approach of mechanical philosophy which is to make a clear distinction between appearances and reality. This brings me to the consideration that maybe Gaia increases our knowledge about let's say our vulnerability but at the same time it increases the accessibility of planetary processes to management.

Jerry Ravetz   I would say that knowledge and ignorance are related in many ways and the easy way to see it is through what we can call criteria of proof or criteria of acceptable demonstration. These criteria do not come from nature; instead they are socially developed and sometimes socially imposed. Thus, if you are in a court of law and you want to say such and such 'caused' this you have one set of criteria and rules of evidence. If you are in a coroners' court you will have another set. If you are in a lab you have another set, or if you are advising a legislator. And always if you say this has not been 'proved' or 'there is no evidence that', then ignorance descends, the thing is washed away and you lose interest. We are then effectively back in ignorance.

   Now your point is that Gaia is still part of the mechanistic world and to answer your last point you need not use Gaia in such a way so as to let the polluters free; you could use Gaia and another set of rules as I have indicated if you have a general principle of not overloading the system. If we are going to use science then we should use science through Gaia. It may be that someone says it is too cold and mechanistic and he may be right, however we will have to take a chance and commit ourselves. It can't prove itself.

143

Nicholas Guppy   A point that appears to have been skirted over is that the science we have is actually a product of the society in which we live and our society as Teddy and others have pointed out is a pioneering society the aims of which are to conquer, to consume and to control. Gaia could easily become just one of those mechanisms which we exploit to serve us. I think that it is vital that we should set out to show the different interworkings of Gaia but we also need to look at our science and our society.

Jerry Ravetz   I think the Gaia hypothesis will help because it will change the idea of science which will then change the idea of knowing. Changing the ideas of the good life and of the nature of humanity may come through Gaia to some extent; but here we are talking about a transformation of consciousness.

Roswitha Hentschel   If we try to control the environment we run into a problem because there is always a time-lag - the ecosystem reacts after a time delay - so that by the time we measure it in many instances we may be too late. We must try to understand the whole system not only to rely on measurements and control we should also develop more awareness and feeling. There is a lack in our civilization of emotional participation in the system.

Jerry Ravetz   I believe the Gaia hypothesis opens the way for a more synthetic and holistic view of the world and through the Gaia hypothesis we can begin to integrate our senses in our own perceptual experience in ways that have not been possible with previous science.

GAIA: SOME IMPLICATIONS FOR THEORETICAL ECOLOGY
by Edward Goldsmith

If we accept the Gaia Hypothesis, then modern reductionistic and mechanistic ecology, as taught in our universities, can no longer be defended. A "New Ecology" is needed; rather than simply return to the "holistic" ecology of Clements and Shelford, however, a more sophisticated ecology must be developed to take account of the work of such thinkers as C.H.Waddington, Paul Weiss, Ludwig Von Bertalanffy and others.

Ecology, as an academic discipline, was developed towards the end of the last century. It came into being largely when a few biologists came to realize that the biological organisms and populations which they studied were not arranged at random but were, on the contrary, organised to form "communities" or "associations" whose structure and function could not be understood by examining their parts in isolation from each other. Both Frederick Clements and Victor Shelford, two of the most distinguished of the early ecologists in the USA, defined ecology as the "science of communities" (Clements/Shelford, 1930).

In the 1930s, the Oxford ecologist Arthur Tansley coined the term "ecosystem", which he defined as a community taken together with its abiotic environment, much as Jim Lovelock sees "Gaia" as the biosphere taken together with its abiotic environment.

It is probable that if Clements or Shelford were alive today they would see ecology as the "science of ecosystems". Eugene Odum, one of the most prestigious ecologists alive today (and also one of the few remaining "holistic" ecologists) defines ecology as "the structure and function of nature" (Odum, 1953). Since he is one of the few modern ecologists to have taken the Gaia thesis seriously, I recently asked him if he would agree to seeing ecology defined as "the structure and function of Gaia" – the overall ecosystem – into which nature is organized. He fully agreed that this was a very acceptable definition.

Ecology, seen in this light, would be indistinguishable from Jim Lovelock's geophysiology. It would of necessity be inter-disciplinary. This was clear to the early ecologists who saw ecology as an all embracing super-science. Barrington Moore, for instance, the first President of the American Ecological Society, saw ecology as "the science of synthesis", and as being "superimposed on the other sciences." "Will we be content" he asked his colleagues, in his address to the St. Louis branch of the society in 1919, "to remain zoologists, botanists, and foresters, with little understanding of one another's problems, or will we endeavour to become ecologists in the broad sense of the term? The part we play in science depends upon our reply. Gentlemen" he warned, "the future is in our hands" (Barrington Moore, 1917).

Ideally, of course, ecology taken in that holistic sense of the term, would be non-disciplinary, rather than inter-disciplinary, since the disciplines into which knowledge has been divided have developed in such total isolation that they are difficult to reconcile with each other, still more difficult to merge into an ecological

145

superscience. What is certain is that ecology, if it is really to explain the structure and function of Gaia, should take into account a whole body of material that was not available to the early ecologists and that has been ignored by modern ones. This would include the Gaia thesis itself; the work of Lynn Margulis on symbiosis, which even the latest ecological literature on cooperation or mutualism in ecology does not mention; and the equally relevant and highly holistic writings of A. N. Whitehead, C. H. Waddington, J. H. Woodger and other members of the Theoretical Biology Club that flourished in the 1940s.

J. H. Woodger, for instance, clearly saw that nature was one. He saw, too, that its functioning could not be understood in terms of a set of separate compartmentalized disciplines, and clearly stated that what was needed was "a most general science, not immersed in a particular subject matter, but dealing with the relationship between various special sciences and trying to synthesize their most general results" (Woodger, 1929).

The similarity between this view and that expressed by Barrington Moore is very striking. Indeed Woodger's *Biological Principles,* now totally overlooked by ecologists, is an important ecological work which we cannot afford to ignore. The writings of other holistic thinkers such as the Cambridge ethologist W. H. Thorpe, the Swiss psychologist and biologist Jean Piaget and the US cytologist and embryologist Paul Weiss, are also of the greatest ecological value.

Equally relevant is the general systems theory of Ludwig von Bertalanffy of which a variant was developed independently at about the same time by Ross Ashby. General systems, which must not be confounded with systems ecology, an essentially mechanistic and reductionistic discipline, provided an indispensable tool for the development of a unified science - what one might call "real ecology" - but is equally ignored by modern ecologists. I shall refer to this again later.

The Perversion of Ecology

However, real ecology is not the order of the day. If modern ecologists take no account of Jim Lovelock's Gaia thesis, of Lynn Margulis' work on symbiosis, or the writings of Whitehead, Woodger, Waddington, Piaget or of Von Bertalanffy's general systems theory, it is because ecology is no longer a "science of communities" nor a "science of ecosystems", let alone a science concerned with "the structure and function of Gaia." As Donald Worster shows in his most illuminating book *Nature's Economy*, (Worster, 1977), Odum is today on his own. Worster documents the extraordinary transformation that ecology has undergone in the last 40 years to make it conform more closely to the paradigm of reductionistic and mechanistic science - and thus to conform with the paradigm of modernism which serves to rationalize and hence legitimize our aberrant and necessarily short-lived modern industrial society. Significantly, a closely parallel transformation has taken place in comparative psychology, genetics, evolutionary theory, anthropology and sociology.

146

Other students of the history of ecological ideas have also noted this transformation. Daniel Simberloff, for instance, tells us:

"Ecology has undergone, about half a century later than genetics and evolution, a transformation so strikingly similar in both outline and detail that one can scarcely doubt its debt to the same materialistic and probabilistic revolution. An initial emphasis on a similarity of isolated communities replaced by concern about their differences: the examination of groups of populations largely superseded by the study of individual populations; belief in deterministic succession shifting with the widespread introduction of statistics into ecology, to realization that temporal community development is probabilistic: and a continuing struggle to focus on material, observable entities rather than ideal constructs" (Simberloff).

As a result of this transformation, virtually all the established principles of the old ecology have been abandoned. Thus the whole is no longer seen as being more than the sum of its parts and is therefore studied by examining the parts themselves in isolation from each other; competition has replaced co-operation as the ordering principle in nature; diversity no longer favours stability; ecological succession no longer leads to a stable climax; and the mere mention of the term "Balance of Nature" elicits from our academic ecologists a condescending smirk if not a belly laugh.

Ecology has in fact been perverted, perverted in the interests of making it acceptable to the scientific establishment and to the politicians and industrialists who sponsor it. In a way, this is understandable. Were it otherwise, as Worster admits, "ecologists might have disappeared as an independent class of researchers and would not occupy today such an influential position among the sciences." That said, however, it is by no means clear that ecologists do in fact exert such influence. Indeed, it is unlikely that those ecologists who view the biosphere in purely reductionistic and mechanistic terms can understand the implications of the devastation being wrought by the modern industrial system, and hence that they can understand what action is required to bring this devastation to an end. This partly at least explains the negligible role played in Britain by the British Ecological Society in awakening scientists, politicians and the general public to the present world ecological crisis which threatens the very survival of man on this planet.

The answer to the question "What are the implications of the Gaia thesis for ecology?" must thereby depend on which ecology we refer to. Clearly the Gaia thesis cannot in any way be reconciled with the ecology that is taught in our universities today. If the thesis were to be accepted, and today's academic ecologists were to face its implications, then conventional ecology would have to be transformed into a more sophisticated version of the old ecology of Clements, Shelford and Barrington Moore, which today's ecologists have been at pains, over the last fifty years, to discredit. For that reason, I agree with Lynn Margulis and Dorion Sagan that "the Gaia hypothesis ....is likely to provide the foundations for a new ecology " (Sagan/Margulis, 1983).

The Pioneer and the Climax World Views

The reductionist and mechanistic ecology of today and the holistic ecology that the Gaia thesis will help us create reflect two diametrically opposed world views. For the purposes of this paper, I shall refer to the former as "the pioneer world-view" and to the latter as "the climax world-view". Let me explain why. A pioneer ecosystem, that is to say an ecosystem in the earliest stages of development, or one that has been ravaged by some discontinuity such as a volcanic eruption or an industrial development scheme, displays a whole constellation of closely related features. In a sense, such an ecosystem is the least "living" of ecosystems or, more precisely, the one in which the basic features of living things are least apparent, for the obvious reason that they have not yet had time to develop. Such an ecosystem is among other things highly productive, which of course endears it to our modern production-oriented society that can cream off the apparently surplus biomass, process it, and put it up for sale on the international market. The reason why it is so highly productive, of course, is because as soon as it is brought into being, so the healing processes of nature are brought into operation and the ecosystem changes rapidly via the different stages of ecological succession until it achieves that state which resembles, as closely as possible, the original climax.

The climax or adult ecosystem, on the other hand, is very unproductive. This must be so both because the climax is the most stable state possible in the local biotic, abiotic and climatic circumstances, and because the achievement of such a stable state appears to be the basic goal of living things. Once achieved, change is kept to a minimum.

The pioneer stage has other essential features that are all closely associated with each other, so much so that to display one of them means displaying the others too. For instance, there is little diversity and little organisation in such an ecosystem, and, as a result, its constituent parts appear to be arranged in a disorderly or random manner.

This being so pioneering ecosystems appear individualistic and their behaviour seems to be explicable by studying them reductionistically on their own. They are also competitive since they are subject neither to the constraints which might be applied on them by the larger whole, of which they are part, nor to self-imposed internal constraints. Instead, only external constraints (competition, predation, "management" etc) operate. Such controls are crude and inefficient; as a result, the life of these ecosystems is punctuated by large and often unpredictable discontinuities which they cannot accommodate without undergoing serious structural changes (population collapses, for instance). In other words they are highly unstable.

Randomness, individualism, competition, crude external controls and instability are indeed the inevitable features of a pioneer ecosystem; they are the features too of a world in which the basic features of living things are still embryonic. They are also the features of the degraded society of which we are part and of the degraded environment in which we live today, both states being the inevitable result of the process of industrial development which we are misguidedly taught to identify with "progress". They are, in fact, the features of what Eugene Odum refers to as a "disclimax" (Odum, Science).

The features of a climax ecosystem, on the other hand, are totally different, indeed diametrically opposed. A climax ecosystem is orderly and its behaviour goal-directed or teleological. Individuals are integrated into larger wholes at different levels of organisation - the family, the small community and the larger society, levels which themselves are part of the hierarchy of the biosphere. For such wholes or systems to exist implies that their parts cooperate with each other. They also possess highly sophisticated internal control mechanisms which enable them to reduce environmental discontinuities either by bringing about the appropriate changes to their environment (changes, which among other things, must serve to insulate them from the rigours of their external environment) or, alternatively, by increasing their ability to deal with such discontinuities. Both such strategies serve to assure the preservation of their basic structure in the face of change and hence, correspondingly, to increase their stability. Such systems are thereby homeostatic, and their fate is no longer dependent on the crude interplay of external forces.

Order, teleology, wholeness, cooperation, stability, and internalised control are the inevitable features of a climax ecosystem as they are of all complex living things. They are also the features of a climax society - that is, a society culturally designed to flourish as part of a climax ecosystem. The only society that fits this description is a tribal society.

If Jim Lovelock's Gaia thesis has caused a major stir in scientific circles, it is largely because it implies a major shift from the pioneer world-view to the climax world-view. In this paper, I would like to show just how it has affected some of the main features of the former world-view as it is reflected in modern ecology. I would also like to carry the argument a stage further to see how the Gaia thesis itself would be affected by what ecology should be - a "Gaian ecology", we might call it, one that takes the climax rather than the pioneer state to be the norm.

Holism

Science is still reductionistic of analytical. Underlying it is the metaphysical assumption that the smaller the particles the more concrete and real they must be. W. H. Thorpe defines reductionism as:

> "the attribution of reality exclusively to the smallest constituents of the world and the tendency to interpret higher levels of organization in terms of lower levels" (Thorpe, 1965).

Atoms are considered particularly real today; however, with the great vogue enjoyed by molecular biology, molecules have also acquired "realness". Francis Crick still insists, for instance, that they are the only reality. In saying this, he and other reductionists are committing what Whitehead called "the fallacy of misplaced concreteness", (Whitehead, 1948), that of abstracting a part and ascribing to it the sort of reality that belongs to the whole.

Science also assumes that for knowledge to be "exact" and "mature", it must be formulated in quantitative terms. This can be done where the subject matter is physics, hence the tendency to seek to understand biology, ecology and even sociology in physical terms. However, as Pantin notes, physics has been able "to become exact and mature just because so much of the whole of natural phenomena is excluded from this study" (Pantin, 1968).

The physicist, by reason of his training, cannot avoid leaving out "so much of the whole of natural phenomena", but then as Paul Weiss argues "there is no reason for us to downgrade nature to meet his inadequacy" (Weiss, 1970).

One of the failings of the reductionist world-view is that it sees the world as dead, machine-like, passive and crude. Indeed, as Von Bertalanffy notes, it makes no differentiation "between physical and chemical processes taking place in a living organism and those in a corpse; both follow the same laws of physics and chemistry" (von Bertalanffy, 1960). He goes on to note: "Concepts like those of organization, wholeness, directiveness, teleology, control, self-regulation, differentiation and the like are alien to conventional physics" yet they are "indispensable for dealing with living organisms or social groups."

The Gaia thesis is holistic - holistic in the extreme. Jim Lovelock notes how "most of us were taught that the composition of our planet could adequately be described by the laws of physics and chemistry" (Lovelock, 1979). He refers to this as "a good solid Victorian view", but it is wrong. Gaia can only be understood in terms of the structure and function of living things. This is one of the most important messages of the Gaia thesis. Lovelock's argument is still more holistic when he tells us:

> "The entire range of living matter on earth, from whales to viruses and from oaks to algae, could be regarded as constituting a single living entity, capable of manipulating the earth's atmosphere to suit its overall needs and endowed with faculties and powers far beyond those of its constituent parts" (Lovelock, 1979).

This clearly means that the behaviour of Gaia cannot be understood by examining its parts in isolation from each other which must follow if Gaia is an organisation and therefore more than the sum of its parts.

Lovelock even compares Gaia to a biological organism, in that, like an organism, it is a cybernetic system geared to the maintenance of its stability or homeostasis. This thesis would have been acceptable to the early ecologists who regarded an ecological community as very similar to an organism. Thus A. S. Forbes stated in 1896 that "a group or association of animals is like an organism" (Forbes, 1887). C. C. Adams, in the first American book on animal ecology, published in 1913, insisted that:

> "the interactions among the members of an association are to be compared to the similar relations existing between the different cells, organs or activities of a single individual..."

Thienemann went further. He saw the living things that made up a lake community, for instance, as "a unity so closed in itself that it must be called an organism of the highest order" (Thienemann, 1918).

Frederick Clement in his book, Plant Succession, published in 1916, tells us that:

> "The unit of vegetation, the climax formation is an organic entity. As an organism, the formation arises, grows, matures and dies. Its response to the habitat is shown in processes or functions and in structures which are the record as well as the result of these functions."

In fact, this view of the ecological community as a "supra-organism" became so well established that Simberloff refers to it as "Ecology's first paradigm."

As Bodenheimer noted at the time that the highly integrated supra-organismic concept of the community was stressed in nearly every textbook of ecology and, "backed by established authority", is generally regarded "if not as a fact, then at least as a scientific hypothesis not less firmly founded than the theory of transformation" (that is, of evolution). "It is above all the concept", he wrote, "that distinguishes ecology from biology proper " (Bodenheimer).

With the transformation of ecology, which I have already referred to, this view was slowly abandoned in favour of one that better conformed with the reductionistic paradigm of science and, hence, with the paradigm of modernism which it serves to rationalize. The resulting reductionistic approach to ecology - which sounds like a contradiction in terms - is normally traced to the writings of H. A. Gleason, whose famous article "The individualistic Concept of the Plant Association", was first published in 1926 and presented and discussed at the International Botanical Congress that year.

Significantly, Gleason used the usual reductionistic argument I have described above. He regarded the association or community as an abstract entity that only existed in the eyes of the beholder, for only the individual was real. The same argument one might add is still used by Neo-Darwinists today to justify their preoccupation with selection at the level of the individual, and their refusal to see evolution as a process occurring at the level of the "unreal" ecosystem or let alone of a still more "unreal" Gaia.

Initially Gleason's thesis was very badly received. In the words of McIntosh, a noted historian of ecological thought, Gleason was "anathema to ecologists" (McKintosh/Gleason, 1975). Gleason himself admitted that for ten years after the publication of his article, he was "an ecological outlaw" (Gleason, 1926). His thesis simply did not fit in with the ecological paradigm of the times. However, as the latter was transformed so as to make it conform with the paradigm of science, so Gleason's ideas became increasingly acceptable.

In the 1930s, Arthur Tansley, whom I have already referred to, and who had originally adopted a firm holistic position, abandoned it in favour of a highly reductionistic one. He denied the basic holistic principle that the whole is more than the sum of its parts and hence that it is not amenable to study by the reductionist method of science. "These 'wholes'", he wrote, "are in analysis nothing but the synthesized actions of the components in associations" (Tansley, 1920). A mature science, in his view, "must isolate the basic units of nature" and must "split up the story" into its individual parts. "It must approach nature as a composite of strictly physical entities organised into a mechanical system. The scientist who knows all the properties of all the parts studied separately can accurately predict their combined results" (ibid).

If this were so, then the very term "community" was superfluous, and he sought to eliminate it from the scientific vocabulary. He denied too that there was anything in common between human associations (which he presumably regarded as legitimate communities) and those to be found among non-human plants and animals. The latter were not "linked by psychic bonds", (ibid), and, hence, for a reason that is not altogether clear, were not true communities.

Today, reductionistic ecology is firmly established. Collier and his colleagues go so far as to insist that the individualistic concept "constitutes one of the most influential and widely accepted views at the present time" (Collier in Boucher, 1986). McIntosh refers to reductionistic ecology as "a viable and expanding tenet of current ecological thought", (McKintosh,) while, Colinvaux, in a well known textbook of ecology, describes the holistic view of the community as a "heresy" (Colinvaux, 1973).

Other modern ecologists go still further and actually claim that their work has provided incontestable proof of the validity of Gleason's philosophy. Curtis, for instance, tells us that "the entire evidence of his plant ecology study in Wisconsin can be taken as conclusive proof of Gleason's individualistic hypothesis of community organisation..." (Curtis, 1959), while Whittaker regards this "gradient analysis" as providing similar evidence (Whittaker).

This sort of nonsense will become more and more difficult to sustain as Lynn Margulis's work on symbiosis becomes increasingly accepted, and as the new holistic ecology develops.

I say "new" because the holistic ecology of the past had major shortcomings. Among other things it never explained the relationship between the whole and the parts, let alone that between the parts and the whole. It never in fact really explained how living things were organised.

The Organisation of Gaia

One reason is that organisation cannot be explained in reductionistic terms, since to admit that there is such a thing implies that systems are more than the sum of their component parts. Organisation is also difficult to quantify. There have indeed been efforts to do so - by Dancoff and Quastler, for instance - but the type of organisation they are measuring, calculated in terms of Shannon and Weaver's reductionistic and mechanistic concept of information, bears no relationship whatsoever to the biospheric organisation with which we are concerned.

To understand this organisation, we must start off by regarding the biosphere as made up of natural systems, operating at different levels of organisation. Natural systems must not be confounded with the systems studied by engineers. They are above all living systems which display all the features of living things already referred to.

It is true that many of the definitions of natural systems are vague and could be made to include the engineer's systems, but this was not the intention of Von Bertalanffy, still less of Paul Weiss who defined a system "as a complex unit in space and in time whose sub-units cooperate to preserve its integrity and its structure and its behaviour and tend to restore them after a non-destructive disturbance" (Weiss, 1970). Weiss's definition is a valuable one since it accentuates the essential aspects of living things such as their complexity, the cooperation between their parts, their tendency towards overall stability, and their ability to restore their basic features in the face of a disturbance - in other words, their capacity for homeostasis.

Lovelock defines Gaia, the all encompassing natural system, in very similar terms as:

> "A complex entity involving the earth's biosphere, atmosphere, oceans, and soil; the total constituting a feedback or cybernetic system which seeks an optimal physical and chemical environment for life on this planet" (Lovelock, 1979).

There is every reason to suppose that this provides an equally good description of such natural systems as molecules, cells, organisms, stable (tribal) communities and ecosystems. The behaviour of all such systems, in fact, can be shown, at a certain level of generality, to display the same fundamental features, which would suggest that they are all subject to the same basic constraints and are thereby governed by the same laws. If this is so, then it is clear how General Systems Theory provides a means of unifying science.

Hierarchy

Natural systems, however, are not arranged in a random way. They form a hierarchy. This means that each system is at once part of a larger system and at the same time made up of smaller ones. Paul Weiss notes how this is true of the cell, the main object of his studies. The cell must be seen:

> "In a double light: partly as an active worker and partly as a passive subordinate to powers which lie entirely outside of its own competence and control i.e. supra-cellular powers" (Weiss, 1970).

Arthur Koestler tried to show how this principle applied to all natural systems or "holons" as he called them. He took the double-faced Roman God Janus, one of whose faces looks outwards and the other inwards, as a symbol of the holon, with its two roles within the hierarchy of the biosphere. Unfortunately, the whole subject of hierarchy is one that has been largely ignored by ecologists and scientists in general. To my knowledge, only two conferences have been held on the subject (one organised by Lancelot Law-Whyte and the other by Howard Pattee) and neither was very enlightening, the participants tending to use the term hierarchy very loosely to mean very diffcrent things.

Once again Eugene Odum seems to be about the only ecologist today to display an interest in hierarchy. He sees ecology as largely concerned with the upper end of the hierarchy of the biosphere, that is "the system levels beyond that of the organism" (Odum, 1953).

To understand the structure and function of Gaia means studying the hierarchy as a whole, which in turn means understanding the two roles of Janus, its relationship to the larger systems of which it is a part and its relationship to the smaller systems that in turn compose it. The former relationship is taboo an ong ecologists today as it is among mainstream scientists in general. Indeed, if, as most scientists seem to, we were to accept the perfectly preposterous thesis of the selfish gene, then we would also have to accept that living things show no concern whatsoever with the survival of the larger systems of which they are part no more in fact than do the inhabitants of a modern disintegrated non-society of today. Those who do are seen as displaying "altruism", which apparently occurs when, on the basis of a cost-benefit analysis, they see cooperation as more likely to favour the proliferation of their genes than the usual much more rational competition and aggression. This may indeed be so in a disintegrated or neo-pioneer society and, in a pioneer ecosystem; it is not so, however, in a climax society, nor in a climax ecosystem whose members can only behave in that way which satisfies the requirements of the hierarchy of the larger systems of which they are part. As Von Bertalanffy writes:

> "... an enormous preponderance of vital processes and mechanisms have a whole-maintaining character; were this not so the organism could not exist at all....." (Von Bertalanffy, 1933).

Ungerer, according to Von Bertalanffy, was so impressed with the "whole-maintaining function" of life processes that he replaced the biological "consideration of purpose" with that of the "consideration of wholeness", (Ungerer, in Von Bertalanffy, 1933), a notion that is considerably reinforced by the Gaia thesis.

The main feature of Janus's relationship with its parts must be one of control. Whitman notes how the organism controls the action of the cells, during development:

> "Comparative embryology reminds us at every turn that the organism dominates cell formation, using for the same purpose one, several or many cells, massing its material and directing its movements and shaping its organs, as if cells did not exist" (Whitman in Chaitanya, 1975).

Paul Weiss (1970) points out how one cannot understand the behaviour of cells unless they are seen as the parts of a larger system which has the power to "integrate" and "direct" their behaviour.

This principle is built into the concept of "order", which is generally seen as the influence of the whole over the parts, and hence of their degree of differentiation and interdependence and corresponding limitation of choice.

Pattee regards hierarchical control as "the essential and distinguishing characteristic of life." It must be a feature of all hierarchies and hence of all natural systems (Pattee, 1973).

Weiss points to the various mechanisms that multicellular organisms develop to coordinate and control the activities of their component cells. He refers to:

> "The nervous system, the hormone system, the homeostatic maintenance of the composition of the body fluids; for in principle, each one of these subsystems operates within its own scope by the same rule of integrative dominance that the higher system exercises over its components" (Weiss, 1970).

Functionally, similar methods of hierarchical control are operative at the level of any ecosystem, though Odum is possibly the only one of today's ecologists to have pointed this out. In a sense, the "wholeness maintaining" behaviour of the parts and the control exerted over the parts by the whole - in other words, the two different

154

roles of Janus - are but different ways of looking at the same phenomenon. Indeed, one can formulate a law that must apply to all natural systems within the hierarchy of the biosphere, to the effect that behaviour that "serves" the interests of the whole must at the same time "serve" the interests of the differentiated parts. If this were not so then there could be no viable whole. I refer to this as the "law of hierarchical mutualism". Let us look at this thesis more closely.

Hierarchical Mutualism

That the behaviour of the parts must serve the interests of the whole is clear from another consideration. Jim Lovelock sees Gaia as creating the environment that it requires to maintain its stability. If we accept General Systems Theory, then one must accept that natural systems, at other levels of organisation, are doing likewise. This means that living systems in general depend for their proper functioning and in particular for the maintenance of their stability on the preservation of their specific external environment.

The term "environment" has never been properly defined. It is used by ecologists in the vaguest possible way to mean little more than "all that is out there". This is also true of Neo-Darwinists, even though they attribute to the environment the capacity for natural selection, a process which is both highly discriminatory and highly teleological.

In reality, "what is out there", from the point of a natural system within the hierarchy of the biosphere, is nothing more than the larger system of which it is a differentiated part, without which it has no raison d'etre and cannot survive. For this reason, the "whole-maintaining" behaviour on the part of any natural system - that is, the behaviour that satisfies the requirements of the larger system - must also be that which satisfies the requirements of the differentiated subsystem. (I say "differentiated", as this would not be true of random parts or parts that are not integrated into the hierarchy of the biosphere). It is in this language, I feel, that one must translate the literature on the subject of morphogenetic fields, a concept introduced in the 1920s (independently, I believe) by Weiss and Gurwitch. Jim Lovelock seems to have little sympathy for this concept. It is nevertheless an essential one, since it accentuates the dependence of natural systems on their respective and highly specific internal and external environments all the way up the hierarchy of the biosphere.

Mutualism

If Gaia is a single natural system capable of maintaining its homeostasis, then its parts must cooperate with each other. Lovelock makes this point very clearly. In other words, the most fundamental relationship between the constituents of the biosphere must be one of mutualism. This was also the view of the early academic ecologists. Indeed, at the turn of the century literally hundreds of papers were published in ecological journals and texts on the subject of mutualism.

Roscoe Pound, an American naturalist, for instance, described, in a celebrated article, all the various forms of mutualism that were known to occur in ecosystems, including pollination and the fixation of nitrogen by bacteria living on the root-nodules of plants. Mutualism in ecosystems was even compared to that occurring in other natural systems such as biological organisms - something which no academic ecologist would dare do today.

The Chicago school of ecology which flourished in the 1940s also saw mutualism as the principal relationship among living things. One of its leading figures, Warder C. Allee, regarded "an automatic mutual interdependence" as a "fundamental trait of living matter" (Allee, 1932). Then came the great ecological transformation already alluded to, and competition became the order of the day, to be viewed by ecologists and theoretical biologists alike as no less than the fundamental ordering principle in nature - as it still is today.

What is extraordinary is the lack of evidence for this thesis. As Peter Price notes in the *New Ecology*, "the body of theory is vast"; however, "little has been tested objectively" (Price et al, 1984).

Connell is particularly outspoken on the subject. Having reviewed the literature, he was only able to find a single study involving serious experimental work designed to determine if competition played a significant role in the interaction between species.

It is not an exaggeration to say, as does Price, that "competition theory lives in a dreamworld where everything can be explained, but the validity of these explanations has not been adequately established in the real world" (Price et al, 1984).

Incredible as it may seem, it is only today that the dogma of competition is being critically examined. To quote Price again:

"....only after fifty years of building an edifice to competition is serious doubt being cast on the evidence for its foundations."

Worse still, the term "competition" has never even been properly defined. Merrell, in his *Ecological Genetics*, provides a veritable catalogue of the different ways in which the term is used. There is no point listing them heré, but his summing up is nevertheless worth quoting:

"Some definitions apply only to animals, others to all organisms - plants as well as animals; some definitions refer only to interspecific competition, others to both intraspecific and interspecific competition; for competition to occur, resources must be in short supply in some definitions but not in others; sometimes the definition is so broad that it does not exclude predator-prey relations, but in others the same trophic level is specified. Given these differences of opinion, it may be hazardous (not to mention presumptuous) to attempt to reach some workable definition of competition" (Merrrel, 1981).

Nor are the various applications of the "competitive principle" to ecology any better defined. The competitive exclusion principle for instance, as Merrell also shows, has been formulated by different ecologists in literally dozens of different ways.

In the meantime, so long as competition was the order of the day, co-operation and hence mutualism ceased to be of any interest to ecologists. Vandermere and Boucher, for instance, point out:

> "Although some of the most spectacular interspecific interactions in nature are obviously mutualistic, relatively little research, empirical or theoretical, has been aimed at understanding this basic and perhaps prevalent form of interaction" (Vandermere/Boucher, 1978).

So too, Risch and Boucher illustrate the extent to which mutualism has been ignored by modern ecologists:

> "A survey of 12 ecology texts published within the last five years clearly substantiates the claim that practically the entire discussion of organismic interactions has centred on predation and competition. Of a total of 718 pages devoted to interspecific interactions in these texts, 321 pages concern predator-prey interactions, 362 pages concern interspecific competitive interactions, and only 35 pages discuss any kind of mutualistic relationship. In addition to the disproportionate amount of space devoted to the different interactions, predation and competition are presented as important organizing principles, while examples of mutualism (such as ... cleaning symbioses) are presented as interesting but eccentric exceptions to the general rule."

In the early 1970s, however, there was a sudden resurgence of interest in mutualism. It seemed to manifest itself independently in the work of ecologists at different universities, who were often unaware of each others work.

Well known ecologists, who had down-played the importance of mutualism, suddenly changed their mind about it. Thus Robert May, in 1973, stated that the importance of mutualism "in populations in general is small" (May, 1973). However, "in only a few years" to quote Boucher, "May's appreciation of mutualism changed considerably". He suddenly announced that mutualism was now seen as "a conspicuous and ecologically important factor in most tropical communities" (Boucher, 1986). Indeed, in recent years May has become one of the leaders in encouraging work on mutualism which he sees as "likely to be one of the growth industries of the 1980s" (Boucher, 1986).

Today's ecologists, for instance, have started looking at the role played by micro-organisms in the metabolism of complex organisms. Boucher, James and Keller, for instance, noted that gut flora are involved in breaking down cellulose and related substances in mutualism with many vertebrates, as well as with termites and other arthropods. Urea is broken down and its nitrogen recycled by rumen bacteria and by the fungal components of some lichens. Toxic secondary plant compounds are also degraded in caeca and rumens by microbial symbionts.

Ecologists have also noted the increasing numbers of parastic or predatory relationships which, on closer examination, turn out to be mutualistic. Thus McNaughton has pointed out that the normal view of the relationship between grazers and the grass they graze is false:

"Ecologists have tended to view plants as relatively passive participants in short-term interactions at the plant-herbivore interface, suffering tissue reduction from herbivory, and responding in evolutionary time through the evolution of novel antiherbivore chemicals and structures" (McNaughton, 1979).

It now seems clear that plants are capable of reacting in a much more dynamic manner to grazing and indeed are capable of "compensatory growth and assimilate reallocation." All in all, McNaughton found nine different ways in which the relationship between grazing animals and the grass on which they graze can be regarded as mutualistic.

Does this then mean, Boucher asks, that mutualism is "destined to be part of a new synthesis, in which Newtonian ecology is replaced by a more organicist, integrated, value-laden view of the natural world?" He is not too optimistic on this score. The reason is that "our present theories of mutualism are still basically mechanistic, mathematical, fitness-maximising and individualistic" (Boucher, 1986).

Unfortunately this is only too true. D. H. Janzen considers that "Mutualisms are the most omnipresent of any organism-to-organism interaction" (Janzen, in Boucher 1986). However, he insists "natural systems larger than the individual cannot be mutualistic" (ibid). The reason is that:

"A mutualism is an interaction between individual organisms in which the realized or potential genetic fitness of each participant is raised by the actions of the other. The participants are called mutualists. Since a species has no trait that is analogous to the genetic fitness of an individual mutualism cannot be defined with reference to species" (ibid).

If a species cannot be involved in a mutualistic relationship, nor can inanimate forces nor even seeds:

"By definition, inanimate dispersal of seeds is not a mutualism. Wind and water have no fitness. Explosive capsules are plants that move themselves. Burrs stuck on horses legs do not benefit the horse. Hard red Erythrina seeds swallowed by a fruit pigeon and defecated entire do not benefit the pigeon. The squirrel does not benefit from the acorn that it buries and never recovers. An ant-acacia whose fruits are eaten by a bird that carefully spits out each seed below the parent ant-acacia does not benefit" (ibid).

Boucher considers it inevitable that ecologists should see mutualism in this narrow reductionistic way:

"While arguing that nature is an integrated whole and that everything is connected to everything else, we continued researching with theories that said that communities are no more than sets of individual organisms. The problem, in other words, is one of cognitive dissonance - the difficulty of working with two sets of ecological ideas, based on different fundamental assumptions and ultimately in conflict" (Boucher, 1986).

What is in fact required is a paradigm change. Mutualism must be seen in the light of a climax rather than a pioneer worldview. The Gaia thesis can do a great deal to help bring about such a transformation.

Stability

One of the basic features of the biosphere is its extraordinary stability. This is implied by Stephen J. Gould and other proponents of the theory of punctuated equilibrium who point to the fact that many forms of life have not changed for hundreds of millions of years. This point is also made by Jim Lovelock who notes the great stability of Gaia over the last few thousand million years. Though Darwin may have been the prophet of evolution and hence of change, he was also impressed by the stability of the living world. Thus, he tacitly admitted in a letter to Lyell that he was not wholly happy with the term 'natural selection'. "If I had to commence de novo" he wrote, "I would have used 'natural preservation'" (Darwin, in Worster, 1977).

Preservation must be important, since without it there can be no structure which displays any sort of permanence. If an organism or community or species or ecosystem has an identity at all, it is because of its persistence. Indeed, a development process whose end-product is not preserved at least for a period of time seems to be self-defeating.

As Piaget puts it "une construction sans conservation n'est plus un developpement organique mais un changement quelconque" (Piaget, 1975).

Indeed within the biosphere, change seems to occur not so much because it is desirable *per se* - indeed it would seem that nature tries desperately to avoid it – but because, in certain conditions, it is necessary as a means of reducing the need for other more destructive changes.

If this is so, then we should accept that stability is the overall goal of life. This was the view of Claude Bernard who wrote:

> "All the vital mechanisms, varied as they are, have only one object, that of preserving constant the conditions of life in the internal environment" (Bernard, 1871).

Though the concept of stability is of concern to modern ecologists, its treatment is rather muddled. Holling, whose writings are occasionally referred to by Jim Lovelock, regards a stable ecosystem as one that returns to an equilibrium state after a temporary disturbance and, what is more, "with the least fluctuations" (Holling in Jantsch/Waddington, 1976). He includes in this category living things that have not undergone change for a very long time. These, he does not regard as persistent. He then contrasts stable ecosystems with resilient systems which are characterised by large fluctuations. Those alone, he sees as persistent.

Holling's work has been taken up by Eric Jantsch and Ilya Prigogine, whose theoretical writings, as I have tried to show in my article "Superscience, its Mythology and Legitimization", (Goldsmith, 1981), serve, above all, to provide the mythology required for rationalizing high-technology, and in particular genetic engineering. It involves singing the praises of individualism, competition, aggression, and instability, and hence of discontinuities or fluctuations such as the wars, epidemics, famines, and climate changes which must necessarily characterize our atomised, high-technology, neo-pioneer society. At the same time, cooperation and stability are deprecated - necessarily so, since they are features which in such a society are conspicuous by their absence.

However, Holling's position does not stand up to serious scrutiny. To begin with, no living system returns to an equilibrium state after a disturbance, but rather it moves to a new position that is as close as possible to the original one. The reason is that unlike the behaviour of machines, the behaviour of living things is irreversible. Each experience must affect a living thing in some way, and such effects cannot be eradicated. The fact is that living things change, though some do so more than others, and indeed must do so in the interests of preventing bigger and more destructive changes. For this reason, a stable system is not an immobile one - such a system could not possibly be stable in the face of a changing environment - but one that is capable of maintaining its basic structure and function in the face of change.

In other words, nothing in the real world corresponds to Holling's stable ecosystem. What is more, the closest approximation to such an ecosystem - say a tropical rain forest - cannot, by the wildest stretch of the imagination be regarded as 'non-persisting'. On the contrary, ecosystems that have lasted without major modifications for more than a hundred million years are obviously highly persistent. They may indeed be facing annihilation today, but then they could hardly have "predicted" the occurrence, let alone the scale, of modern logging activities. Natural systems are neither omniscient nor omnipotent - and cannot be expected to deal adaptively with phenomena that have never occurred during their hundred million years of experience.

It is certainly true that a climax ecosystem has committed itself to an environment of a specific type, which means that it can only survive if the main features of that environment are maintained. This must make the system vulnerable to very radical changes that might affect the main features of its internal or external environments. But then, it is justified in 'expecting' (if I can use such anthropomorphic terms) that they will be so maintained. This must follow from the fact that climax systems - such as Gaia, as Jim Lovelock has noted - exist in an environment whose main features they have themselves created, and which are precisely those that minimize the incidence and seriousness of potentially disruptive changes, and which otherwise maintain those conditions required to safeguard their stability.

Thus rainforests can 'expect' the occurrence of the rainfall they have come to require for the simple reason that they themselves have generated much of it via evapotranspiration, so much so that they are in this respect practically closed systems; the Amazonian rainforests, for instance, appear capable of generating up to 75 per cent of the rainfall they receive.

Rainforests can also confidently predict that the nutrients required for their sustenance will be available, for they themselves have generated these nutrients. Indeed, tropical forests, as everyone knows, grow on very poor soils, but the litter they generate is recycled so quickly, and the trees have developed such effective means of extracting the nutrients from it, that no shortage of nutrients is ever likely to occur.

Many ecosystems that are characterized by large fluctuations or discontinuities, such as grasslands, are pioneer ecosystems which will, if undisturbed by man, eventually develop into climax ecosystems. Others, such as the Californian chaparral, appear themselves to be climaxes existing in biotic, abiotic and climatic conditions which do not favour further development. What seems clear, however, is that all such systems are striving to achieve what, in the conditions in which they exist, is the maximum achievable stability. Their goal remains the preservation of their basic structure and function in the face of change, and they succeed in achieving it to the best of their capacities. One must thereby agree with Waddington that Holling's distinction between 'stability' and 'resilience' is based on "a confusion between two different types of stability" (Waddington in Jantsch/Waddington, 1976).

This fits in better with Eugene Odum's own distinction between 'resistance stability', which he defines as "the ability of an ecosystem to resist perturbations and maintain its structure and function intact", (Odum 1923), and 'resilience stability', which he defines as a system's ability to recover when it is disrupted by a perturbation (ibid). As an example of the former, he takes a forest of Californian Redwoods, with their thick-bark that enables them to withstand fire, but which take hundreds of years to recover if destroyed. 'Resilience stability', on the other hand, he exemplifies by the Californian Chaparral vegetation which burns easily but which recovers quickly.

Significantly, Odum does not suggest that the Redwood forest is not persistent or that the chaparral is not stable. Both assure their survival in the face of the range of changes which, in terms of their experience, they are justified to 'expect', though the former can do so at considerable less cost to its basic structure and function than the latter.

Unfortunately, little work seems to have been done by ecologists to test the thesis that ecosystems can maintain their own stability or homeostasis: however, what work has been done tends to confirm the thesis. The best known experiments in this field are those conducted by Simberloff and Wilson in 1969. These researchers removed all the fauna from several small mangrove islets and then closely watched the way they were recolonised by terrestrial arthropods. Though, in the end, the islets were populated by very different species from the original ones, the total number of species was very much the same as originally.

The same data were re-examined three years later by Heatwole and Levins. Their interest was to classify the different species in terms of trophic organisation, noting the number of species in each of the trophic categories (herbivores, scavengers, detritus feeders, predators etc.). The results were highly significant. They showed that the trophic structure of the communities on the different islets displayed a remarkable stability even though the species composing each of the trophic levels had undergone a considerable change. This experiment clearly illustrates the principle of systemic homeostasis and stability, for the system had undergone change, but its basic structure had been preserved.

Significantly, mainstream ecologists have refused to accept this interpretation. For example, Putman and Wratten, the authors of a recent textbook on ecology, insist that the data do not point to the "recovery of a disturbed system" but rather to the "establishment of a new community after total defaunation" (Putman/Wratten,

161

1984). Simberloff insists the same result could, in any case, have been achieved stochastically - in other words, that it is consistent with the postulate of randomness, a tenet which is critical to the paradigm of modernism. Horn tries to explain the ecological healing process, or successional development towards a stable climax, in terms of the statistical properties of Markov chains, which suggests that, rather than being a device for achieving or restoring homeostasis, it is but a statistical phenomenon.

We are faced here with but another rather pathetic attempt to preserve the credibility of the paradigm of reductionistic ecology or "the pioneer world-view" in the face of yet further evidence of its inadequacy - which demonstrates once more the need for a new Gaia-inspired holistic ecology.

References

Adams, C. C. The Natural History, Ecology, *American Museum Journal*, 7,491-4.

Allee, W. C. "Animal Ecology", *Ecology* 13: 405-7, 1932.

Barrington Moore, Presidential Address to St Louis Branch of US Ecological Society, 1917.

Bernard, Claude. *Les Phenomenes de la Vie*, Paris, 1871.

Bertalanffy, von L. "General Systems Theory", in *Problems of General Systems Theory*, Toronto, 1960.

Bertalanffy, von L. *Modern Theories of Development*, New York, 1933.

Bodenheimer, F.S. "The Concept of Biotic Organization in Synecology", in Bodenheimer F.S. (ed), *Studies in Biology and its History*, Biological Studies Publishers, Jerusalem, 75-90.

Boucher, D.H. "The Idea of Mutualism", in Boucher D.H. et al., (eds.), *The Biology of Mutualism*, Croome Helm, London, 1986.

Clements, F. E. *Plant Succession; An Analysis of the Development of Vegetation*, Publication No 242, Washington. D.C.,1916.

Clements, F.E. and Shelford, V. *Bio-Ecology*, Wiley, New York, 1930.

Colinvaux, P.A. *Introduction to Ecology*, Wiley, New York, 1973.

Collier, J. et al., quoted by Boucher, D.H. et al. (eds), *The Biology of Mutualism*, Croom Helm, London, 1986.

Curtis, J.T. *The vegetation of Wisconsin*, The University of Wisconsin Press, Madison, 1959.

Darwin, Charles. *Correspondence with Lyell*, quoted by D. Worster, op cit.

Forbes, S.A. "The Lake as a Microcosm", *Bulletin of the Science Association of Peoria*, Illinois, 177-87, 1887.

Gleason, H. "The Individualistic Concept of the Plant Association", *Bulletin of the Torrey Botanical Club*, 53:1,20, 1926.

Goldsmith, E. "Superscience, its Mythology and Legitimization", *The Ecologist*, Vol.11, No.5, 1981.

162

Holling, C.S. "Resilience and Stability of Ecosystems", in Jantsch E. and Waddington C. H.(eds.), *Evolution and Consciousness*, Addison Wesley, Reading, Mass., 1976.

Janzen, D.H. "The Natural History of Mutualism", in Boucher D.H. et al., (eds.), *The biology of Mutualism*, Croome Helm, London, 1986.

Lovelock, J. *Gaia, A New Look at Life on Earth*, Oxford University Press, Oxford, 1979.

May, R.M. *Stability and Complexity in Model Ecosystems*, Princeton University Press, Princeton, 1973.

McKintosh, R. "The background and some current problems of theoretical ecology", *Synthese*: 43, 195-255.

McKintosh, R. Gleason, H.A. 'Individualistic Ecologist': His Contribution to Ecological Theory", *Bulletin of the Torrey Botanical Club*, 102, 253-73, 1975.

McNaughton, S.J. "Grazing as an Optimization Process: Grass-Ungulate Relationships in Serengeti", *The American Naturalist*, May 1979.

Merrell, D.J. *Ecological Genetics*, Longman, Harlow, 1949.

Odum, E. "The Strategy of Ecosystem Development", *Science*, 164:260-70.

Odum, E. Personal communication.

Odum, E. *Fundamentals of Ecology*, Saunders, Philadelphia, 1953:1923.

Pantin, C.F. *The Relation between the Sciences*, Cambridge University Press. 1968.

Patee, H. *Hierarchy Theory: The Challenge of Complex Systems*, Brazilier, New York, 1973.

Piaget, J. *Le Comportement Moteur de l'Evolution*, Gallimard, Paris, 1975

Price, P.W. "Alternative Paradigms in Community Ecology", in Price P. et al., (eds.), ibid.

Price, P.W., Gaud W.S. and Slobodchikoff, C.N. "Is there a New Ecology?" in *The New Ecology*, John Wiley, Toronto, 1984.

Putman R. J. and Wratten, S.D. *Principles of Ecology*, Croom Helm, London 1984.

Risch S. and Boucher, D.H. "What ecologists look for", *Bulletin of the Ecological Society of America*, 57 (368-9).

Sagan, D. and Margulis, L. "The Gaian Perspective of Ecology", *The Ecologist*, Vol 13, No 5, 1983.

Simberloff, D. "A Succession of Paradigms in Ecology", *Synthese* 43:3:39.

Tansley, A. "The Classification of Vegetation and the Concept of Development", *Journal of Ecology*, 2:202-4, 1920.

Thienemann, A. "Lebengemeinshaft und Lebensraum", *Naturwissenschrift*, N.F.17, 282-90, 297-303, 1918.

Thorpe, W.H. *Science, Man and Morals*, Methuen, London, 1965.

Ungerer, E. quoted by L. von Bertalanffy, *Modern Theories of Development*, New York 1933.

Vandermere J.H. and Boucher, D.H. "Varieties of Mutualistic Interactions", *Population Models*: 74, 549-558, 1978.

Waddington, C. H. Introduction, in Jantsch E. and Waddington C. H. (eds.), *Evolution and Consciousness*, Addison-Wesley, Reading, Mass., 1976.

Weiss, P. "The Living System", in Koestler, A. and Smythies, J.R. (eds.), *Beyond Reductionism*, Hutchinson, London, 1970.

Whitehead, A.N. *Science and the Modern World*, Cambridge University Press, 1948.

Whitman, 0. E. *Journal of Morphology, Vol.8, 1893, quoted in Krishna Chaitanya, The Biology of Freedom*, Desai, S.R. Bombay, 1975.

Whittaker, R.H. "Gradient Analysis of Vegetation", *Biological Reviews*: 42, 207, 64.

Woodger, J.H. *Biological Principles*, Routledge and Kegan Paul, London, 1929.

Worster, D. *Nature's Economy*, Sierra Club, San Francisco, 1977.

DISCUSSION

Mae-Wan Ho I would like to bring up the notion of control: we haven't for instance mentioned recent developments in contemporary physics, chemistry and mathematics, which have taken us way beyond the mechanistic framework. In fact, Whitehead had already discussed this in 1925 in his *Science and the Modern World*; yet it hasn't seeped down to the general consciousness, and certainly not that of biologists. Now, for instance, through quantum theory some physicists believe that we actually take part in shaping reality.

Not that anyone can yet figure out the implications of all this. Still, we are certainly moving away from the notion of organisms as objects which are subject to push and pull forces. Connected with that control theory is fine, the theory of hierarchy is fine, but we must also take them as a kind of transition away from the mechanistic paradigm and language where we have active versus passive, controller versus controlled. We are therefore thinking in terms of hierarchy as though we have a whole hierarchy of civil servants or mandarins, but the living system when you look at it isn't like that at all. You say there is control, yet I would suggest we don't know precisely where the control is, control is everywhere.

Where is the information? Some of it is written in the environment, some of it is actually in the genes, some of it is in the physiology. Take the notion of mind, for instance; mind is certainly not located in the brain, it is everywhere, it's at my finger tips, it's between us, in this room everywhere. That's the way with the whole of scientific development, it is now part of human consciousness developing itself.

Edward Goldsmith Wherever the information is situated, I think we agree that it is not arranged in atomised and isolated 'bits' as Shannon and Weaver's information is. It is organized to provide instructions and also a model of a systems relationship with its environment, which is used for guiding behaviour, monitoring it and correcting divergencies from the optimum path - what Waddington called the chreod in development.

This information permits sophisticated internalized controls such as those that enable a tribal society to keep down its population - taboos against sexual activity during lactation, during the first years of widowhood for instance. These sophisticated controls must be distinguished in some way from the crude external controls - the four horsemen of the apocalypse - that return into operation when the social system disintegrates and the internal controls are no longer operative.

With regards hierarchy. I'm talking about something that is very much more subtle than the relationship between mandarins and the masses they govern. It involves a two way relationship, through an assymmetrical one. I see systems as trying to preserve the basic order of the hierarchy of larger systems of which they are part, i.e. maintain their stability. It is only in this way that they can preserve their own order and stability, and I see the larger system - Gaia - if you like controlling or coordinating their behaviour, orienting it, and selecting-out those whose behaviour has gone wrong, has become random and no longer contributes to its stability - the individualistic nasty ones - those that ironically enough, the neo-Darwinists see as fit and being selected-in.

165

Lynn Margulis What do we do, Teddy, when your young minds are exposed to the Robert Mays and the Maynard Smiths and the Richard Dawkins who set the paradigms for all academia? William Irwin Thompson says that all innovation is outside the university and will continue to be outside the university because the university in this day and age is playing the same role as the medieval church; in other words it is maintaining and defending the delivered truth.

Edward Goldsmith Well, you see that the trouble is that young minds, if they want to have a role to play in the economy in which we live, have got to be indoctrinated with this sort of stuff. If they are indoctrinated with the kind of stuff we have been talking about they will end up as very marginalized people who will have to live off their wits.

Jerry Ravetz When you mentioned the medieval church there were also the medieval universities and medieval philosophies.

James Lovelock Concerning latter-day ecologists; you mention the Robert Mays of this world. Robert May recently had a paper in *The Proceedings of the Royal Society*, of enormous length. Such people have been moved by the errors of their ways into the most amazing multidimensional quicksand which is the study of the mathematics of chaos and is I think in a sense their punishment.

Edward Goldsmith What has happened is that no-one has talked about mutualism for 30 or 40 years. Robert May was all against it and suddenly he is all for it, but the sort of mutualism people such as he talk about is mutualism only between individuals and then only between two individuals at a time. Therefore it is a mechanistic and reductionistic mutualism and they say there cannot be mutualism between species because species cannot have fitness and if they can't have fitness then you are back again at Richard Dawkins and his selfish gene.

David Abram I much enjoyed what you have to say, Teddy, but I have a few questions about language, like the word *control*, control of the parts by the whole. I myself don't feel as if I control my parts, my organs. In fact, if I try to control them, for instance my heart, it will probably stop beating. I tried therefore to hunt for a better word. One that came to me, but I don't know if it was physically good or not is *integration*. Would you allow that the whole rather integrates the parts.

Edward Goldsmith I think the term integration is fine. But you seem to be identifying yourself with your conscious self. It is your unconscious self that is controlling the circulation of the blood, your digestion etc - and thank God it is too. If you allowed your conscious, rational and so-called objective knowledge to control your metabolism you wouldn't survive a single day.

James Lovelock That is where we are going wrong, trying to manage the Earth rather than letting it manage us. Thank God we are not the stewards of the Earth: this stewards of the Earth business is nonsense.

Edward Goldsmith   Coordination is not a bad word. We are basically talking about cybernetics in the extended sense of the term, i.e. regulation.

David Abram   I think it is important to worry about the words we use because they do influence us, even the sound of words, for instance *hierarchy*, it resonates with higher so that one thinks of higher and lower organisms.

Edward Goldsmith   I think that there are higher and lower systems in the sense that there are wholes and parts. Gaia is in a sense a higher system than its component ecosystems, societies, families, organisms etc and they must all relate to her in a special way by seeking to preserve her integrity or stability.

GAIA: IMPLICATIONS FOR EVOLUTIONARY THEORY

by Mae-Wan Ho

Gaia and the new evolutionary paradigm

I have come to the Gaia hypothesis (Lovelock, 1979) rather belatedly, via a path that led me beyond neo-Darwinism beginning more than ten years ago. The reason it took me and perhaps many others so long to see the relevance of the Gaia hypothesis to evolution is because, contrary to what Jim Lovelock and Lynn Margulis think, there is no real plane of contact between it and Neo-Darwinism, the theory of evolution that continues to dominate much of biology.

Neo-Darwinism is a research programme based on the idea that the natural selection of random variations account for most, if not all evolutionary change. It depends on two main assumptions. The first is the separation between organism and environment, a concept that owes much to the analogy with Newtonian mechanics. Organisms are represented as if they were mechanical *objects* acted on by selective *forces* in the environment (Ho, 1988d). This separation was formalized by Weismann, who split the organism into a mortal body subject to change from environmental exigencies, and an immortal germline insulated from the environment and hence passed on virtually unchanged from one generation to another. Germline and body correspond respectively to the organism's *genotype* – a collection of genes inherited from its parents, and *phenotype* – the organism itself resulting from development. Development occurs under the control of both the genes and the environment; but the environment can have no direct influence on the genes. So-called *Weismann's barrier* ensures that the physiological interactions of the body with the environment do not directly affect the genes, and therefore, acquired characteristics may not be inherited. The second neo-Darwinian assumption means that the variations are independent of the selective force in the environment. Operationally, it also implies that nothing much could be said about the variations because each is the result of an isolated accident. To all intent and purposes, then, the organism is an island of accumulated accidents, existing purely by itself and for itself against the capricious fortunes of unpredictable forces in the environment - hence the Darwinian metaphor of natural selection as the competition and struggle of one against all and all against nature.

In reality, both neo-Darwinian assumptions are invalid. Organism and environment are intimately interconnected at all levels right down to the organism's genes. Form and variation are far from random or arbitrary: they result from dynamic processes which spontaneously generate regular patterns and respond to environmental conditions in predictable ways. The integration of organism with the environment, and the dynamic regularity of process are the very obverse of the neo-Darwinian assumptions. They form the basis of a new framework for studying evolution which I, and a significant number of colleagues all over the world, have already adopted to varying degrees (see Ho and Fox, 1988; Ho and Saunders,

1984). In honour of Alfred North Whitehead (1920) who had foretold the full implications of the collapse of the mechanical world-view nearly seventy years ago, and to celebrate the re-unification of biology with contemporary physics, chemistry and mathematics, I call the new framework *evolution by process* (Ho et al, 1986, Ho 1988a).

Evolution by process, in its emphasis on the integration of the organism with nature, is very much in harmony with the Gaia hypothesis, which says that the totality of the Earth's biosphere, atmosphere, ocean and soil, constitute a single feedback or cybernetic system (Lovelock, 1979). There are, however, two issues which need to be resolved: the relevance of natural selection and the role of human action in evolution. I would like to briefly explain how I understand them in order that the real implication of the Gaia hypothesis for evolution can be better appreciated by all.

First, I believe that the large-scale properties of the system Earth, homeostatic or otherwise, have all emerged spontaneously from the constituent processes, and not from natural selection as Lovelock sometimes suggests. In particular, if we are talking about the survival of the system Earth as a whole, then the concept of selection simply cannot apply. There had not been a number of competing systems, one of which - ours - eventually won out. Rather, we are dealing with the dynamics of change or *transformation* within a single system over aeons of evolutionary history.

The reason Lovelock finds it necessary to appeal to natural selection is because he has adopted the neo-Darwinian assumption that everything must be accidental and random without natural selection. There is now a large body of evidence to contradict the randomness assumption everywhere, from the origin of the universe itself, to the evolution of organisms and mutations in their genetic material or DNA. Astrophysicists tell us that the properties of the universe are remarkably finely tuned, and but for that, neither the universe, nor life and the human species would have come into being (Barrow and Tipler, 1986). Thus, if Newton's inverse square law for gravitational attraction were not exact, the planets would have been unable to form stable orbits; instead, they would either annihilate themselves in the sun, or be lost forever in extrastellar space.

In the same vein, Lawrence Henderson's book published in 1913, on *The fitness of the Environment*, shows how the physics and chemistry of matter are precisely such as to make life possible. Life on Earth did not emerge from a series of improbable frozen accidents. For example, Sidney Fox discovered nearly thirty years ago that amino acids themselves, by virtue of their electronic structure, determine the amino acid sequences of the proteins obtained when mixtures of them are heated together under conditions which simulate those of the primitive Earth (Fox, 1988). These 'thermal proteins' possess an impressive variety of enzymic activities. In contact with water, they readily form hollow spheres which exhibit many protocellular functions, including neuron-like excitability (see Fig. 1). Recently, Simionescu and Denes (1987) reported the synthesis of similar polymers in cold conditions starting from mixtures of methane, ammonia and water. The moral is not whether hot or cold polymerization occurred in prebiotic Earth; it is the robust way in which proteins with a rich array of vital functions can come into being without the help of natural selection or of special creation.

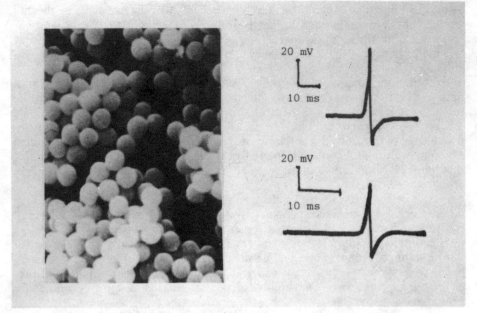

Fig. 1 Microspheres with Neurone-like excitability
    (a)   Scanning electronmicrograph of microspheres formed from thermal proteins in water.
    (b)   Action potential recorded in microsphere (lower trace) compared with that recorded in squid axon by implanted microelectrode. (From Fox, 1986)

Because Lovelock places so much faith in natural selection, he paradoxically downplays the *active* role that humans, and indeed, all organisms have in shaping evolution. And this is my second point of possible disagreement with Lovelock. I get the impression that Lovelock thinks natural selection will take care of whatever chemical and nuclear pollutants the human species let loose on the environment. (Though, to be fair, he does express concern about the devastating effects of the indiscriminate clearing of tropical forests for agriculture, which is turning vast areas of Africa into desert).

As mentioned before, natural selection does not apply to the survival of the single system Earth. Moreover, processes take on a dynamical evolution of their own, *without regard as to whether the outcome is adaptive or desirable.* After all, extinctions of entire species have occurred over and over again, and only Dr. Pangloss would say that *all* is for the best in this best of all possible worlds.

It seems to me that in acknowledging the integration of the human species with nature, we must also acknowledge our effective participation in evolution. By actively shaping the environment in which we develop, we directly influence the developments of future generations. All organisms do that to some extent; but we have more powerful means at our disposal and can choose to do so consciously, for better or for worse. That is to say: we have both power and responsibility for evolution, because we are interwoven within the very fabric of nature as process. This is the palpable reality that envelops us, once we reject the Cartesian duality of the human mind as pure intellect hovering above nature, and the mechanical view of the organism as an object apart in space, and utterly isolated in time.

For the rest of the talk, I shall expand on the premises of 'evolution by process' in order to reveal its deep affinity with the Gaia hypothesis. Then I shall try to draw out the implications for human action that follow from adopting this fundamentally new way of doing science.

Evolution by process is based on two premises:

1. Processes have an inherent dynamic which can spontaneously generate predictable forms and variations.
2. The organism is deeply integrated with nature from the ecological and sociocultural domain right down to its genes.

Within this framework, organisms are seen to evolve in unison with nature through processes nested in space and time, and not as the consequence of the natural selection of random variations.

The ineluctable emergence of form and beauty

The processes generating form and variation are not random, instead, they exhibit organization principles which can often be expressed in terms of physics and mathematics. Let me give some examples.

The honeycomb is a beautiful structure, each cell showing a perfect hexagonal cross-section. Darwin (1875) wrote, "He must be a dull man who can examine the exquisite structure of a comb, so beautifully adapted to its ends, without enthusiastic admiration." This structure Darwin attributed to the hive-making instinct of bees, perfected by natural selection. D'Arcy Thompson (1914) showed, however, that the hexagonal cross-section of the cells, as well as their trihedral pyrimidal ends, are both the result of compression due to close packing. In other words, the impressive symmetry of the honeycomb arises automatically from the physics of the hive-making process (see Fig.2).

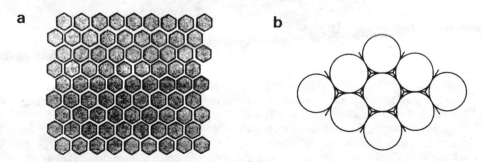

Fig. 2 The symmetry of the honey comb
(a) Cross-section of the honey comb (b) Hexagonal array of cells produced by uniform compression

171

The cellular slime mould is a strange organism which alternates between a multicellular slug that ends up as a fruiting body bearing spores, and a unicellular stage consisting of many amoebae. The amoebae feed and multiply until food runs out, then they aggregate to form the slug. Aggregation starts when a pulse of a chemical, cyclic AMP, is given off by a single amoeba, which attracts neighbouring amoebae to move towards it and at the same time to release a similar burst of cAMP. Thus, concentric waves of amoebae move rhythmically towards the centre of attraction, simultaneously relaying the signal outwards to other amoebae. The resulting pattern is very dramatic, but it is the automatic outcome of the relay process and again requires no extra explanation based on natural selection. Furthermore, it happens to be identical to the alternating blue and orange rings created by an oscillating oxidation-reduction system known as the Belousov-Zhabotinskii reaction (Fig. 3).

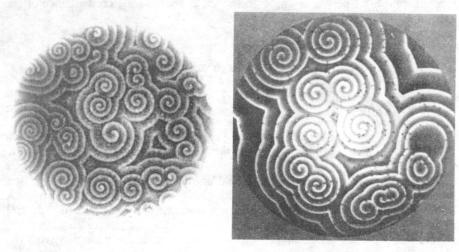

Fig. 3 Convergence between biological and physicochemical patterns. (a) Aggregation of slime mould. (b). The Belousov-Zhabotinskii reaction. (From Winfree and Strogatz, 1983)

This remarkable similarity in form occurs in two systems which differ completely with regard to the detailed mechanisms involved. It was precisely convergence such as these, between physicochemical and biological forms, that convinced D'Arcy Thompson (1914) of mathematical principles underlying the generation of all forms. In his book *On Growth and Form,* he showed how a ring of repeated structures resembling tentacles, can be created by a drop splashing onto the surface of a glass of milk (Fig. 4).

Particular forms and their variations are generated whenever conditions are right, because they represent stable states in the dynamics of the processes involved. Let me show you one more example of repeated structure. These are generated along the shoreline of Cape Cod in Rhode Island, USA, by 'he action of wind and waves. They look to me like the side of some colossal crustacean carrying a series of paddles (Fig. 5).

172

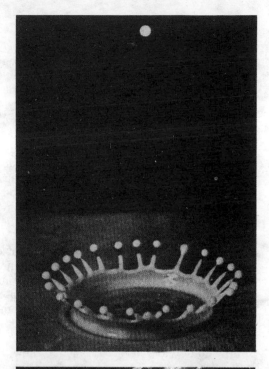

Fig. 4   Photograph of a drop splashing
           onto the surface of milk.
           (From D'Arcy Thompson, 1914)

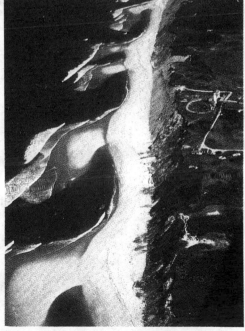

Fig. 5   The shoreline of Cape Cod.
           (From Dolan and Lin, 1987)

173

The non-randomness of variations

I said that particular forms are generated whenever conditions are right. I will now give some examples of variations in morphology as well as in proteins and genes that are repeatably produced in response to specific environmental conditions. They demonstrate most clearly the violation of the randomness postulate so crucial to neo-Darwinism, and at the same time reveal the interconnectedness between all levels of organism and environment.

Although it is undoubtedly true that some changes in the genetic material or DNA may be fortuitous, the resulting variations in the organism are never random because they occur within the context of a developmental system which is highly structured. This dynamical structure in turn *shapes* the variations. A striking demonstration of the shaping of variations by dynamical structures is the observation that similar variations can result either from gene mutations or from appropriate environmental perturbations. There are indeed many cases of these so-called *phenocopies* of genetic mutants.

Many genetic mutants affecting body development in the fruitfly have been isolated and the relevant genes cloned by genetic engineering; they make headline news in the science journal *Nature* .The fruitfly's body is made up of about 14 repeated parts or segments, each of which has a different identity. Some mutations scramble the identity of segments, while others lead to incorrect divisions into segments. The cloned genes have been used most ingeniously to locate the spatial patterns of expression of particular genes. By themselves, however, these studies simply do not address the problem of how the genes become expressed in their particular configurations during development. Spatial organization begins with physicochemical processes which set up spatial patterns in the egg cytoplasm. The latter, in turn, trigger the expression of different genes. We find therefore, that a simple physical perturbation - exposure to ether - is enough to induce a range of segmentation defects (Ho *et al*, 1987) (see Fig. 6). Specific defects are repeatedly induced at precise stages of development. Many of these are similar to mutant phenotypes that have been described, and so may be regarded as phenocopies. On the other hand, a substantial number of the phenotypes obtained have never been described as mutants. It will be of interest to see if they can be *genocopied* in future.

Not only morphological variations, but molecular variations too, can be repeatably produced.

The bacterium *E. coli* metabolizes lactose by first breaking it down with the enzyme B-galactosidase. Special strains in which the B-galactosidase gene is lost have no enzyme activity and do not use lactose if other carbon sources are present. Experimenting with these strains, Campbell *et al*. (1973) found that as the other carbon sources became exhausted, mutant colonies began to appear which can use lactose. The enzyme responsible was not the B-galactosidase that had been lost, but another enzyme altogether, called gencoded by another gene. This gene had undergone mutations that enabled it to breakdown lactose. By itself, this result is unremarkable because it could be interpreted as the artificial selection of a random mutation. However, the experiment was immediately repeated by others, who isolated 34 different lactose-utilizing strains by the same method (Hall and Hartl, 1974). All of these have enzyme activity identical to *ebg*. Moreover, in 31 of the

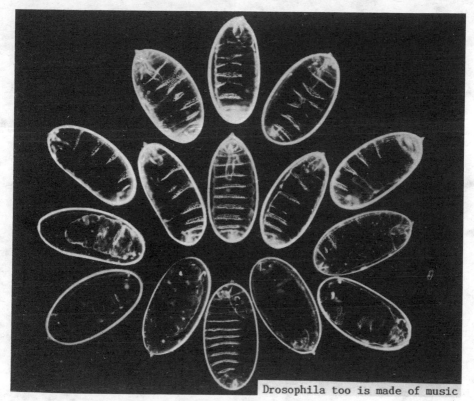

Drosophila too is made of music

Fig. 6   The range of segmentation defects produced on treating early *Drosophila* embryos with ether. The control larva – is in the middle. (From Ho, 1988a)

strains, the synthesis of the new enzyme is regulated by lactose; i.e., there has been an additional mutation in another gene which interacts with lactose to regulate *ebg*. (Hall, 1982). There is nothing accidental in this highly repeatable response to the same environmental challenge, which involves appropriate mutations in two different genes appearing simultaneously.

Remarkable as this example appears, it is really no different from the repeatable production of specific transformations when a given environmental perturbation is applied in *Drosophila* embryos. It is the physiological state of the cell in one case, and the developmental system of the organism in the other, that organically 'selects' the appropriate response. Part of that response may involve specific gene mutations.

These and other instances of directed variations (see Ho, 1988a) demonstrate that the organism responds physiologically to the environment in one *continuous* process. The environment is 'selective' in so far as it selects, *via the physiological system,* or an appropriate response, but no real selective deaths have taken place as required by natural selection. The fact that the response may involve genetic changes shows that the strict separation between genotype and phenotype really does not exist as far as the organism is concerned.

As the variations are generated by the physiological interaction between organism and environment, the persistence of the variations over the generations depends, not on natural selection, but on heredity! The variations would indeed persist in the absence of natural selection, so long as heredity favours them. There is a great deal of conceptual confusion here which some good philosopher of biology should sort out in future. For now, it seems most fitting for us to direct our attention to the nature of heredity itself.

Heredity as process

Until very recently, heredity was supposed to be due to the transmission of something that remains basically unchanged from generation to generation. The widespread use of the term 'inheritance' is significant, as it brings to mind the family heirloom. This concept depended on basic assumptions of genetics that practically everyone accepted as true in the 1960s and early 1970s; they could be found in any genetics textbook of the period:

1. DNA (and in some viruses, RNA) is the genetic material.

2. Genetic information flows from DNA to RNA to protein, but never in reverse.

3. One polypeptide is specified by one gene locus.

4. Colinearity exists between the base sequence of DNA in the gene and the amino acid sequence of the polypeptide it encodes.

5. The genetic code is universal.

6. The codons are read in one direction, without overlap, and only in one correct reading frame.

7. With very few exceptions, the DNA of all cells remain constant during development only the genes expressed differ between different cells.

8. Environmentally induced modifications do not affect the DNA and cannot be inherited.

Since then, all but the first assumption has been violated. (The first assumption remains true only by definition, as it has long been accepted that certain cytoplasmic components of the egg cell also affect heredity, and hence would qualify as 'hereditary material', if not 'genetic material').

By far, the most significant picture to emerge from recombinant DNA research is the dynamism and flexibility of the organism's *genome* (the totality of its genes or DNA located within the nucleus of each of its cells) in both organization and function. This is in striking contrast to the relatively static and mechanical conception which previously held sway.

176

We can get some idea of the functional flexibility by considering the one gene-one polypeptide relationship. This relationship has been violated so many times, and in so many ways that there no longer appears to be any general rule in the matter. All conceivable mappings between genes and polypeptides have now been found.

The functional flexibility of the genome is in part associated with, and indeed, fully matched by its structural fluidity, which in turn locates the genome firmly within the physiological system of the organism as a whole, as we shall see.

There are two main aspects of the recent findings which are most relevant to my thesis of evolution by process (Ho, 1986; 1987a,b; 1988a, and refs. therein).

The first is the so-called fluidity of the genome. This refers to all observations suggesting that DNA is subject to relatively large alterations both during development and in evolution. Genomic fluidity depends on a host of mechanisms which can rearrange DNA, move bits of DNA around the genome, mutate DNA, greatly amplify particular sequences or contracting them, and even convert sequences from one to another in the same or different part of the genome.

Careful comparisons between DNA of related species reveal that there is a relatively high background rate of DNA 'turnover' in all organisms due to cycles of rearrangements, amplifications, deletions and mutations (see Fig. 7). This leads to the genetic divergence of species in the long term, quite independently of natural selection. Furthermore, under certain environmental conditions the same mechanisms responsible for DNA turnover may cause sufficiently large genetic changes to precipitate the rapid formation of new species (Pollard, 1988; Cullis, 1988). This kind of saltatory speciation is also independent of natural selection.

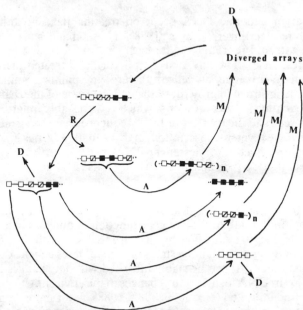

Fig. 7 DNA 'turnover' in evolution. A amplification of sequences; D deletion; M mutation; R rearrangement. Each symbol represents a different sequence of DNA. (Redrawn from Flavell, 1982; Ho, 1987b)

So, the genetic material DNA may be just as responsive and flexible as the rest of the organism, from behaviour to developmental physiology to protein synthesis (Ho, 1986, 1987). In fact, genomic fluidity can itself be regarded as a phenotypic character which varies between strains, between species, and according to the environment and the physiological state of the organism.

The second aspect of the findings from recombinant DNA research is the permeability of Weismann's barrier. This involves all sorts of processes in which the body 'talks' back meaningfully to the germline as part of the functional interactions between different levels within the organism or between the organism and the external environment. I would include, (a) The large scale reverse transcription, or back-copying of processed RNAs into DNA and reinsertion into the germline genome. (b) The non-random changes in germline DNA in certain environments which can become stably inherited in subsequent generations. (c) Certain conversions of genes that go on in all cells of the body.

Reverse transcription plays a large role in shaping the genome of higher organisms. As much as 20 per cent of the mammalian genome consists of reversed transcripts. It is recently reported that a certain family of repeated DNA sequences in primates, may be derived from a sequence encoding a reverse transcriptase, the enzyme that does the back-copying (Hattori et al, 1986). It will be of interest to see whether germ-cell reverse transcription is a normal function of the organism Howard Temin (1971), who got the Nobel prize for discovering reverse transcriptase, suggested this as a possibility almost twenty years ago. I interviewed him by trans-Atlantic telephone for our Open University Genetics Course recently, and he still stands by it.

Directed changes in genomic DNA occur on treating flax and other plant seedlings with different fertilizers (Cullis, 1988). These changes are specific to different environments and reproducible for each environment, and are not just generalized stress responses. The DNA changes occur in all treated plants in the course of development, involving all cells in the growing points simultaneously. Thereafter, the plants improve in growth, so that at least some of the changes may constitute an adaptive physiological response which is then stably inherited.

Gene conversion refers to the transfer of DNA sequences between genes. Many gene conversions involve reverse transcription; in that situation, genes in use which are transcribed and processed into messenger RNA, will convert the ones not in use. So there appears to be a principle of the 'use and disuse of genes' (Krassilov, 1987).

It is clear that DNA is not immune to change as the result of feedback from the environment and from the physiological state of the organism. In fact, DNA changes are involved in the stabilization of gene function as much as in altering it. This only reflects the necessary relationship which DNA has with the rest of the organism. There is nothing special in the status of DNA. States of gene expression (whether it is turned on or off) can be stably inherited without changes in DNA; conversely alterations in DNA instigated by changes in the environment within one generation can become inherited (Ho, 1986; 1987; 1988a,d, for more details).

The real problem of heredity is to account for the stable and repeatable nature of reproduction. This feature was previously widely assumed to be due to the constancy of DNA. One major consequence of the discovery of the fluid genome is to expose the untenability of this assumption. DNA is functionally and structurally as flexible as the rest of the organism. How then should we see heredity? Where does stability reside if not in the constancy of DNA?

Living beings engage in the process of living. Process is an *activity* at all levels from the behaviour of organisms in their ecological and social environment to the expression of genes in their cells. From the beginning of development to maturation and old age, there is almost nothing that remains static and unchanging. Organisms are self-constructed and re-enacted life-histories and not mechanical objects (Ho, 1988c). Whereas the stability of mechanical objects depend on static equilibrium, that of organisms is *dynamically maintained,* and is utterly dependent on activity; in other words, on fluidity and change. The cessation of activity spells death.

Heredity - a name given to the observed constancy of reproduction - must ultimately be looked upon as a process, and not as some *material* which is passed on from parent to offspring. Processes, whether biological or physicochemical, have an inherent dynamic which generates patterns and regularities; and here is where at least part of the stability of reproduction resides. Another source of stability is due to the 'control' of development being *web-like* and *circular* rather than linear and unidirectional (Fig. 8). This means that the 'cause' of development is not just the DNA, but is *distributed throughout the complex interrelationships between the different levels of the organism and its environment.* It may be that the fluidity of DNA plays an indispensible role in the maintenance of the organismic system as a whole, for all components of the system must be able to adjust and respond as appropriate to their particular *milieu.* What is inherited in each successive generation is not only the precise copies of DNA molecules, but an entire experiential repertoire including also, maternal, cytoplasmic effects, the physicochemical, biotic and social environments, all of which conspire to make development similar to the previous generation. (Ho, 1987). Heredity is therefore inseparable from development.

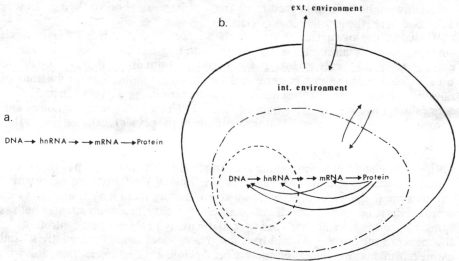

Fig. 8   Two views of gene activity in development. (a)   The central dogma. (b)   The process view. hnRNA, heterogenous nuclear RNA or primary transcript. (From Ho, 1986)

179

Similary, development is directly linked to evolution in two senses. The first is in the formal sense that development, through the dynamical structure of the epigenetic system, defines the sort of changes that can occur under different contingent conditions. The second is by virtue that generations are not separate and the germline not so inviolable as previously held. This means that the experience of each generation will be transmitted culturally and ecologically as well as via physiological influences which may, or may not include changes in DNA.

The old paradigm, in my opinion, is already discredited by the empirical evidence now available. It presents a distorted and reduced view of the organism and its relationship with nature. It imposes a conceptual framework that does considerable violence to reality, not only in theory, but in practice as well. Because science and our perception of the world are interdependent, a distorted science will distort sociocultural reality through the self-fulfilling prophecy (Ho, 1987a; 1988a). In other words, if we see evolution predominantly as the consequence of competition between selfish individuals, then we will tend to create a world governed by profit and self-interest above all else.

The most important reason for rejecting neo-Darwinism is that a new paradigm has already emerged which does not reduce and fragment nature, which accords not only with empirical findings, but also with our deepest experience of nature as a unity (Ho *et al*, 1986). In so doing, it re-establishes a fertile and harmonious relationship between the human spirit and the world we inhabit; and *that* may well be the very soul of Gaia. And, I hasten to add, that the scientists are not alone in this new orientation (Ho, 1988b). They are moved by the same *Zeitgeist* of the human consciousness in revolt against the mechanical worldview (in fact, they are typically far behind, since as conventional scientists, they are *required* to alienate themselves from reality in a fundamental way (c.f. Bortoft, 1986). The signs are everywhere: the rise of environmentalist movements, concern for animal rights, the increasing popularity of homeopathic medicine, the emphasis on holistic living, and as witnessed here, the growing love of Gaia.

What does the love of Gaia entail? It entails a profound knowledge of Gaia which comes out of the realization that we are one with her (as David Abram so stylishly demonstrates). Animals, plants and microbes, mountains and seas, the air we breathe, colour and sound, patterns and forms, are all multiplicity in the unity of nature; each and every part resonating to and encapsulating the whole in itself. Our actions are thus inextricably those of Gaia, and that gives us both power and responsibility to help shape the future evolution of the planet Earth (see Ho, 1988c, for a more detailed argument).

To conclude, I would like to show you the face of Gaia, realized by the New York sculptor, Michael Lekakis, working purely from his artistic intuition (Fig. 9). The discerning among you will take note of the flowing yet structured form which captures the dynamic fluidity and rationality of nature that I have tried to put into words. This is because we touch the same core of reality, artist and scientist both as human beings. I have no ready answers to the many problems that confront us on the matter of the health of Gaia. I have the greatest admiration for the activists and astute commentators among you such as Teddy Goldsmith and Peter Bunyard, who keep us in touch. For me, I see Nature dancing to the harmonics of music, and it is imperative that we must learn again to dance in step with her.

Fig. 9 Photograph of Gaia.
(As realized by Michael Lekakis,
courtesy of Ron Brady)

References

Barrow J. B. and Tipler, F. J. *The Anthropic Cosmological Principle*, Clarendon Press, Oxford. 1986.

Barzun, J. *Darwin, Marx, Wagner*, Doubleday Anchor, New York, 1958.

Bateson, W. *Problems of Genetics*, Yale University Press, New Haven, 1913.

Bortoft, H. *Goethe's Scientific Consciousness*, Institute for Cultural Research Monograph Series No. 22, Tunbridge Wells, 1986.

Campbell, J. H., Engyel, J. A. L. and Langridge, J. Evolution of a second gene for B-galactosidase in *E. coli*. *Proc. Nat. Acad. Sci.* USA, 70, 1973, 1841-1845.

Cullis, C. Control of variation in higher plans, In: *Evolutionary Processes and Metaphors* M.W. Ho and S.W. Fox, Eds), Wiley, London, 1988.

Darwin, C. *Origin of Species*, 6th ed., John Murry, London, 1875.

Dolan F. and Lin, H. Beaches and barrier islands, *Sci. Am.* 1987, 257, 52-59.

Flavell, R. B. Major sources of variation during species divergence, In: *Genome Evolution* (G. A. Dover and R. B. Flavell, Eds.), Academic Press, London, 1982.

Fox, S. W. The evolutionary sequence: origin and emergence. *the American Biology Teacher*, 1986, 48, 140-169.

Fox, S. W. Evolution outward and foward, In: *Evolutionary Processes and Metaphors*, M.W. Ho and S.W. Fox, Eds.), Wiley, London, 1988.

Hall, B. G. Evolution on a petri dish. The evolved B-galactosidase system as a model for studying acquisitive evolution in the laboratory. *Evol. Biol.* 1982, 15, 85-150.

Hall B. G. and Hartl, D. L. Regulation of newly evolved enzymes 1. Selection of a novel lactase regulated by lactose, In: *Escherichia coli. Genetics*, 1974, 76, 391-400.

Hattori, M. Kuhura, S. Takenaka, D. Sakaki, Y. L1 family of repetitive DNA sequences in primates may be derived from a sequence encoding a reverse-transcriptase-related protein. *Nature*, 1986, 321, 625-628.

Henderson, L. J. *The Fitness of the Environment*, The Macmillan Company, New York, 1913.

Ho, M. W. Heredity as process: Towards a radical reformulation of heredity, *Rivista di Biologia*, 1986, 79 , 407-447.

Ho, M. W. Evolution by process, not by consequence. *Int. J. Comp. Psychol.* 1987, 1, 3-27.

Ho, M. W. On not holding nature still - evolution by process, not by consequence. In: *Evolutionary Processes and Metaphors* (M. W. Ho and S. W. Fox, Eds.), Wiley, London, 1988a.

Ho, M. W. Preface in *Evolutionary Processes and Metaphors* (M. W. Ho and S. W. Fox, Eds.) Wiley, London, 1988b.

Ho, M. W. How rational can rational morphology be? *Rivista di Biologia* (in press) 1988c.

Ho, M. W. Genetic fitness and natural selection: myth or metaphor. In: *Evolution of Social Behaviour and Integrative Levels* (E. Tobach and G. Greenberg, Eds.) Lawrence Erlbaum Ass., New Jersey, 1988d.

Ho, M. W. and Fox S. W. (Eds.) *Evolutionary Processes and Metaphors*, Wiley, London, 1988.

Ho, M. W., Matheson, A., Saunders, P. T., Goodwin, B. C. and Smallcombe, A. Ether-induced segmentation defects in *Drosophila melanogaster, Roux Arch. Devl. Biol.* 1987, 196, 511-521.

Ho, M. W. and Saunders P. T. (Eds.). *Beyond neo-Darwinism: An Introduction to the New Evolutionary Paradigm*, Academic Press, London, 1984.

Ho, M. W., Saunders, P. T. and Fox, S. W. A new paradigm for evolution, *New Scientist* 1986, 27th February, 41-43.

Krassilov, V. A. Ecosystem theory of evolution - an attempt at a new synthesis. Proc. Internat. Symp., Praha, 5-11 July, 1987, pp.236-348.

Lovelock, J. *Gaia: A New Look at Life on Earth*, Oxford University Press, Oxford, 1979.

Pollard, J. W. New genetic mechanisms and their implications for the formation of new species. In: *Evolutionary Processes and Metaphors* (M. W. Ho and S. W. Fox, Eds.), Wiley, London. 1988

Simionescu, C. I. and Denes, F. Cold abiotic conditions and the origin of life. Proc. Internat. Symp., Praha 5-11 July 1987, pp.108-1110.

Temin, H. M. The protovirus hypothesis: speculation on the significance of RNA-directed DNA synthesis for normal development and for carcinogenesis. *J. Nat. Cancer Inst.*, 1971, 46, III-VII.

Thompson, D'A. *On Growth and Form*, Cambridge University Press, Cambridge, 1914.

Whitehead, A. N. *Concept of Nature*, Cambridge University Press, Cambridge, 1920.

Winfree, A. T. and Strogatz, S. H. Singular filaments organize chemical waves in three dimensions. 1. Geometically simple waves. *Physica,* 1983, 8D, 35-49.

DISCUSSION

Lynn Margulis I feel there to be a lack of recognition of autopoiesis in your thinking. The idea that we can just go from physics, chemistry and mathematics right into biology is to my mind misleading. You actually said that because you had an action potential on Sydney Fox's proteinoids that they were alive.

Mae-Wan Ho I did not mean that at all.

Daniel Mayer It has been remarked that the single most important weakness of evolutionary biology is the lack of a theory of variation; hence a process by which new organisms are proffered for natural selection. My feeling is that you have been discussing the idea of a theory of regulation, but I don't see how that says much about natural selection

Mae-Wan Ho Natural selection is irrelevant that's what I am trying to say.

Daniel Mayer There are two things I would like to say about natural selection; one is that natural selection as far as I understand it is the non-selection of individuals who have disadvantages rather than the selection of individuals who have advantages. So can you have an individual who has an advantage and doesn't know it?

Mae-Wan Ho That's a very trivial aspect. All you are saying is that if they can't survive, they can't survive. I don't think there are two processes, one variation and the other selection. I see it as a continuum because if you actually look in detail at the interrelationships between organisms and environment it is all of a piece, you cannot actually say this part I call interaction and this part I call selection. This is the difficulty of this mechanical world view that we have got ourselves into, pretending that there is an initial and a final state; in this way of thinking the initial state is governed by the genes which control development and that there is a final state which is then subject to selection so giving rise to the next generation where the process is then mechanically repeated again. It just does not happen this way. The generations are not separate nor discrete; they actually overlap as can be seen from the physiology. Indeed, neo-genetics is telling us that they are not that discrete. I just don't think that there are two processes.

Edward Goldsmith / Even if separately seen they cannot explain evolution. The idea of random genetic mutations is a legacy from the time when we saw the genome as a random assortment of genes - the so-called 'bean-bag' approach. We now know that it is on the contrary a highly sophisticated organization whose specific order is critical and which as Lerner has shown, appears itself inherently capable of preserving.

It is also a legacy of the period when life processes were seen as 'caused' i.e. as triggered off by discrete events antecedent to them in time. Mendelism fitted in with this view. A single gene mutation was seen as causing changes in the phenotype, but it is now known that only superficial changes can be caused in this

183

way - for important changes whole constellations of genes must change - i.e. the organization of the genome itself must be modified. This leaves little room for random changes affecting single genes.

The notion that selection is the ordering principle in nature is equally irreconcilable with today's knowledge. One can draw up a whole list of reasons why this must be so. Let me mention just two of them. Selection acts by sorting out the fit from the unfit but as Piaget has argued, how can a sorting machine actually organize living matter into highly sophisticated forms. How does a sorting machine create a horse or a man let alone Gaia herself? Besides, a machine can in fact only sort things out if they are there in the first place to be sorted out. Selection does not explain organization, it assumes it.

Selection is also the legacy of an age that saw nature as 'red in tooth and claw' and which chose to ignore mutualism, symbiosis and all the other forms of cooperation which as Lynn Margulis and others have shown, have probably played a very much more important part in the development of Gaia than has competition. An organization can only function if its parts cooperate with it. This means that the parts must be selected not for their Rambo-like individualistic and aggressive qualities but for their ability to cooperate with each other and fulfil the differentiated functions within the system of which they are part. It is those that fit in that will in fact be selected by the system, those that are 'fit' in the normal sense of the term, the Rambos in fact, will be selected out that is precisely what the immune system does and a similar mechanism is operative in all natural systems including tribal societies which invariably ostracize or eliminate those that refuse to fit in and observe the traditional law.

Jim Lovelock   I think some of the problems we have here are historical and a bit semantic. I am not a biologist and in trying to sell Gaia I have to convince a lot of hard-nosed biologists. At the same time I never found any great difficulty with the concept that the organism that leaves the most progeny is the one that is going to succeed in the environment. If in writing I have implied that natural selection is all important and that the environment does not enter, that is not what I meant. Alfred Lotka saw evolution as a single process involving both the environment and the organism; one in fact that is completely inseparable. The universe is full of 'givens' and the idea of complete randomness is silly. Of course the universe has also got large pockets of chaos in which there is real randomness, but that's not the business with living things.

Guy Beney   I note that Sabatini has demonstrated that different species of orchid which grow in very different surroundings would evolve some of their forms in very similar ways although far apart. How does that fit in with your idea of evolution by process?

Mae-Wan Ho   I am not saying that, do not get me wrong. The organism is not infinitely plastic to the environment; that is a very banal theory which people think is what Lamarck stood for, and that is not the case at all. Nonetheless certain characteristics even within a single organism are very plastic and certain other characteristics are not. This is a physiological problem; the idea that it is only a

184

genetic problem is just wrong because then you start inventing genes, first major genes, then modifying genes, then control genes and housekeeping genes which are supposed to do all the boring routine work. This kind of language does not explain anything.

Roswitha Hentschel   Darwinism has been a very successful model over the years since it has been invented; there have been modifications but it has not been able to explain the emergence of higher taxa within the natural system. Thus it can only explain intra-specific evolution. I therefore wanted to ask Lynn Margulis whether her theory endosymbiosis might need an explanation and whether she has an explanation for this evolutionary process?

Lynn Margulis   When we get to the criticisms against the neo-Darwinists I completely agree with everything you say. There has been an enormous amount of internal organization that was referred to in this talk and one of those is the symbiotic acquisition of new properties, for example the symbiotic acquisition of a whole photosynthetic unit. Others involve rearrangements at the DNA level, chromosome rearrangements, karyotypic fission, polyploidy; there are many other mechanisms, none of which are random. Randomness is in the head of Richard Dawkins and they are not in the biology of life. Darwin, as has been pointed out by many people, never solved the origin of species, he solved the maintenance by natural selection of species once you have them. In fact the only case we have of origin of species in the scientific literature which I know of is described in *Microcosmos*, the example of Kwang Jeon, which is the origin of a new amoebal species by a symbiotic association between amoebae and rod-shaped bacteria. I don't think symbiosis answers everything, just a small percentage.

Ulrich Loening   I don't disagree with what was just now said but I don't think we should tangle that up with a simple molecular explanation within the context of the molecule. As Lynn pointed out, the fact you can have a few molecules of amino acid having an action potential shows that the chemical explanation of action potentials is beginning to be understood. Not that it is alive, but that we can make a mechanical explanation. Nowhere is such a view a world view, but it doesn't make it wrong.

Mae-Wan Ho   Let me just deal with this action potential of the microsphere once and for all, because it was just a tiny part of my talk and in no way was the root of what I said based on this tiny molecule. In fact, we mustn't think that matter is dead. This is the moral we have to draw on. Moreover I insist on talking about all the levels at the same time, if I can, because they are not separate.

AN AMAZONIAN TRIBE'S VIEW OF COSMOLOGY
by *Martin von Hildebrand*

Tribal peoples throughout the world have survived until this day because they had lived ecologically in balance and in relative harmony with their natural environment. Such survival has not been the simple result of brute adaptation, but instead has been the consequence of profound cosmological experience in which seasonal changes and cycles have not only been noted but sanctified in ritual and tradition.

Tribal peoples concepts of the Earth and their relationship to it and its other 'inhabitants' are quintessentially gaian insofar as they conceive the 'whole' as being necessary for vitality, continuity and sanity in the sense of health. This talk is about one small tribal group living in Colombia in South America.

Ufaina

The Ufaina comprise a small ethnic group of some 150 people who live between the Lower Apaporis and Miriti rivers in the north eastern part of the Colombian Amazon. Their language belongs to the Tukano-oriental linguistic family, while their economy is based on horticulture, hunting, fishing and gathering.

Several indigenous groups live in the area: the Bora and the Miraná who speak Bora, the Carijona who speak Carib, the Matapi and Yukuna who speak Arawak, and the Ufaina, Letuama, Yucuna and Makuna who speak Tukano.

In general terms, after millions of years of exposure to the elements the land has lost most of its soluble minerals and is therefore either moderately or extremely acid. Meanwhile the river Miriti carries little sediment and is of low biological productivity.

In this zone approximately half a degree south of the equator, the prevailing winds converge from either side of the equatorial line making it the most humid area of the Colombian Amazon (3,600 mm a year).

This convergence of the trade winds in the inter-tropical convergence zone (ITC) determines the climatic regimen which is reflected in two rainy seasons: one during April-May and the other October-November, this type of rainfall being known as equinoxial rain. The periods of lower precipitation occur in June and July and heavier rains in December, January and February.

The rites and the annual cycle

For the Ufaina, the period of the Equinox when the weather changes from dry to humid and humid to dry, is seen as favouring sickness. Conversely, the period of the Solstice is considered a healthy one. The rituals performed during the times of health are different from those performed during the times of sickness.

The dry season ends and the rains start at the Equinox at the end of March-beginning of April. The rivers swell and drive from their banks snakes and other

186

animals which often seek shelter near inhabited areas. At this time, *Yufurica* the guardian spirit of wild fruit 'releases' the energy required for trees to bear fruit. To the Indians this is a transitional period from dry to humid, from domesticated crops that are classified as female to wild food, classified as male. It is a dangerous and unhealthy period - it is also the period during which the ritual of *Yurupari*, which lasts 25 days or longer, is celebrated. At that ritual the Ufaina "return to the Mother Earth the heat (a female attribute) accumulated during the dry (female) time." The bodies of those participating are cleansed of the energy accumulated as a result of the excessive consumption of domesticated crops through the imposition of severe sexual and dietary restrictions. That way the tribal group can adapt to the exigencies of the transition. For the young, the *Yurupari* ritual also serves to initiate boys into the masculine world, leaving behind them that period when they were looked after by their mothers and other women of the group.

During the June and July Solstice the rivers remain swollen and the jungle flooded. It is a "healthy' time but fishing and hunting are made difficult by the floods, and when the men fail to bring back solid foods, the women protest and refuse to go to the tilled fields to fetch 'yucca'. This is a source of tension in the community giving rise to much gossip which often leads to conflicts among couples.

During these months, the Ufaina celebrate the 'white feather' or 'heron dance' ceremony, *buja boi buja*, a ritual serving principally to reinforce community ties. Reciting the original myths and performing the appropriate rituals, they 'return' the gossip to the jungle and to the plants. It is then that the wild fruit ripens and is eaten in large quantities by the community. When winter comes, the jungle is flooded, a period the Ufaina classify as 'cold' and as male.

The period of the September-October Equinox is also a rainy one but as the rains come to an end the rivers begin to dry and mud holes are left behind, favouring the spread of various waterborne diseases.

During this transitional time from moist to dry, people begin to select the area in the jungle which they will clear for horticultural use at the end of the summer. It is the time when the cicada sings, which according to the Ufaina is the guardian spirit, *Kanko naifi* of the vital force (*fufaka*) of crops. The cicada then comes down from heaven carrying the vital force required to fertilize the new areas for tilling and in return takes away the vital force (*fufaka*) of those who die during this time (*Myth of kanka-naifi*).

Great ceremonies take place during this period, in particular the fish dance (*wai baja*) *and the 'bamba' dance (wera baja)*[1]. In the first, the Ufaina enact the exogamous alliance between male birds and female fish (*myth of Umabari* and the fish). This ceremony also tells the story of the daughter of the boa, the guardian spirit of fish. She brought domestic crops into the world when she married a nomadic hunter gatherer who lived with the birds, thriving exclusively on wild food (*Myth of Kanuma*)[2]. This ceremony of the alliance between female crops and male wild foods occurs during the transition from winter, with its emphasis on wild fruit,

---

1   This name is derived from dancing to the rhythm of the shaking floor made of wood from a tree of aerial roots locally known as Bamba. (Author's notes).
2   See M. von Hildebrand: *Mitologia Ufaina* . Fundacion de Investigaciones Arqueologicas Colombianas Finarco, Banco de la Republica, Bogotà, 1979. (Author's notes).

and summer, with its emphasis on crops. The main object of the second ceremony - the bamba dance - is to 'return' illness to the guardian spirit of wild fruit.

The Indians consider that during the winter their bodies accumulate an excess of vital force from wild fruit and that this is the reason for the sickness they experience during the time. Just as during the tual of the Yurupariduring the transition from dry to moist, there is a need to 'return' the female heat which can reduce the life-force and to prepare for the world of rains and the cold of winter, so too during the transition from moist to dry ritual is required to 'return' the cold male vital force of winter which has sought to establish itself and instead to prepare the world for the female heat associated with cultivation. During the summer Solstice, the community devotes itself to the preparation of land for tilling, to sowing, and when necessary to the construction of communal houses.

In December the pineapples ripen and the Ufaina celebrate a small dance or 'guarapeada' when through shamanism and song they 'arrange' the recently opened areas for tilling so that they should cease to be lands where wild fruit grow and become instead fields where crops are cultivated.

The second dance is celebrated at the end of the dry season, at the time of the maturation of chontaduro palm (Bactris gasipaes) which grows all round the villages, and from which the beverage for the ritual is prepared. For this ceremony the community invites its allies who dwell in the world under the river where crops come from, to come dressed up as animals. During the ceremony the water creatures who originally gave the vital force to the crops are invited to partake in the harvest. After this dance the March Equinox returns with the yurupari ceremony.

In short there are two great categories of ceremonies: dances for healthy times at the Solstices considered 'gatherings to drink liquor' and which require little shamanistic activity, and dances for unhealthy times at the Equinoxes, considered 'great dances or ceremonies' and which require a great deal of shamanistic activity.

In the picture which follows we show the link between the rituals and the yearly cycle. The summer dances are sometimes celebrated in the winter time, but always in relation to the chontaduro and the crops.

The Cosmos and life-energy: A Gaian imperative

According to the Ufaina, one of the key aims of the great ceremonies is to 'return' the sickness or ills of this world to their 'owners'. Another is to impose nutritional and sexual restrictions upon the community so as to prevent ills from affecting the community in the future. In order to clarify the meaning of this, it is necessary to analyze how the Indians conceptualize the cosmos.

The Ufaina believe in a vital force called fufaka which is essentially masculine and which is present in all living beings. This vital force, whose source is the sun, is constantly recycled among plants, animals, men and the Earth itself which is seen as feminine. Each group of beings, men, plants, animals, Earth or water require a minimum amount of this vital force in order to live.

When a being is born, the vital force enters it and the group to which the being belongs. The group is seen as borrowing the energy from the total stock of energy.

188

When a being dies it releases this energy, and returns it to the stock. It is once again recycled. Similarly, when a living thing consumes another, for example when a deer eats a bush, a man eats a deer, or a tree extracts nutrients from the soil or when people cut down trees to create a clearing, the consumer acquires the energy of the consumed, and it accumulates in its own body.

Since the number of animals, plants, humans, trees and indeed of the amount of inhabited territory is 'limited' the amount of available energy is also limited, and must thereby be treated as a scarce resource. This leads to competition among different species for the available energy, since each must maintain its quota of energy.

What is of importance, according to the Ufaina, is that the vital force continues to be recycled from one species to another, in such a way that not too much accumulates in any one of them, since this would cause another to be correspondingly deprived of his vital force. The delicate balance between a community and its environment makes it defenseless; consequently any disturbance, however slight, necessarily affects the whole.

Human beings, although superior to animals in knowledge, are also part of this energy recycling system, and are subject to the same constraints.

For the Ufaina, each group of beings has a supernatural guardian who assumes that his 'flock' has enough life-energy to survive. The guardian of all hunted animals is the Ant-eater, (*Makuemari*), the guardian of wild fruit is the Tapir (*Yafurica and the Yupari*), the guardian of the jungle is the jaguar (*Yifotsirimaki*); the guardian of the crops are the Anaconda (*Okoa-anafaki*) and the Cicada (*Ka nkonaifi*); the custodian of the fish is the same Anaconda (*Oka-anafaki*) and the captain is the Ray (*Waibaifi*); the guardian of the land is the female mother Earth (*Namatu*)[3]; and the guardian of the energy of each human group is the Jaguar-man or sorcerer (*Yaiko*).

In the tribe's mythology, four heroes who originally established the orders of time, of space, and of the lives of men, animals and plants are responsible for the distribution of all the *fufaka*. They are called the *Imarimakana*, that is "those who have always been".[4]

The guardians are each responsible for their own group. They barter with each other attempting to secure an equitable distribution of vital energy (*fufaka*). Thus they play a central part in Ufaina cosmology as symbolic representatives of the main natural elements which play a part in the ecological balance of the jungle and the demographic balance of the human social groups.

Fufaka or vital energy circulates through the cosmos, which is represented as a great pyramid composed of thirteen superimposed platforms. It is from the top six, referred to as the '*Wehea*' that the *fufaka* associated with males arises. From the lower six arises the feminine life energy of *Namatu* or Mother Earth. The centre platform where *Wehea* and *Namatu meet is where man and nature are born and where the Ufaina live.*

At the apex of the pyramid are the *Imarimakana*, the four heroes who control all life-energy. They live in darkness, without air. The next platform is the abode of

3   Many myths of the Ufaina are related to these 'owners'. (See Von Hildebrand *op. cit.*)
4   *ibid.*

music, the source of *fufaka* contained in the community's ceremonies and trances, considered to be vehicles for the attainment of wisdom and the state of consciousness of the *Imarimakana*. Next comes the heaven of the energy of the dead and then that of the alliance. The last two heavens are those of crops and wild foods; the owner of the crops lives in the first and the owner of hunting and of wild fruit lives in the second, each with its own village. Under the platform where the Ufaina live there are another six heavens which represent various aspects of Mother Earth.

The sun revolves around the cosmos distributing energy to all equally, its summit lying between the abode of the four heroes and that of music. The sun generates energy for the cosmos, but the four *Imarimaka* administrate it.

The Jaguar-man and the handling of life-energy

The jaguar-man is the mediator between all these forces and the Ufaina community. He is selected for this role from birth and from that moment on is subjected to a strict diet forbidding the consumption of various animals and particularly salt, as well as either animal or vegetable fat. The apprenticeship is rigorous, requiring the study of the original myths, community life, animal behaviour, as well as the relationship and interdependence between men, plants, animals and Earth. At approximately the age of fifteen, having attained this knowledge, the apprentice retires for five years with a jaguar-man to specialize in meditation which will allow him access to other states of consciousness. The Ufaina do not take hallucinogens to attain this state, they simply use coca or tobacco as a stimulus. Their discipline implies little eating, little sleeping and abstention from sexual intercourse.

The learning of the jaguar-man is not only limited to the traditional knowledge of the community as expressed in myths, rituals and other customs nor to the practice of meditation and shamanistic ecstasy. It includes empirical knowledge based on the daily observation of the behaviour of the group, of hunting and fishing, of the yield of the land and the gathering of wild fruits, and the behaviour of the fauna and flora.

This information allows him to estimate the load carrying capacity of the area, a capacity which is defined partly by the area of tilled land and jungle surface, but mainly by the density of animals for hunting and fishing, that is providing protein.

Therefore, the jaguar-man has profound theoretical and empirical knowledge of the environment in which he lives. One of his central objectives is to administer the human handling of the nutrients in the natural environment such that the group can remain 10 or 15 years in a single place without the need to migrate. When the time comes it is he who decides when and in which direction to emigrate.

As mediator between his community and the natural environment, the jaguar-man, in regarding animals and some plants as 'people', coordinates and 'negotiates' with the custodians of these so that energy flows and does not accumulate in any group, particularly in that for which he is responsible, so as to avoid illness and the evils of this world.

If the group needs to hunt, fish, collect wild fruit, extract minerals from the jungle for building or to open new areas of cultivation, before taking on the task, it must consult with the jaguar-man. He concentrates and meditates on the state of the flora and fauna, on the carrying capacity of the area, and according to the need, invokes the 'owner' of wild fruit, or of hunting or of the Earth to request a loan of energy. According to his capabilities, the jaguar-man can invoke the 'owners' in various ways: firstly through meditation and shamanic spells, for example on the origin of the Tapir if it is hunting that is required. As he recites his body 'tells' him by muscular contractions whether or not he can proceed with the hunt. Secondly, the jaguar-man 'sees' whether there are many or few; if few he knows he cannot hunt because the 'owner' of the Tapir or of hunting will start to recuperate the energy for his own group, that is, he will send sickness to the Ufaina community. In that case he will search for another group of animals who do not need to 'recuperate' energy at that moment. If the answer to his request is positive, the jaguar-man offers coca in exchange for the animal or plant energy that the group will take for itself. Coca represents energy and has special qualities associated with shamanism like that of stimulating the mind, easing concentration, reducing sensation of hunger and sleep and reducing the need for sexual intercourse. Once the jaguar-man has established that the hunt can take place he will indicate to the men when and where they can find the animal.

To reinforce the jaguar-man's control over the relationship between community and natural environment he can resort to other mechanisms. A person who wishes to hunt, fish or extract any resource from the jungle must purify himself of female heat and of energy accumulated from excessive consumption of some plant or animal. This is accomplished in the ceremonies throughout the year. According to them, animals fall in line with purified men and present themselves to them for consumption, whereas they hide from those who are contaminated. *In other words, he who uses the jungle moderately will have no difficulty in surviving.*

Restrictions and the control of energy

Mechanisms for purification as well as for preserving the purity of individual energy, are founded on obligatory rules which refer mainly to dietary and sexual restrictions.

After the great rituals or certain feasts like that of the jaguar or the sparrowhawk (*Arpía-arpía*) or after having a child, the men must abstain for long periods from eating certain foods (exceptions are yucca in the form of cassava and white tucupi, red pepper and coca) as well as abstaining from sexual intercourse.

During the great rituals, which can last continuously over 48 hours, while the people dance in the communal house, repeating shamanic chants until they enter into a trance, the jaguar-man meditates instead the ecological conditions of the area. This meditation allows him to make a diagnosis of the actual situation of the population in relation to the nutrients in the area and to plan for future management, generally to encompass a one year period. As the ceremonies are celebrated several times a year, the diagnosis is periodically brought up to date.

In the meantime, those who chant are 'returning' illnesses to their respective 'owners'; they are purifying themselves through ritual objects which they wear; they are entering into contact with ancestors; they are preparing for the diagnosis of

191

the jaguar-man and with their chanting, helping him in his meditation.

When the ceremony ends, the jaguar-man should have arrived at a synthesis of the situation and from this he imposes a series of restrictions on the participants. By dietary restrictions he forbids the consumption of certain species for a period of time such that in the long term the community will not lack basic foods.

Protection of diverse species in the environment is interpreted as protection to the members of the community in the sense that the purpose is to avoid *accumulating energy which causes illness*. In these instances one must not eat what the jaguar-man has forbidden. It is no longer a question of asking permission from the 'owners'. This is only done when the restrictions have been lifted.

By means of sexual restrictions demographic growth is controlled, and hence the administration of the carrying capacity of the area is made easier. After each ceremony the participants are forbidden to have sexual intercourse for a period of time equal to the duration of the ceremony, which can be for three days or as long as a month according to the type of ritual. Naturally, during the ceremony these restrictions also apply. Considering that a communal household can easily celebrate four rituals a year, and that its inhabitants participate in those of two other houses, the people are under sexual restrictions more then ten times a year, which effectively allows control.

Beyond sexual restrictions in relation to ceremonies there are others. For instance, women must abstain from intercourse from the time of birth until a child can walk, while anyone who is undergoing training for jaguar-man or singer must abstain for long periods, even years. Other restrictions apply to fishing, hunting, as well as the building of communal houses. The interpretations given to explain such abstinence are two fold: on the one hand, to 'avoid the heat' of women which 'harms' the energy of men; particularly by preventing them from making contact with supernatural beings and impairing their capacity for hunting. Female energy or 'heat' mingles constructively at conception, but in other situations such mingling between the sexes is considered to be destructive. Thus, through daily contact with women, men accumulate female 'heat' which prevents them from identifying their own life-energy with that of animals - both being masculine - and so hinders hunting, or the identification with supernatural beings in order that the world can be administrated. Equally, they try to control their energy to reinforce it and identify it with their own body and not disperse it through sexual intercourse.

Another sexual restriction refers to the prohibition of incest; that is, the obligation to marry members of other groups, in such a way that formal relationships are established between groups. This practice brings with it the responsibility of reciprocal support in communal work as well as having allies should conflicts arise with other communities. It is also a way of ensuring the group's territory through having friends surrounding them who respect their hunting, fish and tilling areas. It is customary to invite allies to the great ceremonies and while the people sing and dance about the centre, the jaguar-men of the different villages sit by the houses and exchange interpretations of the situation in their own communities and environment. This exchange of knowledge and experience allows each jaguar-man to transcend the limits of his area and have a broader and actual view if interrelations between man and environment, allowing for a more efficient administration of the nutrients in the region and coordination with other Indian groups in the region.

Polluted energy and illness

Nevertheless some people in the community who do not obey the restrictions or participate in certain rituals, by their actions cause the accumulation of noxious energy. These are the people who lay themselves open to misfortune.

When a man consumes an animal or a plant he acquires its energy. If the right amount is consumed the energy identifies with and strengthens the consumer. But if too much is consumed, the energy of the consumed animal or plant dominates the man's own energy which makes him vulnerable to illness or misfortune.

Meanwhile when a child is born the new baby contains life-energy in common with all beings in the universe, that is, part of the universal energy has been removed to occupy the body of the newborn child. Nevertheless, this energy does not unite with the body but according to the Indians, extends to animals and plants as though belonging to a jaguar-man. The jaguar-man then takes this energy and through prayer and the original myths of the community identifies it with the ancestors of the tribe. Then, in a second ritual, he identifies the child's energy with his body, that he may 'recognize himself' as an individual. For the rest of the individual's life exercises in meditation as well as dietary and sexual abstinence are all aimed at identifying the energy with the body; reinforcing the person; filling him with his own energy and preventing other energies from entering which can cause illness. In the case of the jaguar-man, his identification is such that he can take part of his own energy to purify the energy of others in the community.

However many people accumulate energy of other beings, establishing a dichotomy in body-energy. When this happens, the contaminated energy becomes visible to the 'owners' or to jaguar-men, not as the energy of the person, but as that of whatever was consumed, whether plant or animal. The jaguar-man can only perceive the contaminated energy when in a state of altered consciousness, through hallucination; in a normal state of consciousness he will not see it. If, for example, he sees tapir-like energy, or deer, fish or pig-like energy and he 'hunts'it, he will take both the energy of the animal as well as that of the person, who will fall ill and may even die. The captains of animals who hunt for polluted human energy are the captain of the armadillo, of the '*borugo*', of the red deer, of the tapir and of the pig, as well as of the tiger, Boa, ant-eater, cicada, *Yurupari* and *Namatu*. When the 'captains' or 'owners' want to take human energy they send snakes to bite the contaminated person or as spirits they hit the individuals over the head with a branch, make them fall off a tree, overturn a canoe in the river, or send ill-winds or sickness. Only a person with contaminated energy is visible and therefore susceptible to these evils. In the case of wild or grown fruits eaten in excess, the energy of the person takes the form of the fruit and is eaten by the Yurupari who administer the energy of this world.

The bodies of people who respect the restrictions are animated with their own energy and hence are invisible to the 'owners' and to jaguar-men, and no harm can come to them. For this reason the community must return energy which is not its

193

own and purify itself through rituals, as well as respecting dietary and sexual restrictions imposed by the jaguar-man on the strength of his knowledge and of tradition.

Purification of energy as a healing system

So far we have spoken of preventative medicine expressed as an ecological relationship. But healing exists too, although for the Ufaina the individual's needs are secondary to keeping the community healthy. The sick are those who have accumulated alien energy and are suffering because the owner is trying to recuperate that which is his or hers. When healing an individual, the jaguar-man enquires about his or her daily conduct and establishes in what way restrictions have been violated. This is in order to decide who is sending the ill, whether the owner of hunting or of fish, or that of wild fruit, etc. But he also does this to show those present at the healing ritual how the sick one is a victim of his or her own imprudence; as a salutory warning. The patient is thus the protagonist of a drama, the evidence of what happens when restrictions are not adhered to. The jaguar-man recites myths and orations with which he underscores the restrictions and situates them in a traditional and supernatural context with the aim of impressing on those attending the importance of the rules. Having concluded the healing he often imposes long and severe dietary and sexual restrictions on those who live in the same communal house as the sick person. If other members of the community do not adhere to these restrictions, the sick one will not 'heal'. Many a time it is said that so-and-so did not heal and died because the brother or the uncle ate something which was forbidden at the healing. In this way, even the ceremony of healing an individual is primarily directed at the community and at reestablishing the rules which maintain group health, preventative medicine, ecological balance, and social consensus.

Nevertheless, when an individual is sick the jaguar-man still tries to liberate him from the polluting energy. The jaguar-man has his own energy at a high level of purity and can therefore use part of it to 'penetrate' the sick, using meditation or some herbal beverage as a vehicle. Once 'inside' the patient he 'approaches' the polluted energy and 'awaits' the arrival of the one who wants to hunt it. Rarely does he have to struggle with the one coming to do harm, because on seeing him, it will not approach. In this way the jaguar-man keeps the 'enemy' away while he 'grasps' the illness and 'takes' it by shamanic prayer and purifies it. For this he 'takes' it to its origins, to the spring from which rivers flow and where all men were born: there he 'purifies' the energy with original energy. He also 'takes' it to where are found the mythical ancestors, particularly those who never sicken like the three major Imarimákana, so that the energy identifies with theirs and becomes pure. He 'returns' it also to the womb where it was first united with the body and makes it be slowly reborn while invoking all ancestors of the group and all the animal protectors of the Ufaina. During the ceremony, the jaguar-man paints the sick person's body with black dye, prepared from leaves of a specially cultivated shrub to purify the individual and forbids the consumption of food, although usually with the exception of yucca (Manihot spp) and its derivatives such as white *'tucupi'* ('cassava') and *'caguana'*.

If the victim's energy has already been 'hunted' saving him is more complicated. The jaguar-man tries to discover who took it and then to retrieve it, but in general these are hopeless cases.

Apart from entering the body through excessive consumption, contaminated energy, which the Ufaina also call *Nenesike* as a general term, may be sent by the jaguar-man of another group who wishes to do harm. In this instance it is generally an attempt to modify the biological or social behaviour of a person. For example, if energy is extracted from wild fruits and introduced into the victim, his body will 'mature and rot in a few months' just like fruit does. If wasp energy is introduced the victim's body will become irascible to the point of not being able to live in his community. If the energy of a sterile plant is introduced in a woman it will sterilize her. In that way the Ufaina consider that the jaguar-man can manipulate the energy of other beings, whether they belong to his own community or not.

According to the Indian groups on the Miriti River, this type of evil shamanism can only be practised by the Matapí and the Yukuna. The Ufaina, Letuama and Makuna can defend themselves and return the evils which are sent to them but can do no harm directly. To heal this kind of ill, the jaguar-man must recite the original myths of the 'birth' of each community or tribe to detect where the contaminating energy comes from. With the same process he then tries to determine which jaguar-man of the tribe in question did it. In both instances, as he recites the myths or thinks about the people during meditation, his body responds with muscular contractions indicating what he is seeking. If the person who sent the ill has no polluted energy he shall not be able to detect him. For this reason jaguar-men, and particularly those who do harm, rigorously follow the restrictions so that no evil can be 'sent' or 'returned' to them.

DISCUSSION

Mae-Wan Ho I am fascinated by this Jaguar man because it is a phenomenon that is common to nearly all the Meso-American cultures. I wonder if you could say whether his role is that of priest or of ruler. Is it only his privilege to mediate and communicate with all these custodians?

Martin von Hildebrand The Jaguar men are the specialists in the community; they are the heads of the community and in charge of the rituals. Hence the person who organizes the singing is the same person who specializes in communicating as mediator between the community and nature, the community and the custodians. He doesn't normally marry and to become a Jaguar man he has to follow a very strict diet right from the beginning. Jaguar men should not eat salt for instance, they should not eat anything that is fat, they should not have sexual relationships, nor do they work in the sense that others in the community do. I can't say it is true for all communities; there certainly have been changes.

Being a Jaguar man used to be inherited, but now because of the impact of our civilization that inheritance has broken down. Sickness has taken its toll and the lineages have disappeared.

Question What about battles between the communities? And how are property relationships organized?

Martin von Hildebrand The communities fight less nowadays because we don't allow them to fight; we keep that privilege for ourselves. Typically they used to fight with the people they knew the best, such as the in-laws, so many of the wars were all to do with the exchange of wives from one tribe to another. Care was generally taken not to kill the women and children, especially since one's own sisters may well be among the women. The women and children were therefore allowed to get out and then the battle would ensue between men over 28; who anyway were considered disposable.

The question of property is extremely complex, but generally an object made by someone belongs to the person who made it; at the same time there is little point in possessing something unless there is someone with whom to exchange it. Hence the importance of objects has far more to do with the relationship that is established than in keeping something for oneself.

Elizabeth Sahtouris Much anthropological and historical research has been carried out on the period of transition between nomadic male-ruled hunting societies and essentially female-based settled agricultural societies. You have discussed tribes that carry out both kinds of activities in cycles and I wondered whether there was any association in the pattern of the cycles with the time of warfare or the actual management of society? You said that during the agricultural phase women played more significant roles in managing the society in some way. Are they therefore in charge of agriculture and is there an association between the wet and dry seasons and the battles? Are the battles more likely in the male season than in the female season?

Martin von Hildebrand   I have problems in answering your question because I have never observed any battles, so I don't know whether battles are more likely to be associated with the dry, male season. At the same time I would not say that women run more of society at a particular season; they always play an important role and through cultivation are responsible for the production of as much as 70 per cent of the food. Nevertheless, it is the men who run the political and social organization of the community; the women come from different tribes and are therefore not necessarily even closely related. Nor do I think it is a question of the women having had the power and the men taking it over. Still I have been talking not of the past but of the present.

Wolfgang Sachs   If I have to think of the absolute contrary of the world you were describing I would point to the concept of *Biosphere II* which Dorion Sagan presented to us yesterday evening - a kind of *ecodisneyland*. On the one hand we have the world you have been conjuring up where knowledge means looking into why things are as they are. Alternatively for us children of modern science we look into things in terms of how they work. Now Lovelock had the genius to call what basically is a book on self-regulatory mechanisms *Gaia* and in so doing gave people the hope that science would limit itself to cosmological concerns about *why*. However we still seem to be caught up in the question as to how it works, the epitome of which is represented by the experiments to create mini-biospheres. Here I think is our contradiction, looking for one thing but being caught up in the other.

Helena Norberg-Hodge   Of course, it isn't just looking at how things work, but it is doing so in order to manipulate them. It is that manipulation which is dangerous.

James Lovelock   To compound the contradiction we have just been faced with I couldn't help wondering as I was listening to the fascinating world presented by Martin how do people there respond to a major perturbation such as an epidemic or a natural disaster - for instance a bug that completely destroys their habitat. I don't know whether these things happen; maybe you've never seen it, but I wonder as to the resilience of the system, and how well it responds to a major disturbance?

Martin von Hildebrand   I have not seen them deal with a major catastrophe in the area; they know how to deal with floods, that kind of problem. However with epidemics they do have a serious problem, particularly with regard to western epidemics since they don't know how to treat them. But they nevertheless have an interesting interpretation, extrapolated from their interpretation of what it is to consume animals. What makes western people different, they say, is their passion for merchandise. Hence the more people of their own communities get interested in merchandise the more the energy associated with it takes over their own thought leading to their becoming white and disappearing, at least as Indians. As they see it they must cut down on merchandise.

Lynn Margulis   I am rather curious about two things related to the botany; one is the use besides coca of hallucinogenic plants, for instance you say that the Jaguar man goes into colour trances. The other is how much do western botanists know and have documented the plants being used? In that respect Professor R. E. Schultes of Harvard University has claimed that 85 to 90 per cent of the plants in the Colombian Amazon are undocumented to science. Does that include the ones being used?

Martin von Hildebrand He is a specialist in the north west region of the Colombian Amazon. In the area I have been working the Indians do not use hallucinogens, but 50 kilometres further north you get all the Tukano-speaking groups that do use *yahe*.

Lynn Margulis So your group doesn't use them at all?

Martin von Hildebrand No, what they claim is that those who use drugs can get into a trance and can learn how to perceive. But they arrive at the same state, so they claim, through meditation. It takes much longer - many years - whereas the others say they do it in six months. In fact, they use coca, tobacco, dancing and feasting.

Ulrich Loening Nicholas Guppy and I have just met Schultes and he repeated that there are thousands of interesting plants and a desperate lack of any understanding or knowledge. The collection at Harvard now runs into the thousands but with scarcely any work being done.

Ted Pawloff Your presentation has been fascinating in helping us in our own understanding of Gaia, and I think we ought to try and transform the information we have been given in some kind of creative and useful way if we possibly can. I was very struck by the way that such communities have an intuitive feel for what we call the balance of the ecosystem and can regulate their behaviour accordingly. Indeed through such mechanisms as their prohibitions they actually manage as it were themselves as an exchange mechanism within the environment. At the same time they have a cosmic connection through what they call *thought*. For instance the energy of the sun is uncoloured but then takes on all the hues as it passes through the ecosystem into the various organisms. Jim Lovelock had the courage of using poetry in helping us to demythify our science in the correct sense. That reminds me of Rudolph Steiner who followed the path of rationality in the highest sense; for instance in his work on agriculture he described the experience of trace chemicals long before biochemistry had been able to show their relevance.

Jerry Ravetz It would be interesting for the microbial ecologists among us to check out how much Steiner actually did say about the importance of such elements in agriculture. Whether he was the first I am not sure, but certainly I know that he warned very early on that growing crops was not simply a matter of plants sucking up chemicals.

Diana Schumacher Are the cosmologies similar among the different Indian groups in the Colombian Amazon, and how vulnerable are these groups to our western civilization?

Martin von Hildebrand The different groups have similar basic ideas but they do vary in the way they interpret the role of the custodians, in their social organization, their specializations and in their political organization. How the Indians react to the impact of western society, that depends very much on certain tribes; some are very resistant. For instance the Kogi from the North of Colombia in the Sierra Nevada are extraordinarily resistant. But the problem is that they become less resistant once we start helping them; that is the dangerous part, that is when they break down.

Take Christianization for example: where I work Christ is considered to be the custodian of White people, for he is seen to be the custodian of merchandise with the priest acting as an intermediary. Thus, if you want to go to the shop and you haven't been baptized or you don't go to Mass on Sundays, then you can't go to the shop. That's perfectly logical because Christ as the custodian would send sickness through merchandise if you haven't made an offer to him and given something back.

Marcus Colchester I just want to cast a word of warning on the implications of this. I don't think I disagree with anything that Martin says. The people I have worked with in the Amazon have many similarities insofar as they have a system which conceptualizes their relationship with their environment. But if we are trying to talk in terms of its implications for Gaia, then we have to ask ourselves certain questions rather similar to the ones that Michael Whitfield asked yesterday in relation to the oceans. Thus, to what extent do these concepts of their environment actually affect their behaviour in terms of its day to day activities, and to what extent do those economic activities have a significant effect on the environment? And should their environment be affected by their economic practices how does that feed back on the behaviour of the shamans?

I think we have been rather loose in assuming that there is a sort of direct feedback, that the shaman actually regulates the environment or regulates human behaviour in response to environmental imperatives. The point I would like to make is that a lot of research has been done to try and show that such feedback cycles exist. In fact the evidence from basic studies indicates that the feedback loops are not there in the consciousness of the people in ways that we seem to be interpreting it here. My only plea is that we must not forget that between ideology and economic practices there is the whole complexity of the social organization which mediates. It is the same for us here: we are all mainly 'green-thinking' people, yet how many of us have motor cars and know that we are being destructive? How many of us drink coca-cola out of aluminium cans?

Helena Norberg-Hodge I want simply to say that at the level of individual consciousness the link is not made, but I see it as having been made collectively, reinforced again and again precisely through social systems, through the technologies that were available to them. It has been reinforced collectively over many centuries; moreover the impact on Gaia has been relatively harmless and their lifestyle has worked since time immemorial so there hasn't been the need of the individual to stop and question his behaviour.

Martin von Hildebrand Just one comment on this. I think we could get in a tangle over this point and that would be a mistake. First I think that it is in the collective consciousness as well as in the individual. It is a shame I couldn't have brought one of those shamans with me because he could have talked about this practically in the same language; it is incredible the amount of abstraction they can make about these things. Anyhow, you can sit all morning and discuss how dangerous it is to eat a particular fish – the salvaletta – because it has fat and other bad things. Then at 3 o'clock, what do they serve up but a salvaletto. It is delicious, and when you query what is going on the shaman says: don't worry, I'll make a prayer and fix it . Four months later there is a sickness and the shaman says: that damned fish I should never have eaten it!

Edward Goldsmith All that is perfectly understandable. Paul Weiss contrasted two things, *macroindeterminacy* and *macrodeterminacy*. That means that you get a little bit of chaos at the lower level, for instance the non-observance of rules like eating the salvaletta, but when you look at the whole you find a much more orderly system. Weiss came to this conclusion after looking inside cells and finding such indeterminacy of behaviour compared with the orderliness outside it.

As regards the second point, whether the knowledge is conscious or not is wholly irrelevant. I don't think that Lynn Margulis' bacteria are conscious that they are part of a cybernetic system: consciousness is epistemologically and cybernetically irrelevant. This brings us back to the whole notion of knowledge and to the epistemology of knowledge. To my mind knowledge is information, and information is organized in the natural world for the purposes of control; thus it serves to mediate behaviour in ways that are orderly. Hence information is organized into the cultural pattern of these tribal communities in such a way that it enables them in some way to achieve homeostasis within their environment. If you reject this view you have to explain how they actually maintain homeostasis of their environment: because they have maintained it for millennia. This brings us again to the great God of Randomness so respected by reductionist scientists. If you admit, as I do, that randomness is total illusion then you have to accept some sort of cybernetic system.

GAIA:
IMPLICATIONS FOR THE SOCIAL SCIENCES
by Matthias Finger

As a professional social scientist, working within the social science university system, I find it very difficult to reconcile the Gaia hypothesis with the social sciences as they are today. Let us see why. The social sciences are still highly mechanistic and reductionistic. Lovelock's thesis on the other hand is based on a very different non-mechanistic and holistic philosophy. Thus Lovelock tells us that "the entire range of living matter on Earth, from whales to viruses, and from oaks to algae, could be regarded as constituting a single living entity, capable of manipulating Earth's atmosphere to suit its overall needs and endowed with faculties and powers far beyond its constituent parts" (Lovelock, 1979).

This statement is clearly neither reconcilable with the mechanistic nor the reductionist thesis.

The social sciences are also man-centred. For them man is an unique animal, quite distinct from all other forms of life with which they show little interest. Thus social scientists are unlikely to accept Lovelock's thesis that "...from its origin the human species has been as much part of Gaia as have all the other species, and that like them it has acted unconsciously in the process of planetary homeostasis" (Grinevald, 1987).

Still less are social scientists likely to accept the following statement by Lovelock:

> "Life on this planet is a very tough, robust, and adaptable entity and we are but a small part of it. The most essential part is probably that which dwells on the floors of the continental shelves and in the soil below the surface. Large plants and animals are relatively unimportant (....). The tough and reliable workers composing the microbial life of the soil and the sea beds are the ones who keep things moving....."

Indeed social scientists would regard it as quite preposterous that man and other large animals are less important than microbes. This brings us to what I take to be a serious contradiction in Lovelock's thesis. If Gaia can survive without the human species, man cannot survive outside Gaia, and he is "condemned to living within Gaia." On the one hand Lovelock sees man as an integral part of Gaia. We can refer to this as the *Gaian view of man,* though we must note that it is also the view that is often put forward by human ecologists. On the other hand man, in particular modern man, is also responsible for the systematic destruction of the biosphere and hence for the disruption of the mechanisms that maintain Gaian homeostasis. If this is so, then rather than being part of the structure of Gaia, man is, in some sense of the word, external to it and again in some sense of the word, parasitical to it. This is probably best referred to as the environmentalist's view of man. Can these two views be reconciled? The obvious answer seems to be that at some point in his history man has shifted from being an integral part of Gaia to being external to it. If this is so, then modern civilisation is not a natural development that can be regarded as contributing to increased Gaian homeostasis, nor can science and technology, which have made possible this modern civilisation, be regarded as part of Gaia's life sustaining mechanisms. But Jim Lovelock does not see things this way. For him, modern industrial civilization is just a continuation of the evolutionary process and therefore a full part of Gaia: "Fluorocarbons which have their sources mainly in the chemical industry, and were never in the air before industrial man appeared, are very indicative of life at work". This fundamentally optimistic conception of evolution places Lovelock in the philosophical traditional of Teilhard de Chardin and explains the success of the Gaia hypothesis within the New Age movement.

Jacques Grinevald accuses Teilhard du Chardin of adopting the same contradictory stance.

> "Le schèma explicatif qu propose Teilhard, à savoir considérer l'Homme comme 'clef de l'évolution', c'est-à-dire 'comprendre la Biosphère par la Noosphère', non seulement repose sur une curieuse conception de la Biosphère, mais est surtout un renversement épistémologique complet, un retour a l'argument téléologique de la téléologie chrétienne, la conception religieuse du monde la plus étrange à la perspective écologique moderne.
>
> (....) L'Homme est nullement remis en place dans la biosphère, tout au contraire, il est placé au-dessus pour la dominer, la transformer, la dédoubler artificiellement. La Noosphère c'est 'une immense machine à penser'! Ni la bombe atomique, ni les manipulations génétiques, ni l'épuisement des ressources, ni la pollution, ni les premiers cris d'alarme des écologistes ébranleront chez Teilhard la foi dans le progrès" (Grinevald, 1987).

In general terms, this contradiction could apply equally well to Lovelock. Lynn Margulis adopts this position even more explicitly than does Lovelock.

> "Not only men are members of the more than 10 million existing species components of the Gaian regulatory system, but so are our machines... We may compare the future evolution of machines to the evolution of life on dry land 400 million years ago. Life may continue to expand by technobic autopoiesis" (Sagan, Margulis, 1987).

Lovelock's view of modern civilisation and its scientific and technological activities as being an integral part of Gaia is consistent with his original refusal to accept their inherent ecological destructiveness. It is only recently that he has admitted that Gaia cannot indefinitely sustain the impact of our industrial activities.

> "It has been said by politically inclined critics" he writes "that the Gaia hypothesis is a fabrication, an argument developed to allow industry to pollute at will since Mother Gaia will clean up the mess. It is true that a system in homeostasis is more forgiving about disturbances. But this is only when it is healthy and well within the bounds of its capacity to regulate. When such a system is stressed to near the limits of regulation, even a small disturbance may cause it to jump to a new stable state or even to fail entirely. In these circumstances,pollution and changes in land use or in ecology of the continental shelves could be the recipes for global disaster. It could be that regulation of the Earth's climate is not far from one of those limits" (Lovelock, 1979).

Facing such a situation, modern man - being the cause of such a possible disaster - not only has, according to Lovelock, a growing "responsibility for maintaining planetary homeostasis", but also has the science and the technology for achieving a better understanding of its functioning. In the tradition of Teilhard, Lovelock sees this as a process of increasing Gaia's own consciousness: modern man with his science and technology are the consciousness of an (unconscious) natural system: Gaia.

But, one should not confuse man's (or Gaia's?) ability to diagnose the disease with his or her capacity to repair the damage done to Gaia. Drawing on Lovelock's medical analogy one can say that the patient may be fully aware of and even understand the functioning of his cancer, but he may be unable to do anything about it, unless he changes his way of life.

By this analogy I want to point out the limits of Lovelock's scientific planetary diagnosis. By placing modern civilization within Gaia, Lovelock is prevented from thinking critically about science and technology. He therefore sticks to a traditional concept of science, the function of which is limited to analyzing and describing the functioning of Gaia, hoping that once the functioning is completely understood, some technical means of intervening will automatically be invented. Significantly, this appraisal does not take into account the historical and social dimensions of science and technology, "the consciousness of planet Earth." Lovelock's interpretation of the Gaia hypothesis may well lead to a scientific description of its functioning, but not to a historical understanding of how and why it now approaches the limits of homeostasis.

In other words, the Gaia hypothesis leaves no room for either society, or the social sciences. To pursue the medical analogy: of course it is always possible to resort to surgery; but why cut off a leg, if a shift to a healthier diet would have achieved the same result?

The development of the Gaia hypothesis is part of a more general movement within the earth and atmospheric sciences, which looks at the biosphere[1] as a global and quasi living system. As Jacques Grinevald has shown, (Grinevald, 1987a), this movement has a long history, going back to geochemist Vladimir Vernadsky (1863-1945) in the Soviet Union and G E Hutchinson (born 1903) in the USA.

Applications of such a global ecological approach to modern society can be found in the works of Barry Commoner, and Howard Odum, in the first Report to the Club of Rome (1972), in the Global 2000 Report to the President (1980), and more recently in a series of studies and publications undertaken by different institutions (Snyder, 1985, Myers, 1985).

I will concentrate here on the three main research projects, which have recently been planned and partly launched, and which have as their objective the study of Planet Earth as a whole system. All three share the spirit of the Gaia hypothesis, even though they do not use the term Gaia nor speak of the Earth as an organism or

---

1   According to Herbert Friedman, "Biosphere is the integrated living and life-supporting system comprising the peripheral envelope of the planet Earth together with its surrounding atmosphere so far down, and up, as any form of life exists naturally.

natural system. Indeed Lovelock is even personally involved in some of these projects. They are:

- The Global Habitability Programme, launched by NASA in 1982 and based since 1983 at the Center for the Study of Global Habitability at Columbia University.
- The International Geosphere - Biosphere Programme (IGBP): a study of Global Change, prepared by the International Council of Scientific Unions since 1983 and formally approved in 1986 (Malone and Roederer, 1985).
- The Integrated Research Programme on the Sustainable Development of the Biosphere, managed by the International Institute for Applied Systems Analysis, Laxenburg, Austria, since 1983 (Clarke and Munn, 1986).

In this paper the term "Global Change" is used for all three programmes. All three see planet Earth as an interactive and "integrated system of the oceans, the atmosphere and the biosphere" (Global Change: Impacts on habitability, 1981) and see life itself as giving rise to the long term development of some kind of life-sustaining equilibrium.

"We live on a unique planet" we read in "Global Change in the Geosphere-Biosphere" "with an ocean of liquid water and an atmosphere capable of sustaining and protecting life. Moreover, the atmosphere, hydrosphere and surface layers of the Earth are not the product of inorganic processes alone, but the result of a synergism between living and nonliving parts, with the former often dominant. What must impress us is the delicacy of the balance that obtains."

Like the Gaia hypothesis, the promotion of these programmes foster a global perspective or "holistic approach, that will deepen and strengthen our understanding of the planet's subtle and often synergetic physical, chemical and biological processes. Such a framework would examine the oceans, atmosphere, lithosphere, hydrosphere, biota and the solar – terrestrial domain as a single system" (Malone, 1985).

In opposition to Lovelock's gaian view of man, these programmes define his role and that of the modern civilization he has created very clearly. Thus, modern man is above all seen as a disturbing factor in the global cycles, as is illustrated by his role in the degradation and desertification of the soil, in depleting the ozone layer or in the building up of greenhouse gases in the atmospohere.

In different IGBP-programmes we can, for example, find the following statements:

"The dominant changes that affect the environment and the course of life on Earth are natural ones (....). But imposed on these is now another set of changes, more recent and immediate in consequence that are the clear result of human activities" (NAS, *Global Change* 1986:1).

"....human impacts have grown to approximate those of the natural processes that control the global life-supporting system" (*Global Change* 1985:xiv).

204

"Human energy production and intensive farming and technology have altered the albedo of the Earth, the composition of the soil and waters, the chemistry of the air, the areas of forests, the balance of the global ecosystem and the diversity of plant and animal species."

More than ten per cent of the land area of the Earth is now under cultivation. More than 30 per cent is under active management for purposes of mankind. Chemical compounds for which there are no natural analogues are being produced and released into the air and water in ever growing proportions, and rates of natural chemical and hydrological cycles have been altered with currently unpredictable consequences for climate and the local and global environment" (NAS, *Global Change* 1986:2).

Thus, in contradiction to the Gaia hypothesis which implicitly states that modern man is still a part of Gaia and that therefore there is no reason to worry, and in contradiction too to Lovelock's gaian view of man as a responsible part of Gaia, who will manage, like the biota before, to bring about a new, life-sustaining equilibrium, the promotion of the three programmes are not as optimistic. They evaluate the present situation as being much more "urgent" and "alarming" (IGBP 1986) than does Lovelock. Understanding the Global Changes is seen as necessary - "essential for survival" (IGBP 1986) - but not a sufficient condition for bringing about a new life-sustaining equilibrium.

We therefore see that the environmentalist's view of modern man as a destabilising element has been adopted by the three above-mentioned programmes. They are thus not only interested in "understanding the way in which the global environmental system operates" (IGBP 1986:2), but also in "the changes that are occurring in this system, and the manner in which they are influenced by human actions" (ibid:3).

I propose to call the underlying hypothesis of the three programmes the "Global Change Hypothesis", distinguishing it from the Gaia hypothesis, which actually is a "global stability hypothesis."

Implicitly, and sometimes even explicitly, the social sciences play an important role within the Global Change Hypothesis. Of all the three mentioned programmes, the IIASA Programme on the Sustainable Development of the Biosphere seems to be most conscious of this role, but none has formulated it as clearly as the American geophysicist Herbert Friedman in 1986:

"Understanding future environmental changes that may be induced by mankind's transformation of the Earth's surface and the atmosphere's composition will require an even greater breadth of investigation that includes the social sciences" (*Global Change* 1986:viii)

As far as I can see it, such social sciences would have to play a double role within Global Change research, following William Clark's distinction between predicting and managing Global Change (Clark, 1985, Clark/Holling, *Global Change*, 1985).

On the one hand the social sciences could help to understand the social, economic, cultural, political, psychological and other origins, causes, aspects and dimensions of Global Change. On the other hand, they could assess the social, political, economic, cultural, psychological and other implications of Global Change on modern civilization. This would in particular include the assessment of

205

the implications on politics, or even the elaboration of policies in accordance with the limits of Earth's habitability (Richards, Parry in Clark/Munn, 1985).

I believe that unless the social dimension is included, a full and adequate understanding of Global Change, i.e. of the interaction between modern civilization and Gaia will not be possible. Nor will it be possible to understand which transformations this civilization has to undergo if it wants to survive.

To date only the Global Change hypothesis in which modern man is seen as part of Gaia, actually offers the possibility of such an understanding.

This does not mean, however, that the social sciences are prepared for such an understanding, or even willing to understand. In fact, participating in Global Change research would require from the social sciences some minimum ideas, concepts and theories about Gaia and the impact of man on it, and it would also require, as Jerome Ravetz points out, a "new style of science, appropriate to this novel and urgent task of coping with biosphere problems" (Ravetz, in Clark/Munn 1986). It is a new type of transdisciplinary, global, policy related science, which admits its ignorance. Such a science is actually under elaboration within the new epistemological field of the Earth and atmospheric sciences through Global Change research. Yet the social sciences continue to refer to the epistemology of classical physics and analytical mechanics.

The social sciences in modern societies

The myth of value-free social sciences, whose role is to observe and understand societies and their problems has to be abandoned. From their origin in the 18th century starting with "political arithmetics", the social sciences were, and still are, part of the enterprise of modernity and development.

This enterprise actually goes back to the philosophy of the Enlightenment. With the Enlightenment society was seen as the product of reason, and later of science, against all kinds of traditional and religious myths. Science has therefore had to furnish meaning to the new rational societies, and therefore has had to indicate the direction in which these societies will be developing (Grinevald, 1975). Today science has not only replaced religion as a new myth, but also plays a significant, instrumental role within modern societies. As such it must be studied as a socio-cultural and a political phenomenon (Blume, 1974, Ravetz, 1971).

The social sciences are of course part of this process of modernization through science. In particular, modern civilization needs the social sciences to bring about the new order needed to replace tradition, more and more seen as being arbitrary and retrograde. In fact, since their origin during the Age of Enlightenment, the social sciences have played a double role: on the one hand they are needed to furnish a new, more rational meaning to modern societies, whereas on the other hand they have the practical function of bringing about and managing a new society based on rationality. As Alain Caille, (1986) one of the rare philosophers of the social sciences has stated:

"Les sciences, socials accompagnent, ..., l'espoit d'une société radicalement autre. Elles sont les prophètes des temps nouveaux.

206

....le 'besoin' pour les sciences sociales est proportionnel au degré d'inadéquation de l'ordre social institué à lui-même, pour autant que cette inadéquation ne peut être palliée imaginairement par l'espoir d'un retour au même ou au passé mais passe, irrésistiblement, à l'invention d'un rapport social nouveau. Les sciences sociales naissent de la reconnaissance plus ou moins explicite du fait de la modernité et de l'arbitraire des symbolismes passés. Parce qu'elles procèdent de la découverte de l'indétermination de l'ancien monde et du désir d'un monde nouveau à accoucher, elles sont demiurges. Et ce démiurgisme est inséparable de leur conceptualisation."

The prophets of these modern times, the "ideologues of progress" as Krishnan Kumar (1978) calls them, are also the first social scientists and the fathers of modern sociology like Henri de Saint-Simon (1760-1825) and August Comte (1798-1857). More than the philosophers of the Enlightenment, these social scientists, the so-called positivists, have introduced the idea of development, which ever since has been an integral part of all the social sciences.

In the beginning, progress meant the perfectibility of man through reason; indeed to the fathers of modern social sciences, progress also came to mean ever more rational social organization, where rationality referred to the achievement of conclusions consonant with the scientific world-view of the time via the reductionist and mechanistic scientific method.

Saint-Simon introduced a new element into the idea of progress i.e. the idea of the stages of development of society. The last of his three stages of progress, the industrial society, is precisely that which is to be brought into being on the one hand by applying science to industrial production, and on the other by applying the social sciences to the task of organising a society's industrial base in a rational way. As Kumar puts it "If the society of the future was the society of science, then the science of society, sociology, had to be considered the master guide to that future" (Kumar 1978:27)

In the late 19th century the idea of progress was further elaborated by Herbert Spencer, who introduced pre-Darwinian biologic evolutionism into the social scciences. From this organic metaphor stemmed the idea of an intrinsic improvement of all "organisms", from individuals to States.

The social sciences therefore have an image of societies and of their constituents (i.e. individuals, families, groups, etc) as being independent and self-referring entities under continuous development, evolution or progress; and this as part of and contributing to a civilization which itself progresses, both materially and culturally.

The role of the social scientist is then to contribute to the achievement of this progress and to the coming of a new, enlightened, self-sustaining and self-referring post-industrial society by propagating the image of a rational society (mechanism or organism) and by contributing to its rational management (social engineering).

Hence, the enterprise of the social sciences, from their beginning, has been technocratic by nature: mythologies and ideologies being replaced by scientific social analysis, "political practice" being replaced by the applied social sciences (Kuper, 1985).

The epistemological dichotomy

We have seen what the social sciences owe to the Enlightenment, i.e. to the "development" of reason. Modern society, which is to be built on Reason through applied science and promoted by the social sciences, is thereby seen as separate from and opposed to nature. This dichotomy is not only philosophical, but also practical: research methodologies considering only reason and cognition i.e. detached and unemotional observation, as furthering scientific progress, whereas "nature" produces subjective, and unscientific ideologies.[2]

As William Leiss has shown, the idea of the "domination of nature", of the "control over nature" or of the "conquest of nature" stems back to the roots of the social sciences, where it was inextricably linked with the expectation of social improvement and improved economic welfare. Economics, for example, sees "nature" either as an instrument for achieving economic development or as an obstacle to its achievement. This relation to nature can also be found in Marxism, which is built on the same epistemological dichotomy between nature and culture. According to Leiss (1972):

> "Marx understood the mastery of nature as a factor in the evolution of the labour-process. At an enhanced stage of development this mastery is expressed in the fruitful marriage of science and industry."

According to the Marxist tradition, each step in the mastery of nature corresponds to a freer society (freer from the constraints nature imposes on society).[3]

Thus mastery over nature is a condition and an instrument for the development of modern societies. Today, a new generation of social scientists (both Marxist and non-Marxist) of which Jurgen Habermas (born 1929) is the most quoted representative - continue to build their theories on the idea of the domination of nature, and to elaborate criteria for social goals which are totally independent from nature. For Habermas for example, these criteria rely on reason.

But not only are economics and modern anthropology based on this "epistemological dichotomy" between nature and culture, so are psychology and psychoanalysis, the impact of which on the social sciences cannot be underestimated.

The father of psychoanalysis, Sigmund Freud (1856-1939), for example, considers the Ego and its development as "squeezed" between the static drives of "nature" (id), i.e. Eros and Thanatos on the one hand, and social norms on the other. "Ego development" is then the result of a successful repression of inner nature, while at the same time an adaptation of social norms. The development of civilization depends, according to Freud, on the use of sublimated energy derived from the repression of nature for socially useful goals.

On the other hand, the life sustaining role of nature is not recognised by the social

---

1 This concept is a central idea of the so-called critical theorists of the Frankfurt school: Theodor Adorno (1903-1969), Max Horkheimer (1895-1973) and Herbert Marcuse (1898-1979).

2 The critics of the (post-marxist) Frankfurt school disagree on this point, believing that the domination of nature will bring about increased domination of man over man, a domination which is necessary to organize rationally and manage the domination of nature. But this is just a pessimistic interpretation of the (optimist) original Saint-Simonian idea of technocratic social sciences managing modern societies.

sciences which is only concerned with man and more precisely with man's rational, cognitive and scientific roles. It is thus unlikely that social scientists will be capable of considering man in terms of his gaian functions.

Instrumentality

Of course it makes sense that social scientists as rational managers of modern societies should elaborate the methods which enable them to fulfil their role. These may be social science concepts, theories, instrumental methods, techniques and the like. But their very nature remains defined by the relation to the world as it was established by the "epistemological dichotomy".

As Friedrich Tenbruck (1985) writes:

"The new world of the social sciences was no longer seen as God's work but as the product of science and technology, hence a new idea of the status of man within the world was born, i.e. the idea that man's destiny was determined by hidden social laws, which a new science would discover in order to enable man once he had conquered nature to become master of his own history."

It is from this basic idea that the double separation stems within the social sciences, as Michel Freitag has pointed out so clearly; thus the separation between society and nature, on the one hand, and that between the social scientist and the objective reality which he analyses on the other (Freitag, 1986). Social scientists are therefore as much separated from the objects they study as is society from nature: they do not see themselves as being part of the society they study. Detachment is actually the condition for the social sciences to elaborate ever more perfect explanations and models of observed social reality.

The history of modern social sciences can also be described as the development of ever better methods and models, creating the ever greater detachment required to elaborate ever better explanations of underlying social mechanisms. As I have shown in another paper, this process is the double evolution from methods to techniques and from theories to models (Finger, 1986). If social science techniques are mainly the result of increased quantification, the development of models is a long process based on imported analogies from the natural sciences, as well as on structuralist and systemic approaches to modelling.

The result of this development is a social science mainly consisting of techniques, each of which gives birth to a new social science speciality. Modern society is not any longer studied as one coherent phenomenon, but as a study of isolated problems and modern social science becomes a purely technical, problem-solving enterprise. Even the "modernizer" Daniel Bell (1982) has seen the main tendencies of this evolution:

"In the 20th century, the social sciences moved away from these sweeping historical generalizations and the building of chambered ziggurats. In theory, the social sciences became ahistorical and analytical; in detail, they became empirical; and in method largely quantitative."

If social sciences are to give meaning and orientation to modern societies, as was the main idea in the 19th century, one has to ask what kind of meaning and what kind of social project can be derived from social technologies (Adorno, 1969). It could be that technology has become a social project in itself, and that the image modern society has of itself is one of a social machinery functioning independently of nature. Michel Freitag puts it as follows:

"Les sciences sociale deviennent en elles-mêmes la société en son mode technicise d'autoproduction..." (Freitag 1986:65).

This evolution can not be separated from the evolution of modern societies themselves, nor from the fact that the social sciences, by becoming social technologies, i.e. useful tools for building up modern civilization, have gradually become a part of modern politics. This evolution finds its parallel in the natural sciences' interpenetration with industry, as Ravetz has pointed out, but also with the military.

The recent history of social sciences can therefore be seen as a process of institutionalization into specialized units, whose only link among themselves is established by the state and by industry. The eminent commentator Horst Kern, thinks that this process will transform the social sciences into mere "administrative and planificatory sciences" (Finger, 1986).

This process of institutionalization within universities (public, private and military ones) and industry-sponsored research institutes, as well as the growing interpenetration of the social sciences with the power structure have progressed significantly with the Second World War. During that period the military for the first time provided finance for the social sciences, in particular for psychology, sociology, geography and anthropology. This resulting dependence on military funding is increasing every day. War has become total and as such also economic, political, psychological, social as well as military (Finger, 1983).

This is not a perversion of the original mission of the social sciences but rather the successful realization of the Saint-Simonian goal of creating a new rational society. Recognized theorists of the "post-industrial Age" Bell and Touraine explicitly continue to advocate such a role for the social sciences. The idea of the "civilization of information or communication", which opens up new horizons for social science management, is the logical outcome of this project.

It is also the logical outcome of the ever growing separation of society from nature - since "information" as conceived by today's science, is taken to be totally independent of any kind of reality, defining its own new reality.

One must therefore conclude that the social sciences, from a historical perspective cannot easily be reconciled with the Gaia hypothesis.

Gaia, Global Change and the Social Sciences

In general social scientists have never really looked critically at their own assumptions. The most fundamental debate within the social sciences, is the so-called "positivist debate". It was part of a more general debate, raise by the counter-culture, by the American "radicals" and the "New Left", which criticized mainstream social sciences (i.e. quantitativism and functionalism) for being conservative and seeking to preserve the socio-economic order. In his book radical sociologist Alvin Gouldner advocated a politically engaged social science, contributing to the transformation of modern societies so as to provide greater freedom for the underprivileged (Gouldner, 1970). This, however, is not a radical proposal, neither with regards the role, nor the basic goal of the social sciences. UNESCO, on the other hand, has at least tried to initiate a more fundamental debate in May 1983; it organized a Symposium on the Fundamental Problems of and Challenges for the Social Sciences in North America. In the background paper for the Symposium it stated:

"The rest of the century will be a dangerous period in human history. On many fronts - the threat of nuclear war, damage to the Earth's biosphere, the exhaustion of vital resources, population growth and the food crisis, persistent poverty - humankind faces problems of survival and deterioration of the quality of life in every part of the world. These problems are not primarily physical or natural but social and cultural; they are problems of human behaviour, organization, social structure and cultural patterns."

The proceedings of this Symposium unfortunately show that the social sciences are still unable to meet this challenge; (Trent/Lamy, 1984), and none of the contributors are even conscious of the type of global problems raised by the Global Change hypothesis. The main identified problems relate to the Third World and its development, as well as to the Arms Race. What seems to fascinate the social scientists most is the global world as a new field of study for the social sciences. They see the "global crisis as a new challenge," not one that could lead them to think critically about the social sciences, but to reaffirm their socio-political role as technocratic managers of modernization, this time on a truly planetary scale. In accordance with the social sciences' tradition, this is done by separating natural global issues from socio-cultural ones. The problems to be examined, as we are told in one of the background papers "are not primarily physical or natural, but social and cultural...."

It is therefore not surprising that the outcome of a social scientist's preoccupation with global problems is not a new debate within the social sciences, but a mere expansion of the field in which they can play their traditional role, a development which is best illustrated by the emerging new "academic" discipline of global modelling (Boudon, 1971).

Nevertheless, there do exist some isolated social scientists who seem to be conscious of the social sciences' profound epistemological crisis. Like Hwa Yol Jung they see this crisis as illustrated by the social sciences' predeliction for social technologies, a development which makes them ever less able to understand those socio-cultural realities which do not fit into their "modernization pattern " (Jung, 1979). This can be illustrated by the studies done on all kinds of new, green and alternative social movements which oppose industrialization as a whole: and which are simply not understood in terms of present social science theories, concepts and methods.

211

In general, the social sciences are totally unprepared for any Global Change issues, as they are completely unprepared for the problems threatening Gaia. The Gaia thesis itself is totally ignored by mainstream social sciences.

One has to be conscious of that, when looking at the social sciences' very recent alleged interest in environment and ecology. Out of all the main concepts required to formulate the Gaia hypothesis (such as Gaia, atmosphere, biosphere, environment, etc) only the terms "conservation" and "ecology" actually appear in the most recent *Social Science Encyclopaedia*. And this corresponds perfectly to the understanding the social sciences have of the environmental issue.

"Ecology", within the social sciences, refers for example to human ecology, a discipline which describes the relations between man and his environment, where man is at the centre of any consideration and the environments are man-made ones (machines, work, cities, etc.) Human ecology seeks to improve these relations for the benefit of man.

By "conservation", social scientists and particular economists refer to the conservation of natural resources that are required to sustain economic development (Dorfman in Repetto, 1985). But what economists actually do is look at the biosphere, or rather the environment, only in terms of the limits it imposes on economic growth. By translating those limits into the economic vocabulary of "scarcity", and by applying "scarcity" to renewable and unrenewable natural resources, they are able to pursue the traditional mechanistic idea of economic growth without calling into question the exploitation of nature on which growth is based. According to economists, all that has to be done is to conserve the natural resources as efficiently as possible; which leads to the concept of the "conserver economy" or "conserver society", best expressed by William Leiss in his *The Limits to Satisfaction* (Leiss, 1978). Other resources-conserving measures are recycling and above all technological progress. This leads to the idea of a "steady-state economy", as advocated by Herman Daly, (1977), or of "sustainable economic development" as recently put forward by the UN World Commission on Environment and Development (*Our Common Future* 1987).

But sustainable growth is still economic growth, given the continued population growth and diminishing returns of technological imports - a steady-state economy can only be sustained by steady economic growth. In other words, economic growth and the domination and destruction of nature are never really called into question, neither by modern society, nor by its economists.[4]

The economy continues to be seen by economists as a sort of developing system on whose development the environment can act as a limiting factor. But then limits can be pushed back by scientific and technological progress. This has in fact become a fundamental tenet of modern economics. So long as economists and politicians continue to believe this - and there is no sign of any change in this respect - it will never be realized that the economic process is not only dependent on the biosphere for its resources but is in fact occurring within the biosphere which it must inevitably degrade and indeed annihilate if it persists long enough.

What is needed is thus a new biospheric economics. There is little sign of it, indeed the only economist who has sought to develop one is Nicholas Georgescu-

---

4 This idea has been put forward by J. Grinevald, drawing on Georgescu-Roegen's 'bioeconomics'; see: Vernadsky and Lotka as sources for Georgescu-Roegen's bioeconomics, 1987, to be published in *Fundamenta Scientiae*.

Roegen (1971) and significantly he has been totally ignored by the economic establishment still more so by political decision makers.

Despite the recent emergence of new fields of social studies such as environmental education and environmental policy research, I must conclude rather pessimistically that social scientists are likely to continue to interpret ecological problems in such a way as to avoid calling their anti-Gaia world view into question. Pressure must therefore come from the outside, but the question remains whether, even under such pressure, the social sciences can really be reformed.

References

Adorno T. et al., *der Positivismusstreit in der deutschen Soziologie,* Darmstadt, Luchterhand, 1969.

Bell, D. *The Social sciences since the Second World War,* London, Transaction Books, 1982, p.4.a.

Blume, S. *Towards a political sociology of science.* London, Macmillan, 1974.

Boudon, R. *La crise de la sociologie,* Geneva, Droz, 1971.

Caille, A. *Splendeurs et misères des sciences sociales*, Geneva, Droz., 1986, cit.p.23,24,33.

Clark, W. C. / Holling, C. S. "Sustainable development of the biosphere: human activities and Global Change", in *Global Change* 1985:474-490.

Clark, W. C. and Munn, R. E. (Eds.), *Sustainable Development of the Biosphere,* London, Cambridge University Press, 1986.

Daly, H. *Steady-state economics,* San Francisco, Freeman, 1977.

Dorfman, R. "Economist's view of natural resources and environment problems", in: R. Repetto (Ed.), *The Global possible Resource, development and the New Century,* New Haven, Yale University Press, 1985, pp.67-98.

Finger, M. *La politisation des sciences sociales,* Université de Genéve, Cahiers du Département de Science politique. No. 19, 1986.

Finger, M. "Sozialwissenschaften und Militär, in: Gsponer et al. *Wissenschaft und Kreig,* Zürich, ETH-VMP, Verlag, 1983, pp.71-92.

Freitag, M. *Dialectique et société* Vol. 1: Introduction a une théorie générale du Symbolique, Lausanne, L'Age d'Homme, 1986.

Georgescu-Roegen, N. *The entropy law and the economic process,* Cambridge Mass., Harvard University Press, 1971.

Gouldner, A. *The coming crisis of western sociology,* London, Heinemann, 1970.

Grinevald, J. "Science et développement - Esquisse d'une approche socio-épistémologique" in: *La Pluralitè des Monde. Theories Developpement* No. 1, Geneva, 1975. pp.31-98.

Grinevald, J. *La Biosphére de la planète Terre*, ECOROPA, Geneva, 1987.

Grinevald, J. "Le développement de dans la biosphére", in: *L'homme Inachevé,* Cahiers de l'IUED, No.17, Paris, PUF, 1987, pp.29-44.

Jung, W. Y. *The crisis of political understanding*. A phenomenological perspective in the conduct of political inquiry, Pittsburg, Duquesne University Press, 1979.

Kern, H. *Empirische Sozialforschung*. Ursprünge, Ansatze, Entwicklungslinien, München, Beck, 1982, p.258.

Kumar, K. *Prophecy and progress. The sociology of industrial and post-industrial society*, Harmondsworth, Penguin, 1978, pp.13-44.

Kuper, A. / Kuper J. (Eds.) *The Social Science Encyclopedia*, London, Routledge and Kegan Paul, 1985.

Leiss, W. *The Domination of Nature*, New York, George Brazilier, 1972.

Leiss, W. *The limits to satisfaction. On needs and commodities*. London, Marion Boyars, 1978.

Lovelock, J. E. *Gaia: A new look at life on earth*, O xford, Oxford University Press, 1979.

Malone, T. F. and Roederer, J. G. (Eds.). *Global Change*, London, Cambridge University Press, 1985.

Myers, N. (Ed) *The Gaia Atlas of Planet Management*, London, Pan Books, 1985.

Parry, M. L. "Some implications of climatic change for human development", pp.407-410.

Ravetz, J. "Usable knowledge, usable ignorance: incomplete science with policy implications", in: Clark/Munn 1986:417

Ravetz, J. *Scientific Knowledge and its social problems*, New York, Oxford University Press, 1971.

Richards, J. F. "World environmental history and economic development", pp.53-70.

Sagan, D. / Margulis, L. "Gaia and the evolution of machines", in: *Whole Earth Review*, Summer 1987, pp.15-21

Snyder, T. P. (Ed). *The Biosphere Catalogue*, London, Synergetic Press, 1985.

Tenbruck, F. *Die Sozialwissenschaften als Mythos der Moderne*, Köln, Adamas-Verlag, 1985, pp.20-21.

Trent, J. / Lamy P. (Eds.), *Global crisis and the social sciences*, North American perspectives, Paris, UNESCO, 1984.

UN World Commission on Environment and Development. *Our Common Future*, Oxford, Oxford University Press, 1987.

DISCUSSION

Paul Blau The social sciences now stand at a crossroads as do the natural sciences. Undoubtedly the social sciences have been instrumental for many of the evil things happening at present. I need only remind you of the terrible role social scientists played during the wars in which they helped to create and propagate enemy images. For instance during the Vietnam War, the evacuation of people from the countryside into special ghettos was described as defending the villages. Recently in Austria a study was undertaken of the behaviour of teachers and it was discovered that a much higher percentage of teachers compared to the general population was described as 'post-materialist'. The conclusion was that such a teacher-population presented a great danger to society because it alienated the younger generation from the rest of society. Now how does the study describe a post-materialist? The answer is that a post-materialist is a person who values human friendship, who tries to beautify cities and other human settlements, who goes in for ecology and green ideas. A materialist, by way of contrast, seeks a higher standard of living, he is concerned with law and order, with job security and is not overly interested in the values held dear by the post-materialists.

Matthias Finger Post-materialist theory has politics built into it, indeed it has been elaborated in order to provide some understanding of the counter-culture of the 1968 movements. The aim has been to try and predict the next time such an uprising might happen by taking opinion polls. Yet, not a single issue deals with ecology; a post-materialist is not who is for or against ecology he has just forgotten to ask about ecology.

Daniel Mayer I would like to point out a danger which it is important not to dodge in our concern about Gaia and it is that social sciences have taken metaphors from biological sciences. The idea is that human beings, if they live in a kind of supra-organism, must fit in, much like the constituent cells fit into an organism. Anybody who does not seem to fit in is considered maladapted or sick and is in need of some kind of professional treatment. The Gaia theory clearly has the potential to be used by social scientists and it is not only the theory itself but equally how the theory is interpreted that matters. I therefore think we have to address the question of how Gaia affects our view of society and what we do about it.

Matthias Finger You are quite right about the metaphor. The point I am making is that Gaia can be translated into a metaphor and even into a model for the social sciences, but it will not alter the fundamental nature of the social sciences. The social sciences have absorbed the metaphor of general systems theory and a new fashion in social sciences is to use autopoietic systems as a new analogy.

James Lovelock It seems to me that most of the social sciences are concerned with people in the cities who may talk about the impact of man on the global environment but they do not have any input from the global environment upon them.

215

Alwyn Jones   One of the problems of the social sciences is that they are described as sciences and that presupposes a mechanistic approach. I think it is extremely important that we break down the division of subjects so that when we look out at the social world we see ourselves as part of that world rather than as something distant from us, which we then strive to manipulate through various endeavours. Indeed by seeing ourselves as part of the world we can then adopt a critical posture to it and can make a new evaluation of those things we have taken for granted such as economic growth, the development of technology and science.

A critical posture towards Gaia would in fact see that the world of Gaia is the world in which human beings reside and since social scientists are concerned primarily with human kind and with the emancipation of human kind from constraints and oppression, part of their study should be to look at Gaia in terms of a critique of a world in which we have become oppressed through our own destructiveness.

Matthias Finger   One line of development in the social sciences stemmed from the humanities and the humanities themselves stemmed back to German romanticism where you find the link between man and nature. This did not develop far having virtually died out with the second World War and the coming up of the new type of social sciences. Where I don't agree is with your interpretation of critical theory because I do not believe that such theory will necessarily lead to a new definition of the relationship between man and nature.

GAIA: ITS IMPLICATIONS FOR INDUSTRIALISED SOCIETY
by Peter Bunyard

Throughout its 4.5 billion year history the Earth has been subjected to all manner of physical trauma, including violent Krakatoa-like volcanic explosions and asteroids such as that which left a crater 1200 metres across and 180 metres deep in the Arizona desert. The evidence suggests that life began as early as 3.9 billion years ago, and once begun retained its grip, not only surviving cataclysmic changes but probably benefitting from them by bursting out in a myriad of new forms to take advantage of novel niches and habitats. As Lovelock and Watson's *Daisy World Models* indicate, Gaia would seem to have been remarkably resilient, always ready to bring in fresh recruits with new biological ideas to help it in the task of creating stability when the old order of organisms had outlived its purpose.

As human beings with a perfectly natural interest in the survival of our children and grandchildren, we may like the idea of Gaia surviving through thick and thin, but in the end our major concern is that the Earth should remain a pleasant, habitable planet for us. One preoccupying conclusion from Lovelock's planetary models is that Gaia can tolerate and accommodate substantial perturbations, up to certain as yet unknown levels. Should those tolerance levels be exceeded the entire regulatory system may flip abruptly to another level, for instance in which surface temperatures become much higher. Bacteria, with their wide range of metabolic capabilities and their remarkable propensity to share in each other's genetic make-up, may well adapt to a hotter planet, (Margulis and Sagan), but would we and those organisms like trees, insects, grass and mammals with which we are familiar and consider to be truly part of the world we live in?

None of us can now dispute that our industrial activities, particularly in the post world war two era, have caused substantial changes to the environment. Our pollutants in the atmosphere, waterways and soil have pushed many recycling, cleansing mechanisms to the limit, overwhelming buffering capacity as in the soils of Southern Sweden, or in some areas actually causing trees to become covered in an algal slime (Bunyard,1986). The millions of motor vehicles on the roads, feedlot, monoculture farming with its heavy inputs in terms of fossil fuel energy and imported chemicals, the wave of tree-felling, particularly in the Tropics, are evidence of mankind's obsession in bringing the entire wealth of the planet into its domain. We are in the throes of trying to create a new Earth with *Nature*, as we know it, banished to a few sanctuaries, conceived more as museum pieces than as essential components in the intricate dynamic of planetary regulation.

We may feel that our modern industrial activities are but a logical step in the process of our development from neolithic agriculture to the present, that our discoveries and applications of technology are inevitable, given our inquisitiveness and ingenuity, and that in the end, having discovered how the world works, we will put our knowledge to rational use and make a better world.

However, the more likely outcome is that the momentum built into our industrialised consumer society, with its mania for growth, will prevent

217

fundamental and vitally necessary action. Indeed, the present approach is to strive for 'business as usual' and to look for ingenious technical fixes to prevent excessive environmental damage, like for instance catalytic converters and lean-burn engines in motor vehicles, or elaborate devices for scrubbing smoke stacks. Our hope then, is that the application of regulations and transnational harmonizations will work well enough to control the pollutability of our devices. Yet our notions of pollution control and what the environment can accept are based on simplistic linear thinking, whereby if one has gone too far one way a simple retraction will take one effectively the other. Again it is an example of our total immersion in mechanistic thinking and our failure to have comprehended fully the fluidity and self- driven dynamics of the Earth's Gaian system. Furthermore, although technology has made the machines we use far more energy efficient, or less polluting, the spread of industrialization and consumerism both within industrialised countries and in less developed parts of the world, have intrinsically taken up the slack granted us through the improved efficiencies now built into machines.

Overall our actions tend to be cosmetic at best. In fact, as part of a dominating, all-pervasive,technology-obsessed culture we in the West have been led to believe that true progress lies in the application of scientific discovery and that all other cultures are basically backward, even though they may have their attractive features. The remarkable, self-evident successes of the scientific approach have been their own ambassador and few other cultures have been able to withstand the forceful power of our own, especially given its connection to profit and finance. In that respect the world is becoming unidimensional, à la Marcuse, and we should ask, like Siegfried Giedion, whether 'the one-way street of logic is taking us into the slum of materialism' (Giedion, *The Eternal Present*).

Gaia and Traditional Cultures

But it is incorrect automatically to assume that our activities *per se* run counter to Gaia. Looking back to the multitude of traditional cultures, or if we are lucky enough to find them, to those still extant, we can find many instances of a collaboration with Nature that enhances richness and diversity. Nothing could be more striking in that respect than the differences between the traditional practices of living off the land among South American peoples and those imposed since the Spanish Conquest some 400 to 500 years ago.

For instance the Quechua and Aymara Indians of the Andean Altiplano developed over the millennia what David Guillet has called *the management of risk*. The climatic conditions at such high altitudes made crop growing at the best of times extremely difficult and, should the frosts be harder or the rainfall less than the average, crops might well fail, especially if they were all of the same variety or indeed species. To counter the risk of failure the Altiplano Indians used a two-fold strategy. One was to grow different crops in any one region, always using a great variety of any one cultivar; the second was to grow crops at different altitudes, using the upper slopes for hardy species such as the chenopodia quinua and canihua, for potatoes as well as for the legume tarsi, and the lower slopes for various beans and maize. The arid, cold Puna high up in the mountains was used for raising camelids such as llamas and alpacas and for deriving water for irrigation. In essence the peasants traditionally employed *diversification* as well as *stratification* in their agricultural activities (Guillet, 1980).

Such a strategy for risk management would not have been feasible if the social and cultural system of the Andean campesinos followed the same pattern as that now prevailing in the Western world, based as it is on individual/family land ownership and on an overriding concern with the production of cash crops for the market economy. As Guillet points out, in the Central Andes the peasants had access to land at different altitudes, moving between the zones as the growing seasons and harvesting dictated.

Remarkably, traditional farming practices among the Quechua and Aymara Indians of Peru and Bolivia survived the Spanish Conquest and domination through the latifundia system, at least until the Second World War. Thus work was organised through both households and what have been called *suprahouseholds* in which relatives through marriage were brought into the system basically to share in the labour and then presumably in its rewards. Through such relationships entire communities became involved, thus ensuring that the infrastructure of terraces and irrigation systems was adequately maintained and that land was distributed through usufruct practices.

Agrarian reform, based as it has been on understandable social pressures to break up the large estates and the exploitation of peasant labour, has not necessarily been a force for the good in the Central Andes. For one, governments have reacted to such political realities by making land available elsewhere, for instance in the tropical lowlands, where agriculture is rarely suitable, at least in the long term. The destruction of tropical forest has been one foreseeable and tragic result. Meanwhile in the altiplano itself land reform and the pursuit of the market economy have begun to destroy irrevocably the traditional communal farming practices that at least ensured survival for all. The land is now falling into private hands and the survival strategies of diversification and zoning are now being replaced by an emphasis on cash crops for the market. Excessive pressure, through overgrazing for instance, is now being put on the environment, and the precarious ecological balance created through millennia of wise practice is now collapsing.

Throughout the Americas, and the same applies to any region of the world, we can find evidence of remarkable adaptations of different peoples to their environments. When we consider the Eskimoes, the Prairie Indians of North America, the peoples of Central and South America we find a host of different cultures and adaptations to the environments in which those peoples found themselves. The now extinct Sinu people of northern Colombia, for instance, converted the *cienaga* swamplands to the west of the Rio Magdalena into an extensive, highly productive canal system that was similar in a number of respects to the water/garden 'chanampas' system developed by the Aztecs and their predecessors around what today has become sprawling, highly polluted Mexico City (Outerbridge, 1987). Through such canals the Sinu Indians controlled the seasonal inundations that occurred throughout the rainy season, thus keeping the cienagas filled and well stocked with fish, while simultaneously trapping sediment that could be used for intensive crop growing in the areas between canals. An appraisal carried out by scientists in Colombia indicates that at least 2000 square kilometres were made fertile that way and suitable for highly productive cultivation (Negret, 1986).

The carrying capacity of the region in terms of the number of people it can now support is now no greater than 70 to the square kilometre whereas an evaluation of the numbers that were and could be supported by the Sinu system indicates a 15-fold greater population density at some 1000 inhabitants per square kilometre. The forests have now been chopped down to make way primarily for cattle and the swamps, those wonderfully productive ecological systems, are increasingly being drained and dried out. The tens of thousands of people who depend on the cienagas and the river systems to provide them with essential protein from fish are being inexorably deprived of the little livelihood they once had. Ironically, the current obsession with hydro-electricity, planned for the Rio Sinu, together with flood control, is the antithesis of traditional practices where the rainy season was seen as essential for replenishing the canals.

Fallen Man

The destruction of community, the desperate search for land, the need to get into the market economy, have all combined in the process of environmental degradation in the developing world. There we see in front of our eyes the brutal consequences of environmental destruction; erosion, desertification, salinization, flooding, gross pollution with agrochemicals.

In effect, we have replaced intrinsically productive and sustaining systems with our own westernised model of progress and development, introducing alien elements into an ecosystem without first evaluating what that particular environment had to offer. There the world's indigenous peoples have shown themselves to be vastly superior; indeed when we look at the sum of our present-day industrial activities we can only conclude that our so-called scientific viewpoint has been environmentally crass. Furthermore, with the profit motive playing such a conspicuous part in development there has been a tendency wilfully to misconstrue the capacity of the environment to assimilate and cope with wastes. The tradition in Britain, for instance, has been to espouse an 'out of sight, out of mind' approach, as if the environment as a whole had an infinite capacity for absorbing and neutralizing wastes.

To a great extent the piecemeal approach to industrial wastes and the setting of compromise standards, which depend for the most part on some rule of thumb notion as to what the environment can take while not jeopardising industry's profits, has to a great extent been mirrored by the activities of the environmental movement. With some justification they have gone for obvious targets such as vehicle emissions, power plant pollution, the aerosol link and the ozone layer, off-shore incineration of toxic wastes, dumping at sea, nuclear power and such bestialities as modern whaling. But with rare exception environmental groups have avoided looking at the whole industrial enterprise. They may be rocking the boat, but certainly not enough to sink it.

220

Our Impact on Gaia

The Gaia hypothesis will undoubtedly have the effect of changing radically the views and actions of environmental groups, transforming them into movements that embrace ecology in the fullest, most general sense of the word. Now we have a hypothesis that enables us to understand far better than before why acid rain is a particular problem of the post world war two era rather than of the late 19th century. Now through the work of Lovelock, Watson, Whitfield, Andreae and others we can glimpse the extraordinary network of interactions that tie the activities of industrial society to sulphur-bearing rain emanating from the seas. We have come indeed to appreciate that sulphur and NO_x emissions from power plants and motor vehicles are just one source of pollution that mixed with a pot pourri of atmospheric chemicals from both natural and anthropogenic sources is causing a fundamental transformation of the oxidation pathways.

Greenhouse gases

As far as changes to the environment are concerned, Lovelock realised from the Gaia Hypothesis that of all the Earth's systems the atmosphere would be among the most sensitive to change and equally, assuming the hypothesis to be correct, the system upon which the biota would have to act reasonably quickly to counteract perturbations, whether the cause was external to the Earth, such as asteroidal impact, or indeed a biota-generated phenomenon such as the release of free oxygen into the atmosphere several aeons ago. In fact, temperature regulation of the Earth's surface by the biota was always one of the most significant features of the *Gaia Hypothesis* and an aspect that distinguished it wholly from other theories of the biosphere, as discussed by Jacques Grinevald. As part of that regulation, given that the Sun has increased in luminosity by between 30 and 40 per cent since the Earth came into being as a planet, the greenhouse gas, CO_2, has had to be dumped, most of it finishing up as limestone like the White Cliffs of Dover, and taking the concentration of CO_2 down some thousandfold to 0.03 per cent today.

Given the importance of climate to human affairs, for instance for agriculture, for flood control and even for such mundane matters as to where to spend one's vacation, it is perhaps significant that one of the areas of greatest concern today is whether or not the emission of greenhouse gases through anthropogenic activities has caused, is causing or will cause fundamental climatic change.

The Gaia Hypothesis indicates that an increase in the concentration of greenhouse gases in the atmosphere must cause climatic change by altering the amount of heat that remains trapped at the Earth's surface; equally, for the hypothesis to be valid, it must be shown that the sum of all biotic activities on Earth will counter, through cybernetic regulation, any such temperature rise. The question then arises as to what kind of time-scale we are talking about. Geologically speaking there is abundant evidence that surface temperature has been controlled within narrowly defined limits, which includes the transition from warm periods to ice-ages. Indeed, one of the results coming from the various attempts at climate modelling is how small a change is needed in the concentration of the greenhouse

221

gases to bring about climatic change.

In that respect the levels of CO_2 in the atmosphere have now risen to some 345 parts per million from about 260 ppm prior to the Industrial Revolution. By 2000 the levels of CO_2 are expected to rise to about 370 ppm and continue their rise upwards to approximately 600 ppm sometime in the middle of the next century, when they will have effectively doubled from what is now taken as base. Thus, at the present time CO_2 levels are increasing at about 1.5 ppm(volume) per year, hence 0.5 per cent per year. To put that change in perspective we have to appreciate that at their peak carbon dioxide levels will comprise just 0.06 per cent of the atmospheric gases.

There is considerable debate over the precise quantities of carbon dioxide being generated by anthropogenic activities. The general consensus is that fossil fuel burning is bringing about the production of some 5 billion tonnes of the gas each year, with land use changes, and in particular deforestation, adding between 1 and 4 billion tonnes on top of that. Where land use changes involve the clearing of one type of vegetation, for instance trees, to make way for highly productive crops, then the difference in CO_2 emission and uptake through photosynthetic activity may be relatively small. In that respect today's exploitation of temperate and boreal forests may not be contributing significantly to the rising levels of CO_2 in the atmosphere. The same, however, is not true of tropical forests, which, particularly when cleared through burning, are adding significantly to the rise in levels of the gas. Nevertheless, controversy over the extent of such destruction of tropical forests is intense. For instance, a report prepared for FAO and UNEP in the early 1980s suggested that some 7 million hectares each year of primary rainforest was being destroyed world wide, which included some 1.5 million hectares per year of the Brazilian Amazon (Houghton et al.,1987, Melillo et al. 1985).

However, the rate of destruction has certainly accelerated since then, and some observers, with the aid of satellite image scanning, are coming up with figures of 20 million hectares of the Brazilian Amazon going up in flames each year. On the basis that between 150 and 300 tonnes of carbon are released as CO_2 per hectare through burning, then the destruction in Brazil alone would be responsible for between 3 billion tonnes and 6 billion tonnes of carbon each year. *That latter amount would therefore be approximately as much as that estimated as released from fossil fuel burning and that is not even taking the remainder of the tropical countries into account.* It would seem that with Brazil's ferocious onslaught on the Amazon the emission of CO_2 from the destruction of tropical forests throughout the world may exceed by a considerable margin that from fossil fuels (Kelly and Karas, 1987).

Ironically, for those who uphold dams as being ecologically clean insofar as they do not involve the burning of fossil fuels and their noxious emissions, W.J.Junk and his colleagues have estimated that the flooding of tropical forests in the relatively low-lying parts of the Amazon such as at the 250 MW Balbina dam close to Manaus for generating hydroelectricity will, if the trees are left to decay, lead to as much CO_2 being emitted from their decomposition as would be released from an equivalent size thermal power plant operating on fossil fuels for some 100 years (Junk and Nunes de Mello, 1987).

Despite the sophistication of today's computers, global climate models are relatively crude when dealing with the real world and no-one is really sure what the overall effect will be of increased greenhouse gases. Nevertheless, there is general agreement among climatologists that the Earth's surface has warmed up by 0.7°C since the mid-nineteenth century, an amount that is certainly consistent with model predictions of the warming-up effects of the greenhouse gases that have been emitted since then and are still resident in the atmosphere.

The seas are a major sink for carbon dioxide both through simple absorption of the gas into water and through the photosynthetic activity of the marine biota. Changes in the biomass of algal plankton will undoubtedly affect the rates of uptake of CO_2 but not in ways that can match today's anthropogenic emissions. For instance, M. Stuiver estimated in 1978 that between 1850 and 1950 some 180 billion tonnes of carbon of anthropogenic origin found their way into the atmosphere, which had it remained there would have been equivalent to an increase of 26 per cent to the total 700 billion tonnes of 'natural' atmospheric carbon. Isotopic studies indicate that only 2 per cent of that carbon is still to be found in the atmosphere and therefore an effective sink has been in operation - just as one would expect from the Gaia hypothesis. The indications are that by 1950 some 64 per cent of the excess carbon had found its way into the first 300 metres of the oceans and 24 per cent had been taken deeper into the bathyal and abyssal zones (Ramade, 1986).

It would seem that the Earth is coping remarkably quickly with the excess CO_2 being generated by our industrial activities, and if we could lay off right now, abandoning our profligate consumption of fossil fuels and our rampant deforestation, not many years would have to pass before the levels of that one greenhouse gas were back to 'normal'. Yet, to date we have not effectively reduced our anthropogenic emissions of CO_2 and the trend would appear to be inexorably upward. Indeed, our emissions of that gas are swamping the natural cycling mechanisms so that according to Ramade as much as 40 to 60 per cent of the CO_2 produced by the combustion of fossil fuels during the decade 1959 to 1969 has remained in the atmosphere with the rest going into the oceans.

Other greenhouse gases

METHANE

Carbon dioxide is by no means the only greenhouse gas that is being emitted through our industrial and agricultural activities. Methane concentrations in the atmosphere, having remained apparently stable for thousands of years, have been increasing substantially since the beginning of the industrial revolution. Pre-industrial concentrations have been estimated as some 700 parts per billion (by volume whereas in 1985 they were more than double that at 1650 ppb with a current rate of increase that is close to 1 per cent per year (Crutzen, 1987).

As Jim Lovelock has pointed out, methane plays a crucial role in the balances of gases such as oxygen in the atmosphere, and since methane is generated by living organisms - anaerobic methanogenic bacteria - here we are seeing a typical and crucial gaian mechanism at work. These bacteria derive their energy and nutrition from carbonaceous material and therefore form a small although significant part of the processes whereby carbon dioxide is returned to the atmosphere. Photosynthesis, whether by cyanobacteria, algae such as those comprising marine plankton, or by higher plants, requires that the concentration of CO_2 be sufficiently high in the atmosphere. Indeed, for life on Earth it is now a race between the levels of CO_2 having to be reduced to lower levels to maintain surface temperatures within viable limits and the cut-off point for photosynthesis. As we now know the so-called C-4 plants with their different photosynthetic biochemical pathway are at an advantage over the C-3 plants at low CO_2 concentrations.

At present about 100 million tonnes of carbon are buried each year, equivalent to the release of 133 million tonnes of free oxygen gas into the air. Not that the oxygen content is increasing, as we know full well, having remained at its present levels for some 700 million years; there are in fact plenty of sinks for mopping up excess oxygen such as volcanic materials or reduced materials in the soil. Broad estimates indicate that as much as 97.5 per cent of the products of photosynthesis are consumed by oxygen-breathing consumers, leaving just 2.5 per cent for anaerobes such as methanogenic bacteria. According to Lovelock the amount of carbon buried each year until the current period has been remarkably steady throughout the history of life on Earth. One must therefore assume that in the Archean, anoxic organisms such as the methanogens consumed most of the products of photosynthesis, but that as free oxygen built up in the environment the place of such organisms was taken over by respiring consumers such as ourselves. Lovelock's conclusion is that the methanogenic organisms, being anaerobic, have had to retreat into murky places away from the highly toxic effects of free oxygen. They now reside in such places as swamps, paddy fields, and the intestines of higher organisms.

CATTLE, RICE AND THE ATMOSPHERE

Why have methane levels been increasing and what do such rises mean? Again it would appear that mankind has had a hand in such rises. The spate of forest clearing has greatly encouraged the termite population, and although there are considerable differences in the estimates of the contribution of these social insects to global methane it is nonetheless significant. Cattle provide another excellent refuge for methanogenic anaerobes, and the eradication of tropical forest to make way for cattle is certainly compounding the contribution from termites. Between 1966 and 1983 for instance, well in excess of 100,000 square kilometres were cleared in the Brazilian Amazon Basin for cattle ranching, such multinational companies as Volkswagen benefitting outrageously from the easy terms offered by the Brazilian government for enormous swathes of land (Shelton Davis). We are now seeing that amount of forest and more going from the Brazilian Amazon alone in just one year – an extremely disturbing prospect.

The devastation of tropical forest in Central America for cattle raising was equally great. Meanwhile, through World Bank and European aid the cattle population has increased greatly throughout Africa and is now being extended further through the EEC funded tsetse fly eradication programme which according to FAO plans is to stretch right across the African Savannah, as if the world were suffering a gross shortage of beef.

The annual growth rate in the world cattle population in the decade between 1970 and 1980 was approximately one per cent per year and the indications are that such growth has been continuing. The area down to rice paddy, another ideal habitat for methanogenic bacteria, has also been increasing significantly, at around 0.7 per cent per year according to FAO figures. Leaks of methane into the atmosphere from coal mining and natural gas production have been increasing at about 2.2 per cent per year over the past decade.

Overall, methane releases into the atmosphere per year have been estimated by Paul Crutzen as amounting to 380 million tonnes divided up as follows: domestic ruminants 80 million tonnes; biomass burning 45/60; natural gas leaks 33; coal mining 34; rice paddies 120; and natural wetlands 70/50 million tonnes.

The annual growth rate in methane of around 1.2 per cent suggests an annual growth of 4.6 million tonnes and therefore just 1.6 per cent of the total anthropogenic source. However, the 2.9 million tonnes of methane arising from the growth in rice paddy production, in cattle ranching and in fossil fuel extraction does not tally fully with the increase in methane in the atmosphere and indicates that some 1.7 million tonnes need to be accounted for. Here, Crutzen suggests that changes in atmospheric chemistry are at play and they closely involve methane.

In the Earth's atmosphere methane is a consumer of oxygen through interacting with ozone and with the hydroxyl radical, itself a product of ozone and water interacting photolytically. Thus laboratory experiments indicate that for each methane molecule oxidised as many as 3.5 hydroxyl radicals are consumed as well as 1.7 ozone molecules. Under such circumstances the levels of both these potent oxidizers will tend to fall drastically once methane levels begin increasing. Crutzen is concerned that the 1.7 million tonnes of methane that cannot be accounted for in the totalling of anthropogenic emissions is the result of the fall in the concentration of both ozone and hydroxyl. If Crutzen is correct then the situation may well deteriorate further.

But there is another angle to the story. Such build-up of methane may well be occurring over tropical areas through forest destruction followed by rice paddy and cattle ranching. On the other hand, where levels of NO_x, in particular nitric oxide (NO), are raised the chemistry of methane breakdown takes a totally different course and one in which both hydroxyl and ozone concentrations are likely to increase. Nitric oxide above certain concentrations, as is indeed the case over heavily industrialised areas with their dense traffic and high concentration of power plants, smelters and cement factories, catalyses the production of half a hydroxyl radical and 3.7 ozone molecules. Undoubtedly the increased oxidative powers of the atmosphere over industrial regions of the planet through the interaction of increasing levels of hydrocarbons such as methane and nitrogen oxides are accelerating the oxidation and deposition of acid oxides such as sulphur oxides as well as nitrogen oxides, leading to acidification of lakes, rivers, and soils where the buffering capacity is poor.

Meanwhile methane is a greenhouse gas which per molecule is some ten times more powerful than carbon dioxide. On the other hand its concentration in the atmosphere is some 500 times less compared with carbon dioxide and therefore its increase, at just over double the rate of CO_2 is leading to a greenhouse effect that is some 20 times less. The methane increase therefore accounts for some 5 per cent of the putative warming of the Earth's surface at the present time.

NITROUS OXIDE

Nitrous oxide, which is generated particularly through biomass burning, fertilizer use and the combustion of fossil fuels is slowly increasing in the atmosphere, having gone up some 20 parts per billion over the past 150 years. Nevertheless, it too is a strong greenhouse gas and moreover it has a residence time in the lower atmosphere of some 170 years compared to approximately 10 years for both carbon dioxide and methane. When oxidized to nitric oxide and present in sufficiently high concentrations in the lower atmosphere, nitrous oxide contributes to the increase in trophospheric ozone.

OZONE

Ozone generated at the surface of the Earth through the catalytic processes involving the oxidation of hydrocarbons in the presence of NO_x remains in the lower atmosphere for a few weeks. Levels of surface ozone have been rising at approximately 0.25 per cent per year in global terms, but locally the rise in the levels has been considerably higher. According to Paul Crutzen, for instance, ozone concentrations in West Germany increased by some 60 per cent between 1967 and 1980. Not only is ozone a greenhouse gas but close to the Earth's surface it is highly toxic to living organisms. Moreover, being a powerful oxidant in the presence of light it can bring about chemical changes in a number of other atmospheric pollutants, helping therefore to create a cocktail of toxic by-products that may indeed be responsible for causing the die-back of trees and 'waldsterben' over many parts of the northern hemisphere.

Stratospheric ozone is generated from oxygen in the presence of light. Equally light breaks the ozone molecule down and in the presence of water vapour the electronically excited oxygen atom will form the powerful oxidant - hydroxyl. Stratospheric ozone is important for life insofar as it screens out much of the ultraviolet B radiation that penetrates the atmosphere from outer space. However, ozone decomposes readily in the presence of light and chlorine atoms and one of the great concerns over the past decade has been the potential interaction of the chlorinated CFCs with stratospheric ozone. That such fears may already be realised comes from recent studies indicating that ozone is rapidly becoming depleted from the stratosphere above Antarctica. It appears that during certain months of the year the ozone levels over Antarctica are dropping by as much as 40 per cent compared with the pre-1960s. Moreover the one hole appears to be getting larger and spreading to lower latitudes.

CFCs

Each of the main CFCs, CFC-11 and CFC-12, have been increasing at a rate of around 7 per cent per year in the atmosphere, one reason being their relatively long residence times of between 80 and 120 years respectively. At present their global concentrations are comparatively low, at some 0.2 and 0.3 parts per billion. Lovelock was initially sceptical that at such low concentrations the CFCs could be responsible to a measurable extent for destroying the ozone layer. He now concedes that ozone depletion is taking place in the upper atmosphere and that it is conceivable that the CFCs are involved. On the other hand, he was one of the first to point out that the CFCs were powerful greenhouse gases, molecule per molecule, being at least 10,000 times more effective than CO_2. At their present concentrations in the atmosphere the CFCs would contribute some 15 per cent to the greenhouse effect of CO_2.

Both methane and nitrous oxide independently are effective in destroying ozone and it could be argued that the disappearance of ozone over Antarctica is the result of interaction between the various atmospheric pollutants that have been generated through man's industrial activities. One mechanism has been suggested which, ironically, results from the greenhouse effect, but from the other side of the coin. Indeed, the greenhouse effect results in the Earth's surface trapping more heat at the expense of the upper stratosphere which, for the energy balance to be maintained, must become colder. The suggestion is, therefore, that the air some 20 to 25 kilometres above Antarctica has become colder resulting during the dark winter months in the accumulation of ice crystals within which are trapped a cocktail of pollutants such as methane, nitrous oxide, the CFCs and other substances. At the beginning of the Antarctic summer, when the sun shines, these crystals melt and through photo-oxidation form a host of new chemicals, some of which are extremely effective at causing the destruction of ozone.

In 1986 Wolfgang Seiler proposed a similar mechanism for the killing of the trees in the Black Forest which appeared to be particularly vulnerable just above the inversion layer, at around 500 metres. While all below may be blanketted in fog, the hills above the boundary layer may be bathed in brilliant sunshine, coincidentally at the same altitude as the plume transporting pollutants from tall factory stacks. At those altitudes, particularly during the winter months, the temperature is likely to fall well below zero. As a result, Seiler suggested, all kinds of substances, including photoxidation products, could become trapped in the ice that formed on the needles. Those compounds could well be toxic and in sufficiently high concentrations to cause damage. Alternatively toxic compounds could be generated as a result of interactions with naturally produced substances such as terpenes and isoprenes released from the needles (Bunyard, 1986).

The Consequences of Climatic Change

Global climate models suggest that a doubling of the CO_2 content of the atmosphere could lead to a global warming of between 1.5 and 5.5°C. Such a doubling is expected by the middle of the next century; if we then add in the contribution from the other greenhouse gases, methane, the CFCs, nitrous oxide and ozone, then the effective doubling time for CO_2 is likely to be brought forward by 20 years to 2030 - just 40 years away. The models, supported by evidence of the climatic history of the Earth, indicate that the warming up, given as a global average, will not be uniform but of much greater intensity at higher latitudes, with the equatorial regions, at least in terms of surface temperature, remaining much at present levels. We are therefore talking of dramatic temperature changes in temperate regions, especially if the higher prediction proves to be correct. It should also be remembered that throughout the past 12,000 years the average surface temperature of the planet has risen by no more than 3 to 4°C (Karas and Kelly, 1987).

One effect of a generalized warming-up will be to increase the temperature of the oceans. Just a warming-up will lead to as much as a one metre rise in sea level before any ice-cap melting has taken place, and the effect of such rises is likely to be devastating for any low-lying areas close to the sea, as for instance along the Eastern seaboard of the United States, many capital cities of the World, including London, let alone the Netherlands. Furthermore, salt water will intrude farther inland, jeopardising fresh water supplies in coastal regions.

A warmer climate will lead to significant, although unpredictable changes in weather patterns and in the kind of vegetation that can be supported. Some models anticipate the virtual loss of boreal climates and the expansion of tropical and warm temperate climates, the net result being an increase in grasslands and deserts, with a sharp decline in the area under forests. Such models have not taken man's activities on vegetation types into account. Agriculture would be fundamentally affected, not least through changes in rainfall pattern, but equally important because the rising CO_2 levels would enhance the growth of C-3 plants at the expense of C-4 plants. Since C-4 plants provide us with many essential crops for both human and livestock consumption, for instance maize, sorghum and sugar cane, and the C-3 plants many of the competing weeds, we may well find increased CO_2 levels jeopardising conventional monoculture food-crop systems.

Are the high winds that struck Britain last winter an indication that the climate has already begun to destabilize? And what about the droughts which afflicted the United States during the summer of 1988, or the heavy rains and flooding of the Sudan, Bangladesh and parts of South America? What about hurricane Gilbert? Circumstances never remain precisely the same and it is a manifestly difficult task to pin any one feature of climate down to a recognizable perturbation, whether it be of natural origin, such as a major volcanic event, or man-caused. Nevertheless, we have sufficient knowledge of the effects of deforestation to come to the conclusion that the flooding of Sudan and the upsurge in the waters of the Nile or indeed the flooding of Bangladesh are not simply the result of climate changes, but are also a direct consequence of the deforestation that has been going on over the past few decades.

Deforestation and Climate

There has been considerable confusion as to precisely what happens to rainfall and run-off after deforestation. It has been noted, for instance, that the total quantities of water carried by rivers during the course of the year may not be significantly less after deforestation than before. However, as various researchers have found, the rains, when they come, tend to be far stronger. H. C. Pereira, for instance, measured rainfall in a region of tropical Africa where rainforest was transformed into tea plantations encompassing just 700 hectares. He discovered that high intensity rainfall went up four times compared to still forested regions. Equally

Snow, who studied the climatic effects of substituting tropical forest for subsistence agriculture in Panama, found that average annual run-off in the region prior to deforestation and after did not change significantly. On the other hand the intensity of rainfall and its intermittence increased once the forest had gone. A principal cause for the seasonal increase in surface run-off was found to be soil compaction and the actual proportion of rain reaching the soil.

Substantial differences have been found between the soil's capacity to absorb water when the forest is intact and when it has been cleared. H. Schubart investigated the changes to soil after deforestation in a region close to Manaus in the Brazilian Amazon. He discovered a 10-fold drop-off in water absorption in a 5-year old pasture compared to the soil still covered in forest. That loss in ability to retain water by the soil, primarily through compaction, is compounded by the increase in rain actually reaching the soil. Luiz Molion of the Brazilian Space Research Institute was able to show, again close to Manaus, that 17 per cent of annual precipitation over the forest is intercepted by the canopy and never reaches the ground. Evapotranspiration is significantly diminished after tropical forest has been removed. Indeed, evapotranspiration may fall by as much as 50 per cent and precipitation by 20 per cent, lending considerable credence to the measurements of Eneas Salati, Molion and others that over an extensive area such as the Amazon Basin a considerable proportion of rainfall is derived from the continual recycling of evapotranspired water (Salati, 1987).

This efficient recycling of water over the tropical forest is a component of Gaia, even though in global terms it may appear small. Indeed, whereas over temperate zones local evapotranspiration contributes no more than 10 per cent to local precipitation over the course of a year, over the intact forest of the Amazon the proportion may be as high as 50 per cent and that of a much higher average precipitation, amounting to some 2500 millimetres per year. That process of evapotranspiration is like a sweating mechanism, keeping that part of the Earth far cooler than it would be if it were as dry as a desert. Between 50 and 75 per cent of the solar energy reaching the Earth's surface is used in evapotranspiration and the remainder in heating the air. Thus the humidity under the canopy is 87 per cent compared to less than 50 per cent just 50 metres away out in a clearing. And soil temperatures are at least 5°C hotter out in the open compared to those covered by forest.

The vapour generated over the forest condenses to form clouds which, with their high albedo (reflectivity), will prevent solar radiation from reaching the ground and will thus also serve to keep the surface in tropical regions cooler. Meanwhile some of that vapour will be carried aloft in the Walker-Hadley circulation of air across the Equator and get transported to higher latitudes, where after condensing and precipitation it will release its latent heat. Although there is considerable contention over the role of the tropical forest in providing heat through evapotranspiration for regions in the sub-tropics and beyond, nevertheless some heat is transported in that way and may serve as one component in averaging out the temperatures over the entire planet. The other important mechanism in this process of heat-transport is that of ocean currents (Molion, 1988).

Salati estimates that of 12 trillion (10^{12}) cubic metres of rain that fall over the Amazon Basin each year, 6.5 trillion cubic metres are derived from evapotranspiration. Daniel

Hillel, responding on behalf of the World Bank to my article in *The Ecologist* on the potential climatic consequences of deforesting the Amazon, is somewhat dismissive of concerns that the loss of primary forest will lead to environmentally damaging reductions in either rainfall or evapotranspiration. For instance, he does not appear to find a fall in precipitation of up to 20 per cent to be a dramatic reduction and one that will perturb unduly the system's viability. If we assume that the reduction in evapotranspiration is 50 per cent, as indicated by Molion, then a simple calculation shows that such a reduction over the entire Amazon Basin would be equivalent to a reduction in latent heat of approximately 240 terawatts ($1 TW = 10^{12}$ watts). The entire human population at present consumes energy at the rate of 10 terawatts and electricity at 2 terawatts. Therefore that simple reduction - hardly dramatic according to Hillel - would be equivalent to 24 times the rate of world energy consumption and 100 times its electricity consumption.

We know full well that the tropical forest is one of the most extraordinary contemporary manifestations of Gaia. There diversity enables a highly efficient energy flow through the system with the net result that essential nutrients can be rapidly recycled and kept within the biomass. All components of the system act in harmony, even intra-specific competition which itself must help determine diversity and optimize the use of available energy and nutrients.

The climax, primary tropical forest is a relatively delicate structure, having been greatly reduced in extent during the last ice age. Vast regions of the Amazon Basin, for instance, turned into Savannah, with the truly forested areas remaining isolated in what today have been termed 'biological refuges'. When conditions improved for the forest slowly but surely it was able to recolonise, this very process contributing to the multiplicity of variation and diversity. The difference between a 'drying-out' of the region and its receiving adequate rain to sustain it may not have been so great. Can we assume that the fall-off in precipitation once the forest has been destroyed will not engender a generalized deterioration in the condition of the remaining forest, particularly in the Amazon Basin where the moisture essentially circulates from East to West in what is known as the Walker Cell circulation? Hillel, for instance, is optimistic with regard to the forest's regenerative powers, basically arguing that vegetation soon returns. Of course it will if the area of forest destroyed does not exceed that necessary for seed distribution and the soil has not been too heavily compacted. Otherwise, as Salati and other Brazilian scientists have pointed out, the recovery of the rich original ecosystem may be painstakingly slow - a 1000 years or more.

We would indeed be foolhardy to imagine that a brutal simplification of the tropical ecosystem as brought about through a wide-reaching forest clearance would leave no noticeable mark on Gaia. The Gaia Hypothesis predicts that *stability* is at its greatest when *species diversity* is high and we are already aware that deforestation in the tropics has many fundamental consequences such as soil deterioration and gully erosion that go beyond changes in cloud formation and energy transfers. Undoubtedly one of the more worrying aspects of forest loss from tropical areas, particularly those growing on weathered soils such as in the terra firme regions of the Amazon Basin is the immediate loss of most of the nutrients that otherwise have been so effectively recycled by and within the biomass, particularly through the tightly bound symbiotic relationships between the root mat of the trees and mycorrhizae. Once gone we can never hope to replace the intricate complex interactions that underlie the forest's undoubted success' as an integrated ecosystem. Moreover, the question also arises whether we can, with our modern scientific approach, improve significantly if at all on the strategies of survival within the tropical forest developed and tested over millennia by the world's forest dwellers.

Man and Gaia

In many of our modern activities we are on a collision course with Gaia. One of the essential attributes of Gaia is that its multiplicity of parts - the biota - have evolved recycling systems that keep nutrients in circulation, between for instance, the seas and the land. Our industrialised activities are interfering directly with those recycling pathways, very often speeding them up so that they swamp the processes that normally control them. The acid rain phenomenon is just such an example. As Lovelock showed more than a decade ago, marine organisms such as the algal coccolithophorids generate sulphur in volatile form - dimethylsulphide- which when oxidised to sulphur dioxide, primarily through the action of the hydroxyl radical, returns to the land. Lovelock and his colleagues have since elaborated the process further by pointing out that the self-same sulphur dioxide provides condensation nuclei for the formation of rain-bearing clouds over the oceans.

We have affected such a recycling process in two fundamental ways. First, we have increased substantially the flow of nutrients from the land to the sea, particularly in those areas over the continental shelves where such sulphur-generating planktonic algae are to be found. And secondly, we have altered the processes of photo-oxidation in the atmosphere through the emissions from smoke stacks, from vehicle exhausts, from intensive livestock raising and from land-use changes such as deforestation. The net result of all these activities is to have brought about a substantial increase in the rate and quantities of acid, both of sulphurous and nitrogenic origin, that are deposited. The consequences, as we have begun to realise, are a swamping of soil buffering mechanisms and the making available of toxic ions such as aluminium and cadmium.

Entire ecosystems are now disintegrating as the result of the changes that have been taking place in the post world war 2 era. Thousands of square kilometres of lakes in Scandinavia are now devoid of fish. Meanwhile soils that were considered relatively robust and insensitive to acidification are showing catastrophic declines in pH - sometimes as much as one unit - with the result that at least half the base cations, among them calcium, magnesium and potassium, have been lost from the soil and replaced by hydrogen and aluminium (Bunyard).

The extent of the changes taking place has taken many scientists by surprise, although it would hardly have done so had they taken the fine-tuned recycling mechanisms of Gaia into account. For instance, the levels of sulphur fall-out in relatively pollution-free areas such as in the more northerly parts of Canada amount to less than 10 kilograms per hectare per year. The average levels in open country in South Sweden are as high as 24 kilograms per hectare per year and therefore

231

sufficient to cause damage to soil and surface waters. In Sweden at least 18,000 out of 20,000 lakes are now acidified to the point where they are incapable of supporting fish.

Meanwhile the precipitation of nitrogenous compounds from the atmosphere has increased by a factor of between 20 and 60 over certain regions compared with 'clean' areas. Thus, over 'clean' parts of the United States and Scandinavia the deposition rate for nitrogen compounds such as ammonium and nitrate is less than 1 kg/ha/year. Over parts of South Sweden as much as 20 kg/ha/year are deposited and at the edge of some forests as much as 60 kg/ha/year. According to Bengt Nihlgard the ammonium concentration in bulk precipitation has increased by 2 per cent per year and nitrate by 4 per cent per year since the 1950s. Compared to the natural biological fixation rate the deposition of nitrogen may be from 10 to 100 times greater. No wonder natural mechanisms for nitrogen use are being swamped.

Much of the ammonium deposited derives from fertilizer, as much as 10 per cent of that used evaporating into the atmosphere before precipitation. In the Netherlands where as much as 580 kg of nitrogen per hectare are applied to farmland each year, the quantities volatilizing and falling out are considerable. Indeed figures exceeding 60 kg of nitrogen per hectare per year, three-quarters of it ammonium, have been measured in throughfall and stem flow in deciduous forests. Up to 90 per cent of nitrates and nitrogen oxides in the atmosphere are now of anthropogenic origin.

Ammonium uptake in the plant through the roots leads to the release of hydrogen ions and hence to the gradual acidification of the soil. In fact, when ammonium concentrations in the soil are high magnesium uptake is impaired leading to chlorosis and necrosis of leaves. Analyses of frost-damaged young spruce trees in South Sweden indicated excess nitrogen in the needles, half of which was found to be non-protein. The most affected trees had a nitrogen content of 3 per cent in their needles compared to normal levels of 1.3 to 1.8 per cent. Levels higher than 1.8 to 2.0 per cent are associated with reduced resistance to frost. Excess nitrogen makes trees vulnerable to fungal diseases as well as attacks by insects, supporting Chaboussou's trophobiosis theory in which unbalanced nutrition leads to excess amino acids in plant cells. In some parts of south Sweden, spruce have been found covered in a greyish blue algal slime, suggesting a kind of terrestrial eutrophication (Chaboussou, 1986).

The dismal truth is that ecosystems are in disarray wherever we care to look. The Gaia Hypothesis has brought it home to us that life on the planet is part of a unified system - the ecosphere - which if sufficiently deranged must inevitably transform into a new state of being. If we accept the notion of Gaia then we must accept that life on Earth, through the process of evolution, has worked towards optimising conditions and bringing about the regulation of physical phenomena so that such processes in turn will better support life. We, as one species, are now threatening that state and inevitably are threatening our own survival. The dying of the forests, the spread of deserts, the death of the Baltic seals, the cycles of droughts and floods are all indications of perturbations. Such perturbations may have underlying natural causes but their accentuation to the point of catastrophe is surely our own doing.

References

Bunyard, Peter. The Death of the Trees. *The Ecologist*, Vol.16, No.1, 1986.

Chaboussou, Francis. How Pesticides Increase Pests. *The Ecologist*, Vol.16, No.1, 1986.

Crutzen, Paul J. *The Geophysiology of Amazonia*. (ed. Dickinson, Robert E.) John Wiley & Sons, 1987.

Davis, Shelton H. *Victims of the Miracle*. Cambridge University Press, 1977.

Detwiler, R.P. / Hall, A.S. Tropical forests and the global carbon cycle. *Science*, Vol.239: 42-47, 1988.

Fernandes, Ottoni Jr. Avanço na selva. *Istoé* Dec.2, 1987.

Guillet, David. *Risk Management among Andean Peasants*. Publication 1 Small Ruminants CRSP, Department of Rural Sociology, University of Missouri-Columbia, 1980.

Houghton, R.A. et al. The flux of carbon from terrestrial ecosystems to the atmosphere in 1980 due to changes in land use: geographic distribution of the global flux. *Tellus*, 39B: 122-139, 1987.

Junk, W.J. / Nunes de Mello, J.A.S. Impactos ecológicos das represas hidrelétricas na bacia Amazônica Brasileira. *Tübinger Geographische Studien*, No.95, 367-385, 1987.

Karas, J. / Kelly, M. The Greenhouse Effect and Global Warming. *House of Commons, The Environment Committee*, March 2, 1988.

Margulis, Lynn / Sagan, Dorion. *Microcosmos*. Allen & Unwin, 1987.

Melillo, J. M. et al. A comparison of two recent estimates of disturbance in tropical forests. *Environmental Conservation*, Vol.12, No.1, 1985.

Molion, Luiz Carlos B. *A. Amazônia e o Clima do Globo Terrestre*. Instituto de Pesquisas Espaciais, Brazil, 1988.

Molion, Luiz C. B. *The Geophysiology of Amazonia*. (ed. Dickinson, Robert E.) John Wiley & Sons, 1987.

Mooney, Harold A. et al. Exchange of materials between terrestrial ecosystems and the atmosphere. *Science*, Vol.238: 926-932, 1987.

Salati, Eneas. *The Geophysiology of Amazonia*. (ed. Dickinson, Robert E.) John Wiley & Sons, 1987.

Singh, Hanwant B. Reactive nitrogen in the troposphere. *Environ. Sci. Technol.* Vol.21, No.4, 1987.

DISCUSSION

Joan Davis One of the things you mention, concerned those environmental groups that have not really picked up the spirit of the possibility of the changes they can bring about beyond the technological fixes. Now perhaps we should start evolving shaping powers that we can use beyond the physical thermodynamic level. It seems to me that the environmental movement has been reacting with standard responses and not really thinking of the power 'beyond'. I don't know whether this is one of the criticisms that you meant to bring?

Peter Bunyard What I find fascinating is how over the past few years, global consciousness has been generated over environmental issues and problems, as well as ways to tackle them. Today an empathy has arisen throughout the world among people from wholly different cultures and with what one might have assumed to be wholly different values. The very fact that Martin von Hildebrand is here among us to tell us about the ecological consciousness of Amazonian Indians in Colombia is extremely indicative, because suddenly this consciousness has become global and not confined to us in the industrialised developed part of the world.

Solange Fernex In your talk you indicated that tropical rainforests shouldn't be cut down for gaian reasons – for instance because of potential atmospheric changes. That is a utilitarian view, but we should not forget the aesthetic view. In fact, Gaia can increase our sense of aesthetic reverence and help us not to harm but to restore. For instance, we have now introduced the lynx into our region, even though it could be claimed that such an animal no longer serves any particular use; i.e. it is not utilitarian, at least that is what people are saying. But in my mind such re-introductions are the minimum we can and should be doing. The main thing is to restore diversity.

Jeremy Faull Two main strands at different ends of the spectrum can be perceived at this conference. One is a re-elaboration of the Gaia hypothesis, a fascinating process in itself, given that if the human race disappears as one of the operations of Gaia, that's it. The other is the feeling we have of total empathy with nature. Being a lawyer, I like to try and find a middle way, to try and find a solution to the problem through compromise. Is it unreasonable to ask whether it is possible for us to manage to modify our environment in order that the human race may survive, but without damaging the environment, so that future generations will live as well? The idea of managing the environment comes into it too, even if 'manage' is abhorrent to us here. In fact, throughout our history there are many instances where unconsciously creatures have modified other creatures or their environment through the process of natural selection to make life a bit easier for them. Many examples where this has happened can be cited indicating an unconscious domestication as opposed to the conscious domestication which we have practised, but the process has basically been the same. It is not necessarily inconsistent with that that the environment should be preserved for all species. Is that too simplistic an approach or is it not a possible way to use the Gaia hypothesis as a means better to ensure our survival and ensure the continuance of the world and its species?

Peter Bunyard As far as the species which are left on Earth at the present time there is simply no need in terms of the resources that we have to destroy them in order that we may survive. We have no real need to accelerate their extinctions; however, if we keep on expanding our needs and our populations that of course will no longer be true. Unfortunately, a considerable degree of the destruction now taking place is the direct result of our models of development which have marginalized people, have pushed people into regions where they should not be. This all comes back to the paradigm of the present, dominant kind of political structure, with its concentration of power. On this point I have to admit to being somewhat pessimistic insofar as the system as we now have it will lead to the destruction of increasingly large chunks of the ecosystem. Of course, Gaia will continue, but without man, and that is important because ultimately we are interested in ourselves and our futures through our children and their children.

Diana Schumacher I would like to add to what you have just said. I think the environmental movement as a whole will be greatly helped and facilitated if we could take a look at some of our institutional frameworks, because with the little time left we are not going to change human nature and human selfishness. Therefore we have to help the process in the most conducive way possible. For example I would like to look at our legal system. What right does the individual have to a clean environment, to clean air, clean water, unpolluted soil? And if one wants to be more radical what right does Gaia have to be threatened by the human species? In other words we have to construct safety nets into the system and try and encourage people through a list of perhaps 'thou shalt' rather than 'thou shalt nots'. I think this requires a major area of study. Another point is that we should involve the major religions far more. The meeting at Assisi of all the major religions was a foretaste of what might be achieved. However, I sit on the Church of England's environmental reference panel and it is doing nothing; it is not even really discussing the Brundtland Report. Still I think we must use the channels that already exist.

Vanya Walker-Leigh As a repentant economist I would just like to point to one of the key anti-Gaian institutions, the international monetary system as it present operates. Countries are forced to wreck their environment, destroy their own people, to pay off debts and to satisfy abstract statistical aggregates which are now only figures on a computer screen or a computer print-out. It is a totally senseless system which we have somehow to get away from and I think the Greens have not focussed sufficiently on this.

Agnes Bertrand A question I ask myself is whether it matters to Gaia whether we die out, or is it just selfishness on our part to want to survive. It's not that we are part of nature but that nature is right within us. You raise the question of self-destruction. If there is a self destruction 'bent' within humanity then it should be recognised through symptoms whereby we are affecting that which nourishes us, not only in physical terms but also spiritual ones.

Jerry Ravetz   Perhaps it relates back to Martin's talk on the way in other cultures people recognise by alternative ways what is going on in their environments. Failure to recognise these signs and all sorts of things can go wrong.

Peter Bunyard   Matthias Finger was talking earlier of the way we suppress our inner natures and the realization therefore of nature itself. I think this is a particular problem of western civilization. How do we cast it out and get back to a different state of consciousness?

Nicholas Hildyard   While we have been talking over the past three days somewhere in the region of 200,000 acres of rainforest have gone. I think we ought to remember that, so that we don't let our appreciation of Gaia become too theoretical. Gaia as a concept is vital to any 'ecological' world-view - but if Gaia is not to be mutilated, we have to take on those who are destroying the Earth. What we are really talking about is a process of destruction through the way we live now; it includes institutions like the IMF, the World Bank; it includes our material consumption at home; it includes the way we govern ourselves and a whole host of other things. Now I think that these are the issues which the environmental movement has got to address and it is on such issues that we must come down to Earth.

I believe the Gaia hypothesis has an enormous amount to teach us because it deals with homeostasis, and perhaps we should have been dealing a little more with homeostatic mechanisms working at the level of society. Which societies display such homeostasis? We heard from Martin von Hildebrand this morning about the cosmology of the Indians in the Amazon. There we have, I would stress, only part of a homeostatic mechanism. In fact, we haven't discussed whether that sort of society is the only sort of society that is actually capable of living in harmony with its environment. We have been talking as if Western man was somehow a model of the only type of western society and that the way we behave is somehow the only way of living. Tinkering around with the system may or may not make us a little more conscious of the environment but we would still be failing totally to deal with the political realities, the social realities of living in a homeostatic society.

GAIA AND BIOSPHERES
by Dorion Sagan and Lynn Margulis

The Gaia Hypothesis and Biosphere I

The Gaia hypothesis is the offspring of the space programme and James Lovelock's lively imagination (Lovelock, 1979, 1988). The view the Earth presents us from space is vastly different from that provided by our flanking 'dead' planets, Mars and Venus. Compared with Mars or Venus the atmosphere of the Earth has far too little carbon dioxide, far too much oxygen and contains a chemically bewildering mixture of gases (e.g. methane, hydrogen and methyl iodide co-existing with 20 per cent free oxygen). Furthermore, the mean midlatitude surface temperature of the Earth is suspiciously close to 22°C, i.e. comfortable 'room temperature'. In contrast to the very acid surfaces of Mars and Venus the Earth enjoys a pleasant alkalinity: the pH of the world oceans is about 8.2. The Gaia hypothesis recognizes these planetary anomalies; with respect to pH, temperature and composition of reactive atmospheric gases the interactive properties of life have resulted in a dynamic regulatory system at the Earth's surface. Metabolism, behaviour, growth and death of billions of responsive organisms have led to an altered, metastable planetary environment. The Gaia hypothesis posits that these chemical and thermal properties of the Earth's lower atmosphere and surface sediments are maintained by life. Life has modulated these properties of the Earth for hundreds of millions of years.

For the first time, attempts have been made within the scientific community to prove the Gaia hypothesis. Atmospheric scientists and environmental engineers, climatologists and meteorologists are beginning to take the Gaia hypothesis seriously as they urge some of their students to learn about evolution and microbiology.

Gaia, the self-regulating system of life and its environment at the surface of the Earth, is 'materially closed but energetically open'. That is, very little matter enters or leaves the biosphere. The biosphere, defined as the place where life exists, extends from about 11 km into the ocean abyss to 8 km in the mountaintops - although most life is at sea level. While meteorites still hit the Earth's surface and hydrogen gas still escapes into space, the total amount of material exchange of the Earth with the rest of the cosmos is miniscule. Energy interchange is vastly different: the entire series of complex interactions maintaining the regulated biosphere depends directly on enormous influxes of solar radiation. At present Gaia is the only effective materially closed, energetically open living system known to us. Gaia can be described as the sum of the live organisms – microbial, plant and animal life - inhabiting and regulating the biosphere.

Now, for the first time in history, attempts to build humanly inhabitable, materially closed, energetically open structures are underway. One example is a several-million-cubic-foot architectural enormity near Oracle, Arizona called 'Biosphere II' (a drawing of it is shown in Fig. 1). Other, less ambitious and far

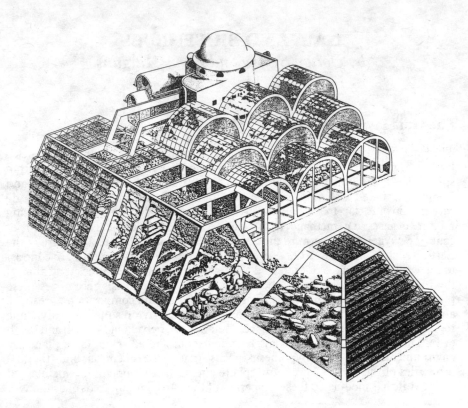

1. Architecture of Biosphere II, Space Biosphere Ventures, Inc. Scheduled to "open" (e.g., close) in 1990. Drawing by Christie Lyons

smaller miniaturized biospheres - such as test tubes and Winogradski columns far too small to contain mammals - have been studied since the nineteenth century, mostly as curiosities.

Central to the Gaia hypothesis is the concept that selected surface features of the Earth (e.g. chemical composition of the reactive gases of its atmosphere, its surface oxidation-reduction state, alkalinity-acidity and temperature) are actively regulated by the biota. The mechanisms of this environmental regulation are obscure and complex but, in general, they are becoming better known. Gaian regulation certainly must involve sensing environmental change, responding by active behaviour and metabolism with concommitant movement of matter, especially gas release. Differential growth of populations of organisms within community structures is also an aspect of Gaian regulation (Brown et al., 1986). Although some scientists reject entirely the concept of Gaia (Holland, 1984) others are actively engaged in testing it (Watson and Lovelock, 1983).

In March (6-12), San Diego, California, the American Geophysical Union held its Chapman conference on the prospects of testing the Gaia hypothesis. At that moment Gaia will have entered polite scientific society as a legitimate topic for investigation and sponsored research.

Biosphere N as Gaia's Ark

Gaia resides in Biosphere I, the place inhabited continuously by life. Recent human construction of secondary, miniaturized 'biospheres' (Biospheres II, III, IV.....N) inspires two kinds of commentary: the first addresses Biosphere II specifically and the second concerns biospheres in general. Biosphere II, a project underway by Space Biospheres Ventures, Inc. occupies two-and-one-half acres sealed entirely under glass near Tuscon at Oracle, Arizona. By the time it is fully operational (stated for 1990) Biosphere II is expected to house some 10,000 known species of organisms including eight people known as 'biospherians'. No doubt many other species inadvertently will be included. Biosphere II grabs our attention because it is the most ambitious attempt to date to form such a controlled ecosystem; this kind of research seems to be a necessary intermediate step in preparation for space travel. We might compare the attempt to build a perpetually recycling biosphere that houses human beings to epic endeavours in the past: to humanity's freeing itself from the embrace of gravity, epitomized by the Apollo landing on the moon or to the flight of the Wright brothers. But despite the majestic symbolism of Biosphere II - building another miniature Earth - we immediately notice a difference between Biosphere II and these other technological triumphs. Both the Apollo moonshot and the Wright brothers' attempts to fly were discrete; they could be definitively accomplished. The Apollo programme has even been criticized as admitting of too much finality. After it was accomplished, nothing was left to be done; all seemed anticlimax. Biosphere II does not have this problem. Indeed, its success will have to be defined negatively, as an absence of failure. Eight biospherians, now being chosen, may live inside it for two years. But will their continued good health in isolation be a definitive success?

What about ten years of closure? Or 200? What if a dozen biospherians survive inside for a century, producing children and grandchildren? What if biospherians confronted with a crisis derived from the century-long accumulation of some toxic waste gas are forced to come out? Will Biosphere II still be declared a success?

Success is elusive and often immeasurable. The urge to be airborne is a human universal, an ancient goal. Even the invention of flight has not ceased. Nor have all attempts been unqualified successes. Consider the development of hang-gliders and human-powered aerodynamic contraptions after the failure of flying machines during the Renaissance. Unlike flying it is difficult to imagine our ancestors yearning to create materially closed, energetically open ecosystems. This is a new quest. Yet regardless of the relative success or failure of Biosphere II the mere undertaking of such a project, its very presence, reminds us that something profound is occurring. We are in the midst of developments far more spectacular than an architectural triumph or a local construction project. Biosphere II may, after minor tragedy and setback, succeed in supporting human beings indefinitely. Or it may degrade into any number of infernos: a giant algal heap; a methanogenic, sulphurous gas trap; a breeding ground for disgruntled, dangerous biospherians. Nevertheless, biospheres themselves seem destined to arrive. There is about them an air of evolutionary inevitability, which leads to some general comments.

From an evolutionary perspective we are witnessing in Biosphere II the budding, the first tentative reproducing of planet Earth as a biological identity. The projected continuation of the evolutionary expansion process is a 'metamorphosis of planet Earth', a 'breaking of the biontic wave' where 'biont' is a biological unit: Over evolutionary time we see the formation of new biological units - cells, organisms, communities, ecosystems, biomes - at ever more inclusive levels of integration. Whereas earlier there was reproduction of cells and multicellular collections of cells in the form of individual bacteria, protoctists, fungi, plants and animals, with the advent of biospheres we now see the first reproduction of ecosystemic enclaves as discrete, semi-independent units. This represents something new not only in the limited realm of greenhouses and human technology but also in the larger domain of the Earth's history (as a living being).

Are we underestimating the extent to which biospheres will be formed on Earth rather than in space? Massuchesetts Institute of Technology physicist Philip Morrison has suggested that the next logical place for human habitation is the oceans: settling the oceans will be far less expensive than living in space. Recycling systems will allow people to live on top of or underneath the ocean surface to bring the environment of land to the water in a reversal of the ancient process by which life encapsulated the wet environment of the oceans in the waxy cuticle of plants or the shells and skin of land animals. The origin of plants depended on the formation of a protective, hard, outer coating by colonies of algal cells; submarine cities, in turn, will depend upon the formation of biospheric enclosures by communities of larger organisms.

This colonization of the sub-ocean, this intraterrestrial exploration can be viewed largely as a positive development, a luxury that expands the living space available for our families and friends. But there is still a more disturbing possibility. This is the chance that the Earth will become a biospheric fractal, a multiform copy of itself, not because a few people desire it but because we have no choice. "Necessity if the mother of invention". "No gain without pain". In this unpleasant view of our collective planetary future, widespread biosphere production will be mandated by pollution of the global commons. As the worldwide water supply diminishes, as garbage bobs in the waves of the Arctic Ocean and the airspace over the Earth becomes polluted, biospheres begin to look more attractive. They become oases. Originally a luxury, biosphere-building eventually becomes obligatory. Survival inside a biosphere becomes more probable than outside.

In his famous paper *Tragedy of the Commons* Garrett Hardin, the biologist and writer, shows how sheep owners pursuing individual gain will not restrain their sheep from grazing (Hardin and Baden 1977). As everyone allows his sheep full reign, the pasture is ruined. In the same way, if individual people, tribes and nations do not restrain themselves from pursuing selfish advantage maximizing individual wealth and national gross product at the expense of communal well-being we will share in the tragic deterioration of our pasture: the global commons of atmosphere and world ocean. And it will not be just the supply line of lamb chops, woollen sweaters and mutton that is threatened, but human survival itself. A recent issue of *Science News*[1] suggests that the correlation between carbon dioxide increase and human population is so close over the last 25 years that census might be better taken by atmospheric measurement. As human populations grew in the past, the

---

1   CO_2/People Connection, *Science News*, p.168, September 12, Vol. 132 No. 11, 1987.

240

shared lands of indigenous peoples gave way to the partitioned lots of landlords and politics; land ownership and national boundaries replaced open territory. We may well see an analogous development with biospheres in the future. As a sort of 3-D private property, biospheres will be required to ensure clean air, fresh water and edible food. In the highly populated, polluted world of the future, biospheres will not be luxury greenhouses and zoos or isolated academic and experimental laboratories. Rather, miniaturized biospheres will be part of the surface of the 'fractalizing' Earth itself.

Finally, although such a scenario has its tragic elements for us, from a larger perspective the fractal break-up of the Earth into versions of itself would appear strikingly natural - like the differentiation of the vertebrate egg into the blastula and morula. The egg fragments into sections as the plant or animal embryo grows. Two billion years ago these biospheric machinations of walling-off and waiting were already in play (Fig. 2). The first protist cells, themselves tightly knit communities of bacteria, formed hard-walled, resistant cysts. Some of these may have persisted in the fossil record as acritarchs. Radiation- and desiccation-proof cells harboured communities of respiring, motile and photosynthetic bacteria so well integrated that with time they became eukaryotes - nucleated microbes and their descendants (Margulis, 1981). Biosphere production - ostensibly such a technological, human process - mirrors previous developments in evolutionary history. Previous micro-biospheric products include radiation- and desiccation-proof structures such as cysts (bacteria, protists), spores (bacteria, protists, plants), tuns (animals), seeds (plants) and eggs (animals).

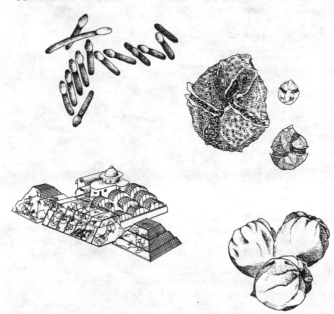

Fig. 2   History of biospheres: bacterial spores, protocist (dinomastigote cysts, seeds (walnuts) and biospheres all examples of resistant structures capable of future propagation. Drawing by Sheila Manion-Artz

How embedded are we in Gaia? Are we as unconscious of doing her reproductive bidding as we are of the beating of our own hearts? Though dependent upon space-age technology, biospheres partake of an ancient process of resistance to threat and environmental menace. Biosphere II, representing the most recent cresting of the biontic wave, becomes a kind of Gaian Ark where the selection for inclusion is fierce. (Perhaps 1 in 100,000 species will be chosen to enter). Biospheres II, III, IV....N represent survival not of cells or multicellular organisms but of multiorganismic ecosystems. New sub-biospheres may be part of the reproductive antics of life as a whole, recalling but transcending past developments in life's history. Seeds, which evolved several times, harbour vulnerable plant embryos. Having the power to harbour human and other life in a protected form, biospheres may presage the dissemination of far future life, not as seeds into the Devonian forests, but as biospheres into space. Viewed from one angle biospheres appear spanking new, part of a technological space-age vanguard. But at the same time they are a very old part of the ancient tradition of forming enclosed protective structures that endure environmental hardships. Regardless of whether Biosphere II or its competitors, Soviet, American or Japanese, succeed, they emphasize that we dwell in an unprecedented time within Earth history. We are presently watching the travail and pangs of a planet struggling to give birth. We now appear not above life but within it as biospheric midwives - aiding in the gestation, delivery and development of the living planet as a whole.

References

Brown, S., Margulis, L., Ibarra, S. and Siqueiros. D. Desiccation resistance and contamination as mechanisms of Gaia. *BioSystems*, 1986, 22: 222-232.

Hardin G. and Baden, J. *Managing of the Commons*, W. H. Freeman and Co., San Francisco, 1977.

Holland, H. D. *The chemical evolution of the atmosphere and oceans*. Princeton University Press, Princeton, New Jersey, 1984, pp.538-539.

Lovelock, J. E. *Gaia: A New Look at life on Earth*, W. W. Norton, New York, 1979.

Lovelock, J. E. *Ages of Gaia: Biography of our Living Earth*, W. W. Norton, New York, 1988.

Margulis, L. *Symbiosis in Cell Evolution*, W. W. Freeman Co., New York, 1981.

Sagan, D. *Across the Universe: Travels of the Fertile Earth*, McGraw Hill Publishing Co., New York, 1989.

Watson, A. and Lovelock, J. E. Biological homeostasis of the global environment: the parable of daisyworld. *Tellus*, 1983, 35B:284-289.

Acknowledgments
We are grateful to Gregory Hinkle and Gail Fleischaker for comments on the manuscript and to John Kearney for manuscript preparation. We acknowledge the support of the Lounsbery Foundation, the Boston University Graduate School and the Columbia University New York City Global Habitability Programme.

Note: "Gaia and Biospheres" is adopted from *Across the Universe: Travels of the Fertile Earth*. For a more detailed discussion of biospheres please consult this work.

This paper was presented during an evening session and there was no time for discussion.

BIBLIOGRAPHIES

Dr Jacques Grinewald, philosopher, historian of science and technology, political scientist, obtained his doctorate in Philosophy at the University of Paris. Teaches at Swiss Federal Institute of Technology, Lausanne, Department of Political Science, University of Geneva, Institute of Development Studies, Geneva. Publications: *La Quadrature de la CERN*, and many papers on the History of Thermodynamics.

Gregory Hinkle is a graduate of Boston University and has worked closely with Dr. Peter Westbroek, University of Leiden (Project: The use of antibodies in dating recently fossilised microbial mats), and Dr. Lynn Margulis as editorial assistant. Publications are "Prostrate gland and epididymis phosphatase isoenzymes: comparison of young adult and aged rats". *Gerontologia* (1988), *Chorella desiccata* sp. nov.: An achlorophyllous cyst-forming desiccation-resistant marine *Chorella* (Chlorophyta, Chlorococcales((1988).

Dr Mae-Wan Ho is reader in Biology at The Open University and Member of Development Dynamics Research Group of the Open University. Publications: "On Not Holding Nature Still: Evolution by process not by consequence", in *Evolutionary Processes and Metaphors* (Ho, M. W. and Fox, S. W., Eds) Wiley, London (1988), "Genetic Fitness and Natural Selection: Myth or Metaphor", presented at the Third Schneider Conference Nov 7-9, 1985, New York (1988), "How Rational can Rational Morphology be? A Post-Darwinian Rational Taxonomy based on a Structuralism of Process" *Rivista di Biologia*, Vol. 81. p11-55, 1988.

Dr Peter Westbroek completed his study of geology in 1964 at the University of Leiden with a PhD in 1967 on a paleontological subject. From 1968 to 1970 he studied biochemistry at the Queen's University in Belfast (N. Ireland) and started a research project on the biosynthesis of 'coccoliths', small, elaborately shaped particles of calcium carbonate that are formed inside special vacuoles of marine algal cells. In 1970 headed together with Professor L. Bosch and Dr. E. W. de Vrind, a modest Geobiochemical Research Group in Leiden, Netherlands. The aim of the work is to help bridge the gap between the life and earth sciences. Apart from coccolith biosynthesis, the major topics are the microbial oxidation of manganese and the study of fossil biopolymers using immunology. He is presently writing a book on 'Life as a Geologic Force.'

Dr. J. R. Ravetz was for many years reader in the History and Philosophy of Science at the University of Leeds, until his early retirement. He is the author of *Scientific Knowledge and its Social Problems* (O.U.P. 1971) and of many papers and essays in this area, particularly in the field of risks and regulation. His current research is on the complementarity and interaction of knowledge and ignorance, particularly in quantitative information.

Dr M. Whitfield is now director at the Plymouth Laboratory of the Marine Biological Association where he has worked for the past fifteen years. His research interests include investigations of the biological availability of trace metals in natural waters and of the evolution and maintenance of the composition of sea water by geochemical and biological processes. He is currently involved in the organisation of a major international programme designed to study biological processes in the ocean on a global scale using remote sensing techniques (Joint Global Ocean Flux Study).

Sigmund Kvaloy is lecturer and researcher at Oslo University: Institute of Philosophy, Council for Environmental Studies, Institute of Zoology 1966-80, Oslo School of Architecture: Research Fellow Environmental Science 1976-80, introduced Eco-philosophy as a field of study at the University of Oslo from 1969, initiated the Cooperative Groups for Nature and Environmental Protection 1969 (presently the Ecopolitical Ring), seven Human Ecology research expeditions to Nepalese Himalaya, presently planning the 8th. Author of one book and co-author of several in Scandinavian languages plus various papers, articles, essays, poems, etc, among these in English: "Ecophilosophy and Ecopolitics", *North American Review*, Summer 1974, "Man, Nature, and Mechanistic Systems", *Alternative Futures*, Troy, NY, Summer 1980, "The Universe Within" — Schumacher Lecture 1983, *Resurgence*, No. 106, 1984. Ecoropa Committee member since 1977, Ass. Ed. The Ecologist, board member on several organizations and committees in Norway and abroad. Main project for last twenty years: Studies in the dynamics of Western society's socio-ecological crisis.

David Abram, author of "The Perceptual Implications of Gaia" (*The Ecologist* Vol. 15 No. 3) has written on ecological concerns for *Environmental Ethics, Orion Nature Quarterly, Parabola* and other journals. A free-lance magician and a Watson Fellow, he has researched the relationship between magic and medicine with native shamans in Indonesia, Nepal and North America. He is currently a PhD candidate in philosophy at the State University of New York at Stony Brook.

Dr Martin von Hildebrand is director of the Fundacion Puerto Rastrojo in Bogota and Head of Indian Affairs in the Ministry of the Interior Colombia.

Dr Andrew Watson is an oceanographer and geochemist by trade, working at the Marine Biological Association in Plymouth. His interest in the Gaia hypothesis stems from a period as a research student of Jim Lovelock's. He has written some of the "mainstream science" papers on the subject of Gaia.

Dr Matthias P. Finger   has a PhD in educational science, University of Geneva, and a PhD in political science, University of Geneva. Since October 1986 graduate assistant at the subdivision of adult education, faculty of psychology and educational science, University of Geneva. Guest professor (March to May 1987) at the Department of Psychology, University of Nice, France. Involved in the research project "Educational proce of adult educators" (Prof. P. Dominice), Swiss National Fund and the research project "The engagement in Swiss political parties"

(Prof. U. Ayberk) Swiss National Fund. Author of many papers. Publications: "L'absence de reflexions ecologiques en science politique", in *Annuaire Suisse de Science politique*, Vol. 21, 1981, pp. 335-352, (Berne, Paul Haupt Verlag), R. Anthamätten/M. Finger/S. Niklaus, *Vomn Lehrling zum Leerling*. (Brig, Tunnelverlag) 1981, 120pp.

Dorion Sagan is a Science writer and magician. A.B., University of Massachussets, Amherst. Dorion has co-authored or edited five books and authored numerous articles and reviews, primarily in the field of geology and evolutionary biology. He is currently dividing his time between a book manuscript *Biospheres. The Technological Metamorphosis of Planet Earth* (McGraw-Hill, expected 1988) and first fiction *The Last Brunch*.

Edward Goldsmith is publisher and joint editor of *The Ecologist*. He obtained an MA at Oxford in Politics, Philosophy and Economics and was adjunct associate professor at the University of Michigan in 1975. He is co-author of *A Blueprint for Survival* (1977) and of *The Social and Environmental Effects of Large Dams* (1984). Author of *Stable Society* publications, including the following on theoretical issues:
"Complexity and Stability in the Real World", *Ecologist Quarterly*: Winter 1978, "Thermodynamics or Ecodynamics?", *The Ecologist* Vol. 11 No 4, 1981, "Superscience: its mythology and legitimisation", *The Ecologist* Vol. 11 No. 5, 1981, "Information Theory applied to the Living World", *The Ecologist*, Vol. 12 No. 3, and "Ecological Succession: Rehabilitated", *The Ecologist*, Vol. 15 No. 3, 1985. *The Earth Report*: Mitchel Beazley 1988 *Great U-Turn* Grccn Books, 1988.

Lynn Margulis is University professor and professor of Biology, Boston University, since 1966; A.B., University of Chicago; M.S., University of Wisconsin; PhD., University of California, Berkeley. Dr. Margulis has held a Sherman Fairchild Fellowship at the California Institute of Technology (1977) and a Guggenheim Fellowship (1979). In 1983 she was elected a member of the U.S. National Academy of Sciences. Her publications, spanning the wide range of scientific topics, include original contributions to cell biology and microbial evolution. She has participated in the development of science teaching materials at levels from elementary to graduate school. From 1977 to 1980, Dr. Margulis chaired the National Academy of Science's Space Science Board Committee on Planetary Biology and Chemical Evolution, which aids in developing research strategies for NASA. She is currently a member of the Commonwealth Book Fund advisory board chaired by Dr. Lewis Thomas, co-director of NASA's Planetary Biology Internship Program.

Professor James E. Lovelock author of *Gaia: A New Look at Life on Earth (OUP) and Ages of Gaia* (1988 W. W. Norton) as well as over 200 scientific papers on medicine, biology, instrument science, aeronomy and geophysiology. He is also an inventor of note having filed 30 patents mainly for detectors for use in chemical analysis. Elected fellow of the Royal Society in 1974 and in 1975 he received the Tswett medal for Chromatography. He was earlier awarded a CIBA Foundation prize for research in Ageing, and in 1980 received the American Chemical Society's award for Chromatography. In 1982 he was awarded an honorary ScD. degree by the University of East Anglia.

Peter Bunyard MA Cambridge and Harvard is co-editor of *The Ecologist* and author of *Nuclear Britain* (New English Library), co-author of *Politics of Self-Sufficiency* (OUP, 1980) and editor of *The Green Alternative, Guide to Good living* (Methuen 1987). He has written many articles in *The Ecologist* and other journals. His latest book is *Health Guide for the Nuclear Age* (Macmillans, 1988).

List of Participants

Carl Amery Drachlstr. 7, D-8 Munchen 90, West Germany.
Well known author and member of Ecoropa. He is the President of the Ernst Friedrich Schumacher Gesellschaft in West Germany.

Mathilda Mortimer Duchess of Argyll, Ardfern, Argyll, Scotland.
The Duchess wrote a series of articles for the *Scotsman* on social and political affairs in France from 1968-1971 and has recently published a philosophical novel *Orian*.

Guy Beney 1 Rue Descartes, Paris 75005, France.
Editor of Science and Culture (Groupe de Reflexion inter et trans-disciplinaire).

Agnes Bergrand 42 Rue Sorbier, Paris 75020, France.
Secretary of Ecoropa and Director of Ecoropa Fund.

Paul Blau Braunerstrasse 10/6a, A-1010 Vienna, Austria.
Until his retirement Head of Institute for Societal Affairs and responsible for environmental policies of the Austrian Chamber of Labour. Now President of Ecoropa and honorary President of the Vienna Section of the Austrian Federation for the Conservation of Nature.

Simon Bradley 16 Ashville View, Leeds, LS6. Since completing his degree in Philosophy and the history of scientific thought, has been preparing for a PhD in the history and philosophy of medicine.

Gerrit-Jan de Bruyn State University of Leiden, Wassenaarseweg 64, 22333 Al Leiden, The Netherlands.
He is an accomplished biologist at the University of Leiden and deeply involved in Gaian related problems. He is co-author of Dr. Westbroek's lecture.

Monica Bryant 5 Fairlight Place, Brighton, Sussex.
Founder-Director of the International Institute of Symbiotic Studies, working with ecological and holistic approaches to Microbiology. Lecturer in "The New Microbiology" at the University of Sussex. Director of Symbiogenesis Ltd.

Marcus Colchester Cobb Cottage, Chadlington, Oxon.
He has a PhD in Anthropology (Oxford University) and is projects director for Survival International.

Joan Davies 8193 Tossaiederen, Switzerland.
Professor of Environmental Protection at the University of Berlin and research assistant at the Federal Institute of Water Resources, Zurich.

Jan Danecki is a sociologist at the Polish Academy of Sciences, Warsaw, Poland.

Ken Dickinson   106 Basingstoke Road, Reading, Berks.
Spent two years travelling the Indian sub-continent. Read Agriculture at Reading University. Since then has been self-employed as a landscape gardener.

Mark Dubrulle   Evreka S.A. 5 rue de la Science, 1040 Brussels.
Born in Ghent (Belgium). He read psychology and sociology at the university of his home town. Now President and Managing Director of a Brussels based consultancy in communications, strategies, specializing in E.C. and environmental affairs. He is a member of Ecoropa and of International Professional Association for Environmental Affairs (IPRE) of which he was a Vice-President for several years. He has written and lectured largely on ecology and 'green' politics.

Jeremy Faull   Solicitor and farmer living in Cornwall. Member of the Ecology Party Executive Council 1974-76. Cornwall County Councillor representing Ecology Party 1977-85. Chairman Combined Arts Panel, S.W. Arts 1983-88. Vice-Chairman South West Regional Committee, The National Trust. Director of The Ecological Foundation. Saw the light thanks to reading The Ecologist c. 1970.

Solange Fernex   68480 Biederthal 80, 40183 France.
Founder and one of the leading figures of Ecologie et Survie, member of Ecoropa and the French Green Party.

Alexander Goldsmith   3 Fernshaw Road, London SW10.
Has a degree in Anthropolgy, (Cambridge) and is co-editor of *The Environment Digest*.

Nicholas Guppy   21a Shawfield Street, London SW3 4BD.
M. A. Cambridge and Oxford Universities. Author of many papers and books particularly on the subject of tropical rainforests and deforestation.

Hermann Graf Hatzfeldt   Schloss Schonstein 5248 Wissen/Sieg, W. Germany.
Education in Economics in Basel, Ibadan and Princeton (M.A.). Staff member of the Ford Foundation in 1968-1970. Since 1971 running a forestry estate in West Germany. Active in several environmental organisations. Special interest: acid rain and energy policy. Member of Ecoropa.

Roswitha Hentschel   D.8193 Ammerland, Riedweg 5, West Germany.
Sociologist and Biologist. Journalist and free-lance writer. Editor (with Satish Kumar) and co-author of "Viele Wege" and "Metapolitik" (The Schumacher Lectures) now working on a new book, the Biography of Rachel Carson. Member of Ecoropa.

Nicholas Hildyard   Corner House, Station Road, Sturminster Newton, Dorset.
Co-editor of *The Ecologist*, author of *Cover-up*, co-author of *The Toxic Time Bomb* and *The Social and Environmental Effects of Large Dams*. Co-editor of *The Earth Report*, a fellow of the Wadebridge Ecological Centre.

Evelyne Hong   37 Lorong Birch, Penang 10250 Malaysia.
She is an Anthropologist and author of *Natives of Sarawak* and one of the organisers of the Consumer Society.

Willem Hoogendijk   Parkstraat 28, 3581 PK. Utrecht, The Netherlands.
Studied law at Leiden University and political science in Paris. Now working at the Foundation for Environmental Education of which he is a co-founder. Member of Ecoropa and author of many publications.

Pip Hurd   Editor for Polity Press, Dales Brewery, Gwydir St., Cambridge, CB1 2LJ.,

Alwyn Jones   Keftom House, Main Road, Gwaelod-y-Garth, Cardiff, CF4 8HJ.
Senior Lecturer in Sociology, Department of Behavioural and Communication Studies, Polytechnic of Wales. Interested in the development of an ecological perspective in social theory. Author of *Rural Housing: The Agriculturel Tied Cottage*, G. Bell & Sons, 1975 and many articles.

Pierre Lehmann   SEDE SE, rue du Midi 33, 1800 Vevey, Switzerland.
MB in Physics from Institute of Technology in Lausanne, Switzerland. His career took him from the physics of nuclear power plants to the intuitive biology needed to operate composting toilets.

Ulrich E. Loening   15 Buccleuch Place, Edinburgh EH8 9LN.
Biochemist and cell biologist. Research background in biotechnology and cancer, University of Edinburgh, Dept. of Zoology, Director, Centre for Human Ecology. Organiser and co-organiser of several recent conferences on tropical forests, the Biosphere and Ecology and Responsibility.

Daniel C. Mayer   Monkey Sanctuary, Looe, Cornwall.
Was born and raised in Mexico City. He has worked in education, mime and theatre with children and studied history and philosophy at a university in the US. Since 1979 he has lived and worked at The Monkey Sanctuary, near Looe in Cornwall where he is now the curator.

Helena Norberh-Hodge   Ladakh Ecological Centre, Leh, Ladakh, Jammu and Kashmir, India.
She is a linguist and has spent most of her time during the last 12 years in Ladakh where she started the Ecological Development Group and compiled a first ever dictionary of the Ladakhi Language.

Ted Pawloff   Beshara Press Ltd, Ambrose St., Cheltenham, Glos.
Was born in Leopoldville in the Belgian Conga (now Zaire) and was educated in France, Austria and UK. He broke off a degree course in philosophy at Sussex University, travelled widely in Europe and Asia and has since attended three

Helena Norberh-Hodge   Ladakh Ecological Centre, Leh, Ladakh, Jammu and Kashmir, India.
She is a linguist and has spent most of her time during the last 12 years in Ladakh where she started the Ecological Development Group and compiled a first ever dictionary of the Ladakhi Language.

Ted Pawloff   Beshara Press Ltd, Ambrose St., Cheltenham, Glos.
Was born in Leopoldville in the Belgian Conga (now Zaire) and was educated in France, Austria and UK. He broke off a degree course in philosophy at Sussex University, travelled widely in Europe and Asia and has since attended three courses at the Beshara School of Intensive Education. He is currently Managing Director of Beshara Press. Member of Ecoropa.

David Pearson   203 Dalling Road, London, W6 0ES.
A qualified architect with 15 years' experience in housing, planning and community architecture. Studied at the Bartlett, University College London and at the University of California, Berkeley. Worked in private practice, Housing Association and Local Authority situations. Also a director of Gaia Books.

Joss Pearson   Gaia Books Ltd, Umbrella Studios, 12 Trundle Street, London, SE1 1QT.
Oxford University Scholar reading English Language and Literature. Editor of Open University Science Courses. Worked for various publishing houses. Formed Gaia Books in 1982.

Alan Reddish   The Open University, Walton Hall, Milton Keynes, MK7 6AA.
A Physicist with many years' industrial research experience and for the last eight years on the academic staff of the Open University. For the last five years also directed the Energy Research Group taking a wide varying interest in energy conservation.

Wolfgang Sachs   Via Timavo 12, Rome, Italy. Also Pennsylvania State University, STS Programme 128 Willard Bldg. University Park, PA 16802, USA. Practical supply and demand issues and energy policy. Member of Ecoropa.

Elisabeth Sahtouris   Metochi, Agistri 18010, Greece.
PhD is an American/Greek biological philosopher who did her post-doctoral research in evolutionary brain development at the American Museum of Natural history in New York City. She has taught courses for the Massachusetts Institute of Technology (MIT), and the University of Massachusetts. She was a science writer for Public Educational Television (the NOVA/HORIZON documentary series, WGBH Boston in collaboration with London BBC). She is co-author of *China: Science Walks on Two Legs*, Avon, NY, 1975, and has contributions in *Cosmic Catastrophes*, Verschuur, Addison-Wesley.
   Dr. Sahtouris has lived and worked as an independent biological philosopher in Greece since 1979, has recently founded an International Institute for the Environment to promote more harmonious relationships between humans and the

Diana Schumacher Church House, Church Lane, Godstone, Surrey, RH9 8BW. Director, Schumacher Projects. Member of Ecoropa and executive member of several other environmental groups. Author of *Energy: Crisis or Opportunity?* and numerous articles on energy/environment

Dorothy and Walter Schwarz The Guardian, 119 Farringdon Road, London, EC1.
Guardian's religious affairs correspondent and author of *The Arabs in Israel* 1959 and *Nigeria* (1968) and co-author with Dorothy of *Breaking Through* (Green Books 1987). Both members of Ecoropa.

Manami Suzuki c/o PERG, 34 Cowley Road, Oxford.
Is a free-lance correspondent and a member of Friends of the Earth, Japan.

Karl Wagner Okologie Instiut. A-1070 Wien, Neubaugasse 64-66, Austria.
Started in 1983 a project for the World Wildlife Fund International to save the riverine forests along the Danube from destruction by the planned hydroelectric power plant Hainburg. The project ended in 1985 with a big success and in 1986 he received the most renowned environmental award of Austria, the Konrad Lorenz Prize (for the WWF Project). In 1987 he left the WWF Austria and joined the Austrian Ecology Institute a private organisation that he co-founded in 1985, current working subject is energy.

Vanya Walker-Leigh PO Box 110, Gibraltar.
Is an environmental journalist.

Mirjam (21), Hanna (20) and Eva (17) Westbroek daughters of Dr. P. Westbroek, University of Leiden, 2333 Al Leiden, Wassenaarseweg 64, The Netherlands.

Bernard Zamaron Enscherangé, 26 Luxembourg, Belgium.
He is a member of the European Parliament and of Ecoropa.